D0500154

THE PARLIAMENT OF ENGLAND
1559–1581

THE PARLIAMENT OF ENGLAND 1559–1581

G. R. ELTON

CAMBRIDGE UNIVERSITY PRESS

Cambridge

London New York New Rochelle

Melbourne Sydney

Published by the Press Syndicate of the University of Cambridge
The Pitt Building, Trumpington Street, Cambridge CB2 1RP
32 East 57th Street, New York, NY 10022, USA
10 Stamford Road, Oakleigh, Melbourne 3166, Australia

First published 1986

Printed in Great Britain by the University Press, Cambridge

British Library cataloguing in publication data

Elton, G. R.
The Parliament of England, 1559–1581.
1. England and Wales, Parliament –
History 2. Great Britain – Politics
and government – 1558–1603
I. Title
328.42′09 JN525

Library of Congress cataloguing in publication data

Elton, G. R. (Geoffrey Rudolph)
The Parliament of England, 1559–1581
Includes indexes.
1. England and Wales. Parliament – History.
2. Legislation – Great Britain – History. I. Title.
KD4197.E45 1986 328.42′09 86-12899

ISBN 0 521 32835 7

UP

Contents

Preface

Virtually all the research for this book was done during a year of sabbatical leave in 1977–78; virtually all the writing of it had to wait for the next sabbatical in 1984–85. So protracted a production poses problems, and I cannot suppose that I have overcome them all. The years of gestation may on occasion have led to apparently contradictory statements, but I think that any such discrepancies arise from the uncertainties of the evidence. My purpose has been to display certain sixteenth-century Parliaments at work – to follow events in both Houses as bills turned into acts or more commonly failed to do so. Much of the available material bore on more than one of the questions I have tried to answer, for which reason it has sometimes been necessary to repeat details in two or three places. This adds to clarity but inevitably also to tedium, for which I am sorry. I have not investigated the membership of these Parliaments. For the Lords, such an analysis has little meaning, especially since we hardly ever know anything about the activities and interventions of particular individuals there; for the Commons the details have been massively collected in the relevant volumes published by the History of Parliament Trust. I take the Parliaments from the point at which, summoned and elected, they have assembled to do business, and it is that business, together with the light it throws on the role of Parliament, that has been my concern.

The chronological limits of the investigation were set by accidents of the evidence (more fully explained in Chapter 1) and by the need not to trespass on other people's preserves. The first seven sessions of Elizabeth's reign form the first period in the history of Parliament for which we have all the formal records, supplemented by some informal material of a novel kind. Before 1559, the Commons Journal is uninformatively thin; from 1584 to the end of the reign it is altogether lost. The collections made by Sir Simonds D'Ewes do help considerably in that later period, but I wished to learn about Parliament from its own records, not from what another scholar had long ago made of them. The less formal materials drawn upon by D'Ewes were all traced by Sir John Neale and are now published in the volume edited by Dr T. E. Hartley which covers the years dealt with in this book; the appearance of his invaluable edition greatly lightened my task and also rendered D'Ewes superfluous to me. I am glad to be able here to express my appreciation for Neale's endeavours, particularly in the search for relevant matter, and I do so the more earnestly because on a great many aspects of the Elizabethan Parliament we differ profoundly. I have tried to avoid too frequent controversy, but Neale's description of a rising House of Commons, employed by a group of ardent protestants or puritans to oppose the policy of the Crown, is so drastically different from what I have come to understand about those Parliaments that I have not been able to omit all argument with my predecessor. It is therefore the more necessary to say plainly that without that predecessor's books this one could not have been written.

One possible kind of material has been used only very patchily. I feel sure that there is much to be found in local records that would further help to explain the terms and fates of bills in Parliament, but it has not been possible to explore those sources unless they were in print or in the Record Office of the Corporation of London. Country-wide searches are the prerogative of the graduate student and the man in retirement; anyone involved in normal academic life will either have to do without them or abandon the idea of ever completing an undertaking necessarily and rightly based on the central archives. It has always been my conviction that all learned works on history constitute staging posts on the road to fuller knowledge, and I prefer setting out markers along the way to leaving the map altogether blank. I hope at least to have provided a usable framework for the pursuit of parliamentary concerns into those counties and towns where they often took their origin.

The eight years that intervened between the start of excavation and the opening of the building provided many opportunities for debates and discussions around these controversial themes. I am grateful to the many fellow-scholars all over the world who patiently listened to preliminary expositions and by their questions and criticisms assisted me in clarifying my own mind on many an issue. Special thanks go to the friends who are working in the same field and have been most generously helpful – David Dean, Michael Graves, Norman Jones and David Lidington. My thanks go to Art Cosgrove and James McGuire, editors of *Parliament and Community* (Belfast, The Appletree Press, 1983), for permission to reprint, as Chapter 2, a slightly altered version of an essay which I contributed to that volume.

The completion of a book is always a relief, but I am perhaps exceptionally relieved to be done with the Parliaments of Elizabeth. There are a good many other things that call the historian to the colours. Prolonged involvement with Parliament has in the end convinced me that the customary concentration on it as the centre of public affairs, however traditional it may be, is entirely misleading. This is a message, it seems to me, that needs to be absorbed into the general history of England. We have been misled by the Victorians and their obedient successors who read the modern Parliament back into history; and I do not except the story of Parliament in the seventeenth century from these reservations. I now wonder whether the institution – one of the Crown's instruments of government – ever really mattered all that much in the politics of the nation, except perhaps as a stage sometimes used by the real contenders over government and policy. But it was a highly sophisticated instrument for the making of law and a means available to all sorts of Englishmen in the pursuit of their ends. It gathered in the particles of the nation and in turn threw light upon their concerns. It did so in a thoroughly skilled and businesslike way, really visible to us for the first time in the reign of Elizabeth. That is the burden of this book, and I hope it will serve.

Cambridge G. R. ELTON
January 1986

Abbreviations

APC	*Acts of the Privy Council of England*, ed. J. R. Dasent (32 vols., London, 1890–1907)
BIHR	*Bulletin of the Institute of Historical Research*
BL	British Library
CJ	*Journals of the House of Commons*
CLRO	Corporation of London Record Office
CSP	*Calendar of State Papers*
D'Ewes	Sir Simonds D'Ewes, *The Journals of all the Parliaments during the Reign of Queen Elizabeth* (London, 1682)
EHR	*English Historical Review*
Ellis	Henry Ellis, ed., *Original Letters Illustrative of English History* (11 vols. in 3 series, London, 1824–46)
HLRO	Record Office of the House of Lords
HMC	Historical Manuscripts Commission
HPT	The History of Parliament Trust: *The House of Commons 1558–1603*, ed. P. W. Hasler (3 vols., London, 1981)
LJ	*Journals of the House of Lords*
LJ/EHR	E. J. Davis, 'The Journal of the House of Lords for April and May, 1559,' *EHR* 28 (1913), 531–42
Neale, *EP*	J. E. Neale, *Elizabeth I and her Parliaments* (2 vols., London, 1953, 1957)
Neale, *HC*	J. E. Neale, *The Elizabethan House of Commons* (London, 1948)
OA	Original Acts (at the HLRO)
Proc.	*Proceedings in the Parliaments of Elizabeth I, volume 1: 1558–1581*, ed. T. E. Hartley (Leicester, 1981)
Rep.	Repertories (at the CLRO)
SP	State Papers (at the Public Record Office)
SR	*Statutes of the Realm* (11 vols., London, 1810–28)

STC	*A Short-Title Catalogue of Books Printed in England, Scotland and Ireland and of English Books Printed Abroad, 1475–1640*, ed. A. W. Pollard and G. R. Redgrave (London, 1926; vol. 2 of the 2nd ed., ed. W. A. Jackson, F. S. Ferguson, K. F. Pantzer, London, 1976)
Studies	G. R. Elton, *Studies in Tudor and Stuart Politics and Government* (3 vols., Cambridge, 1974, 1983)
TED	*Tudor Economic Documents*, ed. R. H. Tawney and E. Power (3 vols., London, 1924)
TRHS	*Transactions of the Royal Historical Society*
TRP	*Tudor Royal Proclamations*, ed. P. L. Hughes and J. F. Larkin (3 vols., New Haven, 1964–9)
Tudor Const.	*The Tudor Constitution: Documents and Commentary*, ed. G. R. Elton (2nd edn, Cambridge, 1982)
YCR	*York Civic Records*, ed. A. Raine (8 vols., York, 1939–53)

Manuscripts for which no location is given are from the Public Record Office in London. Public (printed) acts are normally cited by regnal year and chapter number without reference to *SR*; unprinted private acts are cited by the regnal year and the number given to the OA in the HLRO. I have modernized the spelling, punctuation and capitalization of all quotations. For the facts concerning members of the House of Commons see HPT; the alphabetical arrangement of those volumes usually renders page references superfluous.

PART I

Preliminaries

1

The sources

The limits of this study were set by several circumstances. In the first place, if a really thorough analysis of Parliament at work was to be attempted without making the book gigantic, it became necessary to restrict the chronological sector to some half dozen sessions or so. The Parliaments of Edward VI and Mary I had already been studied by Dr Carl Ericson and Dr Jennifer Loach; for those of the second half of Elizabeth's reign Dr David Dean had started work since finished.[1] But the most important criterion lay in the sources available. In the whole Tudor period, only the seven sessions from 1559 to 1581 are covered by adequate Journals for both Houses. The Lords Journals are indeed continuous and unchanging from 1536 onwards, but things stand differently for the Commons. Before Elizabeth's accession their surviving Journals are exceedingly concise and not very informative; from 1584 to the end of the reign they are altogether missing and have been so since the 1630s at the latest.[2] Though much of what is lost can be recovered from the collections made by Sir Simonds D'Ewes,[3] who used a Journal Book we no longer possess, his copies and extracts are not the same thing as the originals. Thus, since I wished to observe both Houses at work I thought it best to confine myself to that part of the institution's history for which I could follow the labours of both clerks in their original form. That left me with the years 1559–81, seven sessions of four Parliaments. Some years after I had started work on those years my choice of them was rewarded by the publication for the same period of the 'unofficial' parliamentary materials collected by the late Sir John Neale, a publication which saved me from having to repeat his laborious searches.[4] This

[1] Three unpublished dissertations; C. G. Ericson, 'Parliament as a legislative institution in the reigns of Edward VI and Mary' (London, 1974); S. J. Loach, 'Opposition to the crown in parliament, 1553–8' (Oxford, 1974); D. M. Dean, 'Bills and Acts, 1584–1601' (Cambridge, 1984).

[2] Below, n. 17.

[3] Below, n. 23.

[4] Below, n. 24.

restriction to the first half of the reign has its drawbacks. It means, of course, that the analysis stops at a point of no significance though this fact can be useful if it helps to avoid the imposition of supposed patterns of development. All through the Tudor and Stuart periods the quantity of surviving material tends to increase as time progresses; by stopping at 1581 I missed out on some valuable sources that become available thereafter. However, the period chosen is well covered by the systematic production of the parliamentary machinery, and any investigation of that institution as a working body rather than an arena for possible politics must in the first place start from them. We need to understand this Parliament before we use it to interpret the general history of the nation.

After the medieval Stature Roll was abandoned in the reign of Edward IV there remained only one record belonging to the whole institution, the Roll of Parliament. One such was produced for each Parliament and, after some earlier gropings, from 1529 onwards for every session. However, from that opening session of the Reformation Parliament, the Roll in effect became a statute roll: thereafter it contained no more than a recital of all acts passed and assented to. From 1536, the vestigial remnants of what had once been a kind of narrative record vanished as the old formulae concerning the opening of the Parliament – including the appointment of receivers and triers of petitions as well as the election of the Speaker of the Commons – were transferred to the Lords Journal.[5] The outward appearance of the Roll was effectively settled in the reign of Mary by the clerk of the Upper House, Francis Spelman (or, as he usually spelled it, Spilman) who died in office in 1576 and was succeeded by Anthony Mason, from the previous October his partner in the patent.[6] It is therefore no wonder that the Roll retained a virtually standard form throughout the period under review. All seven Rolls survive for the seven sessions in question, and the variations among them are minimal – though not so minimal as to tell us nothing at all.[7] The Roll should have opened with a table (list) of the acts to be enrolled, but that is missing from those for 1566 and 1571. The remaining Rolls carry it, without any distinction being made (as it was made in the sessional printing of the acts) between public and private acts. The numbering of individual chapters of the statute (that is, of the acts of Parliament), which ran continuously, was usually added after the Roll was written up; formulae of assent to bills were sometimes entered by the scribe and sometimes added later by another hand. The clerk was supposed to sign the Roll as examined and collated 'cum recordis' (with the Original Acts), but Spelman did this

[5] For all this cf. *Studies* III, 110–42.

[6] M. Bond, 'Clerks of the Parliaments, 1509–1953,' *EHR* 73 (1958), 78–85.

[7] C65/166–72.

only in 1563. He never transferred the Rolls into the Chancery, as he was supposed to do, but kept them in his office, thereby reserving to himself and his clerks the profitable means of providing copies of private (unprinted) acts if any were required in the course of litigation.

Three acts received uncertain treatment on the Roll – those for the lay and clerical subsidies and for the general pardon always passed from 1563 except in 1572 when no money was asked for and no gracious thanks were therefore required. In the Accession Parliament the laity granted a subsidy but the clergy were spared, probably because Elizabeth resumed the first fruits and tenths which her sister had restored to the Church; the coronation pardon of 15 January 1559 rendered a statutory one superfluous.[8] Those three acts, though public, were always printed separately and did not form a part of the sessional statute, but the Roll indicates a change in the official understanding of the classification of acts. In 1563, 1566 and 1571 the three acts were enrolled right at the end; in 1576 and 1581 they were placed between the public and private acts. Thus an important distinction, long since well established in the sessional print, finally became operative on the Roll in 1576. Details of this kind, as well as the problems attending upon the entering of the royal assent,[9] make it plain that the Roll was put together well after the end of the session, though it may be presumed to have been written out before another meeting of the Parliament; the intervals between sessions should have offered to a clerk otherwise unoccupied plenty of time to get up to date with his duties. There are some erasures and changes of hand on the Roll for 1571 which may have resulted from pressure of time: this was the only session in the period followed by a brief interval before the next Parliament was called.

As a source for the history of Parliament the Roll is thus of limited value. In all seven Rolls there occurs only one entry that does not simply record acts passed. In 1572 the clerk added the order of the Lords in the case of Henry, Lord Cromwell who, arrested for debt at a private suit, was released by privilege; strangely enough, if the Lords Journal can be trusted, he got the date wrong.[10] And even less explicably he added a further note to the effect that on the first day of the Parliament three new peers had presented their writs of summons and been admitted to their places in the House. Nothing else interrupts the formalized recital of acts passed. However, this does not make the Roll and its study totally pointless; as we shall see, it can contribute to our understanding of various aspects of parliamentary procedure.[11]

[8] *TRP* II, 104–8. [9] Below, pp. 127–8.
[10] *LJ* I, 727 dates the order to 30 June 1972; C65/170, m. 15 has it on the 27th.
[11] Below, pp. 50, 53–4, 127–8.

The Roll, though true to medieval practice treated as authoritative by the court and the antiquarians alike, was not, in fact, an original document in the strictest sense; behind it stood the sources from which it was copied. However, in the legal sense it was the Roll that made Parliament a 'court of record' and therefore a member of the curial system in the common-law structure. The public acts it took from the sessional print, and the private ones from the parchment bills in the Parliament Office; the print too, of course, ultimately derived from those Original Acts – the bills that had obtained passage in both Houses and the royal assent, as the notations on them indicate. Both sessional print[12] and Original Acts survive in full, the latter, now in the Record Office of the House of Lords, being in fact the ultimate source on the chief activity of these Parliaments, the making of laws. Both provide evidence for the working of the parliamentary machinery. Thus the two subsidies and the pardon, as the printer's signatures upon them show, were usually printed separately, though they quite commonly got bound up by the purchaser with the sessional print of the public acts; they were printed separately in large quantities because they had to be available to subsidy commissioners and collectors, or alternatively to intending buyers of the pardon, and in all probability were printed first.[13] There is no evidence that at this time any part of the sessional statute was printed before the end of the session, as seems to have happened in 1534.[14] Unlike the Roll and the sessional print, valuable but not very informative, the Original Acts are indispensable to any study of Tudor and Stuart Parliaments. Most obviously, they provide the texts of private acts, not printed at the time and from 1547 left out of the *Statutes of the Realm*. In addition, however, they often contain evidence touching the fortunes of bills during passage, in the form of amendments on the face of the bill, provisos attached to it on parchment schedules, and on occasion paper sheets of amendments proposed by the second House to see the bill which got filed with the act.

Rolls, print and Original Acts constitute the archival production of the whole Parliament; it is worth notice that they all still treat the Upper House as the real centre of Parliament. Its clerk wrote the Roll, prepared the copy for the printer, and filed the assented-to bills. On the other hand, the most familiar source material in the history of the Elizabethan

[12] I have used the conveniently complete collection of what is by no means universally available material in the Pepys Library of Magdalene College, Cambridge, vols. 1994 and 1995.

[13] In 1566 and 1576 the clerical subsidy looks to have been printed with and at the end of the sessional statute; in 1581 this was done for both that subsidy and the pardon. The lay subsidy always got printed separately.

[14] *Studies* III, 101.

Parliaments did not belong to the institution as a whole. The Journals were the product and property of each House separately, or in a sense of the clerks of each House separately.

As a historical source, the Journal of the House of Lords poses hardly any problems. Its form settled in 1536 and never changed thereafter for the rest of the sixteenth century. Prefaced by a list of proxies entered by peers prevented from attending,[15] it records the formalities of the opening and then each sitting day of the session. That daily entry includes a presence list (the list of members in hierarchical order with those present marked with a 'p') and the bill proceedings for the day, with very occasionally a case of privilege. Adjournments and prorogations are noted, and the entry at the end of the Parliament records the dissolution. The Journal is very 'clean', and the eighteenth-century printing of it is entirely satisfactory for the historian's purposes. At times the clerks manifestly failed to enter some stage of a bill and may conceivably have made mistakes in marking up the presence list, though we have no means now to check this. In the Journal for 1559 several pages are missing, having probably dropped out on the occasion of rebinding, but what is absent has been supplied from an early Stuart copy preserved at the Inner Temple.[16] The businesslike conciseness of the Journal testifies to the highly developed clerical organization of the Upper House but severely limits the information supplied; we can track bills and when a vote is recorded usually get the names of those dissenting from the majority verdict; but about actual goings-on in the House we learn virtually nothing.

The Commons Journal presents much more complex problems. For one thing, though a Journal exists for all the sessions in question, we know that some material is lost which was still available for listing in 1633.[17] What we do have are the two journal books called, after the clerks that kept them, 'Seymour' and 'Onslow'. 'Seymour', as Neale showed,[18] consists of two disparate parts – brief notes copied fair for the years 1547–1552, bound in the front of a more proper paper book covering the meetings from the last session of Edward VI to 1566. It is what later came

[15] The problem of proxies awaits further investigation; it cannot be dealt with in the present work. The most serious question arises from the fact that givers of proxies are sometimes found attending the Parliament. See in general M. A. R. Graves, *The House of Lords in the Parliaments of Edward VI and Mary I* (Cambridge, 1981), index entry under 'proctorial representation'.

[16] E. Jeffries Davis, 'Journal of the House of Lords for April and May 1559,' *EHR* 28 (1913), 531–42.

[17] Sheila Lambert, 'The clerks and records of the House of Commons, 1600–1640,' *BIHR* 43 (1970), 215–31.

[18] J. E. Neale, 'The Commons' Journals of the Tudor Period,' *TRHS* 4th ser. 3 (1920), 136–70.

to be known as a scribbled book, that is to say a register written up in the House during sittings, with the compressions and corrections likely to be called for in such circumstances. It is, however, as complete a record as John Seymour ever kept, and from the beginning of Elizabeth's reign his entries, unhelpfully brief to that point, grow rather fuller. Fulk Onslow's book (for 1571 to 1581), on the other hand, is a 'perfected' journal, a fair copy of his scribbled book which itself is lost; it looks as though he discarded his original notes as he had the copy made.[19] Neither book is without faults and inaccuracies – with stages of a bill inadvertently omitted and such like minor slips – but the damage done by such clerical slips would appear to be very slight. The matter recorded in both these journal books is, despite their differing appearance, the same: bill proceedings, some orders of the House, licences for absence, and matters of privilege (usually arising from members' endeavour to avoid arrest by creditors), with a very occasional mention of a protest or a debate, though these last topics get very compressed treatment. Onslow's perfected book finds room for rather more formal accounts of such things as cases of privilege. He entered committees in full where Seymour had noted only chairmen (as the persons responsible for returning the bill to the clerk); on the other hand, when Seymour mentions a division he gives figures, whereas Onslow is content to speak of a majority. In all essential points the two books are alike in purpose and in the information given. They are the clerks' private record of business in the House, intended to aid them in keeping abreast of that business, and the outward differences between terse scribbled notes and the more rounded perfection of the same should not disguise that fact: there are no grounds for speaking, as Neale did, of an evolution from a primitive to a mature state.[20] One particular development, however, still lay in the future: there is no evidence that the House itself took the kind of interest in the Journal and its contents which it began to evince in the first Parliament of James I.

The printed version of the Commons Journal leaves a good deal to be desired. It altogether fails to show the appearance of the record or indicate its component parts; it omits odd notes and scribbles; by introducing capitals and italics, it creates an air of a systematic order of importance absent from the original; and it does not indicate corrections or deletions. The volume now called 'Onslow' actually consists of two separate books now (and certainly since the early seventeenth century) bound together, the paper-size differing between the two; the second,

[19] As Neale and Lambert show, the scribbled book for the rest of Elizabeth's reign was still available to Simonds D'Ewes but has not been seen since. It was never perfected.
[20] Cf. *Studies* III, 165–8.

for the session of 1581, starts on a new set of quires even though seven blank folios were left at the end of the first. Apparently Onslow really wished to produce perfected Journals for each of his Parliaments separately, after running the one-session Parliament of 1571 on into the three-sessions Parliament of 1572–81. In general, 'Onslow', being clean and straightforward, suffers less from bad editing than does 'Seymour', but there are some misreadings and omissions in both books. Most serious are the systematic omissions from 'Seymour' of marginal notes made by the clerk in his manuscript at a later stage. Thus the originals show, as the print does not, that Seymour went over his sessional record at the end of the session, adding where appropriate a note of the assent having been given to his early entry in the margin recording passage of a bill in the House (*judicium*). Since all the business of the assent was handled in the Lords, this was his only means of keeping track of bills that had found approval in the Commons but had either failed in the Lords or been vetoed; the practice indicates that he had no plans to replace his scribbled book by a more elegant copy, as his successor was to do, but on the other hand, unlike his predecessors, meant that record to be kept for the future. Here we see signs of the transition from notes scribbled during sittings for guidance during a session to a permanent register or journal. It was, however, not until after 1660 that the Commons Journal assumed a standardized form, having until then reflected the variable habits and preferences of every clerk.[21]

That exhausts the systematic and, as it were, official sources – those produced by the working life of the institution itself. It is noticeable that they overwhelmingly testify to a concept of Parliament as a laws-producing machinery. Any proper study must obviously begin with this self-generated evidence, but it must not stop there. One kind of record, halfway between the official and the unofficial sort, unfortunately survived very poorly. For this period we possess hardly any of the paper bills introduced into the House and either superseded by the parchment engrossment or dropped before that stage. Whether the very few now found in the collection called Main Papers at the House of Lords represent a once sizable archive, possibly lost in the fire which destroyed the Houses of Parliament in 1834, must be doubted: more survive after 1584, which suggests a similar disproportion before the fire. It is at least likely that record-keeping improved in the Lower House in the course of the reign, as it certainly did in the Upper House or the custody of State papers. In 1633 the Commons clerk still possessed '11 bags of papers

[21] I have corrected my copy of the printed *CJ* from the manuscript and, since it is very inconvenient for the reader to be referred to that manuscript, shall cite from the print, but with emendations silently made where they apply.

of Queen Elizabeth',[22] and in the early nineteenth century the clerks several times complained of ancient papers going back to that reign which crowded the presses in the corridors. Of all this little or nothing now seems to survive, but of what remains almost everything belongs to the 1580s and 1590s. My own guess is that down to the middle of the reign paper bills were not preserved when no longer necessary to the business of the House. A few draft bills – an earlier stage yet – are to be found in private or municipal archives; those now in the State Papers probably came from Burghley's office. Generally speaking, however, the texts of bills that did not pass, or the earlier versions of those that did, can hardly ever be traced. Too often we have to guess at contents from the brief titles invented for the Journals.

However, materials bearing on the history of the Elizabethan Parliaments exist outside the official and semi-official records, and Sir John Neale spent a life-time searching for them. Some had been collected by the antiquarians of the seventeenth century, and Simonds D'Ewes had incorporated a selection in his edition of the Elizabethan Journals.[23] As was said above, Neale's collection is being made available in print, and a first volume, which covers the period of this study, has appeared.[24] The materials there included fall into two kinds. In the first place, there are speeches and memoranda relating to particular occasions; in the second there are diaries of parliamentary proceedings through all or part of a session, kept by members of the Lower House. Hardly any of these materials are originals; we now have only copies made by or for seventeenth-century collectors, quite often several such copies in different collections, nearly all of which have ended up in the British Library. Copies disguise things about the originals, above all authenticity and provenance; as for accuracy, one must obviously be careful about basing any argument on the precise phrasing of copies, though general experience of the practice of the time indicates that copyists were usually very accurate.

The minor difficulties attending the first sort of document have been sufficiently noted by the editor of *Proceedings*. Speeches are a notorious problem for that time and later centuries. If they were recorded by a listener, accuracy is out of the question; if they were produced by the

22 Lambert, *BIHR* 43 (1970), 231.

23 Simonds D'Ewes, *The Journals of all the Parliaments during the reign of Queen Elizabeth*, published by P. Bowes (1682). That edition is notoriously mangled, but a copy corrected from the manuscript is found at the Institute of Historical Research in London. In any case, for the years 1559–81 D'Ewes has been rendered superfluous by the edition mentioned in the next note.

24 *Proceedings in the Parliaments of Elizabeth I, volume I: 1558–1581*, ed. T. E. Hartley (Leicester, 1981).

ostensible speaker we do not know that the script represents what was delivered – or indeed whether the speech was ever delivered at all. The most important speeches, from the point of view of the present study, were the addresses delivered at the opening of Parliaments, by the lord keeper, Sir Nicholas Bacon; these were manifestly taken down eagerly and often copied, and I think we can rely on the transmission. However, the doubts raised by this kind of material are negligible by comparison with the questions that hang about the diaries. Not enough has been done to assess them as historical evidence, which necessitates a word here. Neale used them in his usual selective manner to give colour and detail to a narrative which, had it had to rely solely on the official Journals, would have been bare indeed; but he never wrote a word bearing on the fundamental criticism to which such tricky material must be subjected. Dr Hartley, in his introduction, says some things of value, especially drawing attention to contents (markedly the larger part of the total) that Neale ignored, but he does not seriously address himself to the basic question for what reason and purpose such diaries were ever kept at all.

Considerable labour went into those private records of the business of Parliament. Notes had to be taken in an often crowded and usually noisy House;[25] they had then to be put together in proper shape; no doubt other members and the officers of the House had frequently to be consulted to correct mishearings and omissions.[26] Possessed as we are of copies only, we lack information about the diarist's *modus operandi* which the originals may have provided. The present location of these copies says nothing about the very important issue of provenance and the location of the originals: where did the copyists find them? We are thus deprived of guidance on the central issue: for whose eyes were those diaries meant? The motive behind the keeping of diaries must be conjectured from internal evidence and certain external circumstances, and absolute certainty cannot be obtained. However, one can arrive at reasonably convincing conclusions, and those conclusions differ entirely from Neale's sentimental view that private diaries reflect simply an increasing interest in Parliament and a growing respect for it.

We have no private diaries for the first three sessions of the reign, after which, it would appear, diary-keeping began. Of course, some such documents could possibly be lost altogether, but this is not very likely when we allow for the eagerness with which Stuart parliamentarians searched for information about Elizabeth's Parliaments. The probability

[25] It did not take many members present to crowd the Elizabethan House of Commons which was comfortably filled if only 200 out of its membership of well over 400 attended; the membership grew larger through the reign as more constituencies were enfranchised.

[26] *Proc.* p. xiv.

that 1571 marked a departure in practice is overwhelming. For that year we possess a concise journal kept by John Hooker, alias Vowell, the city official and antiquary of Exeter, which covered the whole session. There is also a much fuller journal kept by an author who remains unidentified, but our surviving copy unfortunately covers only the first three of the session's eight weeks. The rest is more likely to be lost than never to have been written, for the anonymous diarist reappears in 1572 when he covers practically the whole session, though in less detail. In addition, 1572 witnesses the inauguration of the very full and useful diary kept by Thomas Cromwell, grandson to Henry VIII's minister. Cromwell's diary continues in 1576 and 1581 (and beyond), getting steadily thinner in coverage, though it always accounts for the whole session. But that is all: we are evidently in a different world from that of James I's and Charles I's reigns when private parliamentary diaries proliferated. Why, then, did Hooker, Cromwell and the unidentified burgess initiate the practice, and why did they do so in 1571?

There is not much difficulty about explaining Hooker's diary.[27] Though he sat for the first time in 1571, he had been a member of the Irish Parliament of 1569 and had kept a diary then; he wished to collect material for a treatise on Parliament which he published in the following year and which for a time became a standard work of reference;[28] and as dedicated citizen of the city which had returned him to the Parliament he very probably also wished to provide himself with the means for rendering a report to his constituency.[29] Since he did not keep a diary when he sat again in 1586, it may be supposed that the second of these motives formed the chief reason for his doing so in 1571. On the other hand, nothing can be done with the anonymous diarist since the motives of an unidentified person must remain dark; nothing very helpful is to be obtained from internal evidence which shows only that he laboured energetically and showed a serious interest in some bills and debates about them.

That leaves Thomas Cromwell, who kept his diary for four out of the five sessions that he sat in (two of them outside our time limits). The fact that session by session his notes become briefer is sufficiently accounted for by his increasingly active involvement in parliamentary business; he

[27] Throughout this book, information on members of the Commons, if not otherwise footnooted, is derived from HPT.

[28] *The Order and Usage of Keeping a Parliament in England* (1572). The edition by Vernon F. Snow (New Haven, 1977), while not altogether satisfactory in various ways (cf. my review in *History* 63 [1978], 450–1) at least establishes the correct date of publication.

[29] This practice of reporting can only be conjectured in Hooker's case, but it was common and went back a long way. In 1485 the members for Colchester kept a diary specifically for this purpose: N. Pronay and J. Taylor, *Parliamentary Texts of the Later Middle Ages* (Oxford, 1980), 177–89.

was in particular an exceptionally frequent member of committees. That he did not write solely for his own purposes or eyes is strongly suggested by the way in which he refers to his occasional absence from the House: when he reports this reason for his inability to complete the record he certainly seems to be addressing a particular person and certainly not himself. Therefore: for whom was he writing? One clue is provided by a fragment of a diary kept by the clerk, Fulk Onslow, who at times at least made fair transcripts of notes on bills and debates, of which the former can differ from his official Journal, while nothing at all of the latter entered that record. One such fragment survives for 1572 and others can be safely conjectured for later Parliaments. The manifest reason for his preparing these documents lies in the need of Lord Burghley, himself no longer in the Commons, to learn what was going on there; unsurprisingly, the lord treasurer, like his son after him, used the clerk (Onslow was also his client) for that purpose.[30] But Onslow was not Burghley's only client in the Parliament: Cromwell's connection with him explains the series of elections always to seats with which Cromwell had no personal links at all. Quite plainly it was Burghley who placed him in Parliament. In 1571, Cromwell shared the seats for Fowey in Cornwall with Robert Petre, an Exchequer official and another of Burghley's men; in 1586 and 1589 Burghley put him in at Grampound; in 1584 Burghley's old ally Sir Ralph Sadler performed the necessary service to the grandson of his own first patron at Preston. In 1572 Cromwell sat for Bodmin where both Burghley and the earl of Bedford exercised patronage; it would be strange if that election too had not been managed by Cromwell's special patron.

Burghley wished to be kept informed about events in the Commons, so as to exercise a degree of management at some remove; one of his clients suddenly started keeping a careful and complete record of events, a record which he made it plain was not meant just for his own entertainment. Much the most convincing reason, therefore, for Cromwell's diary-keeping is that like Onslow he was commissioned by the lord treasurer, the most avid seeker after information of his day. Burghley may have decided that after his first session in the House Cromwell had learned the ropes sufficiently to be useful, for which reason he set him to the task in 1572. The coincidence of Cecil's transfer to the Lords with the beginning of diary-keeping should not be overlooked, and it is very likely that the anonymous diarist of 1571 and 1572 was another of the lord treasurer's informants. Both he and Cromwell wrote what in structure are very similar accounts, providing a full record of bill proceedings into which they inserted more detailed accounts of particular

[30] *Proc.* 311–16; *Studies*, 169–70.

occasions. This similarity of pattern again suggests a common origin of the practice. And since apparently they served not themselves but an instructor, we can at least be sure that they did not select matters to suit personal taste or because their own particular interests were aroused by this or that event. They certainly did not enter reports of all discussions, and Cromwell, as time went on, confined himself increasingly to listing and describing bills, but by and large, like Onslow, they told their employer things that he, and not they, wished to hear about. This makes it likely that they reported debates fairly, not biassing the effect to suit their own preferences; whether they were, as Neale liked to think, inclined to puritan views therefore matters little. Predictably, it was the record of speeches that caught Neale's eyes, determined as he was to document dispute and opposition, but at least as valuable are the descriptions of bills which quite frequently tell us a good deal more about the contents of some now lost than do the Journals of either House.

Thus we may conclude that it was William Cecil and the needs of management that initiated the private keeping of parliamentary diaries, even though the opportunity for serving other purposes need not have been missed. The manner in which the diarist of 1571 elaborated on the opening proceedings and other matters familiar to Burghley, and the multiplicity of copies, one of which is found in the State Papers where some of Burghley's archive ended up, suggest that the Anonymous author may have utilized his commission to compose an account in which other customers also might be interested. Cromwell's diary contains entries which read as though meant for the information of constituents. Nevertheless, as the use of Onslow and much well attested later practice indicates, the chief purpose was to serve a leading councillor in the Upper House. It may just be remarked that the proliferation of such diaries in the 1620s went hand in hand with the increasing pressure on parliamentary affairs of noble court factions whose leaders also needed to know about events below. At the least it is extremely doubtful whether mere self-importance or a childlike awe at having entered the portals of St Stephen's played any part at all in these valuable scribblings.

Lastly, in this discussion of the sources, we should just note the obvious fact that bills and other concerns of the Parliament could find recorded deposit just about anywhere, in the correspondence of the day, in the reports of foreign ambassadors, in the muniment rooms of municipalities. So far as possible these have been drawn into the net, but it is likely, and to be hoped for, that local searchers will turn up more. One potential but speculative source of information has not been used here. We are concerned with the Parliament, but once it had made an act this act's further life transferred to the arena of the law. It is not impossible that information on the making of laws and the ends intended might lie hidden in the records of the courts and the labours of law reporters, but that barely charted territory, the proper province of which is the application and effect of laws made in Parliament, has had to be left unvisited.

2

Parliament in the sixteenth century

'The most high and absolute power of the realm of England is in the Parliament.'[1] This famous phrase of Sir Thomas Smith's summarizes a concept but falls well short of explicating it. Historians, following a tradition established by the whig victory of the seventeenth century and impressed by the fact that the meetings of representative assemblies inevitably bring together varied and often rival interests, have habitually concentrated on a political function; to them Parliament has been primarily the embodiment of that 'politic' principle which, as Fortescue explained in the fifteenth century,[2] distinguished the otherwise 'regal' monarchy of England from the purely royal despotism that he, rather uncertainly, discerned in France. Thus its history has usually been written around the occasional clashes between the Crown and other politically influential elements, clashes which were exceptional rather than normal. It is not denied that meetings of the Parliament could offer an arena for political dispute, but the essence and permanent function of the institution did not lie in that fact.

It is now nearly a hundred years since F. W. Maitland taught us an essential truth when he explained that from its beginnings the Parliament formed an aspect of the king's government, a meeting in which the monarch and his Council, calling to them the members of the realm, sat to resolve the problems of Crown and common weal.[3] Even in the sixteenth century everyone agreed that Parliament formed the apex of the king's courts: here the errors of the other courts could be amended and its own errors were remediable by itself alone. This, no doubt, represents a somewhat limited lawyer's view, but few except lawyers at the time thought or spoke on such constitutional matters, and they

[1] Sir Thomas Smith, *De Republica Anglorum* (ed. M. Dewar; Cambridge, 1982), 78.

[2] Sir John Fortescue, *The Governance of England* (ed. C. Plummer; Oxford, 1985), 113–14.

[3] F. W. Maitland, introduction to *Memoranda de Parliamento, 1305* (London, 1893); and cf. G. R. Elton, *F. W. Maitland* (London, 1985), 56–69.

recognized that the Parliament's function touched the law rather than politics, for politics defined themselves in legal decrees and laws could be made only in Parliament. Though a court, it sat without the regularity of the bodies more obviously deserving that name, and one should keep in mind the time between particular Parliaments and the advisability of looking at those meetings as particular occasions. Nevertheless, there was an institution properly to be called the Parliament, continuous in its rights, claims, practices and records. Since, however, it came into active existence only at the will of the Crown, without whose decision to issue the writ of summons it could not even meet, the primary attention given to its constitutional role in limiting the power of the executive must from the start seem misplaced. A king's court, therefore, but an odd court, especially in its manner of proceeding: no bench of judges, no counsel pleading at its bar, no litigant parties, no established law to administer. Evidently, the curial definition is inadequate if not entirely inapposite to these intermittent manifestations of 'the most high and absolute power of the realm'. If, therefore, we wish to see it rightly we must first of all become clear about two things bearing on the relations between the institution and the monarchy: what were understood to be the component parts of Parliament, and what was at the time thought to be its normal role in the government of England?

Regarding the composition of the Parliament, we find a certain fundamental confusion throughout the century which complicates what was yet the main accepted definition. Earlier ages had entertained no such doubts: to them the Parliament was the king's court of which he was, as it were, the president but not a member. Instead, its members were the 'three estates' of nobility, spiritualty and commonalty assembled in two Houses, though of those two the Upper or House of Lords occupied a superior position, being the conciliar part of the Parliament (a council of the realm), while the Lower or House of Commons was still regarded as the assembly of petitioners on behalf of the realm. The institutional discrepancy between the Houses had been in process of disappearing between about 1484 and 1523. During the sittings of the Reformation Parliament (1529–1536), a new concept of a High Court consisting of three parts equally participant in its work – king, Lords and Commons – began to gain general currency. It was adumbrated quite unselfconsciously by Christopher St German in 1531, stated plainly in the dispensations act of 1534, and endorsed by Henry VIII in 1542 when he described a Parliament in which he as head and the Houses as members formed 'one body politic'.[4] This doctrine, which placed the king inside the Parliament, was accepted by Sir Thomas Smith when he

[4] For all this cf. *Studies* II, 32–6, 38–40; III, 110–42.

described the institution as embodying the realm in time of peace and as consisting of the prince, the 'barony', the commonalty and the bishops, though he left some room for debate because he seemed to hint at a structure by estates rather than Houses. Smith's opinion has something authoritative about it, not only because he was an experienced member of several governments but also because the office of the secretary of state regarded his treatise as the best guide to the English constitution.[5] It is important to note that his remarks about Parliament were written in the early 1560s and thus described practice and concepts as they stood at the beginning of Elizabeth's reign at the latest.[6] By 1559, the best opinion held that in England the supreme lawmaking power was vested in 'the king in Parliament'.

However, as Smith's choice of words indicates, some room remained for uncertainty. The older concept, which separated the monarch from the Parliament, could still crop up, especially when the misleading notion intervened which viewed the Parliament as composed of estates. In England, the medieval idea of three estates had always been better suited to political and social theory than to institutional analysis. After all, while one might just possibly regard the king, in his capacity as a corporation sole, as an estate, this was not the usual meaning of the word; and neither House of Parliament fitted the estates terminology at all. The lords spiritual presented there no separate existence; they were only members of one constituent part of Parliament and were held to sit there, being summoned individually by the Crown, as tenants-in-chief, not as members of the spiritual estate. The lords temporal did even worse because, according to the doctrine of estates, they should have included not only the peerage but also the knights; thus they appeared to be distributed between the two Houses. And the commons of the realm, the conventional third estate, even if one were to allow citizens and burgesses in Parliament (who in personal status often belonged to the lesser nobility) to represent them, shared a House with the knights of the shires, very definitely by convention reckoned as noble rather than common. The truth, of course, was that the composition of the English Parliament had never owed anything to the representation of the mythical three estates, so that the term produced only mental and verbal confusion; but

[5] Conyers Read, *Mr Secretary Walsingham and the Policy of Queen Elizabeth* (Oxford, 1925), I, 428 – where Robert Beale advises that the book, though in some respects out of date, should be regarded as the fundamental instruction.

[6] In her introduction to *De Republica*, Dr Mary Dewar has conclusively demonstrated that Smith's chapters on Parliament were completed by 1565 and not perhaps inserted or revised for the first printing of 1583, as Sir John Neale, convinced that the pre-Elizabethan Parliaments were too 'primitive' to fit that description, always imagined.

used it was nonetheless, with the result, among other things, that the medieval definition which treated the prince as separate from the Parliament could survive, at least at a first glance, though a second often calls up doubt. At any rate, from the 1530s the correct doctrine, reflecting fact, looked upon the prince as one member of a parliamentary trinity.

The conventional verbiage about the three estates could produce language that might mislead. Queen Elizabeth, right at the start of her reign, signed a proclamation which asked the realm to postpone religious innovation 'until consultation may be had by Parliament, by her majesty and her three estates of the realm',[7] and when James I informed the nation of Gunpowder Plot he declared that the plotters had meant to blow up 'us, our children, and all three estates in Parliament assembled'.[8] Did they separate themselves from the estates in Parliament? It is just possible to read this into James's pronouncement though even there the case is not certain; Elizabeth surely implied that she was a member of the Parliament too. On the other hand, William Harrison, who did not respect monarchy all that highly, noted that the law governing the ordination of ministers was made 'by the three estates of the realm in the High Court of Parliament' and later defined this court in a way that denied the king estate-status: that High Court consisted of 'several sourts of people, that is to say, the nobility, clergy and commons of this realm' – good, oldfashioned estates doctrine.[9] Just possibly this view later received the formidable support of John Selden who in one of his *obiter dicta* declared that 'the king is not one of the three estates, as some would have it (take heed of that!), for if two agree the third is involved: but he is king of the three estates'.[10] Just what he meant by this is as darkly gnomic as so much of his Table-talk, for he cannot have supposed either that an agreement between his three estates in Parliament bound the king to consent (which would ignore the power of the veto) or that the king took no share in the decisions of the Parliament. Perhaps he had it in mind that the king must not be bound by a majority decision which might exist if he formed one of the estates; perhaps – seeing he does not mention it – he was not thinking of the Parliament at all and preferred to use the estates terminology for its original, non-parliamentary purposes only. If so, he helped to lead others away from an identification of Parliament with the three estates, an identification which, however unsatisfactory to a scholar, had great use in clarifying the nature of Parliament and its powers.

[7] *TRP* II, 103 (27 Dec. 1558).
[8] *Stuart Royal Proclamations* (ed. J. F. Larkin; Oxford, 1973), I, 143.
[9] William Harrison, *The Description of England* (ed. G. Edelen; Ithaca, N.Y., 1968), 27, 170.
[10] BL, Harleian MS 1315, p. 70.

The revolution of the mid-seventeenth century, when Parliament by stages dispensed with two of its three 'estates', inclined some people against any teaching which failed to set the king apart from any of his subjects, even in Parliament, a change of mind from Tudor doctrine – and indeed from Charles I's famous declaration in 1642[11] – which was fully espoused by so careful a lawyer as Sir Matthew Hale. Writing after the restoration of the monarchy, Hale expressly denied that the king was one of the estates of the realm and spoke of 'the "three estates of the realm" assembled in parliament, viz. the lords spiritual, lords temporal and commons'.[12] But Hale's confidence covered up a very dubious argument. For his first point he cited no evidence later than 1484, which means that he simply ignored the drastic change that had come over the definition of Parliament from the 1530s onwards, proving himself to be the sort of medievaliser common among seventeenth-century lawyers. His second point he claimed to prove by reference to Elizabeth's act of supremacy in which, according to him, those three estates had recognized the Queen's title. But what 1 Eliz. I c.1 actually says is 'your faithful and obedient subjects, the Lords spiritual and temporal, and the Commons in your present Parliament assembled', which was the conventional description of the two Houses and had nothing to do with any three estates. It was Hale who by inserting a second 'Lords' before 'temporal' managed to create the semblance of an estates structure.

In fact, those of the Queen's faithful subjects who looked at reality knew better than to set her apart from the Parliament or to confuse the truth – three partners in one Parliament – with the fiction, a Parliament of estates. That the Parliament consisted of Queen, Lords and Commons conjoined, to cite Henry VIII, in one body politic, was the view of Lord Burghley who sat in and supervised more Parliaments than any man before the eighteenth century.[13] Arthur Hall, member for Grantham, quarrelled violently with Sir Walter Mildmay, chancellor of the Exchequer, over the antiquity of Parliament, but both of them firmly agreed on this definition of the Parliament, as did William Lambarde, the learned antiquary.[14] All these four also demonstrated how quickly realism could absorb the fiction when they applied the term 'the three estates' to prince, Lords and Commons – of which estates, as Burghley put it, 'consisteth the whole body of the Parliament able to make laws'.

[11] In his 'Answer to the Nineteen Propositions' which enunciated the 'classic' doctrine of the mixed sovereign, the king-in-Parliament: C. C. Weston, 'The theory of mixed monarchy under Charles I and after', *EHR* 75 (1960), 426–43.

[12] Sir Matthew Hale, *The Prerogatives of the King* (ed. D. E. C. Yale; Selden Society, 1976), 11, 134.

[13] D'Ewes, 350.

[14] *Studies* III, 254–73; William Lambarde, *Archeion* (ed. C. H. McIlwain and P. L. Ward; New Haven, 1957), 123.

Not unexpectedly, such easy, and harmless, confusion would not do for Richard Hooker who yet agreed with what Burghley and the rest were trying to say, though in his anxiety to grant authority also to the Church he invented a new confusion by adding Convocation to the Parliament – a dubious proceeding in law, however convenient in polemical practice. (He was concerned to show that Parliament was not 'so merely temporal as if it might meddle with nothing but only leather and wool'.) His definition, therefore, made of Parliament 'the body of the whole realm' consisting of 'the king and of all that in the land are subject to him: for they are all present, either in person or by such as they voluntarily have derived their personal right unto' – the last sentence being nearly pure Thomas Smith.[15]

There were, in fact, three ways of coping with the confusing concept of estates. You could use it without justification, as these exponents of the true mixed-sovereign idea did; you could, like Smith and Hooker, take care to avoid the word; or you could simply pretend that the term fitted the real situation well. Almost predictably, this last solution – riding sovereignly and idiosyncratically over all the difficulties – was adopted by Sir Edward Coke according to whom Parliament consisted of the king 'sitting there in his royal politic capacity' and 'the three estates of the realm' (lords spiritual, temporal and commons); those four parts 'are the great corporation or body politic of the kingdom and sit in two Houses' – the king and the lords in one, the knights and burgesses in the other.[16] Coke's fence-sitting act enabled David Jenkins, imprisoned by Parliament during the civil wars, to deny Prynne's insistence that the king was but one of the estates of the Parliament: he pointed out that even Coke, 'their oracle', had confined the term estates to the two kinds of peers and the commons.[17] Even so, Jenkins held that 'the king is the head of the Parliament, the Lords the principal members, the Commons the inferior members, and so the whole body is composed' – a definition which, by placing the king inside the Parliament, came much closer to Tudor doctrine than to Hale's later swerving from it.[18]

Perhaps it is no surprise that Hale, after the experience of a Parliament which had done without the king, should have revived an estates-based

[15] *The Works of...Mr Richard Hooker* (ed. J. Keble; Oxford, 1888), III, 408–9.

[16] Edward Coke, *Fourth Institute of the Laws of England* (London, 1644), 1–2.

[17] David Jenkins, *Works* (London, 1648), 49. In view of some of the things now being said about the seventeenth century I should stress that when I speak of harmony I do not have 'consensus politics' in mind. The term, transferred from American political science, seems to me inapplicable to Tudor and Stuart England.

[18] Ibid. 19. Yet ibid. 50 we learn that 'the King, as King, is present in his parliament as well as in all his other courts of justice, howbeit he is not there', a statement which by equating the Parliament with, e.g., the King's Bench implicitly makes the king the 'owner' of Parliament rather than a member of it.

doctrine which set the monarch apart from the Parliament, but Coke's ruthless carpentering job described much better what was really practised and held under Elizabeth. Then the legislative authority was defined as resting with an institution consisting of three parts – the king and the two Houses – each separately deciding whether to agree or not in the threefold consensus which alone could make laws. If the three parts had to be called estates, let them by all means take the name; it meant nothing in practice but seemed to satisfy some sort of philosophy. The point was well made by William Camden with that accidental skill that makes the good historian. In the first edition of his *Britannia* (1586) he defined Parliament as consisting of three estates and as representing the whole body of the realm: 'ex tribus enim Angliae ordinibus constat et totius Angliae corpus repraesentat'. The subsequent Latin editions retained this succinct and inadequate description. But when Camden supervised the English translation, to which he added new passages, he put forward a significantly expanded definition for home consumption: 'it consisteth of the king, the clergy, the superior nobles, the elect knights and burgesses; or to speak more significantly after the lawyers' phrase, of the King, the Lords Spiritual and Temporal, and the Commons, which States represent the body of all England'.[19] After the lawyers' phrase: the right legal view spoke of the king-in-Parliament. And he added words to underline the primacy of that view: 'It has the sovereign and sacred authority in making, confirming, repealing and expounding laws, in restoring such as be attainted or out-lawed in their former estates, in deciding of the hardest controversies between private persons, and, to speak at a word, in all causes which may concern either the state or any private person whatsoever.' The English Parliament, which included the king, was above all a sovereign lawmaking body.

How clear were contemporaries, even before Camden wrote, about this supreme lawmaking power vested in Parliament? Definitions tend to result from argument; it is only differences of opinion which produce attempts at clarification. The function of the Tudor Parliament was thus liable to be more precisely analysed during the years of disputation which Stuart methods of government unleashed, and it will serve to start after the event. That reflective and much too talkative King, James I, once offered an interpretation which shows that he understood his second kingdom rather more clearly than historians have done who nevertheless used to speak of his ignorance and his need to be taught better.[20] In March

[19] *Britannia* (1586), 83; (1610), 177.

[20] Cf. J. R. Tanner, *Constitutional Documents of the Reign of James I* (Cambridge, 1930), 202: 'a lecture to a foreign King on the constitutional customs of his realm'. Of course, this applied to 1604, and it could, I suppose, be argued that James dutifully learned his lesson. Did he ever? Or rather, did he ever need to?

1610, addressing the Parliament, he explained the call for reform.[21] Much as he respected the common law, he could not avoid recognizing that it required improvement, 'but always by the advice of Parliament, for the king with his Parliament here are absolute in making or forming any sort of laws'. After running over the kind of revision he wanted – replacing the use of French by English, codification, a review of statutes to remove illogical confusions – he added that furthermore Parliament, as 'the representative body of the whole realm', was the means for bringing the nation's grievances to the king's notice. It is not that James displayed high originality or insight; what signifies is the manner in which he understood the commonplaces of the position, though he took misleading care to separate himself from the Parliament. He knew that Parliament had a definite role to play in the running of the country: it provided a forum for opening up matters requiring attention, and it possessed the power to remedy such matters by the making of laws. To him, as to the Tudors, Parliament was thus an extension of the royal means of government, not a restriction upon them; he thought in terms of habitual cooperation, even harmony – and again this was a commonplace, not perhaps merely a momentary need to appear conciliatory. As a 'Discourse concerning the success of former Parliaments', published in 1642 (the year of final disruption) rather wistfully put it:

It was ever heretofore seen that our Parliaments were rather a strength and advantage to an honourable wise prince than a remedy against a bad and weak one; or, if we change the expression, they were rather an excellent diet to keep a good reign in strength than physic to cure a bad one.[22]

This plea for cooperation between the king, the Lords and the Commons, coming from a supporter of the Long Parliament who wisely confined his historical examples to the years before 1399, correctly stated the role of the institution in the hundred years before he came to write.

Remedying grievances and deficiencies by the making of law: a chorus of Tudor pronouncements lies behind this Stuart definition. St German said so even before the Reformation Parliament demonstrated the consequences that could arise from permitting the law to be enlarged by statute; he knew that the ultimate source of law in England 'standeth in diverse statutes made by the king, the Lords and the Commons'.[23] It was Elizabethan doctrine that the making of law must always have been vested in Parliament, a doctrine maintained even when the evidence of

[21] *Harleian Miscellany* (1744 ed.), I, 12. Cf. *Proceedings in Parliament 1610* (ed. E. R. Foster; New Haven, 1966), I, 47.

[22] *Harleian Misc.* VI, 377–81.

[23] *Doctor and Student* (ed T. F. T. Plucknett and J. L. Barton; Selden Society, 1974), 30–1, 73.

the past appeared to contradict it. That sensible antiquary, William Lambarde, denied any independent lawmaking power in the king alone by blatantly demanding that the evidence for it be ignored:

If you shall find any acts of Parliament seeming to pass under the name and authority of the king only, as there be some that have that show indeed, yet you must not by and by judge that it was established without the assent of the estates.[24]

William Camden, even when engaged in very properly analysing the high claims of the royal prerogative, yet emphasized that revision of the law did not belong to the king alone because lawmaking was a parliamentary function; and he found a good recent example: 'whereof yet if any man doubt let him see the statutes made in the time of King Henry VIII: and let no king desire to be accounted worse than Henry VIII'.[25] A brief note on the courts of the realm, jotted down late in Elizabeth's reign, summed it all up succinctly: 'Parliament: to make new laws and abolish old'.[26]

However, as James I indicated, the matter could not be left so simply at the level of defining a function: what laws were to be made? As James again indicated, the answer lay in the reception and resolution of 'grievances' – anything, that is, that troubled the subject. The petitions that were received and tried in Plantagenet Parliaments for the king's answer had their descendants in the petitions and bills brought in Tudor Parliaments for legislative answers from the parliamentary trinity. However, if Parliament was to bring such matters to public attention, its function clearly extended beyond the purely legislative one: it was then to be seen, and so described, as advising on action, as a council to its head, the king. Even Matthew Hale, writing about the prerogative in full awareness of what revolution had done to it a few years earlier, admitted that Parliament was a great council whose advice should be followed unless there is 'clear reason to the contrary'; and its advice could cover 'all matters concerning the state'. He hastened to add that kings were not constitutionally bound to follow such advice, but he clearly allowed that Parliament (with or without the king in it!) had also a political function.[27] By 1660 it would have been hard to avoid seeing that fact, but the notions are much older and lie, for instance, behind the claims that even the Commons on their own were a council of the realm, able and indeed bound to advise the Crown on political issues,

[24] Lambarde, *Archeion*, 139.

[25] 'William Camden's "Discourse concerning the prerogative of the Crown",' ed. F. S. Fussner (*Proceedings of the American Philosophical Society* 101, 1957), 215. The identification of Camden as the author is doubtful, but this does not matter in the present context.

[26] Inner Temple, Petyt MS 538/54.

[27] Hale, *Prerogatives*, 140–1.

which Paul and Peter Wentworth were fond of putting forward in Elizabethan Parliaments. The semi-public platform of a Parliament – in either House – offered a suitable stage for political argument and general debate, and the inclination to engage in such debate was much stimulated by the decisions taken in the 1530s which demanded from both Lords and Commons a deep involvement in the affairs of state and Church. It is, however, important to understand that conceptually the political function was seen as essentially subordinate to the legislative one: discussion of such high matters was merely a preparatory stage towards the making of statutes designed to improve the law and remedy grievances (the primary purpose for which Parliament assembled), and a meeting which failed to move from the preliminary to the essential stage, as the Parliament of 1614 did, caused not only frustration but also astonishment. 'Bills,' as John Pym noted in 1621, 'are the end of a Parliament': an admirable and memorable definition.[28]

One thing that any modern commentator would surely expect to find mentioned here has so far had no airing: in contemporary discussions we hear virtually nothing about the granting of money to the Crown, that supposedly famous pillar for the power and continued existence of representative institutions. Neither those eager to elevate monarchy nor those concerned to mollify a Parliament would, it is true, be much inclined to remind their hearers of that tiresome subject. Only Francis Bacon, reviewing the first two Parliaments of James I and trying to ascertain why they had been such messy failures, adverted to taxation, and he did so because in his view too open an insistence on it had been a chief reason for the difficulties encountered.[29] He may well have been right, but the way in which one of the most constant preoccupations of any meeting of Parliament is passed over by the commentators remains striking – and a warning against equating their comment too readily with the truth and whole truth. Even those writers who, trying for a systematic treatment, list the uses of Parliament in some detail – writers like Sir Thomas Smith or Richard Robinson[30] – slip the matter of money in very casually and concentrate on activities which require legislation. Doing things no one else could do, and doing them by producing laws: that, in the all but universal view of constitutional theorists, was what Parliaments were for.

Generally speaking, this line of thought also characterizes the notions expressed by people called upon from time to time to explain why a particular Parliament had been called, though they of necessity were

[28] Cited C. Russell, *The English Commonwealth* (ed. P. Clark et al.; London, 1979), 150.

[29] See his analysis, produced in 1615, in *The Letters and the Life of Francis Bacon* (ed. J. Spedding), V (1869), 176–91.

[30] Cf. *Studies* III, 159–60.

markedly less reticent about the need for money. By the early sixteenth century at the latest, it had become customary to open a new Parliament with what was in effect a speech from the throne – an oration in which the speaker (nearly always the lord chancellor or lord keeper of the great seal) laid out the reasons for the meeting about to start and justified the burden placed on members of both Houses by their obedience to the royal summons. As long as chancellors were chosen from among prominent clerics, these speeches were in fact and purport sermons which tended to concentrate on turning the assembled Lords' and Commons' minds to their spiritual duties and gave remarkably little attention to the real reasons for the meeting of Parliament. In 1483, preparing an address to the Parliament of Edward V which was never delivered, and one for that of Richard III which was, Bishop Russell of Lincoln, chancellor, talked a good deal about Christian virtue and spread himself quite interestingly on problems of good governance, but found little else to say.[31] For the first occasion he meant to explain that the sole purpose of the Parliament was to confirm the duke of Gloucester's protectorship, while on the second he vaguely concluded by reminding the assembly that their task lay in the advancement of the commonwealth.

This medieval tradition, which rather emphasized the need to maintain a godly frame of mind than dealt with practical problems or put forward a programme, continued into the reign of Henry VIII, though a small change was coming over these set pieces in the hands of Archbishop Warham who as chancellor opened three Parliaments with sermons summarized by the clerk of the Lords in his Journal book. In 1510, he said much about the needful fear of God and the excellence of the new king, but also added that the Parliament was invited to consider the existing laws with a view to amending what was amiss and repealing what was wrong.[32] The Parliament followed instructions by passing measures intended to prevent a recurrence of the alleged abuses committed by the late king's administration.[33] In 1511, when Henry was planning to join in a European war, Warham expressly 'declared the cause of the summons of Parliament' by drawing attention to that prospect, but in spite of the obvious implication he does not seem to have spoken specifically about supply; after justifying the rapid calling of a second Parliament in the reign with a tedious catalogue of Roman and Jewish assemblies, he merely emphasized the need to prepare for war by seeking the advice of the realm.[34] There are, however, reasons for thinking that in that context 'advice' stood as a euphemism for finding the money. And

[31] S. B. Chrimes, *English Constitutional Ideas in the Fifteenth Century* (Cambridge, 1936), 168–91.

[32] *LJ* I, 3.

[33] Cf. *Studies* I, 92–5.

[34] *LJ* I, 10.

in 1514 (reminiscent of Russell's preoccupations) he spent most of his time in reflecting on the qualities needed in a good ruler and a good system of justice before perfunctorily telling the Parliament to remedy whatever needed attention.[35] They – that is, the Commons – were in effect to be responsible for bringing up the agenda of the meeting. Next time, in 1523, Wolsey was chancellor, but he apparently extended his dislike of Parliaments to the point of suppressing his normal delight in the sound of his own voice. The sermon was instead preached by the bishop of London, Cuthbert Tunstall, who, so far as he was recorded, confined himself to the moral duty of man and the need for good kingship ('where there is no ruler, the people shall perish'); however, he perhaps became more specific thereafter, for 'in a wise and devout fashion the said bishop of London added many things more fully, more penetratingly and more elegantly than is here entered'.[36] On balance, this still sounds as though he elaborated his points of edification rather than presented a list of practical purposes.

The chancellor who opened the Reformation Parliament was Sir Thomas More, more devout than most bishops but a layman and a lawyer, and moreover a practised and conscious orator. From this time, the opening of Parliament usually necessitated a sermon in Westminster Abbey, followed by a speech to all the Parliament in the House of Lords.[37] More's speech thus abandoned the sermonizing of tradition and concentrated on the reasons for the summons.[38] As he explained these, they were the misgovernment of his predecessor, Wolsey, whom he attacked with the abusive severity he usually reserved for heretics, and the need to provide new remedies for newly arisen 'enormities' – in the context either solely or predominantly the problem of heresy. This was More's programme and neither the King's nor the Parliament's which in the event found itself preoccupied with the deficiencies of the Church and the breach with Rome, but at least the chancellor had presented a plain reason for the meeting.[39] Since such addresses remained confined

[35] Ibid. 18.

[36] Ibid. p. lxxv (taken from the Roll, the Journal being lost).

[37] E.g. in 1563, Alexander Nowell, dean of St Paul's, preached on the Queen's marriage before the lord keeper got a chance to direct the Parliament's thoughts to less contentious matters (below p. 358). In 1571, Edwin Sandys, bishop of London, choosing for his text the words of Sam. xii ('Timete deum et ei servite in veritate') showed how religion 'is chiefly to be sought in virtue and truth' and reminded princes that they 'ought to direct their doings in true religion and to govern their people in truth, equity and justice' (*Proc.* 243), before Bacon once again brought things back to reality.

[38] Esp. Edward Hall, *The Union...of Lancaster and York* (ed. London, 1809), 764; and cf. J. A. Guy, *The Public Career of Sir Thomas More* (Brighton, 1980), 113–5.

[39] S. E. Lehmberg, *The Reformation Parliament 1529–1536* (Cambridge, 1970), 78–9. Lehmberg's studies of Henrician Parliaments provide a good account of these speeches, as well as a handy guide to the evidence.

to the opening of new Parliaments, none being delivered at the start of prorogued sessions, there was now an intermission, but in 1536 Lord Chancellor Audley completed the secularization of the speech when he explained at length that the sole purpose of the present Parliament was to provide for the succession to the Crown, in total disarray after the annulment of Henry VIII's first two marriages.[40] Audley's speech is a fascinating mixture of king-worship and frankness about that particular King.

At this point unfortunately the clerk ceased to enter summaries of the opening address in the Journal, and until 1558 we lack all knowledge of what was said.[41] He did, however, note the speeches in the House of Lords with which Audley and Thomas Cromwell introduced the prorogued session of 1540, and although they were addressed to one House only they concern us here because they amounted to statements of government policy. Audley, in fact, spoke twice, on the first day praising good religion but on the second more significantly calling for law reform and specifying the measures he wanted. Cromwell, in a passionate oration, looked for unity in religion (supposedly settled the previous year by the act of six articles) and asked for a new formulary as well as less contentious disputing.[42] At this point, therefore, we find ourselves in the presence of Parliaments called to carry out a legislative programme submitted by government, but it is necessary to remember that the preparing of such programmes was peculiar to the era of Cromwell's ascendancy and rarely followed so vigorously at other times. Naturally, when government wanted certain laws enacted it reminded Parliament that its function lay in the enacting of laws. We cannot even conjecture what may have been said to the nine Parliaments that met between Cromwell's fall and the accession of Elizabeth – and they included the Parliaments that made England protestant and then turned her back to Rome. All that can safely be said is this: in the course of Henry VIII's reign it became customary to tell the assembled Houses that they shared

[40] S. E. Lehmberg, *The Later Parliaments of Henry VIII 1536–1547* (Cambridge, 1977), 84.

[41] As Lehmberg notes (ibid. 56), on the authority of William Dugdale's *Summons to Parliament* (1685), 502–3, the Parliament of 1539 seems to have been opened by neither the chancellor nor by any bishop but by the earl of Sussex, lord chamberlain, who is stated to have explained the reasons for the assembly. Dugdale cites a manuscript in the College of Heralds which is likely to have got it right: the heralds, for their own use, kept accounts of proceedings at the beginning of Parliaments. The most likely explanation for this surprising intrusion lies in Cromwell's illness at the start of the session: as viceregent in spirituals he could have claimed the right to deliver the address. Dugdale's evidence shows that 'speeches from the throne' continued to be delivered and that the silence of the Journal represents only a change in record-keeping.

[42] G. R. Elton, *Reform and Renewal: Thomas Cromwell and the Common Weal* (Cambridge, 1973), 152–3; Lehmberg, *Later Parliaments*, 90–1.

in the tasks of government and were there to be consulted, but that this advice was meant to lead to the making of such laws as the occasion required. Even when supply was to be got and reference made to the needs of the Crown, the actual mention of money seems to have been avoided. In the Cromwell era, with the Council in charge of proceedings and engaged in pushing through a planned policy, reference to new laws became specific rather than vague.

Information comes to us again with the beginning of Elizabeth's reign and is full for the first three of her Parliaments: 1559, 1563, 1571. Prorogued sessions like that of 1566, of course, still witnessed no opening speeches. The reason for this happy state of the evidence lies in the high oratorical reputation of Sir Nicholas Bacon who as lord keeper opened them all. His speeches in and out of Parliament, collected and frequently copied, survive in several manuscripts and have been familiar because Simonds D'Ewes included them – not without confusion.[43] Bacon's addresses, artfully put together and manifestly effective, followed a pattern. He liked to begin by explaining his lack of skill, a proem which must by stages have both amused and exasperated his audience; he claimed always to be conveying the mind of the Queen; and he carefully parcelled his matter in numbered sections with subdivisions. He obviously memorized a careful script and thus gave much clarity to the information and instruction expressed.

In 1559,[44] Bacon made it plain that the Parliament was to do three things: to establish uniformity of religion, to attend to 'the enormities and mischiefs that do or might hurt or hinder the civil orders and policies of this realm', and to consider the effect upon the realm of the recent 'losses and decays' inflicted upon 'the imperial crown of this realm' to the end that they might 'advise the best remedies to supply and relieve the same'. The last point referred specially to the loss of Calais and the

[43] *Proc.* has silently cleared up the confusion, but the editor gives no reasons for his rearrangement. Thus for 1563 D'Ewes (59–61) prints a speech which differs very considerably in phrasing and detail, though not in substance, from that found in BL, Harl. MS 5176, fos. 89–92 and there dated to 1563. D'Ewes (192–5) prints the main part of this latter text as the address of 1572, adding to it a lengthy passage taken from another version of what he correctly prints as the address of 1571. As for 1563, all MSS are later copies and neither version is included in the best collection of Bacon's speeches (Harl. MS 398). However, the Harl. MS 5176 text belongs to 1563, for the following reasons. (1) It refers to a law for attendance at church made in the last Parliament; there was no such law in 1566, whereas the 1559 act of uniformity (1 Eliz. I c. 2, sect. 3) fits well. (2) The speech asks for supply but none was demanded in 1572. (3) The reference to the uncompleted accounts for expeditions of 1562–3 would have been nonsense in 1572. (4) There is no allusion in the speech to the Queen of Scots, the hot theme of 1572. D'Ewes' version for 1563 (taken from BL, Cotton MSS, Titus F.i, fos. 66 seqq.) Neale called a 'lengthy report' (*EP* I, 97, n.1), but it may well have been an earlier draft of the speech

[44] *Proc.* I, 33–9.

possible cost of measures to recover it. The remainder of the address at length elaborated each section. Parliament was given a very broad hint that the religious settlement must avoid either extreme; it was told that remedying mischiefs involved both new problems requiring legislation and a consideration of existing laws; the request for supply was wrapped up in a long declamation about the excellence of the Queen and the miserable state of her inheritance from the previous reign.

Having once found his formula, Bacon varied it only to suit the situation. In 1563,[45] he divided the business of the session into matters of religion and matters of policy, the former 'for the better maintenance and setting forth of God's honour and glory', the latter 'for the more perfect upholding and establishing the Queen's Majesty's honour and royal estate and the preservation of the commonweal committed to her charge'. The first in turn involved two things: doctrine (that is, the enforcement of uniform practices) and discipline (the spiritual improvement of both clergy and laity), but so far as the clergy were concerned he emphasized that both were to be attended to by 'my lords the bishops...and that as speedily, diligently and carefully as can be'. This, of course, was the supreme governor speaking. The only thing here left to the legislature was the problem of making 'the common people' attend church more regularly – unless indeed the bishops, having obeyed the Queen's demand that they should devise remedies for the Church, decided that they wanted an act of Parliament. Here, I think, we hear the lord keeper's own voice. Commonwealth matters Bacon also divided into two sorts: 'good governance' and 'defence against the enemy abroad'. Good governance in turn was declared to consist of two branches: a revision of the existing laws (are there too many, especially too many dealing with the same things?) and better provision for their execution. This last point, we learn, calls for these steps: a careful choice of agents (ministers of the Crown at all levels), 'sharp laws' to put an end to 'sloth, corruption and fear of them' (quite probably a reference to the statute of artificers planned for this session), and – he calls it an idea of his own over which he will defer to the judgment of Parliament – a regular enquiry every third or second year into the conduct of lay officials, similar to ecclesiastical visitations. Bacon recalled the old general commission of oyer and terminer (used by Henry VII and early in his son's reign) but with reason doubted whether it was adequate for the task he had in mind. Admitting that such a check applied to 'the great and open courts of the realm' would make his own burden in the Chancery 'equal with the greatest', he disarmingly declared that he 'would gladly every year hear and feel of such a controller'. Lastly he turned to defence, justifying the need for further taxation by once more

[45] Ibid. 80–6.

reviewing the state of affairs encountered at the Queen's accession and the costs incurred in gaining peace and repairing the inherited deficiencies. The Queen's treasure had been spent, her lands sold, and her credit committed to the limit at home and abroad – 'and all this for your surety and quietness'. Referring to the costs of the expeditions to Leith and Le Havre, he slid over the facts by explaining that the details were not yet available, a trick not unknown in later debates on supply. The Queen, he added, would much rather not have called the Parliament and burdened the subject, but there was no help for it. This address, so far as our evidence goes, came much closer to being a detailed programme for the Parliament than anything previously delivered – and the emphasis, supply apart, was once again exclusively on legislation.

Since Bacon's two remaining speeches were very similar in general structure and particular import, there is no need to discuss them at length. In 1571 he concentrated on the reform of the laws both ecclesiastical and temporal, again reminding his hearers that the former were in the first place the concern of the bishops. There then followed yet another call for money, justified both by the debt of gratitude owed to the Queen for ten years of successful rule, and by the special needs created by the upheavals of 1569–71 (with no reference to actual or possible war).[46] For 1572, the collections let us down and we have no text preserved; instead we must rely on the notes made by private diarists.[47] Such notes are more chancy ground on which to rest, but it would appear that Bacon tried to preempt discussion of the really contentious issues – the fate of the duke of Norfolk and the treatment of Mary Queen of Scots – by suggesting that a short session would be wise for a meeting arranged for mid-summer, with the danger of plague about, rather than for the usual winter season. After apologising, on the Queen's behalf, for so inconvenient a summons, he declared the purpose of the Parliament. Firstly, owing to the detection 'since the last Parliament' of various treasons and conspiracies, new laws had to be made touching the Queen's safety; secondly ('an old common cause in all Parliaments') he wished the existing state of the laws to be reviewed and any deficiencies remedied. He concluded with a warning that 'when they had once begun to deal with matters for the Queen's safety they should as little as might be intermeddle with other matters until the despatch of them'. This attempt to prevent official bills being swamped by private ones backfired: since to the Houses the Queen's safety seemed better guaranteed by the removal of Norfolk and Mary than by general laws, they managed to make the session difficult by concentrating just on those issues that Elizabeth did not wish to see debated.

Bacon's speeches thus truly came from the throne, expressing the

[46] Ibid. 183–7. [47] Ibid. 317, 336.

desires and purposes of Queen and Council, and they overwhelmingly identified the purpose and function of every meeting as taxation (peace-time taxation, on which he says most because it needs most justification) and the making of laws which, as he made plain, would occupy the bulk of the Parliament's time. Like his predecessors so far as we can reconstruct their attitudes, the lord keeper thought of Parliament as an instrument for legislation and of its business as defined by the making, mending and repealing of statutes. Its so-called capacity to advise was to be expressed in the discussion and refining of the bills put before it. This, of course, was a point of view expressed by those who ruled, and the alternative opinion that Parliament was a political council engaged in the conduct and supervision of public affairs can also be found; but in the reign of Elizabeth at least it was held by very few men and must be called eccentric.[48]

From the recognition that Parliament stood at the head of the hierarchy of courts, and from the fact that its chief function was the making of laws, there sprang the doctrine of the supremacy and omnicompetence of parliamentary statute. By 1558, opinion generally agreed on this: even those occasional judges who still treated Parliament as just another court and its pronouncements in consequence as no more than the ultimate judgments available in the system testified to the universal range of statute and the universal obedience due to it.[49] Even the problem of judicial interpretation, which of necessity arose in the course of applying acts of Parliament to cases litigated, would have looked very different if the authority of statute had not been so high as to impose obedience even on judges. Interpretation meant making sense of what blind obedience would have turned into nonsense, or it meant avoiding confusion arising from the equal authority of all acts of Parliament even when they conflicted with one another. If statute had still been regarded in much the same way as the judgment of any court, such difficulties would have been resolved by ignoring the statute, not by seeking to give it a meaning which would work. Thus interpretation sprang from the judges' position as servants of the statute, not from any sovereignty over it that they might seek to claim.[50]

In fact, statute was remediable only by another statute, and there was no appeal against any act of Parliament, against which not even a writ

[48] The view was put forward by Paul and Peter Wentworth but they got so little support in the House that the customary concentration on their interventions distorts the reality.

[49] Cf. L. W. Abbott, *Law-Reporting in England 1485–1585* (London, 1973), 228–9.

[50] For general discussions of this point cf. [T. Egerton], *A Discourse upon the Exposicion and Understanding of Statutes* (ed. S. E. Thorne; San Marino, 1942), especially the introduction; and Abbott, *Law-Reporting*, 229–39.

of error could be brought. As the Queen's Bench explained in Trinity term 1571: though a writ of error would lie against commissioners of oyer and terminer in a judgment of treason, the writ ceased to be available once the judgment had been confirmed by act of attainder. 'That which is confirmed by Parliament is made indefeasible, although it were defeasible before.'[51] That same litigation (*Earl of Leicester* v. *Heydon*: a case brought by bill of Middlesex for lands obtained from a forfeiture arising out of a conviction for treason since reversed) also provides an excellent example of the contortions to which the judges could be reduced in their efforts to combine the provision of justice with absolute respect for the supremacy of statute.[52] It being argued that the confirmatory act under discussion contained misstatements of fact, it was admitted that Parliament 'may be misinformed as well as other courts' but held that 'when they have recited a thing which is not true, it cannot be otherwise taken but that they were misinformed, for none can imagine that they would purposely recite a false thing to be true, for it is a court of the greatest honour and justice of which none can imagine a dishonourable thing'. Thus far can legal doctrine depart from notorious fact. Establishing an error in an act was thus no insult to the supremacy of Parliament which, having been merely misinformed, cannot be supposed to have intended the unfortunate consequences of an erroneous allegation because, had it been better informed, it would have ruled otherwise. Rather daringly the court therefore held

> that when an act of Parliament confirms a thing which is and wants force, the act shall give force to it and shall make it to be of effect where it was not before; but if an act of Parliament is referred to that which is not, and confirms it, as in our case, there the act shall be void to all intents.

The Bench could even cite a recent precedent for the new principle governing interpretation. The act of 1 Ed. VI c. 12, which repealed treasons and felonies created in the previous reign, in sect. 18 meant to exempt the Henrician act against servants who stole from their masters. However, the passage by mistake described the session during which this earlier act had passed as extending from 4 February to 24 April, whereas it had really ended on 14 April: for which error the exception was void, and an act which opinion generally thought valuable stood repealed. In this way, Parliament's immunity to a writ of error could actually be by-passed, and while a writ of error provided a remedy only for errors in the record (under which heading the case of 1 Ed. VI c. 12 could be classified) this judicial doctrine could extend to errors of fact. However,

[51] *Plowden's Reports* (ed. Dublin, 1782), 394.
[52] Ibid. 399.

as the precedent shows, the doctrine was used to frustrate government rather than enhance its powers.[53]

It must again be emphasized that such encroachments upon the sovereignty of statute arose solely from the tenet that statute was supreme and omnicompetent; there would have been no need for these complications if the judges had felt able to treat the judgments of Parliament as they treated other judgments – as guides but not as binding guides. This high position, however, statute had acquired only recently, mainly as the result of the events of the 1530s. Even the virtue of an act confirming a title obtained in the usual way, by donor's grant, had not always been recognized: a legal opinion of 1510 thought it 'not expedient' (not required for better security) to obtain such an act to confirm the testamentary bequests of the Lady Margaret Beaufort upon which the existence of St John's and Christ's Colleges, Cambridge, depended. A confirmation, 'at leisure', by royal patent was thought sufficient.[54] A few years later, a confirmatory act was welcomed in court as validating letters patent in themselves dubious because the King, though possessed only of a reversionary right, had conveyed the estate itself.[55] But even then, doubts (not resolved in the report) could be expressed whether a subsequent confirmatory act would not void even the effects of the attainder it confirmed, and thus become inadvisable.[56] In the course of the 1530s, Thomas Cromwell's and Thomas Audley's predilection for settling the property deals of the Crown in statutes would seem to have terminated these hesitations with regard to both the desirability and the effectiveness of this use of statutory supremacy; confirming acts became quite customary as the best guardians of secure possession.

Of more general significance is the ability of statute to override and abrogate rights established at law. In Hilary term 1529, the courts doubted Parliament's capacity to legislate in matters spiritual;[57] a few months later, the meeting of the Reformation Parliament by stages terminated the immunity of the spiritual realm from statute. There really was no escaping this, though the efforts to do so help to underline the

[53] According to the sensible views expressed in the *Discourse upon the Statutes*, 114, errors mattered only if they occurred in the enactment: 'for it is not the words of the preamble that have the effect of an act of Parliament but it is the body of the statute that hath that force'.

[54] Archives of St John's College, Cambridge, 6.12.

[55] *The Reports of Sir John Spelman* (ed. J. H. Baker; Selden Society, 1977), I, 149.

[56] Ibid. 151. An obscure difficulty. Buckingham's attainder (1521) had led to an inquest which found him seised of the lordship of Holderness; by the attainder and as a result of the office, the lordship reverted to the King who, thus seised, granted the stewardship to Sir Robert Constable. The act confirming the attainder declared all Buckingham's property forfeit, which appears to have been taken as rendering the office doubtful and as freeing the King (now seised under the act) to regrant the stewardship a few years later to the earl of Northumberland.

[57] *Spelman's Reports*, II, 44 n. 2.

novelty of the transformation. Even towards the end of the century, Hooker (as we have seen) still tried to save something by including Convocation – contrary to all the evidence of the statute book – within the body that sovereignly ruled the Church, but even he could not avoid the conclusion that Parliament could by itself legislate for such spiritual matters as the definition of heresy.[58] As the *Discourse upon the Statutes* had noted a generation earlier, 'though an act of Parliament pass without [Convocation's] consent, yet it is firm and good'.[59] The triumph of statute over the law of the Church was complete but recent, and so (despite earlier pointers) was its triumph over the custom of the realm. In 1527, John More J. (father to Thomas More) unhesitatingly denied that Parliament could alter established customs such as gavelkind;[60] twelve years later, the act of 31 Henry VIII c. 3, entitled 'An act for changing the custom of gavelkind', obligingly did precisely that.

Judicial preconceptions clearly changed as a consequence of the work done in Parliament during that decade, a change resulting not only from facts accomplished but also from policy enunciated. If it became accepted that matters spiritual, including the settlement of true religion, were suitable material for acts of Parliament, opinions of the kind that Thomas Cromwell in 1537 expressed in public surely played their part. Presiding over a meeting of bishops convened to discuss the nature of the sacraments, he exhorted his audience to argue the controversies thoroughly (though also 'friendly and lovingly') and to arrive at their conclusions solely on the grounds of Scripture, 'as God commandeth you in Deuteronomy'. The King, Cromwell explained, would not 'suffer the Scripture to be wrested and defaced by any glosses, any papistical law, or by any authority of doctors or Councils', not a very accurate representation of Henry's views but highly revealing of the viceregent's. In addition, the bishops learned that in their own persons they served as investigators and advisers only, for the King would not allow 'any common alteration but by the consent of you and of his whole Parliament'.[61] The outcome suggests that in this, too, Cromwell expressed his own opinions rather than Henry's. The formulary which resulted from that meeting (the *Bishops' Book*) may not have received parliamentary confirmation because Henry did not like it, but the successor of 1543 (the *King's Book*), of which he did approve, was held to be authoritative without an act of Parliament. However, by 1549, when

58 *Hooker's Works*, III, 357–8, 408–9.
59 *Discourse upon the Statutes*, 110.
60 *Spelman's Reports*, II, 44–5.
61 Alexander Alesius, *Of the Word of God against the Bishop of London* (1537: *STC* 292), fos. 1v–2r.

the first act of uniformity formally enacted the Book of Common Prayer, Cromwell's desire for parliamentary authorization had triumphed.[62]

Thus the statutes of the 1530s initiated a change in standing from a high regard to omnicompetent supremacy, a change which, of course, reflects a similar change in the standing of Parliament itself. More particularly, those statutes directly affected the law at its heart, in the training of its practitioners. By its bulk and importance this legislation called forth a new style of reporting, designed to assist the absorption of the statutes by the profession, while by mid-century the Henrician acts had replaced those of earlier periods as the chief subject of instruction at the Inns of Court.[63] In the reign of Elizabeth, readers at the Inns could express regard even for acts that more recent opinion has tended to despise as poorly made: thus Francis Bacon thought the statute of uses absolutely marvellous.[64] By the beginning of that reign the transformation was in fact complete and statute had acquired unquestioned sovereignty. In the words of the *Discourse upon the Statutes*, acts of Parliament ruled common law, being able to add to it, to remedy a deficiency in it, to confirm it, clarify a doubt, abridge or abolish it.[65] That is to confer absolute supremacy in the law of England.

As we have seen, the novelty of that doctrine raised practical problems; quite apart from the need for interpretation, there remained unsettled questions. One such touched the endurance of a statute: did it lose its force with time? A curious question, perhaps, but not unimportant because limitation of prescription applied in so many branches of jurisprudence. It was therefore briefly considered in the *Discourse*. What was at issue was neither the power of Parliament to alter what its predecessors had done – no one doubted that – nor the effect of limitations of time fixed in statutes themselves, a common practice in the sixteenth century, but simply the possibility that the passage of time by itself eroded the meaning and effect of a statute. (The very fact that the issue was raised shows how wrong the influential historians are who deny that sixteenth-century common lawyers had any appreciation of historical change.) The *Discourse* thought it did: true, 'no continuance of time can gain any prescription against' acts of Parliament (mere age would not be an acceptable plea in court for ignoring a statute), but yet time can weaken them – as Livy says, who calls laws as mortal as men.[66] However,

[62] For the victory of statute and common law over the independent law of the Church, whether the pope's or the supreme head's, cf. G. R. Elton, 'Lex Terrae Victrix: der Rechtsstreit in der englischen Frühreformation', *Zeitschrift der Savigny-Stiftung für Rechtsgeschichte: Kanonistische Abteilung* 100 (1984), 217–36.

[63] Abbott, *Law-Reporting*, 67–8; W. R. Prest, *The Inns of Court under Elizabeth and the Early Stuarts 1590–1640* (London, 1972), 120.

[64] BL, Harl. MS 1853, fos. 125 seqq.

[65] *Discourse upon the Statutes*, 143.

[66] Ibid. 165–6.

determined not to be subject to out-of-date laws, the author got himself into a tangle. He pointed out that Magna Carta had by an act of Edward III been declared unalterable for all time and had yet through age ('which all can fret and bite') lost force in many of its clauses. What he really proved here was the impossibility of binding future Parliaments, for insofar as Magna Carta had lost force this was the result only of alteration by statute. No doubt, some of its clauses were no longer applicable and raised no litigation (which may have been in the mind of the author of the *Discourse*), but that disuse had not done away with them; anyone willing to employ them in litigation would still have found them in existence. I incline to thinking that the courts would in the sixteenth century have enforced any statute, however ancient, that had not been repealed; why else did law publishers keep on producing collections of all the statutes back to Magna Carta? However, until we know more about the application of acts of Parliament in actual litigation, a subject little studied so far, the question must remain open.

What, lastly, about the monarch's relation to statute law? How sovereign was this law with respect to our sovereign lord or lady? Were the king *solus* or the queen *sola* as subject to the edicts of the king-in-Parliament as were all other inhabitants of the realm? This question really contains two issues within itself: whether the king could free himself from the constraints of statute law, and whether he could convey a similar freedom to others. As to the first, it was generally held that the royal prerogative had been defined by the common law,[67] so that, in view of statute's superiority over that law, there could be no doubt that Parliament could legislate for the prerogative, both to enlarge and to diminish it. It did so freely in Henry VIII's reign, for instance in the familiar instance of the act of proclamations (31 Henry VIII c. 10) which confirmed and defined one of the undoubted prerogatives of the Crown. Elizabeth, as is well enough known, several times confronted the problem on occasions when she wished to prevent Parliament from interfering, and the fact that she adopted political solutions – avoiding rather than forbidding acts trenching on the prerogative – sufficiently confirms where the right answer lay. If so high a defender of the prerogative (much higher than her father) could never claim that prerogative matters must not be handled in statute and had to confine herself to saying that such matters should be made the subject of an act only if she so authorized it, the fact that statute was recognized as governing the prerogative is confirmed. In 1562 it was laid down in the Queen's Bench (in *Willion* v. *Berkeley*, decided against a Crown patentee for some distant remaindermen) that where the king claimed an estate governed by common and

[67] William Staunford, *An Exposicion of the Kinges Prerogative* (1563: *STC* 23213), fo. 5.

statute law he himself was 'restrained along with the estate';[68] holding an estate in tail, the king could not break the entail by letters patent, contrary to the statute *de donis conditionalibus*, which was in effect what he had done. Opinion went the same way on a different issue altogether. In the Easter term of 1582, Serjeant Gawdy, in Common Pleas, raised a question on the act of 13 Eliz. I c. 12, 'An act to reform certain disorders touching the ministers of the Church'. Suppose an incumbent had been deprived for failing to read the articles of religion from his pulpit and, the living standing vacant, the ordinary failed to inform the patron of the fact, so that no successor was appointed and the advowson, by the act, reverted to the Queen; could she present, even though the notice stipulated in the act (sect. 7) had not been issued? The court held that the Queen was bound by the proviso and would have to give notice, as under the statute. Gawdy, it appears, was preparing his ground, for a little later an actual case was brought which was decided in accordance with this opinion.[69]

There remains the royal power to render an act void by prerogative action. In the reign of Henry VIII, the act laying down standards for cloth-making was at the request of the parties affected several times suspended by proclamation, but it would seem that in the reign of Elizabeth the only approximately similar action occurred in May 1559 when merchants travelling abroad were exempted, to the tune of £4 per man, from the strict statutory prohibition against the export of coin and bullion.[70] It can be said with some confidence that in this reign no power was ever claimed or exercised by the Crown to suspend the law made by Parliament, except of course in the cases where statute specifically authorized such action. On the other hand, the Crown claimed and exercised the right to except individuals from the operation of particular statutes – the so-called dispensing power embodied in great-seal licences *non obstante*. Since many laws were framed categorically, on the assumption that their application would be suitably varied by means of government licences, this power was very necessary to the running of the whole system and never seriously questioned until James II brought it into disrepute. Moreover, it too was governed by a species of interpretation. In its subheading – 'how the king may dispense with statutes, for he is above his laws and may dispense with his laws' – the *Discourse* seems to take a high prerogative view of the royal power, but the text actually points out that this superiority above the law was strictly limited by the

[68] *Plowden's Reports*, 246–8, 322.

[69] BL, Harl. MS 1699 (an Elizabethan commonplace book of the law); fos. 140r, 141v.

[70] *TRP* I, 258, 291, 300, 306; II, 113–4. The Elizabethan proclamation merely repeated one issued by Mary: ibid. II, 62–3.

law.[71] It applied only to *mala prohibita* – individual actions in themselves lawful which had been expressly barred by Parliament.

But for such statutes that have the force of a law and bind men generally and every man specially... that are made, as you would say, for a commonwealth, with such things he cannot dispense.

What this appears to mean is that the Crown could license exceptions from the essentially temporary and very variable statutory regulations governing, for instance, trade and industry, but that licences *non obstante* were not valid against the main bulk of parliamentary legislation. Even if she had wished to do it, Elizabeth could not by the prerogative have licensed anyone to avoid the use of the Prayer Book in the services of the Church or to absent himself from such services without the fear of a recusancy fine, nor could she have found a litigant harmless against a successful defendant's claims for costs (8 Eliz. I c. 2) or permitted anyone to practise usury (13 Eliz. I c. 8).[72] By this interpretation, James II's evasion of the test act in fact offended against Tudor principles, and the bill of rights' seemingly vague phrase about the dispensing power 'as of late exercised' becomes precise.

Thus the developments of the sixteenth century made Parliament (the king-in-Parliament) a supreme legislator, unhampered by other laws though not by the obligations of piety and morality embodied in the unwritten laws of God and nature, and dominant over the executors of the law – both Crown and courts. The doctrine of estates, however handled and however misleading, defined the institution as embracing all members of the realm. The community of England therefore related directly to its Parliament and there expressed itself in sovereign action. Though earlier Parliaments had manifestly pointed towards such a development they had not achieved it. The Parliaments that met after 1529 represented a fundamental restructuring not only of that institution but of the state and its functions, and therefore of its own impact on the nation. They did not, however, shift the centre of political power for by apparently imposing a limitation upon the Crown they in fact greatly elevated monarchical power provided it was associated with the Lords and the Commons in the making of laws. To the making of those laws we shall now turn.

[71] *Discourse upon the Statutes*, 168–9.

[72] Dr Norman Jones tells me that he has found a licence exempting a person from the effects of the usury act, but I have not seen this. If such a licence issued it would imply that usury was not regarded as a *malum in se*, a point of some real philosophical interest.

PART II

The structure of business

3

Public and private

Both bills and acts could be either public or private, but though most private acts originated with private bills and public acts with public, public or private origins could end in private or public outcomes. The only extant Elizabethan list of bills which distinguished between the two kinds gives proof of that.[1] Among the private bills for 1576 listed there, five became public acts: those for clothiers, for the building of bridges at Rochester and Chepstow, for the paving of streets in Chichester, and for a bridge at Oxford.[2] Among the bills not called private and therefore presumably public was that which produced the private act of naturalization for foreign-born children, but this could be a mistake in the list because naturalization acts, profitable to the officers of the Houses, always started as private.[3] Two public acts of 1571 are explicitly stated in Journal to have started together as private bills: those for the paving of Aldgate and Ipswich.[4] It would appear that a bill could in the course of passage be declared to be 'general', as happened in 1571 to the bill for coming to church which passed both Houses and was vetoed by the Queen.[5] There must have been established criteria for declaring a bill public or private, general or particular, but we cannot be sure that later definitions already apply. The first recorded Speaker's ruling on the point occurred in 1607 when it was laid down that a bill affecting only three counties was 'by all former precedents' private,[6] and the bill just mentioned for clothiers (18 Eliz. I c. 16: in Wiltshire, Somerset and Gloucestershire) fits the definition so well that it could have been one

[1] SP12/107, fos. 144–5.

[2] 18 Eliz. I cc. 16–20. All except the first would really have been more suitable for private act legislation, but see below, pp. 316–18.

[3] 18 Eliz. I, OA 37.

[4] 13 Eliz. I cc. 23, 24; *CJ* I, 89.

[5] Ibid. 91. The use of 'general' for 'public' was common in the 16th and 17th centuries. This particular bill cannot really ever have fitted the private category; it is more likely that the clerk erred in first assigning it to the wrong category and had his error amended in the House.

[6] *CJ* I, 388.

of those precedents. If a bill was sufficiently restricted in purpose, its promoter might apparently be able to choose (no doubt by agreement with the clerk) whether he would make it public or private, which argues that the rules were still flexible.[7] In this state of uncertainty one is tempted to follow earlier historians and avoid the subject altogether, but the distinction between public and private acts and bills is one of the peculiarities of the English Parliament and must be discussed.

So far as acts are concerned, the distinction can be established with no difficulty at all. Public acts were those printed by the Queen's printer in the statute of the session.[8] It is important to emphasize the sessional statute. Acts of Parliament were quite frequently printed in later collections and several not at first printed thus got an undeserved appearance in print, for which reason the identifications in *Statutes of the Realm* (concerned only to know whether an act had ever before been printed) can mislead. If an act was left out of the statute at the end of the session it was, irrespective of its import, private by the one criterion which really mattered: in litigation, it could not be pleaded generally but had to be produced in an exemplification under the great seal or a copy formally certified by the clerk of the Parliaments if the court was to take notice of it. No doubt some of the later printing resulted from that fact: litigants might get a copy of a private act printed if they wanted to multiply copies. This happened, for instance, to two private acts of Henry VIII's reign because they were used in a case at law round about 1666.[9]

The acts left unprinted, and therefore left private, in our period include some surprises; now and again one wonders whether the omission occurred on purpose or by oversight, but the effect would nonetheless be the same. Besides, it is always worth considering whether such surprises do not merely testify to false expectations on our part. Thus among the unprinted acts of 1559 we find four which were reasonably general and of public concern: that enabling the Queen to acquire bishops' lands by exchanges, that authorizing her to make orders for collegiate churches and other spiritual corporations (including schools), that restoring her legitimacy by cancelling Anne Boleyn's attainder, and that which once more transferred monastic lands to the Crown – all quite important for the generality but also very particular to the Queen, a fact which may well lie behind the decision not to print.[10] In 1563, four acts got printed later which do not appear in the sessional

[7] Neale, *HC*, 383.
[8] *Studies* III, 92–109.
[9] Ibid. 102, n. 131.
[10] 1 Eliz. I cc. 19, 22–4. The original dissolution act of 1536 (27 Henry VIII c. 28) was also left out of the print. The compiler of an early-Stuart collection of manuscript materials on the Elizabethan Parliament copied cc. 19 and 24 from the Roll: evidently no print existed at that time (BL, Cotton MS Titus F.i, fos. 36–40v, 50–52v).

statute: for the enrolling of indentures in the courts, for the levying of fines in County Durham, for a Welsh translation of the Bible and Prayer Book, and for the assignment of money to the royal Household – and only the omission of the first must strike one as inexplicable.[11] In 1566, the three acts not printed originally but so treated later were indeed, to judge by their contents, private (trials in Merionethshire, and two confirmations of patents granted to individuals), so that the later printing and not the original omission calls for comment.[12] Private interests secured printing at some later stage, but that did not turn those acts into public ones. This sort of thing continued to happen, in 1571 to the act concerning the two universities, in 1572 to the act for London hospitals, and to one altering the custom of gavelkind at Exeter in 1581.[13] The last named was first printed for proclamation in the city and very likely got into the early collection in this way;[14] others may have reached print in the same manner. One act of 1571, promoted by London, was not in the sessional statute but when later it got printed in the collections it crept into the middle of the true public acts, causing some confusion; nevertheless, it was and remained a private act.[15] It is thus essential to study the printing of acts of Parliament from the sessional statutes and not from later collections.[16]

We have already had occasion to remark that three acts were always printed without being included in the statute: those for the lay and clerical subsidies and for the general pardon. Copies of them were needed in some quantities – for the taxcollecting commissioners, for the bishops and their officers responsible for the clerical subsidies, and for persons anxious to know the terms of the pardon so that they might find out whether they should buy one. At the same time, these acts were long and had no effect beyond the immediate time, so that they would have been tiresome in a sessional statute. When, as happens, they are now found there, they have, as the signatures show, usually been bound in from separates. One exception occurred in 1563 when the pardon and the lay subsidy appear in print, signed through with the rest of the publication. Even then it is evident from the absence of page numbers on the subsidy

[11] 5 Eliz. I cc. 26–8, 32.

[12] 8 Eliz. I cc. 20–22.

[13] 13 Eliz. I c. 29; 14 Eliz. I c. 14; 23 Eliz. I c. 17.

[14] Below, n.18.

[15] 13 Eliz. I c. 18, for the river Lea. Neale's account of this act (*HC*, 336) is in error; he supposed that the city managed to get a private act treated as though it were public, for the payment of 50*s* to the clerk of the Parliaments. What the evidence he cites shows is that the city paid the enrolment fee and also acquired a manuscript copy: nothing unusual about that.

[16] A useful guide is provided in J. Beale, *A Bibliography of Early English Lawbooks* (Cambridge, Mass., 1926); the second edition of the *STC*, at present in preparation, also means to indicate distinctions between sessional and later printing. For the collection used here see above, p. 6, n.12.

that the printer used set-up type, altering only the signatures in the form. On the other hand, in 1576 the clerical subsidy, but not the other two acts, got so reprinted for the sessional statute. In fact, the 1576 statute was something of a mess for which the printer tried to compensate in 1581. In the former year he included the three separates in his table of acts printed (as was usual) and, exceptionally, actually printed the clerical subsidy. He altogether omitted the table of acts not printed which had been introduced in 1571 and invariably appeared from 1581 onwards. In that year, therefore, he produced a very peculiar statute. The table of printed acts is followed by the public acts of the session (sigs. A2r–I4v). So far so proper, except that the last act is the one for the clerical subsidy which could have been left out. Then follows the lay subsidy, separately printed (sigs. Aa1–Dd1) and bound in. Next, signed in with the main part of the statute (sigs. K1r–K5v) we get the pardon of 1576, in that year tabled but left out, and (sig. K6r) the table of the unprinted acts of 1576 which should have been in the statute of that session. There follows a bound-in separate of the 1581 pardon (sigs. C1–4, CC1–2) and the 1581 table of acts unprinted. The *finis* at the end of this production signifies a sigh of relief that at least the last two sessions were now, after a fashion, in print as intended. This strange rescue operation also suggests that purchasers liked to collect sessional statutes regularly and expected to bind them together; the printer may well have responded to complaints made to him in 1576.

The session of 1581 also provides the single example of an indubitably private act getting printed sessionally. The so-called c. 13 of that year (for the inning of Erith and Plumstead marshes) was inserted among the public acts but also listed among the private ones with a note to the effect that 'this act by special suit is also printed'. There had been three earlier acts empowering a syndicate to undertake the work of drainage, but they had never managed to finish the work in the time set by the statutes;[17] it seems likely that the undertakers, who now promised to complete within two years, paid for the favour and the printing in order to have a public instrument to hand with which to overawe the local opposition responsible for the earlier delays. Otherwise public knowledge of private acts was confined to the table first introduced in 1571. It should be added that public acts could be made more generally known on occasion by being proclaimed and posted up. For this purpose the bound quarto of the sessional statute was useless; instead, 'broadside' editions were published for which evidence is rare. One, of the act abolishing gavelkind at Exeter, survives in that city's archives.[18] From some accidentally

[17] 5 Eliz. I, OA 36; 8 Eliz. I, OA 25; 14 Eliz. I, OA 14.
[18] HMC, *Exeter*, 341 (23 Eliz. I, c. 17).

surviving accounts we know that on 14 May 1559 the Queen's printer received from the Hanaper of Chancery 22*s* 6*d* for printing 500 copies of the act touching the export of horses to Scotland in proclamation form, no doubt for use in the northern counties, and £2 5*s* for 500 proclamation copies of the act against the export of leather.[19]

Printing made acts public, but how did acts get chosen for printing and (a matter of interest) who was responsible for the order in which they appeared in the sessional print – an order which followed a rough and ready sequence from matters of national importance (the Queen, treason, religion, defence) through reforms of the commonwealth (trade, agriculture, industry, law) to a bobtail of local or individual concerns? Evidence to answer these questions is very slender but it suffices to show that the decisions were made in Parliament, in the course of the session. We may presume that the clerks and Speakers of both Houses knew at least rough guidelines for placing a bill on introduction into the correct category: most bills would identify themselves by their contents as appropriate for either public or private enactment. The distinction is not the same as that between private and public bills (about which more in a moment) though an approximate correlation must have existed. That there were conventions governing this aspect of business appears long before the sixteenth century in the section of the then operative Roll of Parliament called 'common petitions'.[20] Moreover, any such accepted guidelines did not inhibit, as we have seen, the inclusion among the public acts of matters sufficiently private or local to surprise by getting printed, nor the exclusion of matters of public interest if the Crown did not wish to make them generally known. At any rate, in the course of the session the clerk of the Parliaments (with whom finished bills remained until the assent) put together a list of bills that had received the approval of both Houses and awaited the Queen's response, and this list – which included bills to be vetoed – was kept in the order later adopted for the print.[21] It was the clerk of the Lords, and neither the printer nor any member of Privy Council or judiciary, who superintended the selection of public acts and the order which gave them their chapter numbers.

[19] 1 Eliz. I cc. 7, 10; BL, Additional MS 5786, fo. 134; cf. *CSP Foreign, Eliz. 1558–9*, no. 678.

[20] *Studies* III, 118–22.

[21] One such list survives for 1576: SP 12/107, fos. 207–8. It is endorsed by Burghley as 'a note of the acts passed in both Houses;' since he added crosses to 'such as her majesty is thought will not assent to,' it clearly predates the royal assent. It was in fact drawn up too early to include the bill for goldsmiths which became c. 15 and which received its third reading in the Commons on 14 March, one day before the end of the session (*CJ* I, 115). The list sent to Burghley therefore cannot have been drawn up later than 13 March.

For his copy, the printer received the Original Acts, there being nothing else available immediately upon the close of the session, though the risk involved should have worried the clerk. The few Original Acts now missing at the House of Lords Record Office may testify to its reality. The printer could not use the Roll because from 1529 onwards the scribe responsible for making it relied on the print, rather than the other way round, so that only the parchment acts had the texts.[22] In 1510 the precaution had been taken of copying the acts for the printer,[23] but that was done in a more leisurely age and ceased to be possible as printing, in response to demand, came to take place at the latest immediately after the close of the session. The Original Acts of 1581 provide conclusive proof of how things happened because they are marked up – cast off – for printing with marginal notes identifying the start of new pages; the breaks as marked correspond with the pages of the print. One might have supposed that those notes were made from the print and not in preparation for it (though for what purpose?) if it were not for the fact that the marginal notes give separate numbers to each page of each signature, whereas the printer, true to practice, used new numbers only for every folio. Thus the divisions on the acts and in the print coincide but the numbering does not: the marginal note B4 becomes B2v in the print. The former must therefore have been made first, in preparing the Original Acts as copy for the printer.

The table was printed separately and usually first, being a small job worth doing for customers who wished quickly to know what had been done in the Parliament but would have to wait for the full text until that could be run off. In 1581 Sir Francis Walsingham was able to send the table of acts just passed to the earl of Huntingdon a mere three days after the Queen had given her assent, but so far as texts were concerned he could supply only a hand-copied extract from the act for religion which as a privy councillor he knew well and did not need to see in print.[24] The time-lag grew bigger as the acts grew longer. In the reign of Henry VII it was apparently possible for the returning burgesses for King's Lynn to read the acts of the last session before the assembled aldermen and council on 8 January 1496, only seventeen days after the end of the Parliament; but if they really had a printed text available they had benefited from unusual speed.[25] It took just two months from the end of the 1572 session before the city of York could give careful study to the poor law just passed.[26] When York's parliamentary representatives

[22] Above, p. 4.
[23] *L & P* I, no. 485(4).
[24] HMC, *Hastings* II, 29.
[25] HMC, *11th Report*, App. III, 171. In 1555 the printed set appeared three months after the end of the session (*Studies* III, 96).
[26] *YCR* VII, 52–3.

had first come back they had nothing to offer except a list of acts, and on the next occasion this was expressly described as the table.[27] It was the practice to buy the table for quick information and then acquire the statute itself at some opportunity. After the 1563 session the city council of York waited a year before grudgingly authorizing the expenditure involved, but they seem to have learned their needs better and in 1571 acted as soon as the text was available.[28] Like other local authorities, not to mention lawyers and other interested private persons – quite apart from government agencies such as the Exchequer or the Privy Council who got the print routinely delivered – they had come to recognize the need to possess the latest news about acts of Parliament as quickly as might be. No wonder that to the Queen's printer the monopoly of the sessional statutes was one of the most profitable of his privileges.

The texts of private acts, remaining unprinted, might none the less become important, and not only to immediate beneficiaries.[29] Their subject matter made sure of that. Many of them were really local – concerned with the management of towns and counties, or governing the practices of local groups of manufacturers and the like. Even those that seemed to touch only individuals or their families usually had a wider impact. Land settlements might interfere with the rights of relatives. Restitutions in blood seriously affected the interests of those who had legitimately acquired properties taken from persons attainted for treason or felony. Thus the effects of private acts spread well beyond the range of those who promoted them, a fact which accounts for the increasing care taken over their passage. It also accounts for the introduction of the table of acts left unprinted which at least acquainted everybody interested with what matters had received legislative attention and what acts they might wish to study in greater detail. Interestingly enough, the compiler of a collection of parliamentary materials, now among the Cotton manuscripts, went to the trouble of recording the titles of the private acts of each session, with brief summaries of the families and estates affected; he actually read the Roll to do this.[30]

Though unprinted, the texts of private acts were available in two forms. The Original Acts themselves were carefully filed by the clerk of the Parliaments, and since they were not sent to the printer they were less likely to be lost by inadvertence than the parchment bills of public acts. In addition, the clerk enrolled all private acts on the Roll of Parliament, after the public acts, simply copying the Original Acts for

[27] Ibid. 51–2, 115–6. [28] Ibid. VI, 82; VII, 33.

[29] For this study the texts have been obtained from the OA in HLRO and are so cited, unless they have been misleadingly printed, with chapter numbers, in *SR*.

[30] BL, Cotton MS Titus F.i, passim.

this purpose.[31] Though the Roll no longer fulfilled any of its ancient functions as a record of what happened in Parliament, it had acquired the new function of the register of acts passed; during this period it was complete, the subsidy acts and pardons still being copied, though not always in the same place in the sequence.[32] The clerk certainly took enrolment fees from the promoters or beneficiaries of private acts, and since enrolment was in effect compulsory the cost of private bill proceedings always included this item.[33] From these records – Original Acts and Rolls – copies could be supplied, for which reason the clerk during these years appears to have succeeded in evading his duty to transfer the Roll into the custody of Chancery. He wished to maintain his monopoly in the providing of copies certified as correct which were accepted by the courts; one such copy, on parchment, survives among the State Papers and more are found elsewhere in the public records.[34] Unable to produce copies from the records in their hands, the clerks of the Chancery had to resort to extreme measures when a client wanted his copy certified under the great seal. Thus in 1544 the earl of Hertford's agents procured a writ of *certiorari* to the clerk of the Parliaments, ordering him to supply to the Chancery a copy of an act touching the earl's private property, so that a parchment exemplification properly sealed might be made there; and in 1571 the city of Lincoln used the same method to obtain a copy of an act touching its affairs.[35] Hertford, a leading favourite, may not have paid for the service, but in the ordinary way the making of copies was highly profitable to the officers of the Upper House. One odd mention of private acts allegedly printed is just worthy of note because it indicates the confusions that all these technicalities could cause even at the time. In July 1561 the Council of the North sent to the mayor and aldermen of York a printed summary of what they called 'sundry private acts and statutes' whose enforcement they wished especially to urge upon the city's attention.[36] However, the acts mentioned – concerning hides, tanners, poor relief, vagabonds and unlawful assemblies – were all technically public and freely available in the sessional prints. Perhaps the entry in the York register misquotes the

[31] C 65/166–172.

[32] Above, pp. 4–5. Both before and after this period the enrolment of private acts could be selective, and after 1593 it ceased altogether.

[33] Above, n. 15. The enrolment and copying fees combined came to 50*s* but we have no way of separating them; besides those fees were calculated on the number of lines written and therefore varied.

[34] SP 15/9, fo. 24: copy of the act of 1559 (=OA 27) for the restitution in blood of Robert Rudstone. Mr David Lidington has found certified copies in the Exchequer, and there are some in Chancery, class C 49.

[35] HMC, *Bath*, IV, 99 (the act in question was 35 Henry VIII c. 25 – not enrolled); 11th Report, App. III, 53.

[36] *YCR* VI, 24–5.

circular received; perhaps the clerks of the Northern Council were as unsure about the distinctions as historians have been since. The poor law extracted into the circular must have been an old one; no act passed for this purpose in 1559.

To turn to bills. Before we look into the distinction between public and private it should be noted that doubts attend any count of the total number of bills of both sorts that reached either House of Parliament. The Journals do not tell all the story, which needs to be supplemented from such evidence as the list of bills in his hand which the clerk of the Commons on occasion delivered to Lord Burghley. The records may not all match: thus a list of 1572 mentions two bills not entered in the Journal – for the navy and for brewing extra-strong ale and beer – of which only the second appears in Cromwell's diary as having been read once.[37] Two weeks before the end of the 1576 session the clerk had in hand seven bills 'not yet read' of which four cannot be identified with anything mentioned in his Journal, unless the one touching the customs of Cumberland referred to a bill 'for the redress of murders and felonies in that county'; these four, therefore, seem never to have received even a first reading.[38] One touching adultery and incontinence, which might have thrown light on social attitudes, was strangely upstaged by one for 'advowtry and incest' originating in the Lords where a little later it got a single reading.[39] Of the forty-two unread bills in the clerk's possession on 1 March 1581 (with eighteen days of the session still to go) thirty-six never reached the floor of the House.[40] They included one for collectors of the clerical tenth of which a much damaged draft survives in Burghley's papers;[41] one based on a petition from gunners of the Tower and the Navy for the improvement of gunnery;[42] and one for the reform of the London Goldsmiths' Company which drew a careful counterblast before ever it was read.[43] A draft act for a lighthouse on Winterton steeple left no trace in 1581 to which year the document has been assigned; either it never got so far as a first reading or, more probably, really belonged to 1584.[44] There are several petitions and articles submitted to councillors

[37] SP 12/88, fo. 76v; *Proc.* 387.

[38] SP 12/107, fo. 132; *CJ* I, 107, 111, 113.

[39] *LJ* I, 740. These attempts at moral legislation support Keith Thomas's view that legislating against adultery did not begin in 'puritan' England: 'The Puritans and adultery: the act of 1650 reconsidered,' *Puritans and Revolutionaries*, ed. D. Pennington and K. Thomas (Oxford, 1978), 257–82.

[40] SP 12/148, fos. 3–4. None of the missing bills is mentioned in *Proc.* See below, pp. 95–6.

[41] SP 12/147, fos. 200–3.

[42] Ibid. fos. 245–57.

[43] Ibid. fos. 149–50, which describes the bill argued against as 'presented to the honourable and worshipful of the Parliament House'. Presumably it meant to amend 18 Eliz. I c. 15.

[44] Ibid. fos. 204–5; cf. *CSP Domestic, Eliz. 1581–90*, 295.

with a request for action in Parliament which never happened; there is no means of telling whether bills accordingly prepared got nowhere or the petitions were simply ignored.[45] Such uncertainties, together with the fact that we have evidence for bills introduced but not read for only two out of the seven sessions, counsel caution in estimating totals or percentages. What we can say is that in those seven sessions at least 885 bills, public or private, were read in one House or both, of which 146 resulted in public acts and 106 in private.[46]

Public bills do not pose very serious technical problems but private ones do, and since on a conservative count close to a third of that total consisted of private bills the means for identifying them must be discussed. Procedure by private bill throws light on questions of legislative initiative and parliamentary management, so that we need to know which bills were private. Of the two hallmarks mentioned in the record and the opinions deposited in more or less contemporary treatises one would appear to be imaginary and in any case would do nothing for bills that failed to pass, while the other certainly turns out to be genuine but can only very rarely be discovered with respect to particular bills. These hallmarks are the formula of the royal assent and the fees payable for private bills during and after passage.

It was stated categorically by William Hakewill, writing round about 1611, that the royal assent distinguished between public bills (not acts,

[45] E.g. proposals for improving the harbours of Rye and Winchelsea submitted to Burghley in 1576 (SP 12/107, fos. 105–8); a petition of January 1581 for an act to grant a saltpetre monopoly (ibid. 147, fos. 113–14); the articles for the reform of the Church submitted by William Chaderton, bishop of Chester, on 14 Jan. 1581 to the Privy Council with a request for a statute (ibid. fos. 15–16).

[46] The total (derived from an analysis of both Journals) differs from the provisional count I gave in *Studies* III, 161–2. The following table breaks down the outcome of private bills, identified from specific evidence or by proper conjecture. Especially because for failed bills one usually has no more than the often inadequate brief titles given in the Journals, there are uncertainties about these figures, but I have tried to be severe and the numbers represent minima.

	Public acts	Private acts	Failed bills	Total
1559	1	17	14	32
1563	1	20	26	47
1566	4	14	28	46
1571	4	15	23	42
1572	2	4	28	34
1576	6	13	25	44
1581	4	15	19	38
Total	22	98	163	283

as the textbooks say) which got the response *le roi le veult*, and private which got *soit fait comme est desire*.[47] Thus Hakewill, a conscientious and experienced parliamentarian, seems to offer a useful guide at least to those private bills that passed. One could wish it were so. However, what we have there is a fine piece of antiquarianism reflected confusingly in the practice of the clerks but actually on its way out by the reign of Elizabeth.[48] It stemmed from the medieval distinction between matters thought private which were called (first for the king's bills and later for all private bills) 'bille formam actus in se continentes', and public matters collected under the heading 'communes peticiones'. After 1529, when this distinction had been entirely abandoned, the clerk of the Lords, responsible for producing the Roll, still distinguished between bills and petitions but in effect reversed the old terminology: approximately he called public bills *bille* and private ones *peticiones*, assigning *le roi le veult* to the former and *soit fait* to the latter. Apparently he tried to rely on the outward form of the bills, some of which employed petitionary phrases – a bad guide because that form could be used for political reasons rather than technical ones. If the actual assent differed from what the bill's formal structure had led him to expect, and if he had got the Roll written before he learned of this, he altered both description and assent to fit the first to the second. However, neither his use of the assent nor his reliance on a distinction between a bill enacting and a petition petitioning for an enactment coincided with the distinction between public and private acts, nor (in all probability: a precise check is impossible) any longer with that between private and public bills, though it may have done so in the fifteenth century.

In Elizabeth's reign, the Roll at first attempted to maintain this same archaic practice, or at least to presume the *soit fait* assent if the bill was cast in petitionary terms. In the heading formula of the acts transcribed on the Roll, the clerk distinguished between *quedam billa* and *quedam*

[47] William Hakewill, *The Manner how Statutes are Enacted in Parliament by Passing of Bills* (London, for John Benson, 1641). Two editions of this book appeared in that year but this is the one to use since the author supervised it; it is readily recognized by the plaintive preface which explains that Hakewill had obtained the Commons' authority to print because one of the many copies of the treatise, written some thirty years before ('and I think the falsest written of all the rest') had been published without his knowledge. Hakewill relied less on personal experience, which when he wrote extended to only two Parliaments and six sessions, than on a search of the Journals, and he was careful to allege his sources. Without accepting D'Ewes' comfortable assumption (p. 18) that nothing had changed between 1559 and 1610, we may yet use this treatise on many points in the confidence that he was describing practice already current in the first half of Elizabeth's reign.

[48] For what follows cf. *Studies* III, 113–18, 127–8, 130–1, 136–7.

peticio, but from the first with insufficient consistency.[49] Thus he called cc. 1, 3 and 4 of the statute of 1 Eliz. I (the act of supremacy, the recognition of the Queen's title, and the restoration of first fruits to Crown) *bille* – and not without reason, for they were all, of course officially initiated bills. However, because for political reasons they were framed as petitions from both Houses he entered *soit fait* for the assent, which turned out to be wrong; as the parchment acts testify, they all, unsurprisingly, received *la reyne le veult*. The clerk made the same mistake with c. 23 (the repeal of Anne Boleyn's attainder), a private act in the form of a petition and assented to *la reyne le veult*; he called it a bill and added *soit fait*. For the rest of the session's Roll he got it right: that is to say, he entered the assent actually pronounced and apportioned his *bille* and *peticiones* accordingly, even though two of his 'bills' used the form of a petition. Here, as under Henry VIII, the assent governed the formalities of the Roll, and Hakewill's dictum possibly applies. However, by the time that the next Roll came to be made up consistency was on the way out. The clerk mistook only one assent: the act for confirming a grant to Southampton (OA 35), which he justly called a petition, in fact got *la reyne le veult* while the Roll, using the other formula, followed the supposed rules. Thereafter, the clerk just about gave up. He got all his assents right but several times has *billa* standing with *soit fait*. Worse confusion prevailed in the next two Rolls, with a good deal of erasing and altering in 1571, and from 1572 the clerk conceded the battle. Thereafter all bills are *bille*, irrespective of the formula of assent and the structure of the text. The Roll at least had ceased to pretend that the formula of assent distinguished between two different kinds of bills. Although it so happened that in 1581 virtually all private acts did get the 'private' *soit fait* response, one such act spoiled any simple inference by attracting *la reyne le veult*.

One might nevertheless suppose that Hakewill was right and that the assents, once correctly established, would indicate the private or public character of the bills behind the acts, even though the failure of the Roll to maintain an earlier distinction, reflecting a practice that had once been real and akin to what Hakewill asserted, makes this doubtful from the first. Besides, even if we could rely on the assent we could know nothing about failed or vetoed bills. The question can in any case be settled, thanks to the classing as private of certain bills listed by the clerk of the Commons in 1576.[50] He so defined twenty-three of them. Three never reached the assent and three more were vetoed. Of the rest, six became

[49] This discussion is based on the Parliament Rolls for 1–23 Eliz. I (C 65/166–72) and the OA in the HLRO.

[50] SP. 12/107, fos. 144–5.

public acts which all received *la reyne le veult*. Of the eleven that finished as private acts seven carry *soit fait* but the remaining four attracted the so-called public response.[51] That is to say, of seventeen indubitably private bills ten got the assent which by Hakewill's rules was wrong, and only seven the correct one. Plainly the formula does not work; even for bills that passed, the assent is no guide to private or public origin. Why the Queen's assent should have varied so is a question we shall answer later.[52] The matter needed this tedious discussion here because one still finds historians accepting Hakewill's statement as true, though they often fail to notice that he was talking of bills, not acts.

That leaves the second distinction, namely that fees were payable on private bills which did not arise on public ones. Difficulties hang about this, too, but that private bills can be distinguished by the payment of fees is certainly true. Most of the evidence comes from the House of Commons. In 1571 it was stated that the Speaker took £5 for every private bill, the clerk £2, and the serjeant-at-arms £1 (sums that remained fixed for a long time after), but that all this money was due only upon every bill 'passed both Houses and enacted'.[53] Does this mean that failed bills paid no fees? Clearly they did. In 1593 Lord Vaux of Harrowden promoted a bill to free his lands for sale so that he might pay his debts, a bill whose urgency was well illustrated by his inability to pay the fees to the clerk, as a result of which delinquency the bill, which had passed both Houses, was held back in the Commons when it should have been sent to the Lords for the assent.[54] In 1604, a bill for assarting certain lands stuck in the Commons because it was 'a long time not well understood by Mr Speaker, or any other, who preferred and who followed this bill'; in the absence of anyone to pay the fees the bill made no progress. In the end it was discovered that the clerk had been by-passed: 'one Haynes paid fees to Mr Speaker's servant'. Haynes was not behaving properly nor doing himself much good, but the case shows clearly that private bill fees had to be paid in the course of passage if there

[51] The Roll for that year (C 65/171) makes only one mistake in the responses assigned to these seventeen acts.

[52] Below, pp. 128–9.

[53] John Hooker's treatise on 'Order and usage how to keep a Parliament in England', printed in *Parliament in Elizabethan England*, ed. V. Snow (New Haven/London, 1977), 171, 172, 174. In the case of naturalization acts, with their multiple beneficiaries, every person benefiting paid the Speaker £5 'unless he did agree for less': *William Lambarde's Notes on the Procedures and Privileges of the House of Commons*. ed. P. L Ward (House of Commons Library Document no. 10; n.d.). The editor was mistaken in identifying this Lambarde as the well known antiquary of Kent: cf. below, p. 370, n.63.

[54] HMC, *Various Collections*, III, 71. The bill passed (39 Eliz. I, OA 19), so that presumably the money was found in time.

was to be any progress.[55] And in 1607 a bill for mending the highways in three counties was held up because 'it was followed and pressed as a public bill', which meant that the clerk got nothing even though it 'was long and of much labour' to him; the House resolved that 'the ordinary duties should be performed', or nothing further be done with the bill – that is, it should be treated as a private bill and the fees duly paid, or else it would be dropped.[56] Quite clearly, therefore, fees were payable on all private bills, not only on those that made it into acts, and were normally collected in the course of the session. At the same time, it does appear that the Upper House (*noblesse oblige*) could on certain occasions postpone collection until after the end of the session. On 8 July 1572, the city of London resolved to send a deputation to the lord keeper to seek his 'lawful favour for the fees that one Mr Spelman[57] demandeth of the governors of the hospitals within the city' for the act on their behalf made in the session just closed on 30 June.[58]

Our fullest evidence for the payments required to get a private bill through arises from the history of the act for making the river Lea navigable, much contested in both Houses because the interests of riparian owners were involved. Put up by the city of London, it had Burghley's support and was first introduced into the Upper House. The city chamberlain paid the following fees and rewards: £1 to the Lords' clerk for getting the bill before the House; 11*s* to other Lords' officers and 3*s* 8*d* to the keepers of the door; further rewards to the same two groups of 2*s* 6*d* and 12*d*; £6 5*s* to the yeoman usher for hanging up the map explaining the proposals in the House of Lords; 2*s* to the clerk of the Commons for drafting provisos; £5 for the Speaker's fee; to each clerk for his fee, £2; to the lord keeper ('being due to him *ex officio*') £10; to the gentlemen ushers of both Houses 10*s* 6*d* each; for the enrolment of the act and for a certified copy £2 10*s*; and a further 10*s* for the favour of enrolment since, being private, it had been left out of the sessional statute. Altogether, the passage cost the city some £40 because in addition to fees it also lobbied by several times dining men of influence (including Spelman) and paid the expenses of people sent to study the problem on the ground; but just getting the bill promoted in Parliament plus the regular fees for the Speakers and clerks of both

[55] *CJ* I, 197. Haynes was servant to Sir Thomas Leighton knight of the shire for Worcestershire in 1601, who did not sit in James I's first Parliament. It turned out that Haynes was promoting the bill against his master's interests and therefore trying to keep his machinations secret; hence the mystification in the House.

[56] Ibid. 388.

[57] Francis Spelman, clerk of the Parliaments.

[58] CLRO, Rep. 17, fo. 342. The act in question is printed in *SR* as 14 Eliz. I c. 14, but is was not in the sessional statute and is therefore private.

Houses thus amounted to just over £30, not a negligible sum. The accounts also show that while the clerks of both Houses took the same fee, the lord keeper demonstrated his superiority by demanding double what was due to the Speaker of the Commons.[59]

Thus: fees had to be paid on all private bills during passage, while Hooker was categorically certain that the standard fees for the three officers of the Lower House fell due only if the bill got enacted. This also suggests that these officers might trustingly make it possible for the promoters of such bills to walk off without paying: the royal assent having been given, the act stood, and the Speaker, clerk and serjeant might have to whistle for their money, as Spelman apparently had to do in 1572. The resolution of this conundrum lies in one piece of contemporary and one piece of slightly later evidence.

The *Notes* on parliamentary procedure, ascribed to one William Lambarde and written around 1585, state rather obscurely that the Speaker took 'of the subject, for every private bill, for assurance £5 before that he delivers it out of his hand'.[60] The identity of the 'he' may be in doubt, but whether Lambarde meant that the promoter paid when he put the bill into the House, or when the Speaker handed it over after second reading for engrossing or to a committee (and I think he meant the second), it appears either way that the fee due for the enacted bill was paid by way of deposit long before the end of the session. It may be conjectured that the other two officers followed the same practice. Presumably, therefore, the fee had to be returned if in the end the bill did not pass, which supports the view that the money was collected at a point when the bill had made reasonable progress. Secondly, it can be shown that private bill fees included more than those lump sums payable for acts. We have already noted that additional money had to be paid for enrolment because this was a particular service done to the beneficiary, and that thanks to the practice of enrolling everything this fee was in practice compulsory.[61] The first surviving table of fees proves that this was not all. Unfortunately it belongs to 1649, a rather late date for our purposes and applicable at a time when there was only one House of Parliament, but the clerk's £2 was there unchanged, and there is really no reason to doubt (quite apart from the story of the Lea river bill) that in essentials the list reflected long established practice.[62] The whole principle of charging fees to those who used the public service derived from the notion that particular things done by the king's servants for

[59] See below, p. 80.

[60] *Lambarde's Notes*, 70.

[61] Above, n. 15.

[62] Henry Scobell's Table of Fees, in Orlo Williams, *The Clerical Organization of the House of Commons 1661–1850* (Oxford, 1954), 209.

anyone not a servant to the king should be paid for; all public salaries took account of this principle. Thus Henry Scobell's table lists the clerk taking £2 of any person taking benefit of any private act or of any proviso in any act that names him explicitly: this is the end-of-session fee. The table also shows that underclerks took 10*s* for every private bill put into the House; in Elizabeth's reign, before underclerks were created on the establishment, this money must have gone to the clerk or his man. Lastly, fees fell due upon any order made by Journal entry touching any private bill – for every reading and appointment of committee, or in other words for every move forward that the bill achieved. It does seem certain that this is what happened in Elizabeth's reign too. Indeed, the demand for such fees might explain the occasional silence of the Journal when yet we know that a bill had been read a first time and the clerk was presumably still waiting for his payment. We do not know the going rate for this in the mid-sixteenth century. When – if – a bill passed as an act either private or public, the major fees to the officers of both Houses became payable, and it would seem that at least in the Commons payment had to be made in advance by deposit.

We therefore know that when we find evidence of fee-paying the bill was private. Unfortunately such evidence is rare, so that as a rule we have to infer the private character of a bill from circumstantial or internal evidence. Quite often this can be done, but it must be emphasized that such identifications, however cautiously done, remain rather conjectural – safe enough conjecture most of the time, but rarely positive certainty. It is therefore consoling to find that yet another criterion exists which defines a whole group of bills as unquestionably private.

Private bills in Tudor Parliaments divide into two kinds: those that carried the monarch's sign manual and those without it. All sign manual bills were private – promoted by individuals. They included bills on the Crown's own behalf (that is to say, for its private concerns), but of these I find only one in these seven sessions: the Queen signed the act for assignments to the royal Household in 1563 (a private act) before the Commons saw the bill.[63] Unlike her father, Elizabeth did not order her estates or her family affairs by statute, and unlike her grandfather she did not sign or initial bills and provisos at the ceremony of the assent.[64] That one item apart, therefore, all parliamentary bills signed by her deal with the private concerns of a person or a family which had been brought

[63] 5 Eliz. I c. 32, a private act (later printed) which started with a sign manual bill. The bill of 1571 for preventing members of the Household from serving on juries was dashed in the Lords, which suggests that it was not commended by the Queen's signature (*CJ* I, 84, 89, 91; *LJ* I, 694, 697).

[64] Cf. J. I. Miklovich, 'The significance of the royal sign manual in early Tudor legislative procedure,' *BIHR* 52 (1979), 23–36; *Studies* III, 132, n.231.

to her attention. Such bills took the form of a petition to the Queen, setting out the matter at issue and the need in question, and asking for an act of Parliament to resolve them. These petitions, giving the text of the expected act, were presented engrossed on parchment and first sent to the law officers who scrutinized them for any adverse effects they might have on the rights of the Crown.[65] If the attorney general gave them clearance by his signature at the foot, the Queen could then, if she wished, authorize the obtaining of an act by signing at the top. Though such bills therefore entered Parliament on parchment, they still had to pass all the usual stages of three readings and acceptance in both Houses; though, of course, there was no question of engrossment, they could be committed and amended. This happened rarely; normally they went through on the nod.

Bills first submitted to the Queen dealt with three types of cases: restitutions in blood (usually the reversing of an earlier act of attainder which had left the family 'corrupted in blood' and unable to use the law), naturalization (usually of children born abroad to parents of whom at least the father was English by birth), and concerns commonly handled by an ordinary private bill but which the petitioner hoped to get through more easily by soliciting the Queen's special favour (especially settlements of landed property). The first two sorts of cases were always dealt with by sign manual bills, but even among them occasional departures from the norm turn up. Restitutions might escape the law officers' scrutiny, a cheapening and acceleration of the business granted to persons whom the Queen wished to favour: an uncle of Lady Jane Grey, an old acquaintance like Sir James Croft, the children of a victim of the Marian persecution, the descendants of that earl of Surrey whom Henry VIII had executed at the end of his reign.[66] All these got their clearance in the first Parliament of Elizabeth; the many restitutions of 1563 all went through the full procedure, and the only petitioner thereafter allowed speedy redress was Lord Norris of Rycote, a member of a family long linked with Tudor and Boleyn who in 1576 was still suffering the consequences of his father's attainder forty years before.[67] Though naturalization acts at first suffered the delaying scrutiny of the attorney general, an exception was made in 1571 for a Bertie offspring and in

[65] E.g. reversals of attainders always touched the interests of those who had acquired attainted lands. The bills for restitution invariably saved the Queen's rights, which meant that if the reversal was to be accompanied by a restoration of the family estates the Queen had to regrant them by letters patent. She could not regrant what had already been granted away to private persons whose interests were protected by the clause known as 'the general saving', but this could prove insufficient, with litigation resulting or even occasional trouble in Parliament.

[66] 1 Eliz. I, OA 22, 23, 32, 39.

[67] 18 Eliz. I, OA 24.

1576 for a daughter born to the now countess of Bedford in her first marriage to Sir Richard Morison, then ambassador to the emperor.[68] At this point, the administration, faced with a growing flood of applications on behalf of children born to merchants settled abroad, introduced the device of multiple in which any interested party could buy a place by paying the obligatory fees to the officers of the House.[69] These were still framed as petitions to the Queen and for a while continued to be signed by her, but there are no countersignatures and they were treated as routine.

On the other hand, petitions to the Queen seeking to ease through bills for the settlement of jointures, the breaking of entails, the confirmation of purchases and similar matters were too serious to become routine, and only one such ever attracted special favour. Elizabeth signed the bill for the jointure of her friend, Lady Cobham, a thing she would not do even for the estates bill promoted by her favourite, Sir Christopher Hatton.[70] It should be noted that the sign manual did not act as a command to pass the bill: it constituted a strong recommendation and expression of support, not an order, but of course evidence that the Queen favoured a bill was likely to secure preferential treatment for it. Estate acts, however, were bound to affect so many varied and often unknown people that caution and common sense advised against rushing them through or indeed associating the Queen with specially urging them on the Parliament. Most of them, in fact, started without any attempt to involve the Crown, but six are known in this period which vainly tried to petition the Queen and had to make their way without her signature.[71] Quite a few estate bills failed to pass in these seven sessions – seventeen out of the thirty-five put up – which indicates how risky it might have been for Elizabeth to put her name to such petitions. For the sign manual was certainly an efficient aid, and only two bills so honoured failed in Parliament. One was the restoration bill for Anthony Mayne moved in 1576, which started in the Lords, acquired a proviso in the Commons, and then went back to the Upper House too late to go forward. It passed routinely in 1581 when the promoter introduced it in the Commons; the Lords, finding it familiar, read it three times in one day.[72] The other bill which, despite the Queen's signature, failed to achieve its ends caused more serious complications: this was Lord Stourton's bill which led to a quarrel between the Houses.[73]

From the general point of view, the chief problem raised by private

[68] 13 Eliz. I, OA 28; 18 Eliz. I, OA 26.
[69] 18 Eliz. I, OA 35, 37.
[70] 8 Eliz. I, OA 27; 18 Eliz. I, OA 27.
[71] 1 Eliz. I, OA 28; 5 Eliz. I, OA 35, 37, 38, 50; 18 Eliz. I, OA 27.
[72] Below, p. 92.
[73] Below, pp. 306–9.

bills lay in the time they took up and the nuisance they could be to the managers of business. As for the public bills, the good Marthas of legislation from which sprang most of the achievements of these Parliaments, they pose no particular technical problems. In essence they were of one kind, except that some took the form of a petition while most did not. On the other hand, they raise one enormous problem which does not beset their private counterparts. With private bills we are just about always quite sure who stood behind them: they were produced and promoted by the interests whom their terms assisted. But anybody could produce public bills for Queen and country, and many did so. Such bills might be official – coming from Crown and Council – or unofficial, and unofficial origins could mean individuals or groups or localities. They could start with some identifiable private persons but might then be taken up by the official side. Ideas put up by someone could be amalgamated with those coming from another quarter; or a complex proposal might get redrafted into several bills. The big problem about public bills touched the initiative behind them.

4

Initiatives

Our evidence rarely permits a complete understanding of how bills came to be proposed and promoted, but often suffices to tell important things about the initiative behind legislation. When we know the text of a bill we can rely on the probability that a full enacting clause means private promotion while a short clause implies government origin.[1] However, most bills, and especially those that failed, are but titles to us. Older views which tended to solve the problem by assuming that in the sixteenth century public acts of Parliament originated with the government have long ceased to convince. We no longer suppose with A. F. Pollard that before Elizabeth's reign bills for the common good were always devised by the Council, or with Wallace Notestein that only in the reign of James I 'the House of Commons' wrested the legislative initiative from the Crown.[2] Even so, the various ways in which bills came to be put forward and pursued are still not sufficiently appreciated. Yet if, for instance, policy is to be evaluated by means of acts of Parliament it obviously becomes very necessary to gain a clear understanding of the minds and the people behind them: a judgment touching what was done depends on at least some knowledge of who did what.

It also seems to have been generally assumed that every Parliament's output stood by itself; insofar as bills have been studied this has been done within the compass of individual sessions. This, however, will not serve. Acts often resulted from efforts renewed in Parliament after Parliament; failed bills quite frequently reappeared in later sessions, sometimes making it to the statute book after several endeavours. Nor have we yet fully grasped how widely spread the interest in promoting legislation could be. Every calling of a Parliament produced much activity among all sorts of people who tried to get bills ready for the

[1] *Studies*, III, 142–55.

[2] A. F. Pollard in *EHR* 57 (1942), 225; Wallace Notestein, *The Winning of the Initiative by the House of Commons* (Oxford, 1924).

assembly of the Houses. And there is evidence that legislative programmes or proposals could rumble in their promoters' minds in the apparently deadest time between Parliaments. Intended bills leaked out, and people did not always have to wait until the Parliament met in order to discover what was toward. Thus on 29 December 1562 the city government of York knew enough about the text of a bill for apprentices, planned for the forthcoming session, to decide to have 'a like proviso made for York as is for London and Norwich'; yet the session did not start till a fortnight later. The fact, as we shall see, is an important clue to the errors committed in the most recent analysis of the act of artificers.[3]

When, on occasion, we happen to learn something about the genesis of an act, the story even of apparently straightforward measures can be so intricate and half-obscure as to constitute a warning for cases of which less is known. Take the act of 1576 which limited the use of benefit of clergy – to all appearance simply another step in the long-run campaign of the Council to gain better control over crime.[4] The act – four sections and one proviso – declares: (1) Persons convicted of rape, ravishment of women, and burglary shall be deprived of their clergy; (2) felons reprieved by their clergy and branded in the thumb shall no longer go through the ceremonial committal to the ordinary to make their purgation (a process which notoriously led to the swearing of false oaths) but shall be set free at once; (3) the court shall, however, have the power to imprison such felons for one year if it sees fit to do so; (4) unlawful carnal knowledge of a female under ten years of age shall be felony without clergy: (5) persons admitted to their clergy shall nonetheless thereafter be tried for any felony of which they may later be indicted. Quite clearly the act falls within the recurrent sixteenth-century legislation on the subject, reducing the escape routes open to criminals, though section 4 seems to cross an existing t, while section 5, a proviso, seems rather superfluous. The act looks like a simple government measure, an impression confirmed by its brief preamble and its use of the short enacting clause; and it has been so treated by legal historians.[5] Yet in fact it grew from several roots, and its making had a surprisingly complex history.

The first hint occurred a good year before the parliamentary session which made the act. In 1575, William Fleetwood, recorder of London, tried a man for the rape of a child.[6] When the accused pleaded his clergy, Fleetwood, somewhat moved, declared that the first bill in the next Parliament to which he would put his hand would be designed to deprive

[3] *YCR* VI, 50. [4] 18 Eliz. I c. 7.
[5] Cf. W. H. Holdsworth, *History of English Law*, III, 300–1; IV, 504.
[6] BL, Harleian MS 1699, fo. 52.

rapists of their clergy.[7] His indignation seems to have been premature, for the accused was acquitted when the jury learned that the alleged victim's very belated accusation had been extracted from her by her parents' relentlessly long interrogation. Still, this looks like the first germ of the act. However, when the Parliament met Fleetwood did not put any bill into the House; instead, a bill appeared in the Lords which had no easy passage.[8] To judge from the clerk's description ('for the exclusion of clergy and purgation ecclesiastical') it included the first two clauses of the act, or even perhaps was intended only to achieve the effect of the second. The Council had planned legislation along these lines as early as 1566,[9] which suggests that this was an official bill and that Fleetwood abandoned his intentions because he learned of the Council's plans. Contrary to usual practice, the bill was committed on first reading, so that it must have seemed very insufficient to the House. It was passed for revision to one of the assistants (Robert Monson, once a prominent House of Commons man and now a judge of Common Pleas) who brought it back within two days: once more it was read a first time, and once more it was committed. This time it got a proper bill committee – two earls, two bishops, two barons, and two assistant judges.[10] Their labours produced yet another revised bill which received yet another first reading three days later – only to be committed once more, to the solicitor general.[11] This last hesitation, however, evidently involved only some minor technicality: on 29 February the bill was read a second time and ordered to be engrossed, and on the next day it passed and was sent to the Lower House.[12] Since throughout all these proceedings the clerk did not alter his descriptive title we can only guess what happened to it. When it left the Lords it consisted of the first three of its ultimately five sections, and the chances are that clause 3 (which modified the liberal effect of clause 2) had been added in the Lords, but why such a change and (presumably) some verbal redrafting should have led to three first readings and three committals must remain mysterious.

The Commons dealt expeditiously with the bill, giving it two readings on 7 March – and committing it.[13] Three days later they accepted the committee's amendments, passed the bill, and returned it to the Lords.[14] There the changes and additions caused a hold-up, and on the 12th, at the Lords' request, a conference of committees from both Houses reviewed the problem. The Commons received the bill back 'to be

[7] 'Recorder dit que le primer bill in le prochein parleament a q'ill mittera son maine sera de Rauishors de femes seron oust de lour clergie.'

[8] *LJ* I, 734.

[9] Below, pp. 301–2.

[10] *LJ* I, 735.

[11] Ibid. 737.

[12] Ibid. 738–9.

[13] *CJ* I, 111. The entry alleges three readings on this occasion, but that must have been a clerical error.

[14] Ibid. 113.

amended in the former addition of amendment thereof by this House'; they did as asked, and the bill was finally done with that same day.[15] But what had resulted from that last further change? The Commons' original amendments were of two kinds.[16] They sent up a paper schedule of drafting changes, and they added a parchment schedule which in the end contained the last two clauses of the act. The drafting amendments are not uninteresting, being mainly designed to reduce verbiage: a phrase was deleted which, quite typically but superfluously, spoke of crimes as 'daily committed and done more than in former times has been seen', and another went out probably because by recalling that purgation was a right 'by the laws of this realm' it weakened the effect of section 2. There is no sign that the amendments on the paper schedule caused any difficulties in the Lords; they were all put into the bill by insertion and underlining (for deletion). So the trouble must have arisen over the parchment proviso, and this does indeed look as though it underwent a change. Section 4 is crammed onto the parchment above section 5 and was evidently written in later. It would therefore seem, on this evidence, that the clause making rape of a child felony – the very issue that had moved Fleetwood so long before to resolve on legislative action – got into the act at the very last stage. It had not been in the Lords' bill nor in the Commons' additions; it entered the bill on the urging of the Lords who, having already passed the bill, could not now amend it and had to fudge matters by getting the Commons to insert it awkwardly on a proviso that they had already despatched to the Upper House.

That would appear to be the only possible history for the act: but what does it mean? Even if Fleetwood had abandoned his intention to promote a bill because he knew that the Council were about to take action in the Lords, why had he not seen to the addition of clause 4 when the bill was in the Commons? And how had the Lords come to think the addition desirable at that very late stage? Unprovable though it must remain, the most likely answer to these questions is that Fleetwood missed his chance in the Commons because he was not in the House at the right time, a probability supported by his frequent absences on judicial duties and by the fact that he was not appointed to the bill committee. We may thus conjecture that, too late, he realized what had happened but arranged to get word to the Lords – for instance through his regular patron, Lord Burghley – so that at the last moment the purpose conceived months before did produce a legislative result. The story underlines the haphazardness of the process and more particulary the frequent inadequacies of bill drafting. If a Council bill could undergo so much redrafting in the Lords, of all places, one wonders who had written the first version;

[15] Ibid. 114; *LJ* I, 746–7. [16] Evidence of OA in HLRO.

though the usefulness of the legal assistants in the Lords, able to put matters straight, also deserves notice.

Even bills produced by expert Crown servants were not necessarily official (promoted by the Council), as the case of the act 'for the abridgement of appeals of suits in civil and maritime causes' shows (1566).[17] It proclaims its unofficial origin, confirmed by other evidence, also in its use of the long enacting clause. It aimed to prevent endless litigation at civil law, especially in the court of Admiralty, by providing an immediate and final appeal from judgment there to commissioners under the great seal, thus extending to maritime disputes the machinery which in the reign of Henry VIII had been created for ecclesiastical causes. The bill was drawn for the 1563 session by Dr David Lewes, judge of the Admiralty, 'upon occasion of complaints of strangers for their long suits in civil and maritime causes by reason of divers appeals permitted in those causes'.[18] However, it received only one reading in the Commons, even though some six weeks of the session still remained – a sure sign that no one followed it at all determinedly.[19] Indeed, Lewes's professed concern lacks conviction: someone else revived the bill in 1566, and Lewes did not even hear of this until after the first reading on 9 October.[20] No doubt it would again have vanished if Lewes had not at last taken an interest in his brainchild which he now described as 'for a common profit, and that indeed it will redound to the benefit of all those that shall have cause of action in such cases, and prejudicial or hurtful to no person'. He moved the Speaker 'for his favour to have the same pass' and followed up by soliciting Cecil's support as well, reminding the secretary that 'both your honour and I shall have less trouble hereafter with strangers'. The hint worked: on 14 November the bill got its second reading and a fortnight later its third when an amendment was carried to change its inception date from 'henceforth' to the last day of the present session.[21] The Lords got it through in quick time.[22]

This was a brief and apparently uncontroversial bill, but never adopted by the Council and at first insufficiently pressed by its promoter – an acknowledged recipe for disappearance. Lewes's behaviour strikes one as odd. Not only was he urgently involved as an Admiralty judge much bothered by complaints over endless appeals, but as a master in Chancery he worked as an assistant in the Lords and frequently carried bills down to the Commons. He really should have known his way about the Parliament: yet, having devised the bill, he let it die in 1563 and made

[17] 8 Eliz. I c. 5.

[18] Lewes's role emerges from his letter to Cecil of 5 November 1566 (SP 12/41, fo. 23).

[19] *CJ* I, 66.

[20] Ibid. 74.

[21] Ibid. 77–8. The amendment was entered on the engrossed bill by the clerk of the Commons (OA).

[22] *LJ* I, 652–3.

no move in 1566 until somebody else had revived it. Perhaps he needed persuading that the bill would serve, for it certainly did not satisfy everybody; some time later Cecil received a draft bill which planned to remedy a deficiency by giving the Admiralty power to make appellants pay the whole costs of the party to whom judgment had been awarded.[23] Cecil filed the draft, but the matter went no further.

These two small and seemingly unimportant bills well illustrate the need for caution in assessing initiatives whether official or unofficial, as well as the difficulties introduced by the interplay of diverse initiatives. Caution need not, however, terminate enquiry altogether.

Official initiatives sometimes stand out plainly, as with the brief act which prohibited the sale of clothing on credit (1563), a quirky little piece of paternalism of which Sir William Cecil proudly told Sir Thomas Smith he had been the author.[24] Even so he had to allow the Lower House to alter one important detail: whereas he had fixed the limit for the purchaser's income above which credit could be given at £200 a year, this was changed in the course of passage to the absurdly high (and self-defeating) figure of £3000, the traditional minimum income for an earl – which, since the act deprived the vendor of all rights touching the recovery of the debt, meant that no gentleman even would be able to buy apparel on tick.[25] The repairing of the harbour at Dover had been in the mind of the Privy Council since December 1565 when it was thought that the costs were such as to require 'some general assistance of the whole realm', a thing to be arranged 'at Parliament, being now at hand'; in fact, nothing was done until 1581 when a manifestly official bill passed after revision in committee.[26]

[23] BL, Lansdowne MS 105, fos. 191–4.

[24] 5 Eliz. I c. 6; BL, Lansdowne MS 102, fo. 24v.

[25] There is a mystery in the record. £200 was the figure in the original bill (*CJ* I, 66: 25 Feb.); the third-reading entry in *CJ* (26 Feb.) changed this to £3000. Yet in the Lords the bill is recorded as using the £200 limit on first and second reading (*LJ* I, 597–8: 2 and 3 March); here too £3000 appears at the end (ibid. 600: 8 March). *LJ*, but not *CJ*, notes the return of the bill to the Commons after the Lords had passed it; this would have happened only if the second House made amendments to which the first had to agree. The OA, started and engrossed in the Commons, has no changes at all noted on it. It is thus impossible to be absolutely sure which House raised the limit, but the probabilities indicate the Commons. It is more likely that the Lords clerk should have mistakenly used an outdated figure (perhaps still left in the breviate) in recording the reading of a bill, than that the Commons clerk should have doctored his record (for what purpose?) after the bill came back from the Lords. Nor do I think that the bill did so come back. The discrepancy between the Journals touching the last stages of the bill is more convincingly resolved in favour of *CJ*. *LJ* says that 'the last three bills passed' (which should have included this one) were sent to the Commons and that only this bill returned from there, all on one day. The chances are that 'three' was a mistake for 'two' and that the clerk cleaned up his record by putting in a return which brought the bill back to where in fact it had always remained.

[26] *APC* VII, 310–11; 23 Eliz. I c. 6; *CJ* I, 132.

Official origin thus by no means guaranteed unopposed passage: such bills could be treated very critically indeed, as the interesting history of the act of 1581 for fortifying the Scottish border shows.[27] That the bill originated with the government and was not perhaps promoted by the local interests involved emerges clearly enough from the protests raised in the north against the increased burdens which the proposed strengthening of the defences would impose on landowners there.[28] The bill claimed that the defence of the borders was adversely affected by local landlords who, by increasing their tenants' rents, deprived them of the means to fulfil their military obligations. The official bill, which passed the Lords without difficulty, set up commissions which would compel those lords to reduce their demands.[29] The Commons committee, however, produced a *nova billa*, passed in a rush, which changed the penalties to 'pains and bonds'; that is, it chiefly amended the bill by adding the second section; as usual, the addition of an internal proviso to a parchment bill called for a newly written out document.[30] The Commons' action greatly annoyed the Lords who recorded their feelings in a Journal entry of 8 March:

This day the Common House...sent up a new bill and withal returned a former bill that with great deliberation the Lords had passed and sent down before, with the same title; which course the Lords thought to be both derogatory to the superiority of the place and contrary to the ancient course of both Houses; and as they misliked the disorder, so was it their pleasure that this their misliking should be entered in the records of Parliament, lest so evil an example might hereafter be abused as a precedent.[31]

They also asked for a conference at which they communicated their displeasure, though all they got from their inferiors was the answer 'that this House had cause to do as they did and might likewise well do so'.[32] As usual, the Lords did not insist on their anger, even though they seem to have been correct in calling the Commons' action unprecedented.[33]

[27] 23 Eliz. I c. 4.

[28] The Percy archives at Alnwick contained a copy of the original bill, a proviso drafted for modifying it, and a paper of arguments against it (HMC, *Third Report*, App. [Duke of Northumberland], 42a).

[29] *Proc.* 536–7.

[30] Ibid. 542.

[31] *LJ* II, 46.

[32] *CJ* I, 133.

[33] The OA is marked as starting in the Commons, even though the history of the statute began in the Lords: i.e. the Lords bill had been fully and formally replaced, something never before encountered in the reign. The bill against tellers of 1571, started in the Lords, had reached the stage of a *nova* in the Commons when the whole affair was redirected by the arrival of a different bill from the Lords; here the initiative remained from first to last with the Upper House (cf. below, pp. 172–3). Only once before did the Commons return a replacement bill to the Lords: the bill for clipping coin of 1563 (5 Eliz. I c. 11; *CJ* I, 63–4, 66–7). Here, however, the OA now extant started in the Lords, so that apparently, after receiving the Commons bill on 27 Feb., the Lords on 11 March

Burghley at once made himself a summary of the bill as it had come back from the Commons and had the particular changes set out for his consideration;[34] and the Lords contented themselves with a series of verbal amendments.[35] The Commons had certainly sharpened the act, especially against absentee landlords, and they would seem to have done so by going counter to the Council's intentions which had been relatively conciliatory; no wonder that the local peers protested, and no wonder that the Lords' House tried (in vain) to get back to the original bill. This was an official bill of some importance – and yet it ran into such serious difficulties and unofficial alteration.

Indeed, while this bill passed, official origin by no means guaranteed a bill success, even if after amendment. In 1563 an attempt was made to remedy the notorious poverty of many church livings, caused by the engrossing of their incomes by impropriating lessees who maintained vicars on pittances. The grievance was notorious, but the guilty parties certainly included members of both Houses and influential constituents. Remedies were tried. The initiative seems to have been taken by the city of Exeter which put into the Lords a bill for uniting parishes there, to secure a better living for the remaining incumbents. The House remitted the matter to Southcott, J. with instructions to prepare two different versions.[36] One of these left action to the bishops who were to be encouraged to unite livings providing the combined income did not exceed £24; the other wished to empower the lord chancellor to drive the bishops into action by letters of commission. Interestingly enough, only the first prospered, passing the Lords quite quickly but sticking in the Commons after changes which would have reduced the top value permitted to twenty marks (£13 13*s* 4*d*).[37] The other appears to have reached the Lower House, though the record is very poor here; at any rate, it very quickly came to nothing.[38] All this activity, and perhaps the

read a further *nova* of their own which the Commons passed (*LJ* I, 596, 602). Thus honour was saved silently. On the present occasion the Commons cited the precedent of the apparel bill of 1576 (*Proc.* 544–5) which had indeed involved sending up a replacement bill, but the Lords had then refused to proceed with it.

[34] SP 12/148, fos. 87–8, 89–91 (8 and 10 March). This shows that the *nova* included also a lot of changes. A note in Burghley's papers (HMC, *Hatfield MSS*, XIII, 189) for an addition to the act which blamed landlords and farmers for reducing manpower on their lands by converting to pasture, and for letting to Scotsmen, left no deposit in the act as passed. Since nothing of the kind was removed from the *nova* the clause probably belongs to the preparation of the original bill.

[35] *LJ* II, 51–2. The Lords' amendments appear as additions, erasures and substitutions on the OA.

[36] *LJ* I, 600.

[37] Ibid. 600, 602–5; *CJ* I, 69–70, 72.

[38] The similarity of all these bills seems to have defeated the clerks of both Houses but the bills mentioned in *LJ* I, 610 and *CJ* I, 71 are not the same as those in the preceding note; the most probable reconstruction is that offered in the text.

example of Exeter, stirred Winchester into promoting a similar bill for its own parish churches, but this lapsed after two readings in the Upper House.[39] This concentration on the Lords indicates that the drive for improvement involved the bishops; it was the Lower House, supposedly (or so we are told) full of puritan champions of the lesser clergy, that stood in the way and frustrated every effort in 1563. However, Cecil had now become convinced of the need for action, and in 1566 he made strenuous efforts to prepare a bill which would set up diocesan commissions with powers to augment livings either by taxing parishioners or, in the case of impropriations, by assigning sufficient of the tithe to the vicar.[40] A generous but also a drastic measure, it stood little chance of success, even though Cecil started it in the Commons in order to keep it under his eye; in fact, it vanished after one reading.[41] The history of later efforts along similar lines is discussed below.[42]

Less comprehensible is the fate of the sumptuary bill of 1566 which was drafted on the orders of the Council[43] and clearly close to the heart of Cecilian paternalism, as frequent demands for the enforcement of existing acts show.[44] Though officially initiated in the Commons, the bill was twice redrafted by committees chaired by privy councillors. The Lords committed it to a strong body which included the original draftsman (John Southcott, judge of Queen's Bench); perhaps the new bill they produced in effect restored the terms first thought of. This bill the Commons dashed on third reading, and another government initiative over apparel failed in 1576.[45]

Indeed, official bills quite often came to grief. No subtle reasons need be sought for the failure of the 1571 bill to encourage the use of firearms, to the preparation of which Burghley devoted much detailed care; he may well have been responsible for commissioning propaganda material in support which asked 'the Lords and burgesses of the high court of Parliament...to establish some good order for the exercise of the arquebus'. This measure for improving the military capabilities of the nation readily passed the Commons but fell victim to the Queen's preference for short sessions and the general pressure of bills: it reached the Lords on the day of dissolution.[46] The same fate befell an important bill for tightening up controls over trade in goods which could be

[39] *LJ* I, 597–8.

[40] SP 12/77, fos. 177–83; 28, fos. 7–11. Both belong to 1566 and are to be read in this order; Cecil's hand appears on both.

[41] *CJ* I, 79.

[42] Below, pp. 217–19.

[43] SP 12/107, fo. 146.

[44] *TRP*, nos. 464 (21 Oct. 1559), 493 (6 May 1562), 494–9 (7 May 1563).

[45] Below, pp. 271–3.

[46] *CJ* I, 90, 93; *LJ* I, 701. Preparation: SP 12/78, fos. 225–31. Propaganda: SP 15/20, fos. 53–60 (two treatises to much the same effect by the same man, one Saul).

exported only under licence; an official origin is indicated by the short enacting clause, by the survival of the paper bill in the State Papers, and by the urgent message sent from the Lords (who never received the bill) to get it through.[47] It went into committee three days before the end of the session, and that was that.

Official initiative behind bills can, of course, often be conjectured with some assurance from the tenor of the resulting act – treason acts, ecclesiastical settlements, matters touching the Crown, and so forth – even when specific evidence fails us; and powerful probabilities are indicated, as has been said, by the framing of the enacting clause. Unfinished bills, for which texts survive only very rarely, pose essentially insoluble problems without additional evidence, since most of them dealt with 'commonwealth matters' in which official initiative can never be either assumed or denied without proof. Occasionally we are helped by the evidence of pre-parliamentary planning. Although the government of Elizabeth did not go in for such energetic and ranging legislative programmes as those of Thomas Cromwell in the 1530s, the Privy Council did not neglect its duty to produce some reforming bills to meet grievances and to avoid the impression that only need for money moved the Queen to call Parliament. It is probable that the Council always appointed a committee 'for consideration of all things necessary for the Parliament', as it certainly did on the eve of the 1559 and 1576 sessions;[48] and it is interesting that on those occasions the Council looked to the lawyers and not to its own leading members. Those preparatory committees overlapped markedly with the persons who were called by writs of assistance to the Lords where as advisers and draftsmen they continued to guide and improve legislation. They – judges, attorney and solicitor general, masters in Chancery, under the chairmanship of the lord keeper – thus acted from first to last as the government's steering committee for the making of statutes, which underlines the fact that statutes were treated as changes in the law, not as the fulfilment of a social programme.

Rarely only, however, do we know what such preparatory committees advocated. The 'Considerations delivered to the Parliament' in 1559 look like the product of such deliberations, being mainly concerned with laws old and new that touched the economic problems of the day.[49] The memorial called for the revival of expired acts against enclosures, vagabonds, the export of bullion and the import of wine; it contemplated various highly restrictive rules which would have barred merchants as well as husbandmen from acquiring more than a very small quantity of

[47] SP 12/107, fos. 133–7, 144.

[48] *APC* VII, 28; IX, 64.

[49] HMC, *Hatfield MSS*, I, no. 587, printed in *TED* I, 325–30.

land, confined the study of all laws to the upper sort, allowed only peers to employ private tutors for their children (to end 'the decay of the Universities and common schools', one of Hugh Latimer's constant complaints), and so forth. Some of these proposals clearly left a deposit in the comprehensive act of artificers passed 1563, but even in 1559 a bill was promoted (which got no further than a second reading) to give effect to the memorial's conviction that the behaviour and wages of labourers and servants need statutory attention.[50] Four acts of 1559 took up points made by the memorialists: c. 8 for shoemakers, c. 9 for leather manufacture, c. 13 for shipping in English bottoms, and c. 15 for limiting the wasteful production of charcoal by banning iron mills. On the face of it, only the second and third of these were drafted officially, but what seems to have happened is explained in the document: touching shoemakers, it was proposed to call 'a convenient number of the most skilful tanners, curriers and shoemakers, each sort apart, before the Queen's Council'.[51] We may suppose that these negotiations produced bills drafted either by the Council's own experts or by the interested parties under Council urging – so that in the end cc. 8 and 9 in their different ways sprang from a Council initiative. Other ideas put forward in the memorial appeared in later sessions. Attempts to legislate for bankruptcy began in 1563 when the bill passed both Houses but was vetoed as unsatisfactory;[52] the perjury act of that year (5 Eliz. I c. 9) was forecast in the 'Considerations';[53] the notion that no sheriff should be responsible for more than one county became law in 1566.[54] That programme of 1559, as fitted the start of a new reign, was much too all-embracing and ambitious even to secure a general acceptance in government circles, but it certainly left its mark on the statute book and indicates for some important measures an official origin of which otherwise we should not know. Not that the document constituted the whole of the government's programme for the session. Religion and the Church received attention from another committee,[55] and by sheer chance we know that Cecil had planned to deal with the military establishment of Berwick by statute, an intention which was abandoned in favour of telling the captain of the garrison to make his own reforms.[56]

For 1563 we possess a note of Cecil's touching matters to be prepared for the Parliament; as he indicated on it, he meant it for the attention

[50] Ibid. 325; *CJ* I, 60.
[51] *TED* I, 329.
[52] For bankruptcy see below, pp. 297–8.
[53] *TED* I, 328.
[54] The general act, an official bill, was 8 Eliz. I c. 16, but cf. below, pp. 194–5, for the difficulties caused by several shared shrievalties.
[55] Norman L. Jones, *Faith by Statute: Parliament and the Settlement of Religion 1559* (London, 1982), 47–50.
[56] *CSP Foreign Eliz. 1558–9*, no. 600.

of the attorney and solicitor general who no doubt were to do the necessary drafting.[57] He asked for the preparation of the subsidy bill; this was done.[58] His requests for 'such device for the execution of penal statutes as the subjects of this realm may in no such sort be grieved by promoters as presently they are' (for the reform, that is, of actions brought by informers) took some effect and still echoed faintly in 1571.[59] He wanted some statutory modification of lawyers' fees, but predictably the law officers dragged their feet over this; not until 1571, using his new influence in the Lords, could he get a bill started which then passed both Houses with some ease. However, Burghley was frustrated by his sovereign. Though she had specially commended the bill to the Commons when it first reached them from the Lords, she was got at in time to refuse her assent, saying that she would 'in time see the reformation and take order therein'. She never did, and Burghley seems to have given up, even though in 1584 he was presented with a usable proposal by Francis Alford. Evidently he knew when an interest was too powerful for him.[60] In 1563, Cecil also contemplated the act of apparel he failed to obtain in 1566.[61]

The clearest evidence for the manner in which Cecilian government prepared its parliamentary programme survives for 1566, in a paper endorsed 'Articles touching the Parliament'.[62] It is a list of items requiring legislation for each of which a short paragraph of explanation is offered, and against each of which there appears the name of the Queen's legal counsel who was made responsible for drafting the bill. Moreover, despite the difficulties of that session all the bills envisaged were introduced, and where the text survives the short enacting clause testifies to official origin. The attorney general's bill to settle the doubts attending upon the consecration of Anglican bishops became c. 1 of the session, though not without real difficulties especially in the Lords where the third reading passed against thirteen votes.[63] The solicitor general took on the bill which enabled defendants in actions started by informers to recover their costs if the verdict went their way (c. 2). If the lord chief justice followed instructions and drew a bill to consolidate the existing law on benefit of clergy (removing the privilege from cutpurses, rapists and burglars) he wasted much of his effort; the bill, replaced in a Lords committee, became c. 4 which dealt with cutpurses only, leaving the other criminals to wait until 1576.[64] The other three draftsmen fared

[57] SP 12/40, fo. 149, misplaced into 1566. [58] Below, p. 158. [59] Below, p. 103.

[60] *LJ* I, 696, 698, 701; *CJ* I, 93; *Proc.* 255–7; Alford to Burghley, 9 Nov. 1585 (Ellis, III, iv, 54–7).

[61] Above, p. 70. [62] SP 12/107, fos. 146–7.

[63] *LJ* I, 641.

[64] Ibid. 629, 631. Cf. above, pp. 64–5, for the legislation of 1576.

worse still. We have alrady seen what became of the bill for apparel, prepared by Southcott J.: the Commons rejected it.[65] They gave the same treatment to a bill touching fraudulent gifts intended to defeat the creditors of bankrupts (drafted by Dyer J.) and to one swearing under-sheriffs to a faithful execution of their duties which had been assigned to Thomas Carus, serjeant at law.[66] Dyer's bill was to contribute to the making of 13 Eliz. I c. 5, a fundamental law on bankruptcy, but Southcott's and Carus's failed once more when they were reintroduced in 1576.[67]

The official side, therefore, believed in putting together legislative programmes before Parliament met, programmes which after an extravagant start became increasingly modest but even so never got carried out in full. Councillors also, of course, promoted further bills not mentioned in the very patchy evidence we have for such programmes. But even as many public bills did not owe their initiation to the Council, so it is clear that not every large-scale set of proposals represented official thinking. Thus there lies among the State Papers a fairly extravagant effusion, entitled 'Reformation proposed in Parliament', which at first sight one might take to be official.[68] Speaking in the Queen's name, its author lists a series of measures that she is presented as urging upon Parliament; part of the paper is cast into paragraphs and provisos which the author no doubt intended to see used in the statutes he was seeking. This reformer, troubled by deficiencies in the common law and its administration, showed an ominous propensity for giving the Queen power to govern by rather authoritarian commissions. Some were to arrange the codification of the law, others to provide a compulsory and more or less binding arbitration between litigants, others again to establish the proper local customs governing the payment of tithe. The paper deteriorates into a rag-bag of bright ideas. As we shall see, some of it is reflected in actual bills in various sessions down to 1576, but most of it is not; its tone confirms its private origin. The author picked up things that had been tried, added things that no one would dream of trying, and offered his predilections as a programme. At least he provides clear proof that not only the government could think in terms of comprehensive legislative reform.

Initiatives from unquestionably private sources are more plentiful, varied, scattered and directed to practical purposes. At times we get firm evidence that a move started unofficially. Naturally enough, most of this evidence comes from the archives of towns; the efforts of individuals only

[65] Above, p. 70.
[66] *CJ* I, 79–91.
[67] Undersheriffs: *CJ*, 105–6, 108–9. Apparel: above, p. 70.
[68] Discussed in detail below, pp. 277–9.

rarely enjoy documentary survival. Robert Rosse, who in 1576 – being troubled with a lewd wife – offered to settle his lands by act of Parliament on the earl of Rutland with a life interest to himself, never pursued this intention.[69] The supplication submitted by the merchants of Danzig touching the trade in rabbit furs, which in 1571 was read in the Commons and passed to Sir Francis Knollys for action, left no parliamentary consequences.[70] In 1580 the earl of Hertford hoped to promote a bill 'concerning the lands he is seised of or is to demand', but though he maintained that its contents would benefit the Queen as much as himself his plea that she should have it scrutinized by her Council and sign it fell on deaf ears.[71]

An interesting light is thrown on these pre-parliamentary moves by the attempt in 1572 by Sir Richard Fiennes, who did not secure election to the Commons until 1584, to introduce a bill 'for felonious fellows' of the Colleges of Oxford and Cambridge – a bill intended to protect Colleges against members who allegedly were robbing them (in some, to us unknown, fashion). The move caused great excitement, and Fiennes soon had to defend himself to Lord Burghley, as chancellor of Cambridge, who blamed him for talking of his plans to all and sundry, with the result that the lord treasurer had been bombarded with protests. Writing on 19 May 1572, after the session had begun, Fiennes claimed to have shown his proposal only to the solicitor general and to Speaker Bell, both of whom had contributed to the drafting of it.[72] However, he admitted that Thomas Norton, the main draftsman, had also, of course, seen it and had broken his promise to tell no one of it except the two chancellors of the Universities, Burghley and Leicester. 'Wanting in this matter that consideration I wish had been in him, contrary to the trust I reposed in him,' he had shown the bill also to John Whitgift, then master of Trinity College, Cambridge. The result was the spreading about of its contents in the Lower House of Convocation and false reports about its terms: Fiennes had been told 'that I preferred a bill which would discourage scholars from learning and subvert the founders of Colleges'. He had done his best to correct these false impressions, though we never quite learn what the bill was supposed to do. Having met trouble at Cambridge, Fiennes proposed to search out opinion at Oxford, but his doing so finished the bill. A week later, Laurence Humphrey, president of Magdalen College and very well friended in high places, wrote urgently to the two chancellors jointly to prevent further proceedings.[73] As he explained, 'poor men' like himself, used only to the ways of Convocation,

[69] HMC, *12th Report. App. IV* (*Rutland*), I, 107.

[70] *CJ* I, 86.

[71] HMC, *Bath*, IV, 145.

[72] SP 12/86, fo. 194.

[73] Ibid. fos. 220–1.

'cannot understand all mysteries of Parliament'. Two days later, on 28 May, he wrote again to Burghley with a note of various bills touching the Universities' interests – a note the competence of which convicts him of hypocrisy in his denial of parliamentary expertise. The third item in his list reads 'the bill for felonious fellows in Colleges, which is already provided for and therefore needless; I think Sir Richard Fiennes will not bring it in, and yet it is drawn'. There is indeed no sign of the bill in Parliament, and this teacup storm blew over, but it tells a good deal about the way that bills might be shaped even before they reached Parliament.

Town councils were among those most eager to watch what happened in Parliament and to promote their own needs. In January 1559, the city of Lincoln, contemplating the forthcoming session, proposed to advance its interests in becoming the staple town for Lincolnshire and the east Midlands if it were decided to move the wool staple, homeless since the loss of Calais the year before, to England.[74] No such bill was introduced until 1563 when no one pushed it beyond a first reading; Lincoln would seem to have been as unconcerned as everybody else.[75] The city also looked into the chance of acquiring four local parsonages by act of Parliament but did nothing further about it; it would seem that their care in appointing a solicitor (contact man) for their 'burgesses at this Parliament' of 1559 was somewhat superfluous.[76] Exeter, whose town clerk, John Hooker, displayed such activity in the Parliament of 1571, did a little better in 1563 when it promoted two bills. As emerges from the town burgesses' report to Hooker, they showed some sophistication, introducing one bill for the uniting of parish churches in the Lords and the other 'for orphans' in the Commons.[77] The writer trusted that

> by that time we have thoroughly considered that bill for orphans and ready to be sent off to the Lords, the Lords' bill will be ready to come down... If we should have put both in at one place then peradventure the House would not be best contented with two bills for our private city.

These tactics did not work out as intended. The orphans' bill (which confirmed various of the city's liberties) reached the Lords on 17 February and passed easily.[78] The other bill ran into a lot of trouble, being not even first read until 9 March, more than five weeks after the burgesses had given it to the clerk. As already suggested, it got mixed up with Cecil's and the bishops' efforts to improve the remuneration of vicars, and though it progressed a long way it finally lapsed in the Commons.[79]

[74] HMC, *14th Report, App. VIII (Lincoln)*, 49.
[75] *CJ* I, 65.
[76] HMC, *Lincoln*, 50.
[77] HMC, *Exeter*, 51–2.
[78] 5 Eliz. I, OA 34.
[79] Above, pp. 69–70.

Rather more obscure are the efforts made by fishermen from various places. Those of Rye tried to mobilize their members in 1572.[80] They wanted a bill 'for the maintenance of the fishermen of this realm and avoiding of strangers fishermen', as well as banning the sale in England of aliens' catches, a recurring theme of those years which left deposits in the various navigation acts. The men of Rye asked for the mobilization of a nation-wide fishermen's lobby. Nothing came of this in 1572, but when in 1576 a bill was introduced to continue the act of 5 Eliz. I c. 5 (for the navy and shipping), representatives of twenty-eight sea ports from Newcastle to Exmouth on the very next day signed a certificate strongly urging the need for the act.[81] Evidently this lobby had a very definite existence, though on this occasion it acted illadvisedly; the statute of 1563, having been made for ten years from 1564 and then to the end of the next Parliament, was not due for renewal in 1576, and so the bill lapsed. Even less is known of a bill apparently promoted in 1572, 'that it shall be lawful for any Englishman or denizen, taking any kind of fish, to sell the same to any except the Queen's enemies'. It failed to get registered in the Commons Journal, which makes certain that it never made it to a second reading and suggests that it failed to get even a first, but its existence was known to the diarist, Thomas Cromwell. He also knew that it was put up by men from Suffolk, intent upon breaking the monopoly of herring sales which Great Yarmouth claimed by virtue of royal letters patent. Yarmouth evidently counterattacked at once, one of its members protesting in the House that the bill, if passed, would ruin a town burdened with a past expenditure of £12,000 upon the maintenance of its harbour. Yarmouth was profitable to the Exchequer, paying £50 a year to the Queen for the privilege and another £50 for the road built to bring the fish to market; the supporters of the bill should not claim advantages to general shipping because they 'use none but small boats, not fit for navigation'. In the upshot the promoters paid the penalty of trying to use statute against a powerful vested interest – and for not organizing a better campaign.[82]

Of all the lobbies the most active, best organized and therefore most troublesome was the city of London. It had long had experience of using Parliament to solve its problems and notoriously contributed to prolonged sessions through the promotion of bills which, some thought, dealt with matters that could easily have been settled by the city's own

[80] HMC, *13th Report, App. IV (Rye)*, 18–19.

[81] *LJ* I, 745; SP 12/107, fos. 170–1.

[82] *Proc.* 363. A few words in the entry are left blank, presumably because the copyist of the original could not make them out. For Yarmouth and its fishery see my forthcoming article, 'Piscatorial politics in the early Parliaments of Elizabeth I', in a volume of essays dedicated to Donald Coleman.

administration.[83] The court of aldermen (mayor's court) quite often recorded the paying of fees and thanks offerings to the officers of the Parliament, sometimes for services rendered and sometimes in expectation of future favours. The clerk of the Commons would be voted 40*s* at the end of a session, but Speakers were wooed as soon as chosen, on one occasion with six yards of velvet and on another with a purse containing twenty nobles in gold. Exceptionally the city gave the serjeant too 20*s* in 1581, 'for his good will showed to the city in the Parliament time'.[84] This last generosity was called forth by the passage of a very troublesome bill to sort out the testamentary settlements of Sir Thomas Gresham, disputed between the widow and the city.[85] Anxious to secure statutory protection for the recently founded Royal Exchange, the city forked out £18 9*s* in set fees to Speaker, clerk and serjeant, adding 20*s* more to reward the clerk's staff and further payments for a certified copy of the act; they decided that the Mercers Company should bear half the expenditure and presumably extracted the money from them.[86] The court demonstrated its sophisticated experience in 1563 when the London brewers lost a bill in the Commons which would have allowed each brewer to employ more than four aliens in his business; they were advised to reform the bill and reintroduce it in the Lords, 'to try what they can do therein with the help of their friends', but they seem instead to have given up.[87] Perhaps there were not enough friends to brewing in the Upper House.

Wishing to keep some sort of control over these charges and over policy in general, the mayor and aldermen had worked out a routine procedure. When the writs of summons reached the major he informed all the Companies of the impending Parliament and invited legislative proposals. These were then reviewed in court, some being adopted, others turned down, and others again sent for redrafting. When the brewers did try again in 1566 the court did not like the bill and ordered them to desist.[88] The butchers twice ran into lack of cooperation when they tried to get prices reduced and pork-butchering better controlled; both bills were put back for further consideration and neither came to anything.[89] A glovers' bill of 1563 did not please the court who nevertheless agreed to let it go forward if its backers so desired, but the lack of support seems to have ended its life.[90] On several occasions the city government

[83] BL, Harl. MS 253, fos. 33v, 34v. Cf. Helen Miller, 'London and Parliament in the reign of Henry VIII,' *BIHR* 35 (1962), 128–49.

[84] CLRO, Rep 13(1), fo. 251; 14, fo. 161; 19, fo. 39v; 20, fos. 163v, 183v. For more information on payments made to officers of the Parliament see above, p. 56.

[85] 23 Eliz. I, OA 29.

[86] CLRO, Rep. 20, fos. 183, 190.

[87] *CJ* I, 64; CLRO, Rep. 15, fo. 188.

[88] Ibid. 16, fo. 141.

[89] Ibid. 15, fo. 183v; 16, fos. 139v-140r.

[90] Ibid. 15, fo. 177v.

welcomed initiatives presented to them but in the end did nothing – or at least, none of those bills reached even a first reading. In 1563, 'the fishmongers being merchant adventurers' moved for the repeal of the navigation act of the previous year (1 Eliz. I c. 13) and were given expert drafting assistance; in 1571, complaints from the sealer of leather in the city about the state of the law secured a promise that the city's members in the Commons 'shall be moved to and spoken withal for the furtherance' of the desired reform; in the same year, a bill for the paving of Tower Hill and improving the watercourse by Hog Lane was agreed in court; in 1576, a committee was appointed to draw a bill for the truer barrelling and gauging of fish; in the same year, the governors of Bridewell were told to get their charter confirmed in Parliament; in 1581, Thomas Norton received instructions for a bill to improve London's grain supply.[91] Of none of these matters do we find a trace in the Journal of either House; even if the bills got drafted and handed into the Parliament, they evidently were either crowded out or too insufficiently 'followed' to secure even a first reading.

The insistence that London interests were to work through the mayor and aldermen made good sense: it could help to prevent conflicts and superfluities. A comparison of manifest London bills in the Commons with the records of the aldermen's court, however, shows that parties sometimes by-passed this machinery and took their problems straight to the House, with the result that too many such private bills clogged the machinery. The Council were advised in 1572 that these bills should first be discussed with the members for the city, before being read, with a view to sifting sensible from undesirable measures, and also with a view to referring to the city authorities themselves anything they could deal with so as to unburden the Parliament.[92] In fact, by-passing the mayor's court did nobody much good: not one such smuggled-through bill prospered. Most of them never progressed beyond first reading, though this minor showing of a flag may have satisfied their backers: for removing brew-houses on the Thames below London Bridge, for rights of search to be granted to the cutlers (killed by a protest from the cutlers of Westminster), for enforcing the cordwainers' privileges, for 'the assize of weights and measures among innholders within three miles of London' (the wardens of the Innkeepers' Company to have powers of search within that radius).[93] A waxchandlers' bill of 1572 caused a fair bit of pother before being rejected at third reading.[94] A bill of 1576 for

[91] Ibid. 15, fo. 188; 17, fos. 144, 152v; 19, fos. 43, 47; 20, fo. 164v.
[92] BL, Harl. MS 253, fo. 34v.
[93] *CJ* I, 75 (and cf. SP 15/13, fos. 79–80); 76; 84 (and cf. *Proc.* 208, 246).
[94] Below, p. 237.

the assize of wood and coal within three miles of London vanished in committee;[95] one of 1581, designed to ensure that a set proportion of various cloths should be manufactured in England and giving the London Clothworkers powers of enforcement, got a new bill out of the committee, and that was that.[96] Exactly the same fate befell an attempt in the same year to open up entry into the Merchant Adventurers Company, presumably on behalf of outport merchants and against the London interest; not for the last time, the monopolists' arguments, preaching at large of the benefits to state and commonwealth, carried the day.[97] Considering the hold that the Livery Companies had on the court of aldermen, it is not surprising to find that an attempt to open all trades to all the freemen of the city had to go ahead without the city government's blessing; more surprisingly, after failing abysmally in 1572 the promoters tried again in the next session, won in the Commons, and failed in the Lords only because their opponents delayed the second reading long enough to let the bill run out of time.[98] There would appear to have been some powerful London interest in the Commons capable at times of queering the city government's pitch.

Unassisted bills failed, but those adopted by the aldermen's court did not, to tell the truth, do much better. Of the fourteen parliamentary promotions put up by the court which can be safely identified in these seven sessions only four succeeded: the clothworkers' act of 1566;[99] the act of 1571 for the Lea river navigation (after a most difficult passage, even though Burghley had assisted with the drafting of the bill, and at a cost to the city chamber of £7 in promotion dinners as well as £33 2*s* 4*d* in various fees around both Houses);[100] the act banning iron mills near the city moved for in London nine years before it got into Parliament and was hotly contested there;[101] and the act for Gresham's bequests.[102] London initiatives contributed to the legislation on bankruptcy, but the bill owed much also to others.[103] It is probable that the act for the fulling of hats and caps, which passed in 1566 after abortive efforts in the previous two sessions, originated in the city, though evidence for an

[95] *CJ* I, 110; *Proc.* 486.
[96] *CJ* I, 121, 123, 134; *Proc.* 531.
[97] *CJ* I, 128, 130, 132; SP 12/148, fos. 19–30.
[98] *CJ* I, 99, 105–7; *LJ* I, 734, 745; *Proc.* 311, 478.
[99] Below, p. 83.
[100] 13 Eliz. I c. 18 (a private act not printed at the time); CLRO, Rep. 17, fo. 141v; SP 12/77, fos. 244–55 (the paper draft, corrected by Burghley); *Chamber Accounts of the Sixteenth Century*, ed. Betty A. Masters (London Record Society, 1984), 129–30.
[101] 23 Eliz. I c.5; CLRO, Rep. 17, fo. 311v (13 May 1572). The bill passed only because it came to be combined with similar endeavours elsewhere to reduce the manufacture of charcoal.
[102] Above, p. 78.
[103] Below, pp. 297–8.

interest there exists only for 1563.[104] The Haberdashers later failed twice with bills sponsored by the mayor's court; the first (1571) aimed to tighten up manufacturing practices, while the second (1576) tried to limit the number of apprentices employable in the trade.[105] The Thames did no better than the city. A bill to protect fishermen's interests against unlawful netting of fish failed in 1563, thus forcing the city to take direct action nearly four years later,[106] while another promoted on behalf of the watermen was dropped in exchange for a brief clause in the act obtained in 1566 by Trinity House.[107] Strained relations with aliens produced several bills approved of by the mayor and aldermen, but none of them succeeded. In 1571, the city backed 'the poor handicraftsmen' against competition from foreigners, though it was only in 1576 that the bill then agreed to be 'preferred and followed in the Parliament House' reached the Commons where it was so poorly followed that it lapsed after one reading.[108] In 1572, on the other hand and to its credit, the mayor's court agreed to support the outsiders' complaint – aliens, denizens and Englishmen from Southwark – about special impositions extorted from them by the Companies. The bill, read a first time on 24 May, was immediately denounced by Fleetwood as a slander to London; however, he admitted that if the charges were true the extortion deserved punishment. Some four weeks later the mayor's court heard a protest from the Companies accused, invited them to justify their claim that they were only imposing fees authorized in law, and resolved that the recent practice of charging outsiders for the enrolment of letters patent (licences) should cease. Satisfied therewith, the promoters of the bill withdrew it on the following day and put their trust in mayor and aldermen, thus testifying to the good sense of the advice tendered earlier with respect to a reduction in London's bills.[109] On the other hand, when a protest was raised against the alleged practice of certain foreigners to bring their pregnant wives to England, so that the children should be born within the Queen's dominions, even the facts that Norton, the parliamentary expert, drew the bill and that Burghley was solicited did not prevent extensive redrafting in the Commons before the lords let it die of inanition.[110] That a bill to free grain imported into London from all

[104] 8 Eliz. I c. 11. For the earlier bills cf. *CJ* I, 53–4, 58, 68–70; *LJ* I, 586, 598, 600. For the city's move see CLRO, Rep. 15, fo. 177v.

[105] Ibid. 19, fo. 45v; *CJ* I, 84, 89, 107–8, 111; *Proc.* 218, 482.

[106] *CJ* I, 68, 71; CLRO, Rep. 15, fo. 175v and 16, fo. 147v.

[107] *CJ* I, 77–8; 8 Eliz. I c. 13, sect. 3.

[108] CLRO, Rep. 17, fo. 144; *CJ* I, 110.

[109] CLRO, Rep. 17, fos. 323, 335, 337; *CJ* I, 97; *Proc.* 380.

[110] CLRO, Rep. 19, fo. 38v; *CJ* I, 118–9, 121–3, 127–8; *LJ* II, 34, 38. The city agreed to the bill on 3 Feb. 1576, too close to the session of that year to be ready for it; it was thus introduced early in the next session (1581). The doubts raised in the

payment of customs duties got very short shrift is not surprising;[111] but what went wrong with a bill for the purchase of wool by woolwinders which got no further than a single reading?[112]

The parliamentary manoeuvres of the London Clothworkers Company (assisted by the Merchant Taylors),[113] which led to much production of bills and papers, merit more detailed discussion for the light they throw on practice.[114] Because rival London interests were involved the mayor and aldermen only rarely played a public role, but that the endeavours had some sort of official support is nevertheless plain. The Clothworkers were much troubled by the domination in the export trade of cloth left unfinished (monopolised by the Merchant Adventurers trading to Antwerp), as a result of which less and less English cloth passed through their hands to be finished. The relationships were somewhat complicated by the fact that the clothiers of several counties, especially Kent, Sussex and Suffolk, also exported some unfinished cloth (which made the local clothworkers allies of the Londoners) but did so without shipping through the Adventurers' depot in Blackwell Hall (which annoyed the clothworkers' enemies). The London Company tried to secure that a fixed proportion of London's cloth export should deal in finished cloths and to obtain rights of search which would enable them to police such a law. They had tried before, but in the reign of Elizabeth they began their campaign with an appeal to the Privy Council in June 1565. The Council decided to test their claim that they could finish cloth as well as any Antwerper, but the results were at best indecisive.[115]

Commons, where it was much 'impugned', concentrated on its morality ('against charity, against the law of nature') and the danger that it might in time be used to question a lot of people's rights by allegations of alien descent (*Proc.* 528, 532–3).

[111] CLRO, Rep. 15, fo. 189; *CJ* I, 65.

[112] CLRO, Rep. 17, fo. 134v; *CJ* I, 89. There had been an attempt to legislate for woolwinders (to 'buy wool notwithstanding the statute') in 1563; so this may have been a revived bill.

[113] Cf. G. Unwin, *Industrial Organization in the Sixteenth and Seventeenth Centuries* (Oxford, 1904), 114–6.

[114] The story is put together from the following evidence: *APC* VII, 218, 227–8, 304–5, 338 (1565, 1567); BL, Lansdowne MS 24, no. 69 (1577); 8 Eliz. I c. 6 (act of 1566) and its parliamentary history (*CJ* I, 75, 79, 80; *LJ* I, 662–3); *CJ* I, 76 (bill of 1566); SP 12/41, fos. 129–34 (arguments over bill, 1566); CLRO, Rep. 17, fo. 129v (1571); SP 12/77, fos. 169–72 (protests from merchants of the Steelyard, 1571); *CJ* I, 89 (bills against clothworkers, 1571); ibid. 85, 90, and *Proc.* 225, 247 (bill for Kentish and Sussex cloths, 1571); *CJ* I, 109 (bill for Kentish and Suffolk cloths, 1576); *CJ* I, 121, 123, 134 and *Proc.* 531 (bill for clothworkers of London, 1581); *CJ* I, 124 and *Proc.* 535 (bill for clothiers of Kent, 1581). For the general setting see also G. D. Ramsay, *The City of London in International Politics at the Accession of Elizabeth Tudor* (Manchester, 1975), esp. 43–6.

[115] The Clothworkers' claim in 1566 was obscurely worded: the assessors appointed (the lord mayor and other eminent persons) 'by their certificate have declared their judgments of the said workmanship; and yet those cloths... were of the worst they could

So the Clothworkers turned to Parliament. On 25 October 1566 they obtained a first reading for a bill to compel merchants to export one finished cloth for every four unfinished, and to empower the Company to supervise the execution of the act. This led to a vigorous protest from the Adventurers to which the Clothworkers replied at length, emphasizing their ability to produce cloth good enough to sell abroad and the excellence of their supervision of their workmen. Apparently despairing of gaining their main purpose, they also introduced on 6 November a bill simply conveying powers of search, but this was dropped when on 13 December a revised form of the first bill appeared in the House. It embodied a compromise in that it reduced the ratio of finished cloth exported to one in ten, and it passed both Houses readily enough. There had evidently been some forming of alliances, for apart from imposing the more moderate ratio the act also barred the export of unfinished cloth from Kent and Suffolk, an enactment which assisted clothworkers outside London and protected the exporting monopoly of the Adventurers.[116] On the other hand, the right of search was granted only obliquely, in a final clause which conveyed the moiety of the forfeiture suffered for breach of the statute to the Clothworkers' Company: this implied that they would bring the necessary action by information but gave them no policing powers. Perhaps the bill of 6 November should not have been abandoned so readily.

The act proved pretty well unenforceable since the exporters continued to proclaim their inability to sell finished cloth abroad; besides, since it did not apply to merchants licensed for export before its passing (that is, the Merchant Adventurers), its chief victims were the few remaining Hanseatic merchants who complained of being singled out. In the next session, therefore, the Clothworkers tried again. They once more wanted an act ensuring that one in ten ratio, but wished the earlier act to be 'enlarged' and impose heavier penalties; we may suppose that they put up an amending bill to bring in those merchants whom inadequate drafting had left out in 1566. Through the mayor and aldermen they sought 'the aid of the knights and burgesses of this city in their said suit' but got only a promise that their request would be considered. The Parliament met a week later, and the Clothworkers had to go ahead without formal help from their superiors. Probably as a consequence, the bill read a first time on 10 April reached a second reading and the order

pick out'. Thus quite probably the Merchant Adventurers' memory in 1577 that the test went against the Clothworkers was correct.

116 As the OA shows, on third reading it was felt that the term 'Kentish and Suffolk cloths' might be taken to describe a type of product rather than a manufacturing district, so that 'made or to be made in the counties of Kent and Suffolk' was added each time.

for engrossment only on 17 May, too late in the session to do them any good. Perhaps they gained some consolation from the facts that on the same day the House also buried a bill promoted against them, and that a Merchant Adventurers' bill, which tried to direct all Kentish and Suffolk cloths through Blackwell Hall, fared as badly. In the 1576 session, a bill to bring Kentish and Suffolk cloths in line with London's products (by permitting the export of unfinished cloths provided every tenth was finished) died after first reading, which may have pleased the Londoners.[117] The fortunes of the Clothworkers remained at a low ebb. In 1581 both those of London and of Kent promoted bills for their own relief, but the first emerged renovated from committee only two days before the session ended, and the second was dashed on second reading. The London manufacturers had clearly learned that in the face of economic facts and the indifference of the city they could not hope to assert their claims; their one achievement, the act of 1566, remained a dead letter.

In one case only do we know exactly why a London bill failed. In 1566, the Vintners Company, after years of agitating, promoted a bill to repeal the licensing act of 1553 and enable them to step up the sale of wine. The court of aldermen whole-heartedly adopted the bill and noted expressly that the city's representatives 'shall be specially moved for the furthering of the same'.[118] However, the drafts for the bill got into Cecil's hands and greatly annoyed him; in a powerful memorial he attacked a trade which forced up the price of expensive imports, benefited only France, damaged agriculture by reducing the demand for brewing barley, and encouraged drunkenness and disorder.[119] Nevertheless, the city interest put its back into things and forced the bill through, though it took a division (95 votes against 65) on third reading to do so. For once the manager of the Commons had to fall back on the Lords who duly quashed the bill on third reading there.[120] The Vintners were to have their revenge: a year later they got a patent exempting them from the statute whose repeal they had failed to obtain.[121]

117 Hooker (*Proc.* 253) noted such a bill for 1571, but there is no entry in the Journal.
118 CLRO, Rep. 16, fo. 130.
119 SP 12/28, fos. 108–9 (misdated); 41, fos. 68–71, 151–2.
120 *CJ* I, 76–8; *LJ* I, 651–3.
121 Cf. E. Green, 'The Vintners' Lobby 1552–1568,' *Guildhall Studies in London History* I (1974), 47–58. This accepts Fleetwood's story, told in 1585, that the Commons passed the bill on a Saturday, having been 'well dined' by the promoters, but reversed their vote on the Monday when sobriety had returned (told by Neale, *HC*, 375). This, as *LJ* proves, is a fable; if it were true the bill could not have gone forward to the Lords. In the Parliament of 1572 Fleetwood told the story the other way round, as Neale says he did in 1585: the bill had been dashed one afternoon and passed next morning (*Proc.* 383: not a word of good dining). He also then supposed that the bill had become an act. Nothing but muddled memories.

London's influence in Parliament, therefore did not match its ambition to seek legislation convenient to its concerns, though this conclusion cannot, of course, take account of any influence the city may well have brought to bear on the making of government measures touching social and economic problems which concerned it. That one of the Council's most active bills draftsmen, Thomas Norton, was also the lord mayor's remembrancer and a parliamentary agent for the city must surely have had some significance, though at present we cannot do more than guess at it. What can, up to a point, be measured are the direct efforts made by London to promote particular bills, either through the court of aldermen or side by side with it, and here the evidence indicates that though London bills took up much time they were only rarely successful.

Even so, London did markedly better than York, a city which also tried to constitute itself into a regular lobby. York, of course, lacked the easy contacts with the centre of government available to London, the more so because, with the Queen's authority up there devolved upon the Council of the North, a body of small parliamentary influence or none, the important direct relations between suitors to the Council and promoters in Parliament could not arise. The city therefore always used the occasion of a Parliament to promote all sorts of concerns that had nothing to do with Parliament; its members travelled south with a mixed bag of instructions – renewal of charters, purchase of lands on behalf of the city, private affairs – which distracted them from looking after the bills also at times entrusted to them. A second weakness arose from penury or penny-pinching: the city's members seem never to have had the means to overcome lack of acquaintance by judicious feeing, and no bill prospered.[122] Nevertheless, just about every session was preceded by a meeting to draw up instructions; on one occasion, in October 1579 when the recall of Parliament was confidently but mistakenly expected, the mayor expressly asked all councillors to seek out and bring forward 'anything beneficial for this city'.[123] The same desires appear over and over again, which reveals the true position and the lack of achievement. Many of the points raised for the promotion of bills left no trace in either Journal. The most persistent demands concerned apprentices: York wished to have full freedom in taking them notwithstanding any statutory limitations. They promoted a bill for this purpose in 1559, but one reading was the limit of that bill's life.[124] From the next session onwards this demand became formalized as a request for the same exemptions as

[122] In 1563, the members could pay for a confirmation of York's charters only because they happened to have some money entrusted to them by a private person for his concerns; they urgently wrote to ask that the outlay be reimbursed (*YCR* VI, 55–6).

[123] Ibid. 49–51, 55–6, 118–9: VII, 20, 46–7; VIII, 22.

[124] *CJ* I. 54.

were granted to London and Norwich in the act of artificers; the point was solemnly listed in every sessional programme but did not reach the stage of a bill in the Lower House until 1581 when once again one reading was all that could be achieved.[125] York may have been responsible for a bill 'for searching and sealing of woollen cloth' (1559) which lapsed in the Lords,[126] for on the eve of the next Parliament they expressed a wish to have such powers transferred to them by letters patent and in 1571 once more thought about a bill on the subject,[127] but that would appear to be the sum total of their activity in the promotion of bills. York must be considered willing but incompetent; perhaps the report of its members on 14 February 1563 that 'we have put in a bill or two; how they will take effect we know not' well describes the lack of professional expertise behind its endeavours.[128]

Thus when a bill was prepared beforehand for putting into the Parliament, we can at times learn something positive about the initiatives behind it. The other method for starting a bill – namely, raising a problem by question and moving for a drafting committee – ought to tell more plainly what lay behind the measure, but it occurred too rarely to be of much use in this. The method was regularly employed for the production of supply bills, when it provided the government with a way to make its demands palatable,[129] but there were few other occasions. The collecting of 'grievances' in 1571 by means of a committee from which some bills emerged was so unusual as not to recur in the next two sessions.[130] Nor was the method, when used, particulary successful, except inasmuch as some grouch or bonnet-bee might get an airing; most bills came ready-made to the Parliament, whatever changes they were to undergo there. One act showed up the confusion that could result from planning bills in Parliament. In 1581, Mildmay and Norton (the Council's managers) raised the question whether the existing laws against papists were strict enough, and the latter, moving for a committee, linked the issue with that of supply in order to get a more extreme measure through. It turned out not to have been a wise move: the bill produced in committee cut across one started for the same purpose in the Lords, and in the outcome much discussion and compromising became necessary before the bill passed.[131] In 1576, two apparently private efforts to get action on public issues – 'stealing away a man's children by colour of privy contracts' and the safekeeping of parish

[125] Ibid. 127; *Proc.* 537.

[126] *CJ* I, 55, 59–61; *LJ* I, 538.

[127] *YCR* VI, 49, 51; VII, 20.

[128] Ibid. VI, 56.

[129] Below, p. 158.

[130] Below, pp. 101–4.

[131] 23 Eliz. I c. 1; *CJ* I, 119, 123–4, 131; *LJ* II, 44, 46–8. Unfortunately Cromwell's diary has no entry for the day on which Mildmay and Norton made their move; perhaps he was absent.

registers – procured drafting committees, but the first never produced, while the bill prepared by the second merely got one reading.[132] In 1571, Thomas Norton moved for action against the ease with which convicted felons pleading their clergy could purge themselves in bishops' courts and was encouraged to produce a bill single-handedly; he did this and steered it through the Commons, but the Lords let it rest after two readings.[133] Perhaps Norton thought to get better publicity for his bill in this way, for he could as easily have prepared it beforehand and put it in routinely; he had battled over the issue before that session. Anyway, moving for a drafting committee was not yet a good way to follow up initiatives.[134]

[132] *CJ* I, 104–6.

[133] Below, p. 302.

[134] More fully discussed below, pp. 96–105.

5

Bill procedure

OUTLINE

A man, or a corporation, or the Privy Council, having decided to promote a bill for enactment, then had to enter into the complexities of parliamentary bill procedure. The rules were well established by the beginning of Elizabeth's reign. The bills, written on paper, except that bills graced with the royal sign manual appeared on parchment, were given to the clerk of one House or the other who then passed them to his Speaker (or lord chancellor); he in turn was supposed to bring bills before the House in the order in which he had received them, except that bills coming from monarch or Council enjoyed precedence, but it seems that in this respect Speakers exercised a good deal of discretion. The bill received three readings in its House of origin, though as a rule the full text was read out only on the first occasion; thereafter the summary breviate, which if it was not attached to the bill by the promoter the Speaker was expected to prepare for himself, sufficed. The effectiveness of the first reading may be gauged from the accuracy with which diarists recorded the essential provisions of bills which they can hardly ever have had a chance to see for themselves.Their descriptions are often much fuller than the summary titles used by the clerks in the Journals, and since so many failed bills are lost they often give us the best indication of the contents. Occasionally the bill was debated on first reading but practice was against it. The chief debating stage occurred when the bill came up for second reading, after which it might be committed – handed over to a group of members of the House to consider it and propose amendments; in the Lords, this task was often entrusted to the non-voting assistants (judges, law officers, masters in Chancery – all legal experts), especially if the bill concerned law reform or seemed to affect the legal rights of others, but full-scale committees were also appointed frequently. The chairman of the committee then reported its findings for the House to accept or reject, which led to more debate. Either on second reading or after report the order was given for engrossing the bill on parchment. Thereafter amendment became physically more difficult, especially because unlike the paper bill the engrossment left little space between lines. Major revisions quite frequently led to the bill being replaced by an entirely new draft (*nova billa*) which then had to start again at the beginning, with a first reading. When the bill, now engrossed, had been read a third time, the Speaker put the question whether it should pass, a decision which could be obtained by manifest consent, a mutter of ayes (not used in the Lords) or formal division (rare). If the bill passed, the Commons clerk wrote 'judicium' in his Journal and the Lords clerk wrote 'conclusa'.

The whole process then had to be repeated in the other House to which the bill was sent by the hands of delegates. For this the Commons usually employed privy councillors while the Lords invariably used their assistants. The despatching clerk wrote the 'bail' or transfer formula on the bill: 'cette bille soit baille aux seigneurs [or: communes]'; after the other House had done with it, his opposite number recorded this by writing under the bail 'a cette bille [possibly: avecque provisions et amendments] les seigneurs [or: les communes] sont assentuz'. When both Houses had agreed to the bill it was returned to the Lords to await the conclusion of the session and the royal assent; the exception to this was the grant of the lay subsidy which remained with the Speaker of the Lower House for presentation to the Queen on that occasion. At the ceremony of the assent the clerk of the Crown in Chancery read out the titles or descriptions of bills, with the clerk of the Upper House pronouncing the formula of assent or veto. These he read from a paper previously supplied to him, and he was supposed later to transcribe them at the head of the parchment bills, now acts, but this was occasionally forgotten.[1]

These rules, developed out of practice and convenience, rested upon precedents certainly going back into the fifteenth century. Precedents, however, as was said in the Commons in 1584, offered no more than a useful guide to past practice 'and thereby did give the better light how to proceed in matters arising'; since the House was 'a free council' it could at need override such guides.[2] Certainly, neither House hesitated

[1] Neale's discussion (*HC*, ch. 19) supplies a useful though not altogether accurate outline; his efforts to discover meaningful development must be discounted. He relied a great deal on what he called an 'anonymous treatise' of the early seventeenth century (BL, Additional MS 36856) which is actually one of the several extant copies of Hakewill's work, printed several times (see above, p. 53, n.47). This rested on a careful study of the Commons Journals. Most of Hakewill's precedents postdate 1581, but his is a reliable account of the general rules of procedure as they stood in effect throughout Elizabeth's reign; it will be used here though without constant reference to it. William Cecil made some notes on supposed customs which put public bills always before private ones (BL, Lansdowne MS 105, fo. 41), but practice did not always follow these guide-lines.

[2] Northants Record Office, MS F(M). P.2, fo. 35v.

to do what was necessary if some unprecedented hitch had occurred, but the evidence makes plain enough that rules of procedure were usually regarded as binding and were observed with some rigour. Three readings were not only the norm; occasionally they were secured by procrustean methods, as when manifest readings were solemnly declared to have been no such thing in order to preserve the sacred threesome. A very rare fourth reading could arise, for instance, because the bill was recommitted on third reading, the debate on that occasion having revealed further inadequacies which called for amendments.[3] Twice bills had been formally passed when it was discovered that the House had not fully approved one passage; the bills were recalled, amended and passed again on a third reading as though no such reading had yet taken place.[4] Deviations from the norm are virtually always clerical slips that occurred in both Houses; thus when we find two first readings followed by a third we can safely judge the second *prima* to have stood for a genuine *secunda*. Nevertheless, rigour rather than flexibility usually governed practice right through the period. On one occasion the Commons had at third reading passed an amendment to a bill by division, but it was found that the amendment had been read but once. This offended against the rule that all parts of a bill, including additional provisos and amendments, must be read three times. The slip caused confusion and 'sundry motions', but in the end the House recalled the bill, passed the amendment three times, and repeated the vote on division to pass the bill.[5] The Lords once in 1581 refused to accept a bill from the Lower House because its clerk had forgotten to write the 'bail' clause on it; back it went to be completed.[6] Of course, strict procedural rules could be exploited. When, in 1581, Anthony Cope objected to the Speaker expressing a hostile view of a bill without seeking the permission of the House to open his mouth, he was right but it did him no good.[7] The point of weight, however, is that procedure mattered and governed the work of both Houses; it will not do to regard it as meaningless or insignificant. The rules of procedure do not signify any of the politically important things that Neale and Notestein read into them, but they do explain 'the manner of passing bills' the fate of which can be understood only if those rules are kept in mind.[8]

Procedure thus imposed a lengthy course, with many hurdles, but the

[3] *CJ* I, 123, 127.
[4] Ibid. 92, 120–1. Cf. *Proc.* 383 for Fleetwood's reference to the first occasion. His recollection of the bill for wines in the same speech is nonsense and invention, contradicted by the actual fate of the bill in question (below, p. 241).
[5] *CJ* I, 92. [6] Ibid. 132. [7] Ibid. 134.
[8] Sheila Lambert, 'Procedure in the House of Commons in the Early Stuart Period,' *EHR* 95 (1980), 753–81. This thoroughly demolishes the supposed political significance of the procedural rules and their development.

formal description gives little indication of the complex variations possible under it, comprehending which is often the best guide to opinion and purpose. Neale argued that procedure in fact became increasingly rigorous and formalized, with wilful variety disappearing by stages as the Lower House 'matured',[9] but there is really no proof that any such maturing took place in the first half of the reign, or indeed thereafter. The problem lies in the nature of the evidence. We depend on the clerks: some apparent developments may represent no more than the different practices of Seymour and Onslow, or even perhaps only reflect the fact that Seymour's surviving Journal is a scribbled book and Onslow's a perfected one. The possibility of clerical error has already been mentioned and must always be allowed for. In the turmoil of bill proceedings, a whole stage sometimes failed to get recorded when yet it must be beyond doubt from other evidence that it took place: for some enacted bills we do not even find mention of a third reading. The Lords Journal, suspiciously regular, possibly routinely omitted some information; replacement bills can appear there with no previous committing noted, which cannot have happened, and conferences between the two Houses receive more regular mention in the Commons than the Lords Journal. In all that follows such-like deficiences have been ignored. In the state of the evidence, all figures given must be treated as being only as accurate as possible. However, the total number of bills processed was so large, and the doubtful cases are so few that the minor inaccuracies inevitable in this kind of analysis cease to have serious significance. Let us therefore look at what actually happened to bills in the Parliament.

STARTING A BILL

A bill could be introduced into either House, just as its promoter decided.[10] The only exception to this was the rule that bills for restitution in blood (invariably certified by the sign manual as approved by the Queen) started in the Lords. The private act of 1576 for Henry, Lord Norris, which by its title looks like a normal restitution bill, started in the Commons, but on inspection it turns out to be a second restitution bill to amend and perfect an earlier one which had somehow failed to restore all his rights to the petitioner's ancestor; this accounts for the discrepancy.[11] The only genuine restitution bill to break the rule con-

[9] Neale, *HC*, 372 ff.

[10] The House of introduction can be established from the Journals and for bills enacted from the Original Act. The last, however, is not always a safe guide because on occasion a bill starting in one House was replaced by a *nova* in the other, the latter then becoming the parchment bill as enacted.

[11] 18 Eliz. I, OA 24; *CJ* I, 112. The breviate for this bill survives: SP 12/107, fos. 71–2, dated to the first sitting day of the Parliament. See also below, pp. 305–6.

cerned one Anthony Mayne who in May 1565 had stolen some money from his father. When arrested he confessed and was accordingly convicted, but he pleaded his clergy and his father, interceding on his behalf, obtained him a pardon. Nevertheless he remained corrupted in blood for his felony and in 1576 tried to remedy the deficiency by statute. The bill was introduced in the Lords and passed both Houses without difficulty, but on being returned to the Upper House it got caught in the dispute between the two Houses over Lord Stourton's bill which also involved an attaint for felony rather than the more usual treason.[12] Thus Mayne's bill was not ready for the assent and failed. When successfully reintroduced in 1581, it started in the Commons, presumably because in the end the 1576 bill had remained there.[13].

One other form of private bill was supposed to start in a particular House, in this case the Commons, namely any for the naturalization of children born outside the Queen's dominions to parents born within them. In this period eight such acts passed, of which five, including the multiple acts of 1576 and 1581 which between them naturalized eighty-six persons,[14] were indeed put into the Commons House. The three that broke the rule resulted from petitions to the Queen and bore the sign manual, which fact would seem to have decided their destination.[15] However, here we may be witnessing a degree of standardization: a bill of 1576 also signed by Elizabeth nevertheless started in the Commons, as though the practice touching naturalization acts had become settled.[16] Private acts dealing with landed property – estate acts – could start in either House. In general, the status of the promoters seems to have governed choice, with peers and their relatives opting for the Lords; when William Overton, bishop of Coventry and Lichfield, in 1581 tried to secure the payment of a sizable rent (£82 10*s* p.a.) agreed in Chancery between one of his predecessors and a tenant, the Privy Council, to whom he appealed, evidently advised him to proceed by bill in the House in which he sat himself.[17] Freedom of action is well illustrated by the advice, already mentioned, given to the London brewers to reintroduce in the Lords a bill already thrown out by the Commons.[18]

Ordinarily, therefore, promoters could do as they pleased. It certainly looks as though Council bills were a little more likely to start upstairs,

[12] See below, pp. 306–9.

[13] *LJ* I, 747–9; II, 49; *CJ* I, 114–15, 132–3. The act is 23 Eliz. I, OA 16; the delay in 1576 may have been caused by Mayne's less advertised purposes – doing down his uncle.

[14] 18 Eliz. I, OA 35 and 37; 23 Eliz. I, OA 21.

[15] 5 Eliz. I, OA 49; 8 Eliz. I, OA 29; 13 Eliz. I, OA 28.

[16] 18 Eliz. I, OA 26.

[17] 23 Eliz. I, OA 25; SP 12/147, fos. 234–5.

[18] Above, p. 78.

but more important was the place in which the Council's leading parliamentary manager sat. In Elizabeth's reign it was above all William Cecil who involved himself in steering through such government programmes as existed. Thus while he sat in the Commons, that House was the first to see the bills for supremacy and uniformity in 1559, the bill for the Queen's title of the same year, the 1563 bill elaborating the supremacy, the bill for artificers, also of 1563, and in 1566 the bill for the consecration of bishops.

These were all government bills or bills taken over by the government, and they all passed. In 1571 Cecil was created Baron Burghley some eight weeks before the Parliament met and in April he took his seat in the Upper House. The effects of this change of venue showed at once. Of the twenty-two public acts of that session fourteen can for various reasons be assigned to official initiative: nine of them started in the Lords. Among them was c. 6, the act confirming the validity at law of certain copies of letters patent the bill for which had failed twice before – in 1563 because the Commons discovered legal problems, and in 1566 because the Lords proved dilatory. In 1571 Burghley kept it under his eyes in the Lords where legal advice produced a satisfactorily amended bill; the Commons whipped it through in two days.[19] The Lords maintained their fair share of the work on successful Council bills until 1576, but in 1581 policy seems to have changed; there are indications that the Council began to prefer working through the Commons, but a proper evaluation of these hints must await a full study of the second half of the reign.

The Lords' fair share in receiving bills that became acts does not, however, reflect the general practice on introduction. In these seven sessions, 885 bills are known to have been read at least once in the Parliament, 179 starting in the Lords and 606 in the Commons. The discrepancy is largest for failed bills of which the Commons received 464 and the Lords a mere 69: the Lords gained success for over two-thirds of the bills initiated with them, the Commons for just about one-fifth. Of course, these figures in part reflect the preference of the promoters of hopeless private bills, but even of public acts the Lords first saw sixty against the Commons' eighty-six. If the Lords had worked as hard as the Commons they would have completed more of their bills, but on the whole going upstairs first did give a man a better chance of succeeding. Now and again the point seems to have been noted; bill promoters with the right contacts do seem on occasion to have exploited this advantage. Thus the patronage of the earl of Pembroke inclined sponsors of bills

[19] For the failed bills see *CJ* I 63, 71; ibid. 77–8, 80, and *LJ* I, 662–3. For the passage of the act see *LJ* I, 674–5, 677–8, 684; *CJ* I, 87.

for Wales to look to the Lords.[20] Patronage may have assisted to transform some private bills of 1576 into public acts (which meant that the Crown paid for the printing), though it would seem that bills raising a local rate frequently started private and finished public.[21] The act for Plumstead marshes, a private bill initiated in the Lords, was when passed first left unprinted, but patronage worked wonders: as the table in the sessional statute noted, 'this act by special suit is also printed'. It thus became c. 13 of the 1581 session. However, normally promoters of non-official measures approached the Lower House first, thus following the medieval tradition which regarded the Commons as the agents for bringing the needs and problems of the subject to the attention of monarch and Council in Parliament. The tradition, in effect dead by 1529 when both Houses had come to stand on the same footing, remained strong enough to create legends. In 1589 Lord Chancellor Hatton told the Speaker that 'the use of the Higher House is not to meddle with any bill until there be some presented from the Commons', a use which would have left the Lords twiddling their thumbs well into a session.[22] Though this courteous invention still found credit with Sir John Neale,[23] such lack of business sense is highly improbable and in any case disproved by the briefest check on the Journal. Thus in 1566 the Lords had been considering their own bills for ten days before anything arrived from below, and in 1584 (to allow for Neale's thesis of a developing deference from their lordships to the Commons) five days of bill business passed in the Upper House before a bill was sent up by the Lower.

However, the fact remains that the majority of bills started in the Commons. There were various ways in which they could come to the notice of the House. The usual method (as has already been said) was to deliver them to the Speaker, either directly or more commonly through the clerk, as a rule at the opening of the session, though there was nothing to stop them coming in at any time. A peculiar story of an introduction is told in a petition from promoters outside the House – so peculiar that one may wonder at its reliability. On the last day (30 June) of the 1572 session a group of people petitioned 'the right honourable lords of the Queen's majesty's most high court of Parliament'.[24] Five days before, they said, they 'did exhibit a bill and the adbridgement thereof unto her majesty's Common House of Parliament'. The bill is not described in sufficient detail to be sure but appears to have been

[20] G. R. Elton, 'Wales in Parliament, 1542–1581,' *Welsh Society and Nationhood* (ed. R. R. Davies et al.; Cardiff, 1984), esp. p. 121.

[21] Below, pp. 316–17.

[22] N. H. Nicolas, *The Life and Times of Sir Christopher Hatton, K. G.* (1847), 482.

[23] *HC*, 373.

[24] SP 12/107, fo. 183.

concerned with the manufacture of flax and hemp; it was advertised as being for the Queen's profit and the benefit of the commonwealth, providing employment for 'more than 100,000 idle young, old, impotent and lame people from six years to three score years of age'.[25] What then allegedly happened is hard to understand:

> The said abridgement being read in the said House and the burgesses thereby informed of the full content of the said bill, who willingly would have the body thereof read, the Speaker of the said House alleging that he may not read the same without order from her majesty or from your honours [the House of Lords],

the matter lapsed. The petitioners therefore asked that such an order be given. Would any Speaker ever have made such a statement about a 'commonwealth' bill, and why was the breviate read (*prima vice* at that) and the reading of the full bill refused? I can think of no convincing answers to these questions, and the account in the petition may be either hopelessly muddled or needlessly crafty. It certainly looks as though the lobby were much too late in the session in their first approach, and perhaps the Speaker was trying a dubious courtesy in warning them off rather than ruling them out of order.

The story does, however, draw attention to a serious problem of the evidence, a problem which makes it impossible to give accurate totals of bills put into the Parliament. The Journals record bills that reached first reading, not bills delivered to the clerk. There are quite a few drafts and finished-looking bills in the State Papers and elsewhere which cannot be identified in the Journals, and it is impossible to tell whether they represent abandoned intentions or merely failure to get into the mainstream of bill procedure. The latter possibility is underlined by a report on the state of bills in the House in the session of 1581, prepared by the clerk of the Commons for the information of Lord Treasurer Burghley.[26] It is dated March 1st, at which point some six weeks of the session had elapsed and seventeen days, not omitting Sundays, still remained to come. The clerk divided the list into three parts – bills that had passed the Commons, bills read but not yet finished with, and bills not yet read even once. The last section listed the astonishing number of forty-two bills in the clerk's hands which he had not yet been able to put up for reading at all.[27] Before the session ended six of them had got to that stage, but of thirty-six bills promoted by various interests the House never heard at all. The fact that this accidental information enables us to raise

[25] The only bill remotely to fit the case was one 'for hemp and cordage' read twice on 26 June 1572 (*CJ* I, 103). I have dated the protest accordingly.

[26] SP 12/148, fos. 1–4.

[27] There are actually forty-three listed, but one bill (for the freemen joiners of London) by mistake appears twice.

the number of bills promoted but not passed in that session from sixty-nine to one hundred and five must give pause. For other sessions we do not know anything about the bills in limbo. Incidentally, two items on the clerk's list turn up as paper bills among the State Papers: 'against undercollectors of tenths' and for 'maintenance of artillery'.[28]

Still, the majority of bills were prepared before the session and then handed to the managers of one House or the other. This was not, however, the only way to get a bill moving: it was possible for it to be drafted in the Parliament – in the Commons by a committee, in the Lords more usually by one or more of the legal assistants. The evidence of the Lords Journal is not unambiguous, but it looks as though commitment at first reading to a named legal expert hides a proposal for a bill which the expert was instructed to draft. Most of the cases where this seems to have occurred are of failed bills, which makes it difficult to be sure of what went on. The poor relief act of 1572 (14 Eliz. I c. 5) started in the Upper House, with a supposed committal after first reading, to thirteen peers and two assistants; since the next stage recorded was a straightforward second reading they may really have amended rather than drawn the bill.[29] On the other hand, a committee of the same size appointed in 1563, after an alleged first reading of the bill against the forging of deeds, probably drew the bill since the next stage is again described as a first reading.[30] The 'mature' formality of the Lords Journal, as so often, covers up what really happened. Michael Graves has suggested that positive action upon first reading had become very rare by 1558,[31] and the practice of the Elizabethan Upper House confirms his conclusion. Nevertheless, first readings now and again led to action, and the suggestion that by noting a committal contrary to normal rules the Journal hides the appointment of a drafting committee after a motion for action does not seem implausible.

Matters are clearer for the Lower House: there the story really for once supports talk about procedural developments. I have found four occasions in the 1560s when a bill seems to have been drawn in the House, apart, that is, from subsidy bills which in form were always thus produced.[32] It was certainly what happened with the navigation act of 1563 (5 Eliz. I c. 5) whose history began with a motion 'that this House would have

[28] SP 12/148, fos. 200–3, 245–57. The first is too badly damaged to make its purpose clear but is apparently concerned to reinforce the Exchequer's control over such collectors by permitting other men than bishops to be appointed. The second is in the form of a petition from the gunners of the Tower and the Navy; it proposes to remedy deficiencies by setting up an examining board and keeping a register of persons proved competent.

[29] *LJ* I, 706, 708.

[30] Ibid. 586, 588.

[31] M. A. R. Graves, *The House of Lords in the Parliaments of Edward VI and Mary I* (Cambridge, 1981), 157–8.

[32] Below, pp. 157–9.

some regard by some bill to the navy', put forward by William Winter, the admiral. A bill was read a first time two weeks later, which left plenty of time for the drafting, though Winter may have had something ready to follow up his motion; its enacting clause confirms that it was not a Council bill prepared beforehand.[33] The act of 1559 for the preservation of fish spawn and fry (1 Eliz. I c. 17) began with a commitment upon a notional first reading, followed by the real first reading of the bill that emerged from the committee.[34] The same history is recorded for the act of 1566 for sheriffs (8 Eliz. I c. 16). And a brief entry in 1566 – '1[a] touching clerks convict, to sue a pardon. M[r] Norton' – probably hides the same form of action, for Norton did not give up and his next effort, as we shall see, leaves no doubt that he proceeded by a motion followed by a bill; in 1566, the bill never appeared.[35]

The session of 1571 witnessed a number of procedural developments among which the use of committees to prepare and organize bills stands out as especially significant. For once we can be sure that we are not being deceived by an accident of the evidence, nor did what happened have anything to do with the appointment of a new clerk with different recording practices. The developments were, in fact, linked to the partial collapse of management which characterized the opening days of the session – not the culmination of a puritan assault, as Neale supposed,[36] but more probably the consequence of Cecil's removal upstairs and divided counsels among the remaining privy councillors. These circumstances will be investigated later;[37] what matters here is how uncertainty of grasp affected the bringing in of bills. For the first time in the reign, the bill *pro forma*,[38] read *prima vice* on the first working day (4 April) was, so to speak, a real one – the bill for coming to church (an attack on indifference and recusancy) – which after many vicissitudes was to pass both Houses, only to be vetoed by the Queen.[39] The other sign of a

[33] *CJ* I, 65–6.

[34] Ibid. 55, 57.

[35] Ibid. 75. This happened on 24 October, barely halfway through a long session, but other matters came up to distract Norton – hence no follow-up.

[36] Neale, *EP* I, 193–207.

[37] Below, pp. 101–4.

[38] The Journal shows, though the treatises do not, that the practice of establishing the existence of a fully operative House by reading a bill of small moment as soon as the Speaker had taken the chair already existed.

[39] *CJ* I, 82. The Anonymous Diary (*Proc.* 199) records the introduction of the bill on the 5th, and since the admission of the Speaker took place only in the afternoon of the 4th it is just possible that the later date is correct. The diary also notes that no debate occurred on the reading of the bill because the House was then called (i.e. the roll of members was read in order to discover absentees), an action which certainly took place on the 5th. However, the Journal has the Speaker address the House after the reading of the bill, and since normally the first action taken after seating the Speaker was the reading of a bill I prefer the date in *CJ*.

difficult session ahead showed in the willingness of members to put forward motions not connected with any bill before them, an eagerness to take initiatives which delayed business and annoyed the Queen. On the 10th the Speaker informed the House that he had learned from the attorney general of Elizabeth's desire 'that we should speak of matters propounded only, and not to make new motions every man at his own pleasure',[40] but by then sufficient motion-making had occurred to disorganize the passage of bills. Norton, that expert in procedure, quickly took advantage of the tactic to revive his complaint about the abuse of benefit of clergy by perjurers who had turned the privilege into a routine means for escaping the consequences of criminous dealings. On 14 April he moved 'touching the fees of purgation of clerks convict'. He charged the courts Christian with letting off those allowed the benefit by accepting manifestly perjured compurgations. This was, he said, no liberty of the Church 'except they will claim a liberty to sin', and (quite correctly) traced the privilege back to the quarrel raised with Henry II by 'rebel bishop Becket', a holy saint, he added ironically, 'who would not brook to be rebuked by a temporal judge – *hinc illae lacrimae*'. The House expressed its sympathy by encouraging him to 'enquire and deal therein accordingly'.[41] The phasing suggests that he had no bill ready, which confirms that the 'prima lecta' entered in the Journal when he moved similarly in 1566 misleads, as has been here suggested. Indeed, his enquiries took a little time: he did not bring in the bill until 11 May. Though it was very rapidly passed by the Commons it hung for two weeks in the Lords before receiving a second reading, after which it was dropped. A bill attacking episcopal jurisdiction was unlikely to prosper in the Upper House, but Norton got the substance of what he wanted in the act of 1576 concerning benefit of clergy.[42]

Meanwhile two other clusters of problems had led to the appointment of committees which either drafted bills or promoted existing drafts that would not otherwise have come forward. In the atmosphere of 1571, after the northern rebellion and the papal bull of excommunication and deposition, those determined to improve the spiritual state of the nation were eager to get their pet projects onto the statute book. In the end only one truly revolutionary measure came up in all that turmoil – Walter Strickland's bill for reforming the Prayer Book by cleansing it further of remaining 'rags of popery' – and this does not at the moment concern us. What does is the setting up, on 6 April, of a committee for bills of

[40] *Proc.* 207.

[41] *CJ* I, 84, 89–90; *LJ* I, 686, 688, 691; *Proc.* 224, 252. As recorded in the Anonymous Diary the speech has the air of authentic quotation.

[42] 18 Eliz. I c. 7 (see below, p. 302).

religion, the result of 'a motion for uniformity of religion and the mention of certain bills, drawn for that purpose the last Parliament, and for the redress of sundry defections in those matters'. The mover was Strickland, not yet revealed as a rebel; what he called for in particular was the record of the canon law reform (*Reformatio Legum Ecclesiasticarum*) produced by Cranmer and others in Edward VI's reign, of which document he understood Norton to have a copy; but he spoke at length also about other abuses in the Church, especially the existence of unsatisfactory ministers. Norton responded by explaining that the *Reformatio Legum* had recently been put into print, by John Foxe, a point apparently not known to Strickland, and by producing a copy of the book there and then; he added that of Strickland's list of abuses he shared his feelings about the selling of livings.[43]

The committee appointed to consider these matters and undertake remedies to be discussed with the bishops consisted of twenty men (including the five privy councillors in the House),[44] all well respected and mostly associated with the official element, though Strickland, the original mover, had to be included. Its immediate task lay less in producing new bills than in reviving the so-called alphabet-bills (A–F) concerning Church reform which had got nowhere in the previous session and had been put in Norton's keeping at the time. They should not be described as a puritan programme, seeing that the most contentious of them – that for embodying the Thirty-Nine Articles in a statute – had the support of a petition from fourteen bishops asking the Queen to withdraw her order to the Lords to proceed no further.[45] All six bills were read to the Commons on the 7th and one of them (A: for uniformity in Church services) was passed to the committee for action; the remainder were put back for later; to avoid procedural confusion the readings of that day were formally declared not to count as first readings. This left the committee free to frame revised bills if they wished, though in the absence of texts for 1566 we do not know whether they did. In fact, they produced other bills of religion before they managed to deal with A.

Three bills came quickly. The first (Bill B: read on 10 April) emerged as one enforcing subscription to the Articles in the interest of controlling both popish and sectarian deviation; after six weeks it had passed both Houses and become law.[46] Bill D, against the sale of advowsons for terms of lives or years and other corrupt practices in presentations, followed at once, on 11 April; a difficult passage ended with rejection by the Lords

[43] *CJ* I, 83; *Proc.* 200–1. For a fuller discussion of the bills on religion see below, pp. 205–16.

[44] The Anonymous Diary speaks of twenty-one, but the list in *CJ* carries greater authority.

[45] SP 12/41, fos. 100–1.

[46] 13 Eliz. I c. 12; *CJ* I 84, 86–7, 91; *LJ* I, 680, 682, 684, 691, 694.

on 28 May.[47] 13 April saw the first reading of Bill E, against simony; somewhat amended by the Lords it finished its parliamentary career on 22 May and became law.[48] Bill A, given to the committee at the start of the proceedings, did not arrive for first reading until 26 April, a delay which argues that major revision occurred in the committee; though it passed the Commons in two days, the Lords ignored it after a formal first reading.[49] Even greater delays affected Bill C (against plurality and non-residence, and for the provision of regular preaching in every parish – certainly a puritan or at least a reformist-protestant measure); it emerges only on 12 May and after passing in the Commons got the customary cold-shoulder treatment upstairs.[50] Bill F, concerning pensions payable out of Church livings, was not received, but instead a new bill, G, turned up which meant to compel the ordinary to seek the advice of two justices of the peace before he could commute penances into money payments. This bill thus tried to stop another loophole in the effectiveness of punishments imposed on clerks convict and goes hand in hand with Norton's own bill; together with the alphabetical description, this fact demonstrates its origin in the committee. Introduced on 10 May, it got so far as committal in the Upper House on the 21st, but no further.[51] One other bill for religion was read in this Parliament: it attacked the power to grant dispensations vested by a Henrician act in the archbishop of Canterbury. It was introduced on 14 April by George Carleton, one of the thirteen additional members appointed to the committee on the 10th of that month. This bill too ended with committal in the Lords.[52] On the other hand, Strickland's bill for a revised Prayer Book is less likely to have been before the committee, though the possibility should not be ruled out. Since it incorporated the essential points of the speech he made on the 6th, he had manifestly prepared it before the session opened.[53]

Thus this first committee for religion, neither grand nor standing,[54]

[47] *Proc.* 209; *CJ* I, 84, 88, 91, 92; *LJ* I, 685–6, 689, 699. The Lords had in fact passed the bill, with amendments; they dashed it only after the Commons refused to accept alterations.

[48] 13 Eliz. I c. 20; *CJ* I, 84, 87–8, 91; *LJ* I, 684, 686, 689, 692.

[49] *CJ* I, 86.

[50] Ibid. 89–90; *LJ* I, 688–9.

[51] *CJ* I, 88–90; *LJ* I, 688–9, 692.

[52] *CJ* I, 87–8; *LJ* I, 685, 689; *Proc.* 224–4. The text of the bill, either as originally drawn or as revised on second reading in the Commons, survives in SP 12/27, fos. 221–5.

[53] The bill, read once (14 April: *CJ* I, 84), lapsed after a petition to the Queen to proceed was turned down with a promise to get the bishops to do what was necessary.

[54] Standing committees: appointed usually at the start of a session, to receive all bills concerning its named set of issues. Grand committees: the four regular standing committees (for religion, privileges, trade and courts of law) which in the early seventeenth century it became customary to appoint. The first clear example was that for elections and privileges appointed in 1597. I am grateful to Sheila Lambert for this information.

had promoted five bills surviving from the previous session, plus one of just possibly three new ones, not a bad record in exploiting the novel principle of the making of bills in committee, after a motion for such an action. Two of its bills passed into law, also not a bad proportionate record. The method had proved workable. What is less comprehensible is the further appointment, on 28 April, of yet another committee (actually a four-men subcommittee of the earlier body) 'to sort the bills for religion in such order and course for preceding one before another as they shall think meetest'. By that date only two such bills had not received a first reading.[55] Perhaps the subcommittee was meant to superintend the subsequent stages of all the bills none of which had yet passed the Commons, a task commonly left to Speaker and clerk; if so, this would have been another interesting innovation, though not one with much future to it. The appointment, on the same day, of a sizable committee for placing so far unread bills for the commonwealth in order of precedence, on the other hand, took up the effect of the setting up of the original committee for bills of religion.[56] What it may have done and how effective it proved cannot now be discovered.

The other interesting attempt of 1571 to use a general drafting committee for the preparation of bills – interesting both because it marked an innovation and because it proved futile – arose out of another managerial slip at the start of this session. It was usual for a private member to be put up to initiate discussion of the subsidy mentioned as required in the lord keeper's opening address, but in 1571 the manoeuvre misfired.[57] The man chosen, Robert Newdigate, used the wrong tone: his obvious and extreme deference towards the Queen and his eagerness to give away the subject's money caused his speech not to be 'liked of the House'. Also, by speaking so early in the session (7 April) he had evidently jumped the gun, before the Council was prepared for a debate on the subsidy. Thus the senior privy councillor present, Sir Francis Knollys, had to back him up in an impromptu speech which the diarist called 'long, needless'. Once again the absence of Cecil, who had handled this delicate operation brilliantly in earlier sessions, made itself felt. In the debate so inauspiciously initiated several members are recorded as speaking – Robert Bell, John Popham, William Lovelace, Sir James Croft, Thomas Sampole and Henry Goodere. They were all either active or aspirant government men with careers to serve; in Bell and Popham they included two future Speakers, and Goodere was so far from being a man of opposition as to have sympathy for the Queen of Scots. However, the first five took the opportunity, after paying lip-service to

[55] *CJ* I, 86. [56] Ibid.

[57] See below, pp. 157–9, for general practices concerning subsidy acts. For what follows see *Proc.* 202–3, 245; *CJ* I, 83.

their personal willingness to pay a subsidy, to raise 'grievances'. Bell complained about the burden caused by monopolists and informer actions; Popham added the practice of receivers of Crown revenue who used the money in their hands for private ventures, deliberately going bankrupt when the time came to pay the Crown's money to the Queen; Lovelace threw in purveyors and the sums collected by the Exchequer in fines for respite of homage; Croft, controller of the Household, tried to cool things by promising to use his office to discipline purveyors; Sampole added details to the complaint about revenue collectors. Goodere then put a stop to this recital of mostly pretty ancient complaints about agencies of government, pointing out that 'already more was remembered than in one Parliament could be reformed'. This again displeased the diarist (whose bias is pretty plain) and perhaps the House, but it did terminate the debate. It was decided to appoint a committee to draw bills with respect to four of the grievances recited – collectors of revenue, purveyors, respite of homage, and oppressive process out of the Exchequer. Hooker's diary adds dispensations and promoters (informers) as well, and the clerk's list could have been incomplete. The complainants – 'those that made the motions' – were asked 'to collect notes and bring them to the commissioners to be considered to the drawing of books [bills]'.

It is small wonder that this committee has been treated as the first example of a regular committee of grievances, at a later date one of the standing committees appointed at the start of a session.[58] That it was not: the first committee deserving the name appears to have been appointed on 15 February 1610, on the motion of Sir Edwin Sandys, when no grievances had yet been mentioned and the committee was designed to receive any that might yet come up.[59] What happened in 1571 belonged to the convenient handling of motions for bills, no more; it also proved singularly ineffective. The committee (thirteen familiar members including Bell, Popham and Sampole) was chaired by Sir Owen Hopton, lieutenant of the Tower, who on 10 April reported to the House 'a paper of the motions made' and asked for additional members, including the privy councillors; this is the last we hear of the committee, and Hopton's request suggests that members had failed to turn up.[60] On the other hand, some of the grievances entrusted to their care do appear in bills of this

[58] Neale, *EP* I, 220: in future 'a prime factor in winning the initiative in public...legislation', 'a new device' which would in due course 'provide the House, as it were, with a Privy Council of its own'. Cf. against these rhapsodies, Sheila Lambert in *EHR* 95 (1980), 759.

[59] *CJ* I, 394. In the last previous attempt before this to coordinate 'grievances' it had been moved to have them considered by the committee for the subsidy, but a special committee seems to have been appointed instead (ibid. 267).

[60] *CJ* I, 83.

session: did the committee fashion them? If Hooker is right and 'dispensations' were assigned to them, the bill already discussed might be counted to their tally.[61] One act actually dealt with the grievance raised by Popham and Sampole – that which made the private property of receivers of Crown revenue available for the payment of their official debts (13 Eliz. I c. 4). But its origins had nothing to do with the committee, or indeed the Lower House: the bill started in the Lords where evidently the Privy Council had decided to tackle a problem of at least as much concern to the Crown as to the subject. It had a very complicated history in Parliament, with several replacement bills in both Houses, but when it reached the Commons it was referred to a special bill committee, not to the alleged committee for grievances.

However, two bills do seem to have come out of that committee's deliberations. On 12 April, a bill for respite of homage and another Exchequer exaction objected to was read in the Commons; this we may safely associate with the committee of grievances.[62] It was immediately reformed by a bill committee and after much labour, including a conference of both Houses, led to yet another *nova* in the Lords. At this point the Queen caused it to be put by, much to the grief of the Commons, a grief she attempted to assuage by a mendacious promise to see 'in time' to solving the problem.[63] She vetoed the bill to control the activity of informers, probably drawn by the committee but immediately voted down in the Commons as bearing the stamp of Exchequer drafting; another committee produced a more acceptable bill which the Lords slightly amended.[64] While the fate of those bills proves the reality of the grievance – the veto here acted to protect Crown servants and interests – it cannot be said that interposing a coordinating committee contributed usefully to their production. One very contentious matter handed to the

[61] Above, p. 100.

[62] To judge from the summary of the bill in *Proc.* 211–12, the complaint arose from the Exchequer's ability to inform sheriffs of a man's possessions so that he could attach them for debt or distraint, plus the fact that that information was often out of date; for a remedy it was proposed that Common Pleas and Chancery should issue certificates of transactions known to them (feet of fines and licences to alienate), so that people would not find themselves distrained of property they had acquired, on the supposition that it still belonged to the Exchequer debtor.

[63] *CJ* I, 83–4, 86–8; *LJ* I, 681–3, 686; *Proc.* 257. The earl of Rutland's informant mistakenly thought it had passed on 15 May when on that day it had in fact just been committed in the Lords (HMC, *12th Report*, App, IV, i, 92). An earlier attempt to legislate for this grievance had been made in 1563 when the Commons rejected the bill on second reading, after much argument (*CJ* I, 64–5).

[64] *CJ* I, 83, 87–8, 91; *LJ* I, 685, 690, 696; *Proc.* 245, 248. Though not introduced until 23 April, it had been in the clerk's hands for some time before the 20th (SP 12/77, fo. 111). As this bill and its circumstances are being studied by David Lidington I will give it no more attention here. In 1576, the Queen permitted legislation on this issue (18 Eliz. I c. 5).

committee produced no action: they did nothing about purveyors, and the act of the session which covered a small part of the problem by protecting the Universities against their depredations (13 Eliz. I c. 21) sprang from a Council bill started in the Lords.

However, the method of motion followed by committee did persist and indeed gained a little ground. It came in useful in an attempt to remedy a muddle. As we have seen, the 1571 session opened with a bill that was not *pro forma*, but that did not prevent the normal *pro forma* bill for the preservation of woods from being brought forward by the clerk on 6 April. Bell, clearly rampant on his pet griefs, intervened on what was meant to be a formal occasion by bringing in purveyors and proposing an approach to the Queen for remedy. This rendered the original bill, which dealt only with the environs of London, inadequate; it was dashed and a committee appointed to draw a new one dealing with general purveyance of timber. That bill, once more replaced with a revised one, got as far as the bill committee in the Lords where absurdly it was linked with the bill for rendering the river Lea navigable (13 Eliz. I c. 18); and in that committee it died.[65] In 1572, a bill for the manufacture of firearms originated in a paper of articles moved in the House and sent to a drafting committee; agreed by both Houses, the bill was vetoed, probably because of representations from armament manufacturers.[66]

In 1576 the practice of moving motions out of the blue caused the Speaker – of all people, Robert Bell, who in a way had started it all – to propose some regulation of procedure: 'that for expedition's sake, upon every motion made, certain might be appointed to consider whether the matter moved was fit to be committed to bill before any argument should be used of the matter'. This method of a vetting committee was used for the act (at last accomplished) concerning informers, whose history began with the appointment of a committee to draw the bill.[67] Three failed moves followed the same path. The committee appointed to draw a bill 'against stealing away men's children by colour or privy contracts' never reported; that trying to answer the demand for a reformation of Church discipline presented a petition for freedom to proceed which the House sent to the Queen, only to receive yet another gracious promise that she would cause the bishops to take action; a third committee did draw a bill for the safe-keeping of parish registers, but it lapsed after a single reading.[68] In 1581, management adopted the method – if indeed it had not been there all along. Early in the session Sir Walter Mildmay moved

[65] *CJ* I, 83, 85, 88–92; *LJ* I, 690–1; *Proc.* 202, 245. The original bill survives: SP 46/25, fos. 22–5.

[66] *CJ* I, 96, 99, 100; *LJ* I, 717–19, 723; SP 15/21, fo. 72; *Proc.* 372.

[67] Ibid. 476; *CJ* I, 105; 18 Eliz. I c. 5.

[68] *CJ* I, 104–5, 109–10, 113.

for a consideration of the laws against papists and Thomas Norton supported him with a proposal for a drafting committee; this committee prepared the first draft of the severe treasons act of the session (23 Eliz. I c. 1). Mildmay and Norton streamlined procedure by linking the need for supply to the matter of treason, and the committee dealt with both, for which reason the clerk described it as being 'for the great causes'.[69] Again, this was not a grand or standing committee; nothing further was referred to it, not even Thomas Digges's motion for a navigation act which was instead put to a committee of all the Privy Council in the House together with anybody acquainted with the proposals (these ultimately derived from the publicist Robert Hitchcock). The committee, however, slept, no doubt aware that the Upper House was about to consider cognate proposals; it was these that resulted in the navigation act of that year (23 Eliz. I c. 7).[70] Lastly, a committee sitting on a Lords bill touching the misbehaviour of undersheriffs and similar officers off its own bat prepared a bill concerning fairer jury trials; both bills were rejected on third reading.[71]

Thus these various attempts to turn the Lower House into a body capable of generating legislation from within itself, interesting though they are, never got very far or achieved very much. The normal manner in which either House became acquainted with legislative proposals continued to operate through bills prepared outside Parliament and delivered to the clerk of one House or the other.

PROGRESS

Of the bills so delivered, an unidentifiable number never went forward at all, and a probably larger number terminated at first reading. It being the rule that proper judgment on a bill required reflection after their first presentation, formal rejection at that stage was very rare, but it did occur four times. In 1571 the Commons threw out a bill touching the payment of tithe;[72] in 1572 one for the punishment of persons poaching conies at night and in disguise;[73] as well as another forbidding anyone to engage in the export trade who had not served a seven-year apprenticeship or twelve years as a merchant;[74] in 1581 a bill against the multitude of common inns and alehouses.[75] In these decisions the House displayed a robust common sense in the face of obsessional lobbies. Thus the second bill so much hated rabbit-poachers that it allowed them to be

69 Ibid. 119, 123.

70 Ibid. 121; *LJ* II, 34, 36, 40, 43, 53. For the circumstances of Digges's initiative see my forthcoming article cited above, p. 77, n.82.

71 *CJ* I, 121, 129, 133–4.

72 Ibid. 89.

73 Ibid. 96; *Proc.* 371.

74 *CJ* I, 99; *Proc.* 384.

75 *CJ* I, 121.

killed on sight; the third, as Recorder Fleetwood remarked, was designed to freeze an existing monopoly; the last would probably have created yet more officious interference with the people's pleasures. In these cases, the breach of normal procedure looks likely to have been well intentioned.

Far more bills, however, simply never reappeared after a single reading. Nineteen in 1559, twenty-five in 1563, thirty-nine in 1566, thirty-two in 1571, ten in 1572, twenty-three in 1576, and seventeen in 1581 – 165 altogether, eighteen of them Lords bills. Thus just about a third of all failed bills stopped at this stage. One possible reason lies in the brevity of sessions: for bills first read, as some were, close to the end there may simply have been no time to proceed. But most of them could have gone on by at least one stage, and in this majority of cases one must conclude that what was lacking was intent to push them. Many of them were, of course, private, and one obstacle to their further passage, it may be guessed, lay in unwillingness to pay the fees which alone would move them on to the next stage. But even public ones needed 'following' – an active interest seeing to their reintroduction – and the need was manifestly great in sessions overwhelmed by far more bills than there could have been time to pass them. It therefore appears that a sizable number of bills represented no more than an expression of a potential concern and a search for possible support: experimental balloons. Failure to stir such support caused those bills to vanish into limbo. The practice says something about the role of Parliament in the nation's affairs: it could be simply a sounding-board whose tone might determine whether a particular project was worth pursuing further.

However, the majority of bills, including of course those that passed or failed only at the assent, went on to the second reading, the main stage of debate. This reading could lead either to a rejection by manifest will or vote, or to an order to engross for a third reading, or to the appointment of a committee to revise and amend. The committee stage was still optional, and the grounds for interposing it were well summed up by Hooker (speaking of the 1571 bill for coming to church): the bill was read a second time, 'and the same being in certain parts impugned was committed'.[76] Bills went into committee if the debate made it plain that they needed altering before becoming acceptable. The House of Commons already enjoyed a reputation for argumentative speechifying, irrelevant discourse and eagerness to express often pointless opinions, one of the truly enduring characteristics of the assembly, and one that was responsible for most rules of order and procedure. In April 1559, John Carnsew, a London lawyer who sat for one of the Cornish

[76] *Proc.* 245.

boroughs, complained of one Thrower, servant to the master of the rolls, who had remarked 'that if a bill were brought in for women's wires in their pastes[77] they would dispute it and go to the question'; Thrower added that 'he had heard the lords say as much at his master's table'.[78] In 1581, the Speaker (John Popham) tried to prevent waste of time by appealing to the House early in the session:

to use reverend and discreet speeches, to leave curiosities of form, to speak to the matter, and – for that the Parliament was like to be very short – willed them further to forbear speaking to bills at the first reading and not to spend too much time in unnecessary motions or superfluous arguments.

The voice of management, speaking sweet reason.

In practice, debates in the House were often noisy, prolonged and time-consuming, and that not only on such manifestly important and contentious issues as the bills for supremacy and uniformity in 1559, or the treasons bill of 1571. The subsidy act of 1559 was delayed by three days of arguments over the oath to be taken by the assessors of the tax.[79] The bill against corrupt presentations to livings produced, in 1571, such long arguments on the first reading that on the second it was hurriedly sent to be engrossed.[80] The poor law bill of 1576, on the other hand, was argued over in the House for two days before being committed; the committee came back with a new bill.[81] Nor did Speaker Popham's exhortation do much good in 1581. A bill to prevent frauds involving the counterfeiting of official signatures and seals, though at once committed on second reading, came back as a *nova*; at the third reading this produced two days of debate before it was passed after a study of both bills and further argument; after all that the Lords dashed it 'unanimously' after giving it two formal readings.[82] A bill, which in the end got lost in committee, attempted to outlaw the sect called the Family of Love; its passage was interrupted by long arguments 'whether pains of death might be inflicted to an heretic. Agreed to be argued further the next day'.[83]

In the laborious passage of bills such long debates on the floor needed, if possible, to be avoided, and the setting up of a committee, while it did not by any means always solve the problem, was justly thought to be useful in speeding things up. However, committing was still relatively

[77] Stiffening in head-dresses.

[78] *CJ* I, 60. Though the offender, brought before the House, prudently denied saying any such thing, Carnsew's appeal to the Commons' touchiness landed Thrower in the serjeant's custody, but nothing further seems to have happened in the three weeks remaining of the session.

[79] *CJ* I, 65.

[80] Ibid. 84, 88.

[81] Ibid. 105; *Proc.* 478.

[82] *CJ* I, 118, 120–2, 124, 127–8; *LJ* II, 36, 41; *Proc.* 527–8, 531, 535, 537.

[83] *CJ* I, 127–30; *Proc.* 536, 538.

rare and was not resorted to if there seemed insufficient doubt about the terms of a bill. Understandably enough, the highest percentage is found in public acts – 62 out of the 146 passed were committed in the House of Introduction, and 32 of them (not necessarily the same ones) in the second House. For private acts the figures are low, which is not surprising, seeing how many of them dealt with the concerns of individuals and had received the approval of the Queen's sign manual: 19 out of 106, but as many as 17 were committed in the second House, a fact which mainly registers the Commons' unwillingness to accept estate bills on the nod. Of the 299 failed bills that made it to a second reading 154 were committed – a higher proportion than for acts passed – which shows that bills did usually receive serious consideration. Thirty-four committees in the second House attended to the 205 failed bills that managed to pass the first House; here committing clearly seemed as a rule superfluous.

Contrary to certain claims made, I can find no meaningful trend in the practice of either House.[84] Figures and percentages varied session by session, but in no significant manner. Perhaps practice developed more visibly in the second half of the reign, but in the first committees were appointed as required. Nor can I understand why committing of bills, patchy or general, should in any way be thought of as testifying to an increasing maturity or some sort of political ascendancy in the House of Commons. The most impressive committees – archbishops and earls and leading judges – are naturally found in the Lords where the chances of a purposefully judicious review of a bill were markedly greater. Commons committees by no means always, as we have seen, produced a bill immediately acceptable to the House. It is altogether unlikely that larger numbers, or the addition at a later stage of more members, in a committee, testify to a growth of power or even of wider concerns with the work of the House; far and away the most likely reason for such 'developments' resides in the difficulties always encountered in getting the committee members to attend. The same reason lies behind what may well be an increasing inclination to appoint dates and places of meetings to committees upon their appointment; without such officiousness the chance of the committee ever meeting at all were much reduced.

The most important point to emerge from the use of committees is the frequent appearance of a totally redrafted bill, a *nova*. True, *novae billae* after engrossment need not signify very major revisions, though if they come from the second House, which if it had wished could have considerably revised by adding provisos, they do suggest principled

[84] Neale, *HC*, 272–3.

objections. *Novae* that replaced a paper draft, written out so as to make cancellations, insertions and alterations easy, firmly testify to major recasting and can equal a total rejection modified only by another effort to deal with the matter. And such substitute bills are not rare. Occasional lapses in the Journals and occasional occurrences of several replacement bills in the history of a single measure hamper precise calculations, but it can be said with confidence that at least 36 of the 146 public acts came to the assent in a form quite different from that in which they had been first introduced. One would not expect to find *novae* among the private acts, and indeed only 3 of the 106 bills were so replaced during passage. But among failed bills, the 188 committals (in both Houses) produced 74 replacement bills, and any so treated should be regarded as the ones most seriously pursued without ultimate success. The frequency of *novae billae* needs to be remembered in any study of the history and meaning of bills: very often, especially for statutes, we have only the text of the replacement and little idea of what it replaced.

The increased use of bill committees – increased by comparison with the pre-Elizabethan Parliament – led to separate developments, one mostly for public bills and one for private. Though no standing committees were set up to whom bills concerned with a given subject or area of policy might be assigned, a practice grew up by which new matters could be referred to a bill committee already in existence. Sometimes the fact is expressly stated; sometimes it has to be inferred from the fact that a bill got merged with another. For example, on 15 May 1571 the Lords referred the bill for corrupt presentations, received from the Commons, to the committee which was on the same day appointed to consider the bill for ecclesiastical benefices.[85] On 17 February 1576, the Commons for obvious reasons appointed a single committee to deal with two bills about brewing and innkeepers; on 17 February 1581, they referred two bills of law reform to the same committee.[86] The practice obviously saved time and energy, potentially speeding procedure; the most striking and most sensible use of it occurred in the Lower House on 1 March 1576 when four items out of the constant flow of bills for the cloth industry were given to one committee.[87] Only one of these passed – 18 Eliz. I c. 16 – and since that dealt with clothiers in three counties only it is not likely to have absorbed any of the other three.

Such merging of bills did, however, occur, though it cannot always be traced, and bills taken up into other bills that became acts should by rights be subtracted from the total of failed bills. In 1563, a proposal to free tanners from a statutory prohibition concerning the purchase of raw

[85] *LJ* I, 686. [86] *CJ* I, 106, 127. [87] Ibid. 109.

hides became section 9 of the general act for leatherworkers (5 Eliz. I c. 8).[88] To judge from their titles in the Journal, in 1566 a later-entered bill concerning the dissolution of the chantries and its effect on property rights absorbed one presented earlier.[89] The bill for separating the sheriffwicks for Oxfordshire and Berkshire was in the Lords incorporated into the general act for a number of joined counties: the two counties always appear at the end of the list of shires recited, having been added to the bill in the Upper House by the way of amendment.[90] That bill had died in the Commons at second reading, so that the Lords had had to be moved to act by its promoters. Oddly enough, a bill to do the same service to Buckinghamshire and Bedfordshire remained separate, passed both Houses, and was vetoed.[91] The bill for the watermen on the Thames was added to a general bill for mariners, which passed.[92] Two more examples occurred in 1571. A bill for protecting against arrest all persons going to and from church was added to the general bill touching attendance at church, which was killed by the veto; a bill for the harbours of Devon absorbed another concerning malpractices by the Devon stannary courts, as its first mention in the Lords showed. Both merged bills failed.[93] I have found no certain cases of merging in the sessions of 1572 and 1576, but there may well have been hidden ones. In 1581, a private act which confirms sales of lands to two quite different people, both transactions arising out of one private act of 1576, looks very much like the merging of two separate bills, to the extent that the visibly second half starts again with a full enacting clause. Convenience may have suggested combining the two; there should certainly have been no reduction in the fees payable by both beneficiaries.[94]

Splitting, the opposite of merging, occurred only once, and that is perhaps once more than one might expect. In 1559, a bill passed the Commons which revived a number of crimes abolished inadvertently (or so it seems to have been thought) in the first year of Edward VI in the act that repealed most of the felonies and treasons created in Henry VIII's reign. The bill concerned itself with conjurations and witchcraft, prophecies and buggery. The Lords gave it a second reading, and there the matter rested.[95] It was , however, quickly reintroduced in 1563 and

[88] The bill was read a first (and only) time two days after the bill that was to pass had been committed, and the committee did not report until some six weeks later (*CJ* I, 64, 70).

[89] A bill 'touching' these matters was read on 23 October but on third reading was described as being designed to explain the Henrician dissolution statute. The Lords let the combined bill die (*CJ* I, 75–6, 78; *LJ* I, 658).

[90] *CJ* I, 76, 78; the paper of amendments if filed with the OA of 8 Eliz. I c. 16 at HLRO.

[91] *CJ* I, 78, 80; *LJ* I, 660, 662.

[92] 8 Eliz. I c. 13; *CJ* I, 77–8.

[93] Ibid. 86, 89–92; *LJ* I, 538–9.

[94] 23 Eliz. I, OA 27.

[95] *CJ* I, 57, 59–60; *LJ* I, 538–9.

at once amended to include also the Henrician protection of masters against robbery by their servants; in this form it passed the Commons on 11 February.[96] The Lords received it, and that was the end of it.[97] Instead the Upper House dismembered the Commons' comprehensive bill, replacing it by four separate bills on embezzlement by servants, prophecies, witchcraft and sodomy, all of which passed into law.[98] The last three were official bills and began their careers in the Upper House round about 9 March; the first, which looks like a piece of unofficial drafting, did not start until 22 March.[99] What had happened was approximately this. In 1559, the whole business started as a piece of private enterprise, and its failure seems to have alerted the Council to the need to do something. They encouraged the revival of the bill in the next session but received advice that separate acts would serve better. It was decided to use the Lords, and the necessary three bills were put in hand. However, in the Lower House somebody urged that the matter of corrupt servants be not overlooked and got it added to the bill there. It formed a peculiar defect in the law because no one had ever intended to repeal it in 1547; the repealing statute had expressly exempted the act of 27 Henry VIII c. 17, but because in doing so the reservation had given wrong dates for the session of 27 Henry VIII the exception had been disallowed by the courts.[100] When the portmanteau bill reached the Lords it was realized that preparatory labours had not dealt with this last issue and a separate bill had to be belatedly drawn. The fact that that act, alone of all the four, preserves the long (unofficial) enacting clause may suggest that the Commons bill was used to draw it up.

In private bill procedure the most important development stemming from the use of bill committees lay in the increasing practice to bring interested parties before the committee, in order to establish the rights of a case and settle differences.[101]

AMENDMENT

Throughout their history bills were liable to amendment, even if no *nova billa* made its appearance; changes could be proposed and accepted both in the first House of passage and in the second. Until engrossment, such changes were made on the paper bills few of which survive; virtually all our information touching amendments comes from the parchment bills

96 *CJ* I, 63.

97 *LJ* I, 591.

98 5 Eliz. I cc. 10, 15, 16, 17.

99 *LJ* I, 600–1, 607. No first reading is recorded for the bill on prophecies, ordered to be engrossed on second reading on the 10th.

100 See above, p. 33. The act of 1 Edward VI c. 12, sect. 18 (*SR* IV, 22) did indeed make this mistake.

101 Below, pp. 311, 315.

of acts passed – the Original Acts in the House of Lords Record Office. Changes were made either by simple amendment or by provisos, which are additional clauses engrossed on parchment, attached as schedules to the bill, and read three times in both Houses. The schedules should indicate the House of origin by the inscription of transfer clauses and usually do. If they were produced in the second House they had to be returned with the bill for the approval of the first, and it was rare for them not to be accepted; rejection involved a further return to the House that had produced them. These later stages were not always faithfully recorded in the Journals and on occasion have to be inferred. The bill for the act of 1581 concerning the excessive number of iron mills in the neighbourhood of London, a threat to standing timber in those parts and therefore to the city's fuel supply (23 Eliz. I c. 5), started in the Commons where it had a much contested passage from 27 January to 8 March. When it finally reached the Lords that House added a schedule of three provisos excepting three named landowners from its terms. The Commons deleted two of them, and the Lords asked for a conference. To judge by the bill enacted, they gave way on this occasion, but their Journal makes no mention of either provisos or conference.[102] However, that sort of clash was not usual; nearly always provisos stood, whichever House had promoted them.

Amendments concerned smaller changes, very often purely verbal – to tighten the precision of the phrasing or amend the legal language employed – but sometimes more far-reaching. Additions and deletions on the parchment bill were supposed to be made only by the pen of the engrosser, either the clerk of the House of origin or whatever assistant he had employed to do the writing, and nearly always the rule was observed. If they were made in that House they appear as emendations on the face of the bill, with no further indications. The second House, unable to touch the engrossment, listed its suggested emendations on a sheet of paper where they were keyed to the line in the engrossed bill and given in detail sufficient to make plain how the bill was to be reworded. If approved by the original House they were entered by the clerk, usually with a dot in the margin as he counted to find the line in question. Quite a few such sheets survive rolled up with the Original Act to demonstrate the manner of proceeding. Thus the haberdashers' act of 1566 (8 Eliz. I c. 11) has a number of verbal corrections which can be assigned respectively to the Lower House, where the bill started, and to the Lords whose paper of amendments survives.

The 1572 act against those who would 'rebelliously take or detain' the Queen's castles and fortresses (14 Eliz. I c. 1) well illustrates the practices

[102] *CJ* I, 120, 125, 127–9, 131–4, 136; *LJ* II, 51–3; OA.

used in amending. The bill started in the Lords, and the Commons proposed seven alterations. Considering these, the Lords changed the proposed wording in two places, and these changes were written into the paper of amendments – one by Burghley (not accepted) and the other by the clerk. The Lords returned the paper with their comments to the Lower House whose reactions were noted in the margin by their clerk. The Lords had accepted five suggestions but proposed further changes in the other two. These additional revisions are annotated 'contenti sunt' with a 'sic est' at the foot. All the proposed amendments are identifiable on the face of the bill where they were entered by the Lords' clerk. Changes were not, however, always so insignificant. In the 1571 act for providing better uniformity (for subscription to the Thirty-Nine Articles, 13 Eliz. I c. 12), which started in the Commons, the first section had originally demanded obedience to the Articles 'or so much of those Articles as be or shall be allowed or confirmed in this present session of Parliament or in the Convocation now holden'. Aware that intended alterations had already been disallowed and anxious to block any suggestion of a forthcoming revision, the Upper House replaced the phrase with a markedly more neutral one; the Commons accepted the put-down.[103]

Harmony, willing or reluctant, did not always come so easily, for which reason a further means existed for ironing out persistent differences between the two Houses. This was the joint conference held by committees sent from both – a third use of committees, additional to bill and drafting committees, available in the procedure. The rule was that only the House that at the time had the contested bill in its keeping could ask for a conference. Both Houses then named the necessary members who met in a chamber adjoining the House of Lords. Conferences were the only remaining occasions on which the social superiority of the peers was emphasized in parliamentary proceedings. The Commons always sent a larger number of members, though the later rule of two men from the Lower House for every one from the Upper does not yet seem to have been established. Their men stood whereas the Lords sat, and the commoners bared their heads. Nevertheless, though words about great men overawing their inferiors were heard in the House, conferencing seems in practice to have been courteous and evenhanded, with exceptions.

Such meetings to discuss differences of opinion arising over bills going through both Houses would seem in effect to have been a procedural innovation during the first half of Elizabeth's reign. Representatives had held meetings before (they are vouched for from the beginning of the

[103] For this change and its meaning see below, pp. 210–14.

extant Commons Journal in 1547), but the device had not been part of regular bill procedure. Almost all those pre-Elizabethan conferences attended to such politically difficult issues as the great repeal act of 1547, the drafting of the bill that restored England to the Roman communion in 1554, or the subsidy bill of 1557 when the Upper House played a constitutionally doubtful role in squeezing money for King Philip's French war. Only once in those pre-Elizabethan days did the Houses confer on an ordinary matter (a bill for cloth manufacture in 1552); otherwise they met for what on one occasion was called 'weighty affairs of the realm'.[104] Nor did the situation change quickly in the new reign. In the first three sessions there were only two such meetings, both rather haphazard ones – nothing like the organized conferences of later days. On 3 March 1559, the attorney-general, coming from the Lords, asked that ten members of the Commons might 'attend certain of the Lords tomorrow' to consider a proviso that the Commons had attached to the treasons bill of the session. The Upper House delegated six peers – two earls, two bishops and two barons – to meet the ten commoners, and the meeting seems to have persuaded their lordships to accept the proviso.[105] In 1563, the Commons committee sitting on the Lords bill for the garrison of Berwick had an unproductive conference with some of the Upper House.[106] That seems to have been all the conferencing done in the very busy sessions before 1571.

In that session, however, the device became adopted into normal procedure. An early move to associate both Houses in an approach to the Queen concerning the reform of religion marked no innovation; that was in step with those earlier efforts to present a united front in 'weighty affairs of the realm' and produced no more than one of Elizabeth's customary evasive answers.[107] Then, on 1 May, the Lords asked for a conference on the bill against popish priests going about disguised as serving-men, and this move opened the gates. The Commons delegation reported back on the 2nd that the Upper House would welcome a regular arrangement by which legal experts from both Houses would sort out a bill, and the Commons, 'liking well of the course of the proceedings', agreed that conferences should be sought for the bill concerning receivers of Crown revenue, bulls from Rome 'and such like bills as hereafter shall come from their lordships'.[108] The entry in the Journal conveys an air of light dawning upon the House, or at least on some influential members of it; more probably, the move was coordinated between the managers

[104] Graves, *House of Lords*, 137, 139, 150, 168, 177.

[105] *CJ* I, 56; *LJ* I, 552. The proviso in question is the last section of the act which called for two witnesses in accusations of treason. It was added to the bill on a separate schedule and stood as sent from the Commons.

[106] *CJ* I, 64.

[107] Ibid. 84, 87.

[108] *CJ* I, 87.

in both Houses. In the remaining four weeks of the session eleven further bills, six of which passed into law, became the subjects of conferences between Lords and Commons. The tally included the bills against papal bulls (c. 2) and touching receivers (c. 4), though in the former case it was left to the Lords to call for the meeting. It also included the treasons act (c. 1): though the Lords called the conference, the Commons had taken care to appoint their committee before they sent the bill up, in the evident knowledge that the meeting would be asked for. Conferencing had established itself as a useful way to sort out disagreements and thus, it was hoped, of speeding things up.[109] It should be remarked that the Lords took the initiative on nine out of the twelve occasions. This supports the suspicion that the innovation constituted a Council device, designed to use the Lords to improve business methods in the Commons.

The Commons did not take long to recognize certain risks in the introduction of a stage in a bill's history at which the Lords could exercise the direct influence of their standing, their experience and their close relations with the Council. In 1571, when the Lords asked for conferences over the bills for expiring laws, vagabonds and timber, the Lower House sent 'the former committees in the bill for coming to church', even though particular bill committees existed for all those three measures; it looks as though they wished to use men of weight who had already had experience of dealing with the peers. On the eve of the 1572 session, Christopher Hatton's adviser – most probably Thomas Norton – expressed reservations about conferencing which must have arisen out of the previous session's new practices.[110] He admitted that it 'may do and does good' but held that 'much of it sometimes does more hurt'. 'There is,' he continued, 'no one thing that has so shaken the true liberty of the House as often conferences' by removing some of the leading members of the House at crucial moments, and by overawing 'men's opinions'. It was not that the Lords went about to 'terrify men', but the Commons' representatives 'coming up among them espy their inclinations, and knowing that in the Common House there is nothing secret they gather other avisements'. Anyway, 'over-many conferences work many courses to prolong the session'.

Such doubts were understandable, but conferencing continued energetically because it was useful. In the 1572 session, apart from joint moves against the Queen of Scots,[111] three acts and two failed bills were so

[109] 13 Eliz, I c. 1: *CJ* I, 89–90; c. 2: ibid. 88; c. 4: *LJ* I, 684.
[110] BL, Harl. MS 253, fo. 35v. For this advice see below, pp. 322–8.
[111] In this business Elizabeth herself intervened, calling upon the two Houses to appoint respectively twenty-one and forty-four members 'to consult and deliberate upon matters concerning the Queen of Scots' (*CJ* I, 94). The story of joint committees thereafter suggests, however, that the request proved ineffective.

handled; in 1576 the numbers were five and seven; in 1581, three and one. These figures do not give the full use of the device. Thus in 1576 the Lords wished to appoint a steering committee 'touching such private bills in both Houses as upon their conference together shall be thought fittest to be expedited',[112] and the Journals do not permit us to discover how many bills were so treated. But while most conferences operated smoothly, Norton's fears that the Commons might see their liberties threatened received reinforcement during the complicated negotiations over the bill by means of which Lord Stourton tried to escape the consequences of his father's attainder for murder.[113] Both Houses found opportunity to mount high horses. After the bill had reached the Commons, the Lords sent several messages that went unheeded and ultimately asked for a conference. They were out of order and were told so: 'According to the ancient liberties and privileges of the House, conference is to be required by that court which, at the time of the conference demanded, shall be possessed of the bill'. The Lower House would so require 'if they see cause and think meet'. In fact, the Lord's intervention had been engineered by Stourton, afraid that long debates might kill a bill that the Queen had signed and the Lords had passed unhesitatingly, but the Commons grew seriously annoyed at being told how they should handle their business. When a conference finally met – with the Lords calling it after the amended bill had returned to them – the Lords expressed their displeasure by keeping the Commons' delegation waiting and then accusing them of misbehaving: had they not, by amending the bill at all, ignored both Queen and Upper House? The Commons delegation refused to reply to the charge: their task, they said, was to hear what the Lords wished to say and report this back to their House. They did so and returned to convey the outcome of what turned into a fairly impassioned debate. While remaining polite they stood firm on their liberty to discuss and amend any bill that reached them, no matter what its form. The sole cause of conflict seems to have been a Commons proviso which the Lords regarded as superfluous; acerbity arose from false charges by Stourton regarding the Commons' treatment of himself. In fact, the Lords climbed down and accepted the Commons' explanation of their behaviour, but the proviso stood and because of it the bill was lost. The spokesmen for the two Houses were Lord Treasurer Burghley and Sir Walter Mildmay, chancellor of the Exchequer, two men who ordinarily worked hand in hand.

Though this storm blew itself out quickly enough once both sides understood how they had been mishandled by the petitioner and his legal advisers, it had hinted at the ways in which conferences might be used

[112] *CJ* I, 112.

[113] Below, p. 335.

to overawe the Commons: when even Burghley, a man not usually tactless, could employ high-horse tactics against the Commons they had cause to wonder. And Norton had not forgotten his earlier suspicions. In the next session, before any conference had been called, he moved for an order to limit the possible dangers. On future such occasions, the Commons committee were to 'use any reasons or persuasions they shall think good in their discretions, so as it tend to the maintenance of anything done or passed this House before such conference had and not otherwise'; but they were forbidden to agree 'to any new thing proposed there until this House be first made privy thereof and give such order'.[114] The Lords in manner retaliated by formally recording their displeasure when the Commons returned a Lords bill together with the replacement bill they had produced. This the Lords declared to be 'both derogatory to the superiority of the place and contrary to the ancient course of both Houses'.[115] Derogation is a matter of opinion, but in respect of the ancient course the Commons had done the proper thing: they had the right to replace any bill sent to them, but if they exercised this right they were supposed to return the discarded bill together with the *nova*, as in this case they had done. It may be supposed that the Lords were really complaining because the Commons that thrown out their own carefully considered bill without even seeking a conference. The Commons then added to the impression that in 1581 relations between the Houses were somewhat strained when they delayed for two days before returning a harmless private bill which had reached them from the other place with a special emphasis on urgency. They had in fact spent five weeks on it.[116]

It was not unknown for devices designed to improve procedure to backfire, and conferences between the Houses at times could do so. Normally, however, they proved useful, and except in 1581 relations between Lords and Commons were perfectly amicable. In 1566, when the Commons raised a protest against the appointment of a commission for the enforcement of the penal laws – they thought the licensee unqualified – they sought and got the Lords to join them in a move that probably involved petitioning the Queen, though even this produced no result.[117] We have seen that in 1571, over the bill for coming to church, similar efforts, equally fruitless, to work in harness were made. The only complaints from the Upper House tended to touch on the Commons' failure to keep them supplied with work to do by not processing bills fast enough,[118] a justified worry because with the Queen insisting on short

[114] *CJ* I, 123 (7 February 1581; Cromwell's diary [*Proc.* 533] misplaces the order on the 8th).

[115] *LJ* II, 46.

[116] *CJ* I, 124, 133–4.

[117] Ibid. 81.

[118] E.g. ibid. 91, 115.

sessions that slowness often brought bills into the Upper House too late to get them through the three readings. Towards the end of every session bills came pouring in from the Commons, and while some of them, especially private bills, received rapid treatment, even several readings in one day, anything a bit more debateable needed longer time than remained. It is not possible to quantify such statements. When a bill failed it was either because it was formally dashed in the first or second House of passage, or because the Queen vetoed it, or because it ceased to make progress in either House, or because in the end no time was left to pass it. The first two causes are vouched for in the record; the other two can only be conjectured by a look at individual cases.

FAILURE

The problem of unfinished bills greatly worried the management, especially Lord Burghley, as measures taken in the 1571 session indicate most clearly. The session opened on 2 April, and after three weeks Burghley asked the clerk of the Commons for a full account of the state of bills then in that House.[119] The clerk's return indicated the stages reached by the bills – some passed and sent to the Lords, some read twice or once, and sixteen not yet read at all which 'came to my hands since Easter eve' (14 April). Onslow added that 'we have sitten but eleven days', which was true; in addition to Sundays, there had been a four-day recess over Easter (Sunday to Wednesday). The long list of bills awaiting attention troubled Burghley, and on Monday the 24th the House was made to pass an order for 'the titles of all the bills offered into the House' to be read out the next day, 'to the end the House may make their choice with which of them they will first proceed'. When this was done (on Wednesday) a committee for sorting the priorities was appointed, but (as was noted above) we cannot tell whether this committee achieved anything.[120] Burghley persisted. On 10 May he obtained a list of bills passed in the Commons and either sent on or about to be sent on to the Lords; four bills passed in both Houses remained with the Lower awaiting return to the Upper for the assent.[121] On the 21st the clerk of the Lords made a similar return of bills passed by both Houses, or passed above and sent down, or in process of going through the Upper House – twenty-eight of these last, of which four had had no first reading.[122] On top of all this, the Lower House at the start of the month held a long list of private bills still not read even a first time, and the Council must have known by this time that the Queen meant to bring

[119] SP 12/177, fos. 111–12, endorsed and annotated by Burghley.
[120] *CJ* I, 88. [121] SP 12/78, fo. 35. [122] Ibid. fos. 57–8.

the session to a close within eight days. They had before this instructed Thomas Norton to get more work out of the Commons. Precedents existed for sitting in the afternoon, and on 9 May Norton therefore moved for an order to sit from three to five o'clock on Mondays, Wednesdays and Fridays, solely for the purpose of giving a first reading to private bills.[123] The House buckled to, but the only effect was to get those bills started; they progressed no further. So on 21 May, with the end now well in sight, the House decided to sit every afternoon and allow second readings; in fact, the afternoon sittings came to be used as simple extensions of the morning's business.[124] Even so, when the Parliament went home on the 28th some twenty-seven active bills remained unfinished.[125]

Burghley continued to keep himself informed: lists of bills supplied by the clerk of the Commons survive for 24 June 1572 (a week before the close), for 3 and 5 March 1576 (two weeks), and for 1 March 1581 (sixteen days to go).[126] Afternoon sittings resumed without special orders – in 1572 on 25 June, with five days remaining, and in 1576 on 3 March, leaving still twelve days before the close. But in 1581, a session when management several times looked unhappy, the House only once, on 4 March, sacrificed its afternoon. In the event, thirty-eight, forty and forty-one bills remained over at the end of those three sessions whose failure must in the main be ascribed to lack of time. In the three sessions of 1559, 1563 and 1566, before (so far as our evidence goes) systematic pressure to speed things up had begun, the corresponding figures were thirty, thirty-nine and thirty-five: not at first sight significantly different. However, if we allow for the drastic shortening of sessions which marked the years after 1571 we can point to some managerial success. In the sixties the length of sessions averaged ninety-one days and in the seventies fifty-two – these being total lengths with no accounts taken on Sundays and recesses. It looks as though the drive for efficiency scored some points at least.

Not every failed bill vanished for ever. Quite a few came up again in

[123] *CJ* I, 88. To judge from the outcome, the order was obeyed literally, so that the bills so brought forward provide information on which bills were private. Many of them (including a number that later would have been classified as local) might otherwise have been thought to have started as public bills.

[124] Ibid. 91.

[125] The figure is obtained by subtracting from the seventy-four failed bills of the session the thirty-two that never went beyond a single reading, the nine rejected in one House or the other, and the six vetoed.

[126] SP 12/88, fos. 76–80; 107, fos. 131–2 and 144–5; 148, fos. 1–4. There are minor problems of dating and contents about the 1572 and 1576 lists: they contain a few bills allegedly read which do not appear in *CJ* and others read on dates which call the dating of the list in doubt.

a later session, though even a second chance did not often prove successful. Since so many bills are known only from their often uninformative titles it is not possible to offer a precise count of such reintroductions: the many bills for the wool trade and cloth manufacture, for instance, of which few passed, may well at times have been the same as earlier bills for the same general purpose. However, examples can be cited. A bill for unlawful assemblies passed only the Commons in 1559; reintroduced in the Lords two sessions later it died in committee. A bill touching the taking of bail in the court of Common Pleas got no further than first reading in both 1572 and 1576. A bill for the haberdashers, rejected in the Commons on second reading in 1571, was buried in committee there in 1576. In 1571, a bill for planting hops reached the Commons too late for proper action; reintroduced in 1572 it was not pursued, probably because of conflicts among interested parties – in 1581, a bill to control the import of hops was the only one of that session to be vetoed. A bill for handguns ran out of time in 1571, was vetoed in 1572, and died in committee in the Commons in 1576. A bill to make Stafford into an assize town got one reading in 1563; it came back nearly a decade later in 1572, only to be vetoed. The efforts to prevent simoniacal presentations to livings (one of the alphabet bills pushed by the reforming clergy and their lay assistants) was read once in 1566, rejected by the Lords in 1571, and vetoed by the Queen in 1576. The interested parties anxious to create more opportunities for gentlemen to become sheriffs by dividing joint counties shrievalties persisted through repeated disappointments. A bill for separating Buckinghamshire and Bedfordshire, after getting vetoed in 1566 and 1571, ran out of time in 1572; another for doing the same service to Cambridgeshire and Huntingdonshire ran up against the veto in both 1571 and 1572.

There were, of course, also successes in this game of trying again and again. The prehistory of the 1571 bankruptcy act (13 Eliz. I c. 7) including a vetoed Commons bill of 1563 and a Lords bill dashed in the Commons in 1566. The bill for preserving pheasants and partridges, so long delayed in the clerk's hands in 1571 that it got only one reading, proved so difficult in 1576 that it fell victim to the short session; it finally made it in 1581 (23 Eliz. I c. 10). The 1563 bill for the making of hats and caps, passed by the Lords but dashed in the Commons, became an act in 1566 (8 Eliz. I c. 11); a bill for Exeter, too late to pass in 1572, did so two sessions later (23 Eliz. I c. 17). As we shall see, several vetoed bills got through the second time round. Of course, this study deliberately terminates in 1581, and it is entirely possible that several of the lost bills reappeared after that date; some lost in the session of 1581 certainly did.

The fate of bills dashed or vetoed is naturally more certain, though the reasons for their rejections do not always become plain. In those seven sessions, and leaving out the complex manoeuvres over the 1559 bills for supremacy and uniformity which led to modification, not to the rejection, of bills, only sixty-nine bills were formally dashed in the Parliament, forty-six of them in the House of introduction. The twenty-three dashed in the second House reflect, one must suppose, either more mature deliberation, objections on the part of the second House (in the case of the Lords, sometimes manifest doubts on the part of the law officers), or quite probably successful lobbying by some person or persons adversely affected by the bill. The theory that the Lords helped to control the Commons on behalf of Crown and Council ought to rest on a quite noticeable activity on their part in rejecting Commons bills. They dealt thus with twelve bills (the Commons killing eleven of theirs), and nearly always the bill went through all stages before being voted down on third reading. Political motives – pressure from above – might be suspected in at most two such cases: a bill of 1559 empowering the Queen by commission to restore incumbents deprived in the previous reign, and one of 1571 preventing members of the royal Household from serving on juries[127] – and in the first of these instances the motive looks to have been hostility to the new regime. The remaining rejections manifestly depict doubts raised in the House, by outside influences or legal advice, as when the Lords defeated bills for haberdashers and banning the import of horses. Of course, the Lords could kill an objectionable bill by refusing to proceed with it – burying it alive, as it were – but our evidence does not permit the identification of bills so treated, except very occasionally. On the face of it, and in actual fact, late arrival was at least as good reason as deliberate neglect why bills lapsed in the Upper House.

In the Lords, a dashed bill was always voted on, with each peer, in ascending order of seniority, pronouncing his 'content' or 'not content', but the clerk rarely noted more than the fact of rejection. Since on one occasion he went out of his way to speak of unanimity,[128] one might suppose that the remaining occasions led to a division but this seems unlikely, the more so because two such divisions are expressly recorded: the repeal of the Edwardian statute of wines was voted down by all the spiritual peers but only a majority of the temporal ones, and the 1576 bill reforming errors in fines and common recoveries was defeated by a majority.[129] The act of 1559 which empowered the Queen to force exchanges of spiritual for temporal revenues upon newly appointed bishops was naturally, though unsuccessfully, opposed by the spiritual

[127] *LJ* I, 541, 697.

[128] 24 May 1581: *LJ* II, 41.

[129] *LJ* I, 653. The latter bill was put up in every Parliament and invariably lost until it finally became law in 1581 (23 Eliz. I c. 3). Cf. below, p. 295.

peers in the Upper House, and their voices were recorded.[130] An odd thing happened in 1581 when a bill explicating the forgery act of 1563 (5 Eliz. I c. 14) came to its third reading in the Upper House: even though for once proxies were voted the Lords divided equally, for which reason the bill (which the Commons had passed) was 'commanded to be laid up in the desk till the next Parliament'.[131] In such events the Speaker of the Commons had a casting vote; the lord chancellor or whoever in his absence presided upstairs had none.

In the Commons, all decisions concerning bills required the putting of the question (its content depending on the stage reached) by the Speaker; this terminated debate. The House expressed its opinion by acclamation, with those for the reading, committal, engrossing or final passing shouting aye, those against it (if there were any) shouting no. The House divided only if the Speaker decided that the shouting of the voices left him in doubt about the larger side. Those voting aye went forth into the lobby (the old ante-chapel of St Stephen's), being counted at the door by two tellers; the rest, remaining in the chamber, were counted by two other tellers as noes. In the years 1559–81, the Commons Journal records ten divisions, six of them while Seymour was clerk – and he entered the actual votes cast. Going through the years: in 1563 the installation of gig-mills in Devon was dashed by 84 votes to 47, and a bill for voiding gifts made within eight days of death suffered defeat by 89 to 63; in 1566, a bill compelling persons in sanctuary to pay their debts was lost by 77 to 61, the expiring acts renewal bill failed by 97 to 51, a bankruptcy bill went down by 95 to 65, and the act for wines triumphed by 95 to 65.[132] These figures show that the Speaker could feel uncertain about the acclamation even when the difference in numbers is clear enough; they also suggest that even on occasions of serious disputes the House could not expect more than about 130 or 150 of its members to be present out of a total rising by stages to 450. Unfortunately, Onslow did not follow his predecessor in recording numbers in divisions of which only four occurred (or so he tells us) in the four sessions of 1571 to 1581: the act for hats and caps went through by a majority (1571), a bill for the preservation of timber passed the Lower House on a division only to die in committee in the Lords (1571), a bill for great hosen survived on third reading by a majority of one but never reached the Lords (1571), and in 1572 the bill for the water supply of Worcester was after long debate

[130] *LJ* I, 571, 740.

[131] *LJ* II, 40. Proxies were given to other members of the House by peers who had to absent themselves from the Parliament (by the Queen's permission). They remain full of mystery. I have found only this single reference to their being used.

[132] *CJ* I, 66, 72, 79, 81, 80, 78.

defeated on third reading by a majority of six.[133] How often the Speaker felt that his question was answered positively by the shout we cannot tell, but the Commons Journal records forty-five decisions to reject which apparently required no division.

THE ROYAL ASSENT

After a bill had surmounted the hurdles of Lords and Commons it still had to face the third member of the Parliament. On a very few occasions the Queen intervened during the discussions in the Houses. Though her sign manual on private bills testified approval it also constituted (as we have seen) no more than a recommendation to Lords and Commons; sign manual bills required the assent at the end of the session like all other bills. In 1571 Elizabeth formally commended to the Lower House a bill for cutting down lawyers' fees which the Commons dutifully passed, only to find it vetoed at the assent, a sufficient warning not to take the frequent use of her name in parliamentary (or other) affairs to guarantee her personal interest and involvement.[134] Otherwise the Queen sometimes intervened to put an end to proceedings on a bill. In 1572 the Commons had spent four very laborious weeks over a private bill touching a dispute between the earl of Kent and Lord Compton when, just as things were nearing a settlement, they received a message asking that the bill be put by because Compton had been ordered to accompany a French envoy to Dover and could not attend the hearing before the committee. Burghley, supporting the message with a letter to the Speaker, hinted whence the order came.[135] But there were four positive occasions when Elizabeth managed to stop bills she did not like. She told the Lords to cease proceedings on the 1571 bill for homage, as the Commons to their distress discovered at the assent,[136] and she three times arrested bills for religion. When in 1576 the Commons thought to embarrass her by petitioning for her reaction to a bill for church services and such like, they got what they should have expected – a gracious answer ordering a stop.[137] But the Commons tried petitioning that time because earlier efforts to reform the Book of Common Prayer (1571) and to limit the rigours of uniformity to papists (1572) had been peremptorily arrested by messages from her.[138]

This tally does not exactly demonstrate frequent or highly improper interference, but there always remained the veto, her final chance to say

[133] Ibid. 88, 90, 100. The fusing of the two treason bills was voted through on second reading (ibid, 86).

[134] Ibid. 93.

[135] Ibid. 102.

[136] Above, pp. 102–3.

[137] *CJ* I, 113.

[138] Ibid. 87, 97. Cf. below, pp. 210, 216.

no. Since she exercised it thirty-four times in these seven sessions it might be argued that she kept a firm hand over any proceedings that might have threatened the Crown's interest. However, vetoing quite manifestly did not necessarily imply action to protect the Queen's own concerns. Eight of the vetoed bills later without difficulty passed into acts. Acts for the bowyers of London (8 Eliz. I c. 10), for bankruptcy (13 Eliz. I c. 7), and for the protection of grain seed against birds (8 Eliz. I c. 15) had all been preceded by bills vetoed in 1563. One vetoed bill of 1566 became the act for courts of justice in Wales of 1576 (18 Eliz. I c. 8). In 1571, two bills were vetoed which, reintroduced in later sessions, became acts for the town of Shrewsbury and against promoters (14 Eliz. I c. 12 and 18 Eliz. I c. 5). Two private acts for Lord Latimer's heirs and for the rebuilding of Cringleford in Norfolk (14 Eliz. I, OA 28, and 23 Eliz. I, OA 19) had previously been vetoed. In such instances, as the case histories make evident, the veto was used to postpone a decision, information having reached Queen and Council which suggested that the bill, if passed, would cause serious dissatisfaction or even perhaps represent a one-sided victory won by trickery. The passage of the act for Shrewsbury, designed to repeal an earlier act for the town, was preceded by a passionate plea from the town to Queen and Lords, declaring that the earlier act had been obtained by the drapers, 'being few in number', with the great majority knowing nothing about it, and this appeal succeeded in getting the repealing bill, stayed previously at the instance of the drapers, through the Parliament.[139]

The veto could thus be used to promote local negotiations for the production of an agreed bill, or it could lead to second thoughts in the Houses. In 1572, both Houses passed a bill to confirm a lease to that well known London worthy, Mr Customer Smyth, which he had negotiated with the dean and chapter of St Paul's and in return for which he proposed either to maintain two poor scholars at the Universities or to endow a weekly sermon at St Paul's. Someone, possibly the law officers, had doubts about the bargain, and the bill was vetoed. Reintroduced in the following session it was dashed in the Commons because the lease was for a period of years so long as to prejudice the rights of the succeeding cathedral chapters; also it was held to contravene an act of 1571.[140] A bill of 1576 for an explanation of the 1539 act for the dissolution of the monasteries proposed to exempt all colleges at Oxford and Cambridge from that earlier act's provisions. After it had passed both

[139] HLRO, Parchment Collection, Box A. The petitioners, to prove their numerical superiority, collected the signatures of J.P.s, the officers of the town, the gentlemen of worship of the town and franchise, the common council, the occupants of suburbs and liberties, as well as of members of most of the guilds – mercers, shearmen, coursers, weavers, tanners, butchers, tailors, glovers, saddlers, carpenters and bowyers.

[140] *LJ* I, 726; *CJ* I, 107.

Houses, Burghley received representations to the effect that it would injure the Queen's interest and also, despite its professed intent, damage certain colleges because the exemption provided for them might call in question the monarch's right to use monastic lands for the endowing of corporate bodies, thus threatening the title of colleges set up on such endowments. A counter-protest also received by Burghley asked that the matter be committed to expert investigation. This was done, and Burghley got two judges, one serjeant-at-law, the attorney and the solicitor general to look into the matter. They either agreed with the enemies of the bill or could not report in time for the end of the session, which took place about twelve days after the matter was passed to them; at any rate, the bill was vetoed and never brought back.[141] Here, perhaps, sectionally motivated protest had overreached itself.

Of the twenty-six bills killed off by the veto, five at most affected the interests of the Queen. For the remainder the veto played the important role of a last defence against ill-considered, partisan or even corruptly obtained acts of Parliament. They would have dealt with the sale of feathers, the buying of wool in northern counties, the sale of coarse wools in East Anglia, the allocation of Hexhamshire to the bishopric of Durham, harbour repairs at Hartland (Devon), vexatious suits, the separation of sheriffs in joined counties (several times), the diets of assize judges, legal fees, a land dispute at West Ham (Essex), the making of handguns, assize towns on the Midland circuit, college property, tithe payments at Reading, Old Bailey sessions, the deceitful packing of hops with a 'mixture of dross, sand or leaves', and the corrupt sale of fellowships and scholarships at colleges and schools. Whatever may have been the rights and wrongs in these cases, plainly the veto here served the general interest and not the Queen's.

That leaves five instances in which, it might be alleged, the will of the monarch had nullified the will of Lords and Commons, thus indicating who really mattered in the parliamentary trinity. One such veto killed the 1572 bill against the Queen of Scots which Elizabeth seems to have allowed to proceed because she could use it as a threat against her unwelcome, and captive, guest; she never intended that it should become law.[142] Another vetoed bill (of 1563) concerned the Queen as Queen: it attacked purveyors.[143] The remaining three occasions all concerned the supreme governor of the Church of England – the bill for coming to

[141] Ibid. 108; *LJ* I, 737; SP 12/107, fos. 110–13.

[142] When the Lords sent the bill to the Lower House they misleadingly claimed that the Queen wished them to proceed in the matter (*CJ* I, 100). Cf. below, p. 376.

[143] *CJ* I, 67, 71–2; *LJ* I, 616–18. And cf. the proposal, which may be associated with this bill, for buying out rights of purveyance by a permanent annual grant (BL, Harl. MS 4243, fos. 7v–8). This recognized that the Queen was being asked to surrender an aspect of the prerogative.

church, and a bill twice passed affecting the rights of patrons of livings. It is certain that the Queen disliked the first where her veto frustrated her own bishops; as for the other, it must remain doubtful whether she was interested for herself or responded to protests from other quarters. Anything to do with rights of patronage touched a very large number of usually influential people. At any rate, the most severe scrutiny can find only four bills which Elizabeth might have thought sufficiently contrary to her own rights to be stopped at a late stage. It is plain where the normal use of the veto lay, as it is plain that if the Queen thoroughly disliked moves made in the Lords or Commons she preferred to put an end to them during the session. But that too she did only four times in seven sessions. It will not do to exaggerate her disregard for the high court of Parliament.

In any case, she normally, of course, agreed to any bill that had passed both Houses. The royal assent was given at the end of the session in a sitting of the Lords, with the Queen present and the Commons standing at the bar; after it the lord chancellor dissolved or prorogued the Parliament. The framework of the occasion was as fixed as that of the opening ceremonies. The Speaker made an oration – in 1566 Richard Onslow prosed on for two hours[144] – and presented the subsidy act as the Commons' free offer. The lord keeper then replied on the Queen's behalf, after which the assent was given to the bills of the session. Quite often Elizabeth took the opportunity just before or after this to express her own, usually pungent, views of the session just passed. Thus in 1563 she assured the Parliament that she would take her own steps about the succession over which she had been much pressed, and in 1571 she interrupted the assent in order to complain about the way in which the treason bill had been foolishly enlarged in the Commons before later amendments once again made it acceptable to her.[145] The assent itself followed an ancient routine. The clerk of the Crown in Chancery read out the titles of the bills, and the clerk of the Parliaments read out the royal responses in the set formulae: *la reine le veult*, *soit fait comme est desire*, *la reine s'avisera* (the veto), and the thanks for the money bills. It is quite certain that the formula used in each case was settled beforehand and arranged between the two clerks with the Privy Council: Burghley's notes of 1576 confirm what is in itself clear enough from the necessity of the case.[146] However, some complications arise for us from

[144] *CJ* I, 81.

[145] Ibid. 72; *Proc.* 257. In 1572 she interrupted Nicholas Bacon when he referred to 'a strange answer' given to the bill against the Queen of Scots, to point out that that answer (the veto) had not yet been mentioned (ibid. 418). The Queen's contributions to the closing meetings of each session are fully described in Neale, *EP* I.

[146] *Studies*, III, 181.

the distribution of the formulae and from discrepancies in the record – complications which throw some more light on procedure.

The assent was supposed to be inscribed on the Original Acts as well as entered on the Roll against each act recited there; where the two disagree the former obviously presents the correct version. The entry on the act was made at a later stage, after the clerk of the Lords had returned to his office with the list of assents he had written against the lists of bills, and on occasion he failed to see to this being done. That several times he ignored the subsidy acts and the pardon matters little. In six of these sessions, one single private act (that of 1559 which turned a chapel in Carmarthenshire into a parish church)[147] was missed out; one may postulate a minor clerical error. But the formula of assent is missing on all the public acts of 1581, except for the subsidy and the bill for c. 13 (draining Plumstead marshes); the latter had originally been private but before the printing of the sessional statute it had been given public status 'by special suit'. This is the session for which the printer's casting-off notes in the margins of the Original Acts prove that for once the parchment bills themselves, instead of copies, were sent to him,[148] and c. 13, possessed of both the assent (as are all private acts of the session) and printer's marks, tells us something about the usual sequence of events. Evidently the clerk had sent the public acts to be printed before the assent; after the assent he had entered the formulae on the private acts still in his hands; he then received new instructions about c. 13 which he sent off to the printer still comfortably in time for it to be inserted in the make-up and casting off of the bills before setting. But when he got the public acts back from the printer he forgot to transfer the assent onto them, leaving us with only c. 13 complete and only the Roll to indicate what formulae were used at the assent.

The Roll, as was stated earlier,[149] took the public acts from the print, following the printer's sequence, or rather the sequence arranged by the clerk when he sent the material to be printed.[150] The order of the private acts on the Roll, which corresponds to that in the printed table, differs noticeably from that in which the Original Acts are now numbered; evidently they got disordered after enrolment and were numbered at some later date in the sequence in which they lay in the press. The print, however, did not give the formulae of assent, for which the writer of the Roll had to resort to the Original Acts or to the clerk's notes made during the ceremony. A few discrepancies occur which have already been touched upon.[151] But what decided which assenting formulae should be

[147] 1 Eliz. I, OA 35. [148] Above, p. 46. [149] Above, p. 6.
[150] The order roughly followed the supposed convention: matters of Crown, Church and state first, followed by matters of the commonwealth. [151] Above, pp. 53–5.

applied to which bills? The textbooks tell us that public acts got *la reine le veult* and private ones *soit fait*. In our seven sessions only one public act did not get the supposedly correct assent for its kind: this was that of 1556 for bowyers (8 Eliz. I c. 10) upon which *soit fait* is inscribed, while the Roll puts *le veult*. It must have done so because the scribe had inspected nothing but had used what by this time he knew was the normal formula for all the printed acts from which he worked. The unconventional assent to the bowyers' bill either hides a favour of the sort later accorded to the draining of Plumstead marshes, or is a clerical error. Although the Roll continued until 1566 to distinguish between *bille* and *peticiones*, according to the acts' outward appearance, it never made the mistake about assents again and from 1572 it called all bills *bille*, reality having at last replaced a tradition which had had a real meaning in the fifteenth century.

Thus it was the rule under Elizabeth that acts made public by printing did indeed always get *le veult* at the assent. But it does not follow that acts not printed, and therefore private, always received *soit fait*, as the manuals have it; quite a few got *le veult*. Was there some principle that governed the choice of formula? It would be tedious to lumber through the whole lot, but a possible, and at first sight surprising, conclusion does emerge from a complete review of the acts in question. That conclusion says that a distinction already existed between what later ages called local and private acts, the former being concerned with the affairs of towns and other localities, the latter with those of single individuals. In this period the former got *le veult* and the latter *soit fait*. Both, it must be stressed, were private in the sense that they were not put into the sessional statute and paid fees: the act for the river Lea, for instance, for which, as we have seen, much money was disbursed in regular fees,[152] bears *le veult*.

As one comes to expect in this period, the distinction does not work with perfection; a strict interpretation would seem to bring up exceptions which must be considered if the conjecture is to be made credible. Of the 106 acts in question, seven at first sight break the conjectured rule. Three of them look like local acts but get *soit fait*; four look like personal acts but get *le veult*. The first group includes the act for the endowments of a grammar school at Guildford which the town was having some difficulty in collecting; the act for transferring the weekly market at Battle (Sussex) from Sundays to Thursdays; and the act for settling disputes stemming from the union of Weymouth and Melcombe Regis (Dorset) thirty-five years earlier.[153] The Guildford bill was presented by the

[152] Above, p. 80.
[153] 5 Eliz. I, OA 33; 8 Eliz. I, OA 34; 13 Eliz. I, OA 26.

mayor and corporation, but it concerned a personal settlement made in the reign of Edward VI and involving the archbishop of York; the market at Battle was solicited in a very personal petition by Viscount Montague; these two bills could have been interpreted as personal on those grounds. Nothing, however, can be traced to make the bill for Weymouth anything other than local. Of the four personal bills that got *le veult*, one cleared up an old lawsuit that had gone as far as the Star Chamber and in which the public interest was much involved since what was at issue included rape, forcible marriage and fraudulent dealings in land: extending over several people and more than one county, it deserves to be considered a local act after all. The remainder remedied a collapse of family settlements caused by deaths and minorities, the lord keeper himself being an interested party; naturalized the wife of Lord Grey de Wilton; and settled some of Sir Christopher Hatton's lands, he being at that time a great favourite of the Queen.[154] These last three therefore concerned people capable of claiming special treatment, though it would help if one could show why getting assented to *le veult* should bring advantages to a bill at any stage. There is no sign of preferential or especially speedy treatment in the Journals, and our evidence for the payment of fees is much too meagre to let us know whether these 'local' and 'private' acts operated to different scales. The fees payable to the lord chancellor, the Speaker and the clerks of both Houses were certainly the same. Nevertheless, it now appears that of the seven superficially discrepant assents closer inspection really leaves only one; two more could well have been regarded as local, and the four personal acts given *le veult* all represent special cases. I therefore conclude, though somewhat tentatively because the discovery was really most unexpected, that the parliamentary machinery distinguished in the formula of assent given to what were unquestionably at the time called private acts between local and strictly private, in much the same way as the eighteenth century did by explicit classification and separate numbering.

While this analysis of the assent to private acts therefore indicates a respectably systematic treatment, the assents to the subsidies and the pardon rather disconcertingly tend to deny any such thing. All three, of course, were ephemeral, the first two being effective only till the money granted had been collected and the third always superseded by the next such act. The assent hardly mattered in any case because by rights the

[154] 13 Eliz. I, OA 34; 14 Eliz. I, OA 16 (for the lord keeper's interest see *Proc.* 372); 18 Eliz. I, OA 26, 27. The first of these did not clear up all the consequences of the frauds committed. In 1572, Francis Alford, burgess for Reading, introduced a further bill concerning his own sufferings at the hands of the offenders, which led to a hearing before a Commons committee and an agreement to pursue the matter in the Chancery (*Proc.* 291–3, 362, 380).

Queen should have done no more than thank the grantors in a set formula and should have said nothing at all to the pardon which she herself had given of her own free will and under her sign manual. It is not, therefore, altogether surprising to find no assent noted on four of the six lay subsidies, one out of the four clerical subsidies, and three of the five pardons. The formula of gratitude appears on one lay subsidy and two clerical ones, but since the lord keeper in his closing speech always expressed the Queen's thanks for the generosity of her faithful Commons it looks likely that when the formula is missing on the act it had nevertheless been pronounced, though no one later bothered to enter it upon bills which at the time had been with the printer. The presence, however, of *le veult* on the lay subsidy of 1559, the clerical subsidy of 1563, and the pardons of 1563 and 1576 is simply improper and wrong in principle; most probably the quite unsuitable words got put on by inadvertence, during the general and belated inscription of the assent on the Original Acts.

In sum, the royal assent to bills confirms the fact apparent also from the earlier stages of bill procedure. Business methods in both Houses had by this time become pretty thoroughly routinized. A species of office memory secured continuity and regularity across the gaps between sessions, gaps which could be sizable. Even though each meeting of Parliament needs to be treated as a separate occasion, possibly varying in attitudes, behaviour and concern, each was a meeting of a well established institution.

6

Repeal and continuance

REPEAL

Acts made by Parliament, everybody agreed and agrees, can be unmade only by another Parliament. In view of the labours involved in getting a bill through to the statute book, a repetition of such efforts in order to remove the product once again was unlikely to occur frequently, and that indeed was the experience of the 1560s and 1570s. Of course, the setting up of the protestant Church of England required the formal repeal of the statutes by means of which Mary's government had reunited England to Rome and had made possible the active persecution of dissenters: the act of supremacy of 1559 predictably began with a wholesale abolition of earlier legislation, some of it itself the instrument of an earlier repeal.[1] The effort seems to have exhausted those anxious to cleanse the law of what in their view were unfortunate statutes. In the session of 1559, 1563 and 1566 no further act was repealed, though in 1566 the London vintners vainly attempted to get rid of the Edwardian act for the control of the wine trade,[2] and someone as vainly tried to reverse the sensible transfer of a parish church in Wales to a more populous part of the region in question.[3] Even in the 1570s, total repeals remained exceedingly rare; only one act can confidently be cited. That was the repeal in 1572 of the 1566 act for clothmaking in Shrewsbury (8 Eliz. I c. 7), obtained by a minority of the town's cloth interests; an earlier repeal bill had been vetoed in 1571, in the hope of promoting a peaceful agreement within the town.[4] A private act of 1571 abolished the corporation of merchant adventurers at Bristol, but its purposes and implications are not altogether clear.[5] No earlier act establishing such a

[1] 1 Eliz. I c. 1.

[2] Above, p. 84.

[3] See my remarks in *Welsh Society and Nationhood* (ed. R. R. Davies et al., 1984), 118. The act for the parish church of Abernant is 1 Eliz. I, OA 35.

[4] Above, p. 124.

[5] 13 Eliz. I, OA 22.

corporation can be found, and it would seem that the instrument abolished by the repealing act was a royal charter under the great seal.

This event led to an interesting debate.[6] William Fleetwood, after wondering why Bristol should want to undo what it had done so recently, questioned the wisdom of an act which by cancelling letters patent attacked the Queen's prerogative, a prerogative which 'she is sworn to preserve'; but others held that the charter set up a monopoly hostile both to the common weal and by reducing the customs revenue, to the Queen herself, so that the proposed legislation would be generally beneficial. Francis Alford pointed out that the act of 1563, which confirmed a patent granted to Southampton,[7] showed that the Queen's letters by themselves 'were not sufficient', a point eagerly taken up by John Popham, at that time recorder of Bristol. The mention of the act for Southampton was a good tactical move, for on the very day of this debate a bill to continue that act was read a first time: and that renewal had been arranged over an earlier intention to leave the act stand until repealed by letters patent.[8] But Popham, if he is correctly reported (and his speech was long), then confused things considerably by mentioning an act of the last session (1566) in the drafting of which 'covin' had been used; he therefore wanted the act reversed but the letters patent to stand, to have their validation according to the law. No such act or bill for Bristol is to be found in 1566, and my guess is that the reporters got confused by Popham's discourse; perhaps he too had the case of Southampton in mind. In the end the Commons risked offending the prerogative, without a murmur from the Queen.

As for failed attempts at general repeal, we find the vetoed effort to do for Shrewsbury in 1571 what was achieved in 1572;[9] we find a mysterious bill in the Lords to repeal an unidentified act of Henry VI;[10] and we find a bill 'touching the repeal of certain statutes' concerning the 'shipping of Suffolk cloths and Kentish cloths'.[11] No known act dealt specifically with the cloths produced in those two counties, though both separately appear linked to other counties in various failed bills in these sessions. Clothmaking bills pose very complex problems, as has already been shown,[12] but it may here be conjectured that the bill probably proposed a partial exemption from existing laws and therefore asked for

[6] *Proc.* 209–11.

[7] 5 Eliz. I, OA 35.

[8] In 5 Eliz. I, OA 35, the limitation cause was changed from leaving termination to a great seal patent to 'the end of the next Parliament', which meant that the act needed continuing in the session of 1571. It was so continued by 13 Eliz. I, OA 23.

[9] *CJ* I, 84–7; *LJ* I, 679, 681–2. the bill was, of course, private (*Proc.* 218).

[10] Read once: *LJ* I. 739.

[11] *CJ* I, 128, 134 – first readings of the original bill and a revised version.

[12] Above, p. 82.

only a partial repeal of earlier legislation. The practice of giving certain regions immunity from legal provisions which they could argue harmed them exceptionally is well vouched for; statutory exemption was clearly more definitive and therefore preferable to a *non obstante* licence. In 1566 an act originating in a private bill, promoted in the Lords, freed all Fenland from the act of 1540 which had laid down the sizes of horses to be bred; the fens justifiably claimed that on marshland one could not raise such large animals.[13] In the same year, the London coopers successfully petitioned against the prices fixed in an act of 1531 for the manufacture of barrels; they accepted the main provisions of the act but asked that the inflation of costs be taken notice of.[14] And a third act of the same year sorted out, by the removal of some clauses, a confusion over the trial of crimes committed in Merionethshire, a confusion arising from the various Henrician acts for the settlement of Wales.[15] Partial repeals could create freedoms for the generality too, as was demonstrated in 1563. The navigation act of that year repealed a section of the 1559 act for shipping in English bottoms which had barred small English vessels from trading overseas;[16] even so, it left untouched the much more important and contentious provisions of an act against which the London Fishmongers tried to move in that Parliament.[17] Such partial repeals, as another act of the session demonstrated, could also limit concessions already made. A statute of 1547, prohibiting the export of horses, permitted *bona fide* travellers to take their own mounts with them after swearing an oath that the animals were to be used solely for their own transport; but, said an act of 1563, this privilege had been much abused and was hereby revoked.[18]

Repeal, especially partial repeal, thus provided a possible instrument for usefully varying the effects of legislation, and a few more attempts were made to exploit the possibility but failed. A mysterious bill of 1563 wished to repeal an unidentified clause in an unidentified act 'for journeymen with tailors'; the reform of the clothmaking statute of Edward VI was approached in 1563 through a series of partial repeal bills; religious motives lay behind the vain attempt of 1571 to abolish the 'Wednesday fast' (sometimes called 'Cecil's fast') introduced by the 1563 navigation act; and in 1581 parts of the Edwardian code for

[13] 8 Eliz. I c. 8 allowed fen horses to be thirteen hands high, as against the fifteen limited by 32 Henry VIII c. 13.

[14] 8 Eliz. I c. 9, modifying 23 Henry VIII c. 4.

[15] 8 Eliz. I c. 20; cf. *Welsh Society and Nationhood*, 110.

[16] 5 Eliz. I c. 5 repealed 1 Eliz. I c. 13, sect 3.

[17] CLRO, Rep. 15, fo. 188 (9 February 1563): a fishmongers' bill for the total repeal of the act received encouragement, but no bill resulted in Parliament.

[18] 1 Ed. VI c. 5, sect. 6 was repealed by 5 Eliz. I c. 19.

clothmaking again came under attack.[19] It is sometimes clear and sometimes very probable that at least some of the bills coming from various cloth interests, inadequately described as they are, asked for what in effect were partial repeals of earlier statutes – like the bill of 1566 which proposed to alter the statutory regulation of the size of cloths by doing away with the penalties by which that size was protected.[20] Cloth bills very rarely succeeded, but efforts of this sort appear to lie behind some of the bills that were entered with no clear indication of their purpose.

LIMITATION OF TIME

However, when all is said, repealing earlier acts or parts of them was both a clumsy and a rather expensive way of modifying the law in order to suit an interest; with royal dispensations by letters patent available for the more obviously burdensome laws for manufacture and trade, it is not surprising to find this road travelled pretty rarely. Nor should it be overlooked that too much repealing would have cast doubts on the standing of acts of Parliament; reluctance to keep changing the law thus also reflects the manifest respect for the authority of parliamentary legislation. In any case, the Parliament possessed a more acceptable means to provide against possible mistakes: instead of making permanent laws which might justifiably be repealed, it could and did make laws valid for a trial period and then subject to scrutiny before continuance. Such time-limited acts a few decades later received the name 'probationers' which shall here be used now and again, for the sake of elegant variation.

In the seven sessions between 1559 and 1581, twenty-nine public acts out of 146 (just about one fifth) carried time-limitation clauses. The terms so set varied. The supposedly most usual formula – 'to the end of the next Parliament' – occurs nine times; this required reconsideration during the possibly several sessions of the assembly following next upon the one that made the law in the first place.[21] An interesting modification, which is found four times, compelled review in the first session of the next Parliament; this appears to reflect an expectation that Parliaments might extend over several sessions with longish intervals between them.[22] Several acts were made to terminate at either of these points after a stated span of time. Thus two acts of 1559 (inhibiting the sale of leather and confining general exports to English vessels) were to endure for five years and then to the end of the next Parliament;[23] the major navigation act

19 *CJ* I, 66–7; 68; 89–90 (passed Commons, buried in Lords); 128, and *Proc.* 537.
20 *CJ* I, 77, 80.
21 1 Eliz. I cc 17, 18; 5 Eliz. I cc. 6, 7, 9; 8 Eliz. I c. 15; 13 Eliz. I cc. 15, 20, 21.
22 5 Eliz. I cc. 2, 3; 8 Eliz. I c. 10; 13 Eliz. I c. 5.
23 1 Eliz. I cc. 10, 13.

of 1563 had ten years from Michaelmas 1564 before it lapsed at the end of the next Parliament;[24] for the two poor laws of 1572 and 1576 the initial period was set at seven years.[25] Another kind of formula could restrict the time span allowed without altering the time of expiry but by postponing the date from which the act took effect: the much disputed act concerning informers, which by the rules should have stood from the beginning of the session in which it passed (8 February 1576) was made to start operating at the following Easter (22 April) and endure to the end of the next session – a loss of two and a half months.[26]

A special category of acts was made to expire together with the Queen – that is, they were to last during her life only. Three of these pose no problems: the two acts concerning seditious words and the one for rebellious assemblies simply followed the precedents of Mary's reign.[27] There was some sense in reserving the possibility that a new monarch would wish to change policy in these respects, and indeed both offences lapsed at the beginning of James I's reign. But two acts carrying this limitation in time are odd. That of 1571 concerning fugitives out of England, and that of 1581 for the better defence of the northern border, were to endure only for the Queen's life, a term which in those contexts makes no real sense.[28] Both of them cost much anguish and debate, the chief worry on both occasions arising from apprehensions that too many existing rights of property might be infringed by them,[29] and in both cases the time-limiting clauses were later additions to the original bill. In the fugitives' act the effect was achieved by an amendment in the Commons (the House of origin) which deleted all mention of 'heirs and successors' after every reference to the Queen and repeated the point in an explicit addition, but a surviving paper draft, clearly used behind the scenes after the bill had been engrossed in the Lower House, shows that Burghley was responsible for these changes, probably in an endeavour to assuage fears expressed in the Commons' debate.[30] The act for fortifying the borders originated in the Lords but was replaced by a new bill in the Commons; even so, the time-limitation clause was added there as a special proviso inscribed in the Lower House before engrossing, presumably to help silence similar objections. On both occasions a limitation to the Queen's life would seem to have emerged as a compromise between the Crown, who wanted permanent acts, and protesters

[24] 5 Eliz. I c. 5.
[25] 14 Eliz. I c. 5; 18 Eliz. I c. 3.
[26] 18 Eliz. I c. 5.
[27] 1 Eliz. I c. 6, replaced by 23 Eliz. I c. 2, a very different measure which, however, repeated the limitation to the Queen's life; 1 Eliz. I c. 16.
[28] 13 Eliz. I c. 3; 23 Eliz. I c. 4.
[29] Cf. *Proc.* 237, 536–7; the bills had a difficult passage, with many amendments in both Houses.
[30] Cf. OA, and SP 12/77, fos. 206–35.

in the Commons who wanted an opportunity for later reconsideration and quite probably had at first called for the usual limitation to the end of the next Parliament.

Nor were these the only acts whose limitation in time came in as an afterthought. In the tillage and poor laws of 1563,[31] the clause, written over an erasure, represents a Commons amendment to a Lords bill; the erasure is so effective that we cannot tell whether the amendment replaced permanency or (more likely) merely altered the time-limit. On the other hand, the bills of the same session for imports and for perjury,[32] all three of which started in the Commons, were amended to become probationers rather than permanencies. All three time-limited acts of 1566 started as permanent but were changed during passage: the Commons thus altered the Lords bill for bowyers as well as their own bill for the preservation of grain, while the Lords repaid the compliment on the Commons bill for the division of sheriffwicks.[33] In 1571, leaving aside the fugitives act, it was the Upper House which showed a preference for caution, adding time-limits to the Commons bill for usury and to two of their own bills (preventing the use of small vessels in overseas trade and qualifying the exemption of the University towns from the activities of royal purveyors).[34] Perhaps one may suspect the hands of the judges assistant in this. The poor law bill of 1572 started in the Lords where the limitation was added as an afterthought; when that of 1576 started in the Commons without such a provision it was added in committee expressly because it had been in the former act.[35] The Lords also limited the time in the act for bridges and highways in Oxford which had started as a private bill looking for permanency.[36] Thus it is plain that thought was given to whether an act should be permanent or not, and at times it was only reflection and discussion which suggested that some things needed a probationary period. The increasing practice to limit in time, and the confusion of the limits set, did, however, create real difficulties in keeping the statute book up to date and in a proper condition – the problem of in time continuing or, where inadvertent lapses had occurred, reviving statutes which under those clauses would have expired. The story of expiring laws continuance acts needs to be taken back to its beginnings in 1536.

[31] 5 Eliz. I cc. 2, 3. All this information comes from the OA.

[32] 5 Eliz. I cc. 5 (added by the Lower House on a separate schedule), 7, 9 (added on the act in a hand other than the engrossing clerk's).

[33] 8 Eliz. I cc. 10, 15, 16.

[34] 13 Eliz. I cc. 8, 15, 21.

[35] 14 Eliz. I c. 5; 18 Eliz. I c. 3.

[36] 18 Eliz. I c. 20. The relevant proviso to this Commons bill is on a separate schedule and in the hand of the Lords clerk; it bears the Commons' agreement. For the original status of the bill see SP 12/107, fo. 144.

CONTINUANCE

Limiting the life of an act occurred occasionally in the reign of Henry VII and in the earlier part of Henry VIII's. Thus the famous 'statute of retainers' of 1504 (19 Henry VII c. 14), often spoken of as the chief instrument in the Tudor campaign against baronial independence, died with that king and was never revived. There were, however, few such acts, and they either got swiftly made permanent or after one renewal were allowed to lapse.[37] Nor did it seem to matter much if an act had been overlooked at the right time – as a rule in the Parliament next after its passage. When care was taken it seems to have been because private interests watched out. Thus the act for the harbour at Southampton, passed in 1497 and limited to twenty years, strictly speaking expired when there was no Parliament sitting at the crucial time; the necessary bill, passed in the next Parliament to be called (1523), took care to point out that the act had been in abeyance for six years.[38] In general, however, the picture is one of haphazardness, nor do we at present know how the judges treated statutes that technically had lapsed.

In this respect, as in all others, the Reformation Parliament marked a new beginning. Its seven sessions not only produced more time-limited acts than ever before had emerged from one Parliament, but also, as 'the end of the next Parliament' receded ever further into the future, postponed the need to attend to them. Yet in Thomas Cromwell's hands the management of Parliament and legislation achieved a novel sophistication which called for a more careful review of laws that would expire unless explicitly continued by further acts.[39] Thus the Parliament of 1536 attended to the problem, but the resulting confusion indicates the novelty of the exercise. Altogether four continuance acts were passed, promoted severally in both Houses but to all appearance stemming from the Council: 28 Henry VIII c. 1 singled out four acts of the Reformation Parliament – concerning sanctuaries, petty treason, refusal to plead to an indictment, and buggery – the third of which had actually not been limited in time.[40] The reason for this selection of legislation on crime became plain in the next Parliament. Still in 1536, cc. 6, 8 and 9 continued twelve time-expired acts, including the buggery act for a second time. Things had become better organized in the Parliament of

[37] E.g. 1 Henry VIII c. 8 (control of escheators) made permanent in the next session (3 Henry VIII c. 2); 5 Henry VIII c. 4 (making of worsteds), forgotten in two parliaments but made permanent in 1533 (25 Henry VIII c. 5); three acts of 1512 (4 Henry VIII, cc. 1, 3, 4), never continued.

[38] 11 Henry VII c. 5; 14 & 15 Henry VIII c. 13.

[39] G. R. Elton, *Reform and Renewal* (1973), 43.

[40] 22 Henry VIII c. 14; 23 Henry VIII c. 1; 25 Henry VIII cc., 3, 6.

1539–40. In the first session a single act continued the twelve listed in the three later acts of 1536;[41] in 1540, the measures singled out in the first continuance bill of 1536 were all made permanent.[42] This suggests that an intention to do this on the earlier occasion had either been abandoned at a late stage or, more likely, been defeated in Parliament. The next Parliament was twice prorogued before being dissolved, but the continuance act passed in its first session (1542) in which two of the hitherto time-limited acts became permanent; the remainder of the tally was continued till the next Parliament, with the addition of the sole probationer passed in 1540.[43] Even so, things had still not become organized in a proper routine. The continuance act of Henry's last Parliament (1545) referred back to that of 1539, ignoring its successor of 1542; in consequence it made five new additions of which one had already appeared in that act. When Henry VIII died, fifteen of the acts of his reign remained in force only to the end of the next Parliament, the earliest in the list being that of 1529 for the making of cables and hawsers (21 Henry VIII c. 12) which remained the front marker for quite some time.

The first Parliament of Edward VI lasted for four and a half years and four sessions, which meant that strictly speaking nothing needed to be done until the spring of 1552. But Parliament and even government lacked powers of prophecy, with the effect that proper continuance bills were introduced in both the first two sessions. It could be that the dates on which such bills were abandoned establish the dates on which it was decided to prorogue rather than dissolve; failure to bring in the relevant bill at all during a session may signify an early decision to keep the Parliament in being. At any rate, in 1547 the bill, starting in the Lords, reached the Commons two days before the prorogation; in 1549 the roles were reversed, with the Lords giving the Commons bill a first reading again two days before the prorogation.[44] The session of 1550 passed without a continuance bill, though several attempts to renew particular acts were introduced; only the act for sewers of 1531 was expressly renewed, but that met the special case of an act which had been limited to twenty years.[45] In the last session (1552) the necessary general act

[41] 31 Henry VIII c. 7. In effect it covered thirteen acts because the beggars act of 1536 (27 Henry VIII c. 25) was treated as a mere modification of that of 1531 (22 Henry VIII c. 12) and was silently renewed as well.

[42] 32 Henry VIII c. 3. Confusion could have arisen over the buggery act, continued to the next Parliament in 1539 and made permanent in 1540; the second was to prevail.

[43] 33 Henry VIII c. 17. Omitted were 25 Henry VIII c. 9 (pewterers) and 21 Henry VIII c. 10 (export of metals), made permanent by 33 Henry VIII cc. 4, 7. Added was the act for jeofails (32 Henry VIII c. 30).

[44] 1547: *LJ* I, 311–12; *CJ* I, 48. 1549: *CJ* I, 10; *LJ* I, 350–1.

[45] 3 & 4 Ed. VI c. 8; 23 Henry VIII c. 5.

passed at last.[46] It added one act of 1545 and one of 1550 (35 Henry VIII c. 17; 3 & 4 Edward VI c. 17): both had been given fixed expiry dates (seven and three years respectively) and were thus up for renewal. It also appeared to repeal three Henrician acts by omitting them. One of them, the beggars act of 1531, had in fact already been repealed by 1 Edward VI c. 3, but it looks as though only inadvertence removed the other two. The acts for the keeping of gaols (23 Henry VIII c. 2) and for sowing flax (24 Henry VIII c. 4), both regulars so far, did not vanish for long, being revived in 1553 and 1563 respectively. Edward VI's second Parliament, called in the spring of 1553 mainly to secure the position of the duke of Northumberland against the King's expected demise, found time for a continuance act – an indication of the degree of routine that now attached to these measures; it dropped a late Henrician act for wine but added the ten time-limited acts produced in the previous Parliament's four sessions.[47]

Thus by the time that Mary came to the throne the continuance of probationary acts had settled into the routine of parliamentary business, seventeen years and six Parliaments after Thomas Cromwell had first thought it necessary to institute such regular inspections of the statute book. Unlike her brother, Mary believed in dissolutions, so that four Parliaments met in the five years of her reign, but that reign produced five expiring laws continuance acts because both sessions of her first Parliament produced one.[48] There is no point in pursuing these acts here in detail, except to note that they were done with care, some acts being deliberately allowed to die and others properly added as they came up. Two matters only deserve notice because they influenced what was to happen under Elizabeth. Mary's first continuance act left out the Edwardian law against unlawful assemblies, silently replaced by an act for the same purpose designed for the new monarch.[49] And Mary's last continuance act, which had added two measures passed in the previous Parliament, contains two afterthoughts on separate schedules. The second of these added the poor law from that same earlier session, apparently overlooked in the original drafting.[50] The first, however, is a bit of a mystery: a proviso to the effect that the omission of any mention of the act concerning the sale of wines and spices 'made and ordained

[46] 5 & 6 Ed. VI c. 17.

[47] 7 Ed. VI c. 11.

[48] 1 Mary st. 2 c. 13 (c. 14 revived the act for gaols, inadvertently omitted in 1552); 1 Mary st. 3 c. 12 (a clearing up operation which deleted five acts, including the old list-leader for cables); 1 & 2 Philip & Mary c. 16; 2 & 3 P. & M. c. 21; 4 & 5 P. & M. c. 9.

[49] 3 & 4 Ed. VI c. 5, replaced by 1 Mary st. 1 c. 12 (continued by subsequent acts). Also omitted was 3 & 4 Ed. VI c. 15 against prophecies: regarded as a protestant measure.

[50] 2 & 3 Philip and Mary c. 5.

in this present Parliament' should not be read as rendering that act of no effect. No act answering to that description passed in that Parliament or in any other of the reign, but a bill embodying the stated effect had passed all stages in both Houses five days before the prorogation, which took place on 7 March.[51] The Lords Journal makes no mention at all of the continuance bill, even though it originated, as was the usual custom, in that House; the Commons received it on 3 March and passed it with three provisos in the morning of the day in the afternoon of which the Parliament was prorogued.[52] The list of acts passed in the session[53] includes the continuance act but not that for wines and spices which must therefore have been vetoed, as is the more likely because when it passed in the Lords there had been voices against it. It thus would seem that the Commons proviso had been anticipatory and was rendered meaningless by the veto. Could it have been taken out? The Commons had added three provisos of which only two survived into the act, so that one was certainly removed; perhaps the clerk of the Upper House in his necessary haste removed the wrong one before the assent. The phrasing of the survivor is sufficiently laboured to hint that the Commons had an inkling of the forthcoming veto; perhaps they hoped to secure by their action that the continuance bill might be held over to the next session in November (terminated by Mary's death, as it turned out), which might give them another chance to obtain their purpose, whatever that purpose was. The history of this act displays, at the end of a series of competent measures attending to expiring laws, an uncharacteristic confusion, but let us remember that the confusion was caused by the Commons' desire to add to the bill sent down from the Lords.

That brings us back to our proper place and theme – expiring laws continuance acts in the reign of Elizabeth. The seven sessions from 1559 to 1581 comprised four Parliaments, so that there should have been four such acts in that time. In fact, only three passed. There was nothing peculiar about the first of them which followed precedent so slavishly that, except for the dropping of certain statutes, it was a verbatim copy of Mary's last.[54] Even the afterthought expressed in that act by the proviso for the poor law of 1556 appeared in a separate section for continuing that measure. Taken off the list were the two acts which had been similarly treated on Mary's accession – unlawful assemblies and seditious rumours. Both were in fact continued by separate acts, probably on the grounds (expressly stated for seditious words) that some doubts existed whether the earlier acts covered the person of a new monarch.[55] Only one act disappeared altogether, namely that of 1531 prohibiting the

[51] *CJ* I, 48, 50; *LJ* I, 530–2.
[52] *CJ* I, 50–1.
[53] *LJ* I, 535.
[54] 1 Eliz. I c. 18.
[55] 1 Eliz. I cc. 6, 16.

export of horses, a matter of some contention which was settled in a revised form in 1563.[56] Naturally enough, the Marian proviso for a bill on the sale of wines, having proved abortive, disappeared.

However, conventional and straightforward though the act appeared to be, its passage contained a moment which recalls Mary's last Parliament, and which in the light of later events assumes significance. The bill started in the Lords and passed both Houses at speed. But when it came back to the Upper House it contained a Commons proviso 'to which the Lords would not agree but sent it down again to be passed by the leaving out of the proviso'.[57] On this occasion the Lower House did not persist. We have no means of telling what that proviso meant to do, but whatever its import it would have been the one serious variation from the established form not called for by government policy.

In 1563 Parliament met for the first session of what turned out to be a two-sessions assembly, and it is therefore of interest that the session passed without the normal continuance bill being introduced. It looks as though the Council knew from the first that the session would not end in dissolution. However, two of the failed bills of that year touched on continuance. One attempted to revive the poisoners act of 1531, repealed in the general repeal of Henrician felonies at the start of Edward's reign; presumably the mover wished to reintroduce the specially savage punishment for poisoners of boiling them alive, for in itself the offence was murder and therefore covered by the law anyway. Read only once, it looks like a private move of little moment.[58] On the other hand, the second bill looks to have had official initiative behind it because it proposed to render permanent certain probationers (we do not know which); introduced into the Commons it was there committed on second reading and then vanished, very probably because the Council had decided to postpone the whole business of expiring acts to the next session.[59]

Thus a full-scale continuance bill appeared in the session of 1566. It did not pass, so that its terms remain unknown to us, but the form of the acts of 1559 and 1571 strongly suggests that originally it must have been a straightforward measure listing expiring acts and decreeing their continuance. Its defeat has made the bill notorious: it has been interpreted as the Commons' revenge for the Lords' refusal to pass certain bills for religion.[60] That interpretation depends very much on the supposition

[56] 5 Eliz. I c. 19. The 1532 act against the export of horses to Scotland, lapsed some time before, was revived by 1 Eliz. I c. 7. Thus a proclamation of 7 May 1562 (*TRP* II, 201) erred in ascribing that revival to the general continuance act.

[57] *LJ/EHR*, 541.

[58] *CJ* I, 69.

[59] Ibid. 69–70.

[60] Neale, *EP* I, 168–9.

that an opposition group in the Lower House demanded the enactment of the bill for the articles of religion which the Queen wished to avoid, and that the Commons used the continuance bill to express their petulant displeasure. The first point, as shall be argued later, is in serious doubt; the second looks improbable. The history of the bill, however, contains its mysteries. Contrary to precedent it started in the Commons, perhaps because the Council's manager of legislation, William Cecil, sat there. The Journal tells us that after being read a first time on 10 October it disappeared for eleven weeks. Then it was read a second time, with an additional clause concerning the export of grain, and passed within two days.[61] The Lords read it three times on the day they received it (24 December), evidently because the session was meant to end before Christmas; their Journal provides no further information.[62] However, it seems that they had raised objections: the bill went back to the Commons for amendment by the removal of 'all the provisions and articles besides only the continuance of acts', a demand which the Commons met with a division, upon which the bill was lost.[63]

Neale read the long interval between the two readings in the Lower House as a deliberate manoeuvre intended to keep an important measure in reserve in order to prevent an early dissolution, but that is to place the Speaker and the clerk in the service of an unofficial leadership, which is an absurd supposition supported by no evidence whatsoever. The delay is quite sufficiently accounted for by the major issues of the session – the problems of the succession and of the subsidy – which explain why a bill that had never caused any real difficulties before was left lying until later. The interval may possibly hide a committee stage which the clerk (not for the first time) failed to notice in his Journal, but if that was so it seems to have produced but one addition to the bill, a proviso banning the export of grain. An attempt to legislate for this had been made in 1559 when the bill failed at third reading,[64] and the only information on its possible contents is found in Cecil's notes for a legislative programme which he put together on the eve of that first Parliament of the reign.[65] These include the draft of a proviso which empowered the Crown to make the ban so enacted effective by proclamation. If this was the proviso which the Lords excised from the continuance bill of 1559, it is beginning to look as though Cecil tried once more in 1566. Supposing this reconstruction to be correct, and it does at least hang together, it follows that in the preparation of the 1566 bill he incurred opposition to the introduction of an innovation into a continuance bill; legal opinion may be suspected of objecting. When he tried to circumvent this by adding

[61] *CJ* I, 74, 81.
[62] *LJ* I, 664.
[63] *CJ* I, 81.
[64] Ibid. 60–1.

the proviso to the bill as prepared, he found he had overreached himself: the Lords, guided by their legal experts (lord keeper and judges) not without reason protested at this abuse of a conventional measure. On this reading, therefore, the obstacle to passage resided in a pet project of the secretary of state.

The addition for grain export is the only one mentioned in the Commons Journal but need not have been the only change forced into the bill; the Lords demand, after all, as entered in the record of the Lower House, spoke of additions in the plural. We cannot disallow the possibility that the secretary was trying to use the continuance bill for a wider revision of the statutes, of the sort that, as we shall see, appeared in the continuance acts of 1571 and 1572. For whatever reason – and the most likely one would be a legal conservatism which argued that such changes should be made by separate acts – the manoeuvre failed in 1566 and annoyed both Houses, but not on the grounds tendentiously conjectured by Neale. The adverse vote in the Commons makes much better sense if it was intended to express displeasure at being forced to curtail the bill than if it was to express petulance: rather no continuance act than one that did not do what the conciliar leadership of the Lower House wanted. This would make Cecil appear as willing to lose, at least for a time, a whole raft of statutes, which on the face of it does seem highly improbable. Strangely enough, the possibility nevertheless receives support from the list of complaints about the events of the 1566 session which Cecil drew up to present to the Queen at the end of it.[66] Among his grievances about things not achieved, all gathered round failures to pursue the policies he advocated, the loss of expiring laws does not appear. So far as his own words go, it did not trouble him. Thus the loss of the bill – its rejection in the Commons – must be said to have more probably resulted from matters touching the law and from a mix-up between the two Houses than from puritan resentment at the Queen's religious policy.

At any rate, the expiring laws had now properly expired, and it would seem that the fact was noticed in the courts.[67] That is to say, the expiry caused real difficulties, and since no Parliament was to meet for five years nothing could be done about this death of the probationers for an uncomfortably long time. At least, and despite the hectic events of 1569–70, there was also plenty of time to prepare the remedy, and in 1571 the bill for 'reviving and continuing of certain statutes' got a first reading in the Upper House on 5 April, the first working day of the session. It

[65] SP 12/41, fos. 196–7.
[66] SP 12/41, fo. 76.
[67] Mr David Lidington tells me that *qui tam* prosecutions in the Exchequer on some acts that informers had regularly used ceased during this interlude.

was at once committed to four bishops, four lay peers and three judges – Cecil, now Burghley, not being one of them. Alas for preparations: two weeks later the committee presented a new bill for first reading. Though this passed readily enough it did not satisfy some interests in the Commons where provisos were at once added concerning the Edwardian act against regraters (5 and 6 Edward VI c. 14), made permanent in the bill, and the Elizabethan act against the sale of apparel on tick (5 Eliz. I c. 6), due for renewal. Anxious to avoid a repetition of 1566, the Lords asked for a conference which took place even though, the bill being with the Commons, they had acted out of turn. The conference produced two other agreed modifications, as further did the third-reading debate, and by 26 May the bill was through at last.[68]

Not all the effects of these discussions and amendments can be clearly identified in the act as passed, but that it was the product of much argument and some compromise is plain.[69] In the place of a single section reciting expiring acts followed by the enactment of continuation, we find six substantial clauses and three provisos appended on separate schedules. The act began by making five probationers permanent – three from Henry VIII's reign and one each from Edward's and Mary's.[70] We are unlikely to err in supposing that this section derived from the failed bill of 1566 which had proposed so to provide for acts not named. Next, six expired acts were revived until the end of the next Parliament, it being expressly stated that they had been lost by the failure of the 1566 bill.[71] Three acts, superseded by more recent legislation, disappeared.[72] There then followed an odd interpolation: the old act for the building of gaols, last renewed for ten years in 1563, was extended for another like period after including Cambridgeshire within its provisions, from which it had been left out in 1532.[73] Lastly, the bill dealt with measures of the last Parliament which, while time-limited, had not, of course, expired in 1566. To the first of these the Lords added a proviso that its ban on the import of foreign manufactures was not to be prejudicial to agreements

[68] *LJ* I, 669, 677–8, 699; *CJ* I, 86, 89, 91–3. It is unfortunate that the Anonymous Diary for 1571, which gives much detail of debates, breaks off on 21 April, a week before the bill reached the Commons.

[69] 13 Eliz. I c. 25.

[70] 23 Henry VIII cc. 3 (jury verdicts), 17 (winding of wools); 36 Henry VIII c. 17 (preservation of timber); 5 & 6 Ed. VI c. 14 (regraters); 2 & 3 P. & M. c. 3 (milch kine).

[71] 24 Henry VIII c. 9 (killing of weanlings); 3 & 4 Ed. VI cc. 19 (cattle sales), 21 (butter and cheese); 1 Eliz. I c. 17 (fish fry); 5 Eliz. I cc. 2 (tillage), 3 (poor law). This last was included here by mistake: time-limited to the end of the first session of the next Parliament it was still in force in 1571.

[72] 2 & 3 Ed. VI c. 9 (currying of leather); 2 & 3 P. & M. cc. 2 (tillage), 5 (poor law).

[73] 23 Henry VIII c. 2, last renewed by 5 Eliz. I c. 24. The act of 1532 had omitted to mention several counties, but only Cambridgeshire seems to have been worried by this.

arrived at in commercial treaties.[74] On the face of it, this looks to be the only change, possible verbal ones apart, that distinguishes the bill as it left the Lords from what it should have looked like when first introduced; all that their committee probably did to the bill concerned such lesser modifications, though they may have called for the amount of rewriting which provoked the making of a *nova billa*.

The Commons' effect upon the act can be read in part from the provisos they appended and in part from the issues very briefly alluded to in their Journal as the bill underwent its vicissitudes in the Lower House. It was the Commons who had the acts against the export of leather and the sale of clothing removed and thus repealed.[75] Their separate clauses also reflect some of the points mentioned in the Journal: the Henrician act for the preservation of timber (35 Henry VIII c. 17), now made permanent, was amended by extending enclosure after felling, to encourage regeneration, from seven to nine years; the now permanent statute against regrating (5 and 6 Edward VI c. 14) was made not to extend to wine and all foreign imports except fish and salt; and retailers of corn and victuals were in future to operate under licence, as did drovers by the act of 5 Eliz. I c. 12.

This laborious recital should have shown how very far from simple these continuance acts had become. The Council prepared its bill, but lawyer-like scrutiny at once revealed enough defects to call for revision and replacement; thereafter all sorts of people raised questions about existing probationers and specific provisions in them which rendered continuance bills some of the slowest in passage that the age encountered. It would be exceedingly rash to suppose that the difficulties of 1566 differed drastically from those of 1571, except that in the latter year the final outcome was better managed; and those of 1571 manifestly arose not from political disputes but from cross-cutting endeavours to clean up the statute book, keeping what had proved desirable but modifying or abandoning what various people, from the Council to private members, wished to delete. After all, that sort of thing had been the reason in the first place for passing time-limited acts; and after all, that kind of exercise in revision had been asked for by the lord keeper at the start of almost every session.

The next Parliament met in 1572 and was by repeated prorogations to endure until dissolved *in absentia* on April 1583. It was therefore just as well that the expiring laws continuance act passed in the first session;[76] if the Council had waited until later, the bill might easily have failed to

[74] 5 Eliz. I c. 7; also 5 Eliz. I c. 9 (perjury), 8 Eliz. I cc. 10 (bowyers), 15 (crows).
[75] 1 Eliz. I c. 40; 5 Eliz. I c. 7.
[76] 14 Eliz. I c. 11; *LJ* I, 719–21, 724; *CJ* I, 102–3.

appear in the expectation of a session after that of 1581. Passage in the first session also indicates that this Parliament, like its predecessor, had been intended to last but the one session. It had mainly been called to deal with the affair of the Queen of Scots, and the decision to keep it in being evidently came at a late date. The continuance bill, like its predecessor, started in the Lords but unlike its predecessor was not introduced until 7 June when the two Houses had been sitting for just about a month, at which date, therefore, a dissolution was still in prospect. The bill finally passed on 27 June, three days before the end of the session, and I suspect that Elizabeth opted for prorogation only right at the end. The decision to veto the bill concerning Mary Stuart while pretending that after due study it would come back may lie behind a choice which made that pretence more credible; so also may Norton's opinion, offered at the start of the session, that prorogued Parliaments caused less trouble than new ones.[77]

The passage of the bill again posed problems, including yet another conference between the Houses at which the Lords agreed to all the amendments proposed by the Commons. In the Lords, the official bill passed quickly and without any changes, but once again the Lower House wished to use the occasion for the modification of several of the acts renewed. The result was to give the statute a very odd appearance. As the Original Act shows, the Lords bill was a simple measure, following precedent by reciting the acts to be continued in one long preamble and then enacting their prolonged life in the single section of the act. However, a parchment sheet bearing the Commons' amendments was then interpolated between the last act recited and the continuation formula, adding six sections to the act and just about doubling its length. The original recital made some changes in the law. Somebody discovered and added the act of 24 Henry VIII c. 7, touching the killing of calves, a probationer which had never been renewed because c. 9 of the same statute seemed sufficient to cover the ground; this at least testifies to a searching scrutiny of the acts and a serious attempt to keep the record straight. 5 Eliz. I c. 3 (vagabonds) disappeared because it had been repealed by another act (14 Eliz. I c. 5) which had passed only three days before the continuance bill started on its career;[78] this indicates that the new act was included in the Council's pre-sessional planning.[79] The four acts of the previous Parliament which required continuation were, of course, added to the tally. The Commons did not attempt to vary that list. Rather surprisingly they secured the repeal of the saving clause in the act of 1571 which had exempted commercial treaties from the ban on foreign imports, no doubt a victory for native manufacturers but

[77] Below, p. 324.
[78] *LJ* I, 716.
[79] The act has the shortest enacting clause possible: 'Be it enacted that'.

probably of little practical effect since no one just then was engaging in making such treaties. The main import of the Commons' intervention amounted to a tightening up and beneficial modification of two acts passed in the previous Parliament concerning leases of ecclesiastical lands and of lands owned by colleges and corporations.[80] The amendments tended to the protection of lessees and the proper use of monies obtained in recompense for dilapidations.

By 1581, where we leave the subject, the problems of probationers and their renewal had thus emerged in complex and contested continuance acts which took up much time. The practice of continuing this or that probationer by special act, still common in the 1560s, had not entirely ceased but it had grown very rare. This probably reflects a better search by the makers of the official bill for what needed renewing, so that gradually nothing was left over to be caught up by separate acts. In 1571 only the statute for separating certain counties hitherto administered by the same sheriff needed this treatment, and no act at all received it in 1572, 1576 and 1581. Expiring laws continuance acts had become routine; they increasingly attended to all expiring laws; and they always raised debate, difficulty and delay. Each session, of course, added further to the problem by enacting new probationers, and by the reign of James I the practice was extended to a good many local acts, always wasters of parliamentary time. Things were then further complicated by the occurrence of Parliaments in which no acts passed at all; these were conveniently declared to be no Parliaments, so that the experience of 1566 did not recur and the expiring laws survived. None of this assisted efficiency in controlling probationers. From 1587 (with an earlier tentative example in 1584) continuance bills always started in a Commons committee, in an attempt to get all interested parties to contribute their demands to the bill as first presented, but it soon became apparent that this device only aggravated delays. So in 1621 the Council tackled the problem more effectively by setting up a committee charged with revising the statute book before the session opened, in the hope that the resulting bill would prove uncontested; one of the members of that committee of lawyers, William Hakewill, then chaired the Commons committee which rested its drafting labours on that preliminary exercise. This became practice, but it had taken a long time to settle the routine of reviewing time-limited legislation with real efficiency.[81] Only the statute-law revision committees of the Interregnum, and really only those of the nineteenth century, in the end succeeded in clearing the jungle created by the policy of permitting revision of laws without the laborious process of separate acts of repeal or amendment.

[80] 13 Eliz. I cc. 10, 20.
[81] For all this cf. Lambert, *EHR* 95 (1980), 779–80.

PART III

Bills and acts

7

Supply

As everybody knows, parliamentary consent was required for the levying of all money coming to the Crown, except for its own proper sources of revenue – Crown lands, the profits of justice and the courts, and the income derived from the monarch's position as head of the feudal pyramid (the so-called prerogative revenue, especially wardship). Supposedly, the Queen covered all ordinary expenses concerning herself, her court and the government of the realm with the means gathered under her independent entitlement, and called upon Parliament only when exceptional needs, especially of defence, demanded extraordinary supply, but even in constitutional theory this is not quite accurate. Two items of the so-called ordinary revenue had also to be voted to the Crown in Parliament before they could be collected since neither stemmed from the prerogative – the regular income from the Church, and the customs duties.

The clerical Tenths (a 10 per cent income tax) and First Fruits (one year's income payable by every newly appointed occupant of a benefice), which were first allocated to the Crown in 1534,[1] had been restored to the Church by Queen Mary, so that if Elizabeth was to recover this revenue she needed in her first Parliament an act to repeal her sister's repeal.[2] The relevant bill, manifestly coming from the Council though cast in the form of a petition from both Houses, was introduced in the Lords on 30 January 1559, just a week after the session had opened; evidently it had been prepared ahead of the meeting of Parliament. Its course did not, however, prove to be as smooth as one might have expected, and its history is obscured by the fact that the Original Act now extant was manifestly copied out afresh, in the form of a roll, at the end of its passage, so that it is no longer possible to identify the sources of the various changes that occurred. The original Council bill passed the Lords quickly enough and without amendment; it reached the

[1] 26 Henry VIII c. 3.

[2] 2 & 3 Philip & Mary c. 4; 1 Eliz. I c. 4.

Commons on 6 February.[3] There it staggered, being surprisingly committed both on first reading and on second. William Fleetwood took charge of it on the first occasion, but on the second it was quite properly left to Sir Richard Sackville, chancellor of the Exchequer, to preside over the revising committee.[4] All this reconsideration produced some provisos – five, according to the Lords Journal – and it took over a fortnight to return the amended bill to the Upper House.[5] Instead of contenting themselves with the Commons' desires, the Lords committed the revised bill to the law officers and then, against the opposition of eight Marian bishops and the last abbot of Westminster, approved an additional list of six more provisos of their own.[6] Because of these further alterations it had to be once more seen by the other House, and though the Commons made no more changes the bill was not done with until 22 March, some seven weeks after its first appearance and just before the date originally intended for the end of the session.

The recopying of the act renders obscure what was done to it during its passage. One correction on the Original Act adds 'heirs and successors' to 'the Queen's majesty' in the main clause, a very necessary amendment if the revenue was to belong to the Crown beyond Elizabeth's life, but the words, written in on the copied parchment, probably correct only a scribal error. Two lines are erased in section 2, but what they may have said cannot now be told; the section makes straightforward sense as it stands. According to the Journals, eleven provisos were added after the bill had first reached the Commons, which means that the original bill included only the long preamble (reciting the history of First Fruits and explaining the financial needs of the Crown) and two sections – one reassigning the revenue in question, and the other forming the conventional general saving clause. The rest of the act – a series of exemptions and closer definitions – was added in Parliament. Several of these additions brought back modifications of the law passed after 1534 and before Mary gave the money back to the Church; they restored the position of 1553. The wonder is that the short and categorical version which the Council seems originally to have wanted passed the Lords without opposition, whereas the modified bill met resistance there; the bishops seem to have been slow to rally. At any rate, Universities and colleges, among others now exempt, had cause to bless a procedure which made piecemeal amendment possible. One proviso failed in the Lower House, and its promoters tried, with some effrontery, to gain their ends with a hurried bill exempting lay farmers of Church lands (impropriators)

[3] *LJ* I, 544–5; *CJ* I, 54.
[4] Ibid.
[5] 21 Feb.; ibid. 55; *LJ* I, 552.
[6] 15 March: ibid. 563.

from the tenth; though the bill got two readings and was ordered to be engrossed, it vanished thereafter.[7]

The other regular finance bill ran into no difficulties, which was just as well because the solvency of the Crown depended upon it more than upon any other single measure. This was the bill for tunnage and poundage, that is to say, for all customs duties on exports and imports. Following the standard practice of making the grant to the monarch in person, it created the life interest that had become customary in the course of the fifteenth century and that necessitated a fresh grant at the beginning of every reign. The justification offered – assistance in the defence of the realm – was also conventional and in practice quite meaningless; a great many things were charged on the customs that not even the liveliest imagination could have classified as defence expenditure. In form a petition of the Commons, who claimed to be acting with the advice of the Lords, it asked (section 4) that the grant offered be enacted by the full Parliament, but the practice of transmuting the text of such formalized petitions into properly phrased enactments had been abandoned in the reign of Henry VII (together with the translating of the English petition into the French of the statute), so that this clause looks vestigial.[8] Oddly enough, it is not; it belongs to a drafting convention which began after the time that acts were rephrased from petitions. The pattern followed by the Elizabethan act goes back no further than 1547, the accession of Edward VI, when the medieval device of a contract between king and Commons (in the form of an indenture) was replaced by a normal act of Parliament, the transformational effects of the 1530s having intervened since the last previous grant of 1510. The bill started in the Commons and, though slightly delayed by other business in the Lords, passed all stages in three weeks; there is no sign that either House tampered with what the Council prepared.[9] It must be remembered that the tunnage and poundage act really represented an endorsement of current practice rather than an authority for a start; the act became law on 8 May 1559, when Elizabeth accepted the grant, with effect from 23 January 1559, the first day of the Parliament, but she had, of course, been collecting the customs since 18 November 1558 when she ascended the throne.

These life grants added to the regular income of the Crown. That leaves genuine grants of taxation – grants, that is, made on particular occasions for one stated set of collections. Taxation in this strict sense consisted of the subsidy of the clergy and of two taxes voted by the laity – the old fifteenth and tenth (a levy on movables fixed at a

[7] *CJ* I, 55–6 (28 Feb., 3 Mar.).
[8] *Studies*, III, 129.
[9] *CJ* I, 53–5; *LJ* I, 548, 551, 557; 1 Eliz. I c. 20.

standardized sum in 1334 and rated on localities) and the new subsidy, a levy on every form of income which had been devised and perfected in the second decade of the sixteenth century. The granting of the clerical tax was the business of the Convocations of the provinces, but since 1540 these grants had always been confirmed by act of Parliament. In this symbolic demonstration of the supremacy of statute the Parliament's role was purely formal. On the five occasions that the clergy were asked for money (1563, 1566, 1571, 1576, 1581) the bill was introduced in the Lords soon after the middle of the session and passed all stages in a few days without a hitch.[10]

It was, of course, a different story with the taxation for which Parliament was directly responsible – that taxation which, as Sir Nicholas Bacon's speeches so delicately hinted, usually formed the Crown's chief reason for calling a Parliament at all. Only in 1572, when the problem of the Queen of Scots persuaded Elizabeth into facing a Parliament only about a year after the previous one had gone home, was no supply requested. It would have been difficult – or at least an unwelcome return to the intensive taxing days of the 1540s – to ask for money at a time when the second payment of the subsidy granted in 1571 was still outstanding. Otherwise, every single session called voted supply, and thanks to the practice of granting each time two fifteenths and tenths and one subsidy, all collectable in two yearly instalments, half of the twenty-four years from 1559 to 1581 (in none of which the Queen was formally at war) witnessed the activities of tax collectors. As is well known, assessments for the subsidy had lost the accuracy prevalent under Henry VIII and the Queen never got what she should have had from the nation, but even so, this regularity of 'extraordinary' taxation calls for some rethinking of received notions touching Tudor finance.

Here, however, we are concerned not with the efficiency of tax collection or the use of the money but only with what happened in Parliament, though the ease with which burdens could be evaded by the well placed and well connected may have played its part in rendering the Commons readier to vote those regular grants. They did so throughout in response to appeals from the throne that emphasized the needs of the Crown and attempted, with some embarrassment, to maintain a trace of the traditional justification for supply, namely the fact or threat of war. Bacon liked to make play with foreign dangers and the costs of maintaining coastal defences, but he could rarely afford to be specific. Elizabeth's

[10] 5 Eliz. I c. 29 (*LJ* I, 597, 599, 602; *CJ* I, 67–8); 8 Eliz. I c. 17 (*LJ* I, 655–7, 663; *CJ* I, 79–80); 13 Eliz. I c. 26 (*LJ* I, 687–8, 690–1; *CJ* I, 91, 93); 18 Eliz. I c. 22 (*LJ* I, 738–40, 745; *CJ* I, 110, 112–13); 23 Eliz. I c. 14 (*LJ* II, 41, 43–4; *CJ* I, 131: the bill passed on the question after one reading).

anxiety to appear as a prince of peace meant that the lord keeper never mentioned actual fighting even when he could have done, while the preambles of the acts, drafted by the Council, justified grants of supply on the very general grounds that government as excellent as that provided by Elizabeth deserved support. Thus everybody accepted that regular peacetime taxation had come to stay and that the ordinary rather than the extraordinary tasks of government obliged the nation to assist the Queen financially. Notions of the monarch 'living off his own' had vanished in the middle of Henry VIII's reign, when grants of money were demanded just after the King's own had been enormously enhanced by the wealth of the Church; in Elizabeth's day even echoes of that ancient concept are exceedingly rare.[11]

However willing the Commons may have been to do their patriotic duty, the business of getting the subsidy through was always and obviously a delicate one, if only because in consenting to a grant members of the Lower House burdened their constituents whom they would have to face on returning home. In addition, the constitutional principle that in making a grant the House, apparently of its own free will, offered generous support to the Crown, opened the way to anyone who wished to raise a grievance or discover some offence to feelings in the handling of the issue. Supply was thus always a potential occasion for trouble. Francis Bacon, reviewing the sessions of 1610 and 1614 in an effort to account for the mess they had got into, put his finger on the financial demands of the Crown and identified two major errors in management. The worst thing done, he maintained, was to make it plain

> that the end and cause of calling a Parliament was to pay the king's debts and supply his wants, which in itself did great hurt by putting upon the king the person of a mendicant and was contrary to the honourable form of all former Parliaments (wherein, were the cause of want never so manifest, it was never acknowledged by the State, but fell in upon the bye).[12]

He had offered much the same advice even before the Addled Parliament met when he had urged a return to 'the ancient form (for I account it but a form), which was to voice the Parliament to be for some other

[11] *Studies* III, 216–33, and J. D. Alsop, 'The Theory and Practice of Tudor Taxation,' *EHR* 97 (1982), 1–30. G. L. Harriss ('Thomas Cromwell's "New Principle" of taxation,' ibid. 93 [1978], 721–38) has tried to maintain that this sort of peacetime taxation still obeyed medieval rules as to entitlement, but he mistakes conventional phrasing designed to persuade for the reality of policy; he also ignores the regularity of taxing and the regular use of taxes for general purposes. When a rumour circulated in January 1579 that the Queen would be offered, and accept, the rulership of the Low Countries, informed opinion at once concluded that this was 'a device for a subsidy' (*The Papers of Sir Nathaniel Bacon of Stiffkey*, ed. A. H. Smith, I [Norwich, 1979], 182).

[12] Spedding, *Letters and Life*, I, 179.

business of estate, and not merely for money; but that to come in upon the bye, whatsoever the truth be'. Not that he wished to advocate deceit, but if the King was to maintain an ascendancy it was desirable to make sure 'that the people have something else to talk of and not wholly of the king's estate'.[13] The second error committed in the recent past, he added, was to have the issue of money raised, as it were, officially, instead of putting up somebody (in 1604 this had been that 'honest gentleman', Edward Montagu) to open the subject; this sound practice he alleged had been abandoned on Salisbury's initiative in 1606.[14] Bacon claimed to have learned these necessary ways from his experience in Queen Elizabeth's time 'in whose reign things were so well settled and disposed, as if she demanded anything it was seldom denied, and if she pretended any it was never enquired'.[15] His political sense outranked his memory of history.

Make sure that the Parliament has business other than the Crown's needs to consider, and arrange for the response to the statement of need, given in the speech from the throne, to be initiated from the floor of the House: that way you will get what you want, and no one will look too closely at the needs set out. Bacon did not, of course, mean to suggest that the raising of a supply should genuinely be left to the spontaneous good will of some private member; he would assuredly have agreed with Norton's advice in 1572 that, while it was always tactful to avoid raising possibly contentious issues too obviously through the official element in the House, business must be speeded up by thorough preparation beforehand: it was wise, for instance, to have 'the subsidy book ready written in paper and parchment' (first draft and engrossment).[16] That conscientious manager of Parliaments, Thomas Cromwell, who always took great care to have his bills ready for the session, would have applauded.

Let us therefore see whether these managerial principles were indeed observed between 1559 and 1581, and whether the Queen really did succeed in getting what she wanted without the sort of disputations which questioned the needs she put forward. She certainly did get a grant every time she asked for one, in which she did even better than Henry VIII who had failed to gain agreement to a subsidy in 1532.[17] However, the history of subsidy bills makes plain that the Commons, at least, did not take their grants lightly; getting them through generally took up a large part of the session, giving point to Norton's comment that members, suspecting that once the subsidy was through the session was likely to

[13] Ibid. 372. [14] Ibid. 178. [15] Ibid. 177.
[16] BL, Harleian MS 253, fos. 34v–35.
[17] Lehmberg, *Reformation Parliament*, 133, 157.

end shortly, were liable to 'give as many delays to that matter as they may'.[18] In 1585, when the session continued after the granting of the subsidy, political gossip supposed that some important news was expected from abroad which would need the attention of the Parliament.[19] Usually discussion of the bill started early in the session – within two to nine days from the opening – except in 1566 when nearly three weeks were allowed to pass. Twice only, however, did it conclude within three weeks – in 1559, when the beginning of the reign no doubt assisted patriotic generosity, and in 1576 when perhaps the memory of the previous session without any demands speeded passage. Usually, discussions and interventions in the Lower House span things out to about seven weeks all told, while in 1566, when for once the opportunity of tieing political demands to the granting of supply was seriously contemplated, the bill took nine weeks to get through (in a session lasting three months which included Christmas). Thus Norton was evidently right in part: a House, many of whose members had business to promote that would suffer from a short session, knew how to keep Parliament in being by not passing the subsidy too speedily. On the other hand, the facts do not bear out the reported suspicion of their sovereign: the passage of the bill never terminated the session. A little leeway was obviously necessary because the Lords, in this matter always very expeditious, needed to give their formal consent; but in fact Parliaments always remained in being for some time even after all money business was ended. The unexpected extension of the 1559 session arose from special causes,[20] but in 1563 nearly six weeks remained before the prorogation, and the shortest continuation (1581) ran to ten days. If Elizabeth really wished to close sessions as soon as she had her money, the pressure of business defeated her.

To judge from the history of the various bills, Norton's advice touching preparation at most enlarged on practice.[21] The Council entered the session with a bill in hand certainly in 1563 and possibly in 1576 and 1581; on every occasion it had carefully prepared the essential terms of the grant, even if the actual bill had not been written out beforehand. In any case, it could always expect so many discussions and at least the possibility of changes that a prepared and engrossed bill could well become merely a waste of parchment. It looks as though the engrossing stage was always real. Francis Bacon's notion that it was unwise to let the matter be raised by a councillor was only patchily reflected in practice. Surprisingly enough, it was tried several times but

[18] BL, Harleian MS 253, fo. 35.

[19] *CSP Foreign Eliz.*, XIX, 359.

[20] Jones, *Faith by Statute*, passim.

[21] All this analysis rests on *CJ* and *LJ*; the evidence is cited in more detail below.

then abandoned, at least for a time. We do not know who first mentioned supply in 1559, but an unnamed burgess took the necessary steps in 1563, unquestionably under instruction; he was at once followed by Cecil who made the real speech for supply. Cecil also did the serious talking in 1566 though the first words were then spoken by Sir Edward Rogers, comptroller of the Household and a very elderly, respected and ineffectual councillor. In 1571, taught by experience, the Council held back and the move came from Robert Newdigate, a fact which puts him with some certainty among the Council's 'men of business'; he was backed up by Sir Francis Knollys, treasurer of the Household and privy councillor – Cecil having moved to the Lords. However, in the last two sessions under review the business was handled from the first by a councillor – Sir Walter Mildmay, chancellor of the Exchequer – nor does this seem to have caused any problems. It looks as though the House had got tired of this piece of flummery: everybody knew that the subsidy was a chief cause of the session and feelings were not ruffled by an open admission of the fact, so long as no obstacles were put in the way of a proper debate.

All the evidence suggests that none ever was; in the House of Commons, at least, the production of the subsidy act went forward in a serious, responsible and sometimes disputatious manner. The Lords, of course, were not supposed to alter a grant and did so only once, in 1559; in their House, the subsidy bill always went through routinely, within three or four days. In the Commons procedure had apparently been settled long since, for it was followed with some regularity from the first. After the question of supply had been raised, the House appointed a committee to consider what should be done; the committee reported 'articles' (an outline scheme of the rates and dates of payment to be enacted) which, when approved, were turned into a bill either by the same committee or by some legal experts; and the bill then went through the usual stages of readings, engrossment and passage, after which it was despatched to the Lords. Procedure differed, however, in one detail from that appropriate to other bills: whereas all these after passage in both Houses were gathered in by the clerk of the Upper House in readiness for the assent, the subsidy bill was supposed to return to the Commons for the Speaker to present it to the Queen at the close of the session. In 1581, the Lords, who had been somewhat at odds with the Commons throughout the session, pretended otherwise. When the message came that the session was to end that day it was discovered that the subsidy bill still lay with the clerk of the Parliaments, and when the Commons recovered it it came with a message 'that the use is indifferent, either to take it there or send it hither'.[22] The Commons firmly denied

[22] *CJ* I, 136.

any such indifference, but if the Journals are to be trusted the Lords had indeed more commonly before this retained the bill for the assent. Either the Commons' claim was innovatory, or the Journals, by negligence, missed out the last transfer back to the Commons – and the second possibility is the more likely because certainly at the closing ceremony the Speaker regularly made a presentation of the grant.

Subsidy bills thus were not foregone conclusions and could always involve real difficulties; they therefore required constant management. On the other hand, they always went through; that is to say, they got that management. In 1559 the story is brief and simple. On 31 January, in effect the second working day of the session, the Commons appointed a committee of four lawyers to draft the bill which then received its first reading on 3 February. This makes the odds very high that the committee worked on a scheme prepared beforehand by the government rather than that it started from scratch. Even the writing out of the paper bill (which in the printed edition runs to thirteen very large pages)[23] would have filled the time allowed, leaving none for the hammering out of its originally thirty sections. The four days between the second and third readings (6 to 10 February) just permitted the engrossing of the parchment bill which on the 11th went to the Lords.[24] These intervals should be regarded as normal and indicative of an unhindered passage; longer ones on other occasions can alert one to events in Parliament. For once the bill was held up in the Upper House, being handed to the attorney and solicitor general after first reading and passed only with some corrections whose insertion the Lords demanded.[25] However, there was nothing sinister about this. What caused the Lords to intervene was a petition they received from the inhabitants of Wales and Cheshire, seeking exemption from the subsidy on the grounds that they already paid the special payment to a new monarch called 'mises'. Evidently the petitioners had either supposed that this routine item would appear in the bill or had been too late to get their case before the Lower House; their use of the Upper reflected a slow uptake rather than insolence. Assured by the lord keeper that the Queen had no objection, the Lords authorized the exemption and commended it, as propriety demanded, to the Commons; it accounts for sections 31 and 32 of the bill.[26] Since these are not the tail end of the bill, and since no sign of insertion can be seen on the Original

[23] *SR* IV, 384–96. This is about the usual length; subsidy acts changed very little in detail.
[24] *CJ* I, 53–4.
[25] *LJ* I, 548–50 (11–16 Feb.).
[26] BL, Cotton MS Titus F.i, fo. 15. The decision was taken at the second reading, on 15 Feb., and this exemption came to be a standard part of subsidy acts. For the effect of Welsh mises cf. G. R. Elton in *Welsh Society and Nationhood*, ed. R. R. Davies et al. (Cardiff, 1984), 110–11.

Act (a roll of parchment membranes sewn together), it looks as though at any rate the last membrane was written out afresh, a step which by itself would have required returning the bill once more to the Lords. At any rate, there it went and there it stayed. By seeking the Queen's agreement to the exemption, the Lords had made it indiscreetly plain that the subsidy bill originated with the Crown and that the appearance of a voluntary gift meant nothing. Of one more move to escape taxation there is no trace on the act. When preparing for the Parliament the city of York instructed its members 'if it happens any tax to be granted to the Queen's majesty at this Parliament then they to make suit to release an abatement thereof to the city's use'.[27] However, York was not seeking exemption so much as redirection of the cash, and a later note indicated that we have here another well-established routine: after the passage of the act (and following precedents going back to Henry VIII) the city's members in the Parliament apparently petitioned for royal letters to the collectors which released something like one-third of the fifteenth and tenth assessed on York into the city's coffers.[28]

Naturally enough, the first Parliament of a new reign saw everybody anxious to get off to a peaceful start. The government never again found the obtaining of supply quite so easy and untroubled. In 1563 and 1566, the money bill got entangled in political moves designed to make the Queen act over her marriage and the succession to the Crown, matters which shall be discussed properly elsewhere but cannot be left out altogether here.[29] In 1563 nothing was left to chance, as Cecil's memoranda of late 1562 show. He noted that he would 'have the book of subsidy put in readiness' and scribbled the names of those appointed to draft it ('Mr Attorney and Mr Solicitor') in the margin. A second note reminded him to appoint someone 'to offer unto the Lower House the necessity her majesty has to require a subsidy' with an explanation that the session was to be short and the Queen would wish them to 'forbear to deal in unnecessary matters'.[30] The latter intent misfired: the session was to last three months, chiefly because of the campaign for the settlement of the succession but also on account of the considerable bulk of legislation undertaken. However, the passage of the subsidy bill contributed its share to the delays; it must seem as though the warning concerning a short session had produced only a determination not to

[27] 10 Jan. 1559: *YCR* VI, 2.

[28] Below, n. 38.

[29] Below, pp. 357–74.

[30] SP 12/40, fo. 149. The date (wrongly given as 1566 in a modern note on the document) is established by Cecil's addition, 'Mr Walsingham to be of the House'. Walsingham, who had sat in 1559, was elected to the second Parliament of the reign for its first session, of course, not the second as Conyers Read had it: *Mr Secretary Walsingham and the Policy of Queen Elizabeth* (Oxford, 1925), I, 356.

agree too quickly to supply and thus avoid an early termination. The fact that the 1563 bill imposed a heavier burden than that of 1559 will have helped by offering material for debate. When 'a burgess' rose to move for it on the ninth day of the session he was evidently carrying out the plan put up by Cecil himself who then followed with a powerful statement of needs.[31] Five days later, a large committee – all the privy councillors in the House, twenty-four knights of the shire and six Welsh members – was appointed to draft the bill, with Sir Edward Rogers in the chair; revealingly enough, the stage of preparing articles was left out. However, even though the committee presumably had before them the draft mentioned in Cecil's notes they did not bring in the bill for a first reading until 6 February.[32] Writing the next day to his friend Sir Thomas Smith (on embassy to France) that 'a subsidy is agreed in the Common House', Cecil rather rashly assumed that the committee's proposals would go through without any hold-up.[33]

This was not to be. The second reading led to three days of debate, and though no doubt the burdens of taxation were mentioned, and though perhaps (there is no evidence to that effect) some tactics concerning the petition for the succession may have been involved, the only thing we know to have caused trouble was the oath demanded of the commissioners for the assessment.[34] It seems that objections were raised against compelling people to swear to the truth of assessments when everybody knew that these were commonly fudged: to cause people 'to forswear themselves' for a trifle was thought unwise and unjust, with speakers citing the precedent of the bill for the export of horses (1 Eliz. I c. 7) from which an oath-taking clause had been removed for similar reasons.[35] The issue is not as innocent as perhaps it looks: if assessments were ever to be made realistic again, it was very necessary to compel commissioners to do their duty. Three days of arguments around this matter in fact suggest that the government, unwilling to accept the

[31] *CJ* I, 63. Neale (*EP* I, 123) ignored the pre-sessional preparation and called the motion one of 'spontaneous loyalty...of a Puritan zealot'.

[32] *CJ* I, 63, 65. Neale (*EP* I, 124) asserted that the committee 'certainly' rewrote the preamble and introduced the rather lavish praise for the Queen; he spoke of a 'genuine outburst of feeling'. This assertion thereafter plays its part in explaining propagandist activities ascribed to the 'opposition'. There is no evidence for this at all, nor any reason for conjecturing it.

[33] BL, Lansdowne MS 102, fo. 20v. Agreement had also been prematurely forecast by Geoffrey Tothill, member for Exeter, when writing home on 31 Jan. (HMC, *Exeter*, 52).

[34] *CJ* I, 65.

[35] Strype, *Annals of the Reformation*, I, 453: speech by Robert Atkinson on the bill for treason. Neale's ascription of the scruple to 'the puritan conscience of the House' (*EP* I, 125) is unsupported guesswork; Atkinson was later expelled from his Inn for popery (HPT I, 362).

pointlessness of the oath, was determined to restore some virtue to subsidy assessments, after the mid-century collapse of the tax-gathering machinery. However, they lost on this occasion and indeed for good. After they gave way the bill was ordered to be engrossed and then passed on third reading on 19 February. It too drew some queries from the Lords on some point not known to us, though they passed it in three days; it therefore once more returned to the Lower House and was finally despatched on the 27th.[36] On that same day, Cecil – who had led the delegation that carried the finished bill up – could properly tell Smith that 'a subsidy and two fifteenths are granted'.[37] York made its usual request for relief and this time recorded its success: it received £100 out of a fifteenth of about £270, by writ to the Exchequer.[38] The session intended to be short lasted another five weeks and more after the subsidy was done with, and the Queen's business finished. The reason lay in a massive tally of bills, and while these had been somewhat delayed by the early-session agitation over the succession and the mid-session debates over supply it is plain that there was in any case too much legislative business, much of it the Council's, crowding the agenda for a short session to be feasible.

In 1563, the subsidy had possibly been affected by politics, inasmuch as the House was in a difficult mood after the Queen had stalled over their succession petition. As we have seen, some efforts to prolong the session had been made by delaying over supply, but in the end the bill had not been put to any direct political use. In 1566, politics and money were to interact more positively. That that session witnessed attempts to use the Queen's need to force her into a public settlement of the succession and a declaration of her intention to marry need not be questioned, though it is a deal more doubtful whether this attempt was widely supported and organized by something to be called a puritan opposition group.[39] In any case, it is quite wrong to treat the disputes solely as a reflection of the political argument and to ignore the clear evidence that the demand for money by itself caused considerable difficulties. There were two problems. In the first place, in 1563 the Queen had committed herself to promises that such demands would not be repeated.[40] In 1566

[36] *CJ* I, 65–6; *LJ* I, 593–5.

[37] BL, Lansdowne MS 102, fo. 24v.

[38] *YCR* VI, 50, 56, 66. The writ issued on 16 April 1563, immediately after the end of the session. In recording its desire for relief, the city council noted that it had always had it, back to Henry VIII and forward to 1559. After the 1566 session the writ was long delayed; it issued only in Jan. 1568 after the city had brought matters to a head by retaining the usual abatement without authority (ibid. 129, 132). In 1576 the writ came within two weeks of the close of the session (ibid. VII, 155–6).

[39] As Neale claimed: *EP* I, 135–64.

[40] BL, Harleian MS 5176, fo. 91.

no recent defence commitments could be pleaded, as came out clearly when Cecil re-used the expedition to Le Havre which had already done duty on the previous occasion; the new tax unashamedly constituted a peacetime imposition, naturally enough a sore point with the Commons who had to think of reaction at home if they returned with yet another grant made that did not meet traditional criteria of 'need'.[41] In the second place, the subsidy proposed in 1566 was larger than its predecessors – three instalments (that is, three separate annual levies) instead of two. Even if supply had never got entangled with succession, it would on those terms have led to trouble.

The Council's embarrassment emerged from the start in its failure to follow up the lord keeper's announcement of financial need by setting the usual machinery in motion. It looks as though on this occasion no unofficial member could be found to introduce the granting of supply, though whether the exceptional delay – twice as long from the opening of the session as the longest interval experienced in any other Parliament – reflected a jostling for tactical advantage between succession-hunting oppositionists and a government unwilling to risk that subject coming up must be questioned. When at last the subject was tackled, the indications of prearrangement are strong, but the planning was done by councillors.[42] On 18 October the Council itself moved for supply, with a delicate remark from the comptroller, Rogers, that the House might 'have consideration of the Queen's majesty', a hint brutally glossed by the clerk as 'meaning for some aid'. Cecil followed with a long speech in an effort to rouse a patriotic willingness to pay.[43] Though the usual committee was appointed – all privy councillors, the master of the Rolls, and forty members of the House – this was done, if the French ambassador is to be believed (and he probably is), after some acrimonious exchanges during which the Queen's needs were firmly called in question and an enquiry called for into the way in which earlier grants had been spent.[44] Francis Bacon's recollection that Elizabeth's financial needs were never doubted seems to have been mistaken. Next day, John Molyneux introduced the linking of the succession question with supply, but did so in order to get the second moving after the protests it had encountered; that he was not speaking in opposition is confirmed by the support he immediately received from Sir Ralph Sadler, one of the Queen's most experienced and most loyal privy councillors.[45] Money, it seems, rather than politics had caused the hitch in the well prepared proceedings.

On this occasion the committee did not even pretend that it itself

[41] Neale (*EP* I, 173) recognized the point and then forgot it.

[42] As Neale agreed (ibid. 135–6).

[43] *CJ* I, 74.

[44] Neale, *EP* I, 137.

[45] Below, pp. 365–73.

devised the details of the subsidy. Cecil took charge of it when it met on the 18th: he held the list of members, recorded the agreed rates to be levied, and on the 19th reported them to the House.[46] However, from this point onwards concentration on bringing the Queen to a point over the succession caused mounting delays in which the subsidy got intermittently involved as a tactical instrument for forcing her hand.[47] Actually, the Commons rather overestimated her determination to raise the money, and the weapon in effect broke in their hands, but Cecil certainly, and not surprisingly, seems to have worried over supply. The bill was not read a first time until 28 October, nine days after he had reported its terms, and it reached second reading nearly a month later. Even then the bill was read only because on that day (27 November) Cecil could tell the House that the Queen had graciously remitted the third instalment of the subsidy, thus restoring its terms to those imposed in 1563.[48] It was this concession, and certainly not earlier peace moves over the succession, which at once mollified the House and brought the bill out of limbo, a sequence of events which clearly indicates that resistance had derived from objections to financial demands rather than from political manoeuvring. Trouble was still not over. At this late stage a drafting problem arose and the bill was – most unusually for a money bill – committed on second reading.[49] It seems that what caused trouble was the preamble. Some people deeply involved in the political campaign did want to use it to record the Queen's supposed promise to settle the succession and to marry, so that her conciliatory message (by which she had no intention to abide) would become public property and thus bind her.[50] Her outraged fury scotched that manoeuvre at once, but this did not terminate delay. On 29 November there occurred that bane of parliamentary managers, a full sitting spent in arguments ('for a preamble to be had to the subsidy bill') before the order to engross could pass.[51] However, once again politics were not the problem; the real dispute arose over phrases which made it seem that the House was giving subjects' money away too readily. In the evening of the 29th, Sir William Cordell, master of the Rolls, saw two of the more active burgesses of the Commons, Robert Monson and Robert Bell, who still felt that as the

[46] SP 12/40, fos. 190–1; *CJ* I, 75. On the list Cecil marked those present; of the forty 'ordinary' members only half attended. His note on the rates shows that only two details were adjusted in the discussion. Englishmen, who were to pay altogether 27*d* in the £ on goods, were at first put down for instalments of 7*d*, 12*d* and 8*d*; this was changed to 7, 10, 10. For strangers the first instalment was increased from 20*d* to 2*s*.

[47] Below, p. 371.

[48] *CJ* I, 75, 78.

[49] Ibid. That the committal was for drafting only is indicated by the fact that Thomas Seckford, master of Requests, was put in charge: he seems never to have acted in the House except as a technical legal adviser.

[50] Neale, *EP* I, 162–4.

[51] *CJ* I, 78.

preamble stood it showed Parliament offering more than the Queen, after her earlier concession, had expressed her willingness to receive.[52] It was this open-handed generosity – evidently a relic of the preamble drafted when three instalments were demanded – and not the disappearance of the mention of the succession that troubled Monson and Bell. Cordell was able to satisfy them, but even so the bill did not pass until 12 December. After all this noise and delay, the Lords shot it through in two days.[53]

So in the end the Queen got her money – the usual, not the exceptional amount – and even had to fight a little to have her concession accepted by those who wished to blackmail her by generosity into agreeing to a settlement of the succession. The session had certainly been difficult, and Elizabeth had encountered a remarkable degree of determined trouble-making. Among those left far from satisfied was, as we have already seen, her secretary of state. Cecil was well aware that the Commons (egged on by whom?) had 'offered largely to the end to have the succession established',[54] but some notes he made during the business indicate that he did not stand aside from that manoeuvre. There he linked the willingness of the House to grant supply with gratitude for the Queen's inclination to marry and with further pressure to get the whole problem firmly sewn up.[55] His sour summing up of a session which had ended pretty unsatisfactorily reveals his disappointment: nothing really settled about succession or marriage, various important measures frustrated, and so forth.[56] Among the unsatisfactory results he included 'a subsidy to be levied'. The man responsible for financing the conduct of government would undoubtedly have lamented the loss of the third instalment, but he was not, of course, displeased by getting something. He regretted not the subsidy as such but the fact that it was one of the few pieces in his programme that had got through. Elizabeth had indeed won (as Cecil's notes hinted, contrary to her councillors' wishes) but at some cost to relations with the Parliament and more cost to her temper. She had beaten off or sidetracked the political attack, and she had got her supply – professedly all she wanted – without having to satisfy grievances.

In 1571, the subsidy caused no trouble at all but it was once again caught up in parliamentary manoeuvring. This was the first Elizabethan Parliament in which the Commons lacked the leadership of William Cecil, now Lord Burghley; management was in less experienced hands

[52] HMC, *Hatfield*, I, no. 1121 (and cf. Neale, *EP* I, 162).
[53] *CJ* I, 79; *LJ* I, 660.
[54] BL, Harleian MS 36, fo. 353.
[55] SP 12/40, fo. 194.
[56] SP 12/41, fo. 76.

and relied more than hitherto on non-councillors. Once the House had got itself a Speaker and settled to business, the first thing to happen was that the usual bill *pro forma* was replaced by a bill for compelling a more regular attendance at church.[57] Contrary to certain automatic expectations, this was no 'puritan' bill but one demanded by the bishops and forecast as long ago as 1563 in Bacon's opening address. A measure much desired in government circles, it was clearly produced at this stage by the Council itself, perhaps in the hope that introduction at the beginning would help to get it through. Nevertheless, starting the session on this note proved to be a mistake, a piece of clumsy management, because it gave their chance to those who wished to promote more drastic reform in the Church.[58] With a debate thus threatening on religion and bills for settling it, it became plain to the Council that only an arranged intervention could bring the House back to the business the Queen wanted to see despatched. Robert Newdigate therefore rose to remind the Commons of the Crown's needs and to propose the granting of a subsidy 'unasked'. The House, we hear, did not like his speech, but to judge from the sequel this reaction was prompted less by objections to taxation than by annoyance at a move (successful at that) to interrupt their running away on religion. That Newdigate's motion did not spring from his own mind – an unlikely event in itself anyway – is indicated by the immediate support he received from the senior councillor, Sir Francis Knollys.[59] The tactics of 1563 were being repeated.

However, as tactics the move turned out to be only partially successful, or so at least it looks on the surface. Launched now on a debate touching supply and unwilling just to proceed to the appointment of a committee for articles, several members proposed to link the grant with a petition for the redress of various grievances. Those events have already been analysed,[60] and it is here necessary only to emphasize that no opposition manoeuvres were in question. The Council, anxious about supply, secured the appointment of two committees, one to draw articles for a subsidy bill, the other to draw bills touching the grievances raised. Thus the making of the grant went ahead without interference from various discontents, the latter achieving little while the former returned to the normal practice. After its complicated start the subsidy bill encountered no more problems. Articles were brought in on 10 April,[61] but the committee to draw the bill appeared to take a little longer than one would have expected if they had had a prepared draft before them. Almost certainly, however, the bill had reached the clerk's hands quite quickly, after which he could find no place for it in a crowded agenda; when

[57] See above, p. 97.
[58] See below, pp. 201–2, 208–9.
[59] *CJ* I, 83; *Proc.* 202.
[60] Above, pp. 98–102.
[61] *CJ* I, 84.

Burghley, impatiently, looked into the state of bills before the House on 20 April he was hurriedly assured that the subsidy bill would be read next day.[62] So it was. One rash member, perhaps recalling 1566, began hesitatingly to question whether the country could stand any more taxes, but he seems to have found the House so little in sympathy that he broke off and sat down.[63] Though there was a further delay while the bill was engrossed, no more questions arose, and it passed peacefully on 8 May, passing the Lords also quickly and without mishap.[64] York looked for and got its customary relief, but a novel attempt by the city of Lincoln to secure 'a discharge...speedily' probably failed; at least there is no evidence of success.[65] Such difficulties as had attended the passage of this subsidy had nothing whatsoever to do either with any reluctance to pay taxes or with anti-government tactics. There had been some confusion among the inexperienced managers but that had been retrieved; signs of a mature opposition are visible only to the eye of committed innocence.

In any event, with this session all attempts to make political or factious, or even merely reformist, capital out of the Queen's demand for money came to an end. In both 1576 and 1581, the subsidy bill had a totally untroubled passage. It was brought forward quite early in both sessions: almost at once in 1576, and as soon as a small revolt over a political fast could be got out of the way in 1581.[66] Both times introduction was entrusted to the efficient hands of Sir Walter Mildmay whose careful, informed and informative speeches left no room for doubt or for questions about need. He even had the good sense to pander to the self-esteem of the House, giving some details on the use of the money which, he said, they had no right to know but might be interested to hear.[67] Both times the House duly appointed the usual committee to draw articles, and those prepared in 1576 survive. They list the various rates and dates of payment proposed, and they note that in form the bill was to be identical with that of 1571.[68] On both occasions the actual drafting was left to the law officers (no more drafting committees) who presented their efforts for first reading within three days. Engrossing again took a few days. Since effectively only the old act needed copying, it is likely that neither paper nor parchment draft was ready in advance; very probably the Council thought it enough to have the essential variables

62 SP 12/77, fos. 111–12.
63 *Proc.* 242.
64 *CJ* I, 85–6. 88; *LJ* I, 684–6.
65 *YCR* VII, 22, 33–4, 37; HMC, *14th Report*, App. VIII, 65.
66 *CJ* I, 104–5, 119.
67 Mildmay's speeches (printed after a fashion in D'Ewes; for the second see *Proc.* 502–8) are cited at length in Neale, *EP* I, 346–8, 382–5, and S. E. Lehmberg, *Sir Walter Mildmay* (Austin, Texas, 1964), 130–1, 173–6. This makes extended quotation here superfluous.
68 SP 12/107, fos. 73–4.

prepared and did not wish to risk any expensive recopying of the bill.[69]

Thus by 1581 the peacetime subsidy had become pure routine, in step with the routinizing of its yield at a level so low that it could not be regarded as a serious burden to tax-payers. Only once in those seven sessions had a serious effort been made to question the Crown's demands, and only one other time had supply offered an opportunity for the promotion of reforming bills. Both times the hand of the Council, frustrated by its mistress over action and measures it desired, had been more manifest than that of 'opposition'. The famous formula, 'redress of grievances before supply', had never once been heard. To all appearance, the House of Commons had come to accept that a session of Parliament would make a grant – that taxation was a regular incident of life – though it continued to like to hear reasons stated and gentle managerial persuasion applied. It is hard to see in those introductory speeches and committees for articles – advocating predetermined needs and settling predetermined details – anything more than a formality, though evidently a necessary formality.

Ancillary problems remained less formal. Since statute alone granted taxes, their incidence and administration could naturally become the subject of parliamentary attention. In various ways they did so, usually but not always through Council attempts to improve the collection and yield of revenue. Since customs duties, for instance, were rated *ad valorem* and the value of exports and imports was declared by their owner, the suspicion always existed that the Crown lost on the transaction – a suspicion very probably justified, especially as no one could trust the Elizabethan customs service to perform its duty without corruption. A bill 'for the true answering of the custom of merchandise' received a first reading on 7 April 1559 (too late in the session to do much good) and no more was heard of it;[70] perhaps its import, unknown to us, was thought satisfied by the brief navigation act of that session (1 Eliz. I c. 13). Nothing further along this line was attempted until the Lords read a bill 'for the due answering of customs and subsidies' on 5 March 1576, ten days before the end of the session; again, one reading was the end of the matter.[71] It is very hard to see who other than the Queen's government should have wanted to tighten up declarations of the value of customable goods, but it is also hard to understand why the Council should have given bills for that purpose so little chance to prosper. Still, not only the Queen failed to win over customs duties. In 1563, the city of London, worried over the capital's food supply, promoted a bill to lift

[69] *CJ* I, 106–8, 119, 123–4, 127, 130; *LJ* I, 737–9; II, 40, 42, 47.

[70] *CJ* I, 59.

[71] *LJ* I, 741.

all duties on bread grain imported into London, and instructed its two senior members in the Commons (Alderman Sir William Chester and the recorder, Ralph Cholmeley) to follow it in the House 'to the best of their power'. The bill was duly introduced on 11 February – only two days after the Common Council had resolved on it – and received a second reading the following day, but even after such prosperous beginnings the best efforts of two influential men could get it no further.[72] A bill 'requiring the impost to be taken away' stuck at first reading in 1566; we can only guess its purpose but most probably it aimed to remove the new duties introduced by Mary's government and recently extended to all wines.[73]

The only successful bill affecting the Crown's indirect taxation got through at the second attempt. First introduced in 1563, it proposed to provide a better control over the manufacture and sale of cloth produced in Lancashire by imposing new penalties on clothiers who failed to get their product sealed by the ulnager for the Palatinate (a matter of financial interest to the Crown); it betrayed, however, its undoubted origin in the private interest of the manufacturers by altering the decreed standards of size and quality in their favour. It passed the Commons, with some delay so that it reached the Lords too late in the session.[74] Reintroduced quickly in 1566, it experienced further difficulties but was in the end forced rapidly through the Upper House. No doubt, the fact that its real purpose – easing the problems of the clothiers – hid behind the ostensible purpose of tightening government control helped it through, even as its real purpose may well account for delaying tactics and the need for thorough revision in the Commons.[75]

These were ordinary aspects of parliamentary business. An attempt to free sheriffs from burdens in their financial relations with the Crown produced more interesting manoeuvring. As collectors of various ancient (and now rather minimal) revenues, the sheriffs were responsible for paying the expenses of justices of the peace at Quarter Sessions, but the Exchequer refused to allow them this item against their accounts: sheriffs had to entertain the justices out of their own pockets, rather an unfair imposition on them. A bill to remedy this grievance had lapsed in the Commons in the first Parliament of Mary, and though it passed the House in 1555 the Lords did not even read it once.[76] This hint of stubborn Exchequer opposition – Lord Treasurer Winchester in that reign often

[72] CLRO, Rep. 15, fo. 169; *CJ* I, 65.

[73] Ibid. 78; F. C. Dietz, *English Government Finance 1485–1558* (Urbana, 1921), 209.

[74] *CJ* I, 67–8, 70, 72; *LJ* I, 615–16.

[75] For the act see 8 Eliz. I c. 12. The original bill was replaced by another; even so, its passage took two months. The Lords gave it its first and second readings on one day (*CJ* I, 74–7, 80; *LJ* I, 660, 662).

[76] *CJ* I, 31, 45.

chaired the Upper House – was well confirmed in Elizabeth's reign. The campaign resumed in her first Parliament when the bill, revised in committee, went swiftly through the Commons; the Lords read it once but no more, though there was plenty of time left before the end of the session.[77] Nothing daunted, the sheriffs (or whoever represented their interest) tried again in the next Parliament; once again the bill was replaced in committee, and once again the Lower House passed it. This time, however, the Lords looked likely to abandon their role as protectors of the Crown's selfishness. The bill got as far as a second reading, and when it was about to be read a third time the lord keeper stopped proceedings by conveying a message from the Queen who proposed 'to take order therein herself'. The same message reached the Commons, significantly enough through the mouth of Sir Richard Sackville, chancellor of the Exchequer: the Queen would investigate and 'order should be taken for the discharge thereof'.[78] This promise went the way of most of those that Elizabeth made to her Parliaments, but it sufficed to keep the item off the agenda in 1566. In 1571, the sheriffs' interest, having no doubt lost faith and hope, for charity's sake tried yet again. This time the Queen avoided messages: she let the bill pass through all stages and vetoed it.[79] This was not in any sense a prerogative matter, and not even Elizabeth pretended that it was. Since both her sister and herself put up determined resistance we need to look for a reason not personal to either: Elizabeth may have been parsimonious but Mary was not. It follows that in all probability both were acting under pressure from the Exchequer bureaucracy; quite possibly Winchester, who died in 1572, stood behind this economic refusal to remedy a just enough grievance. Thus the steps taken to stop the bill, from using the Lords through sending a message to applying to veto, indicate not personal decisions of the monarch's but Council policy.

In the difficulties over the last bill to concern us here several interests clashed, but the Queen's personal intervention played no part in them. The matter at issue was the behaviour of those who collected and administered the Crown's revenues all of whom were liable at intervals to hold considerable amounts of the Queen's money. Commonly they employed such reserves for their own advantage, 'borrowing' them to purchase lands or make loans at interest. Not infrequently, therefore, the money turned out to be unavailable when required, for which reason revenue officials quite often died heavily indebted to the Crown – that is to say, with balances of money in their care remaining unpaid into the

[77] Ibid. 54, 56–8; *LJ* I, 566.
[78] *CJ* I, 63, 66–7, 69; *LJ* I, 596, 599, 605.
[79] *CJ* I, 86–7; *LJ* I, 680, 688, 691. Hooker's note on the bill (*Proc.* 249) confirms that an allowance in the Exchequer was in question.

central coffers. So far the problem was one of concern to the government, at odds with its own officials. From the point of view of the generality, revenue officers appeared as rapacious, extortionate and potentially corrupt. Controlling them properly therefore constituted an ambition in which Queen, Council and Commons could feel united. On the other hand, the interest attacked did not lack power. In the patronage structure which governed social and political relations they were both beneficiaries and benefactors; they often supplied the necessary help of the investment banker without whom many a private enterprise would have lacked sinews; and the means at their disposal could be useful in securing support in all the circles in touch with government and Court. Even though high officers, such as the lord treasurer or the chancellor of the Exchequer, might wish, in the national interest, to prevent peculation and defalcation among the officers who actually handled the cash, they could not afford totally to disrupt the fiscal services by too stringent a pursuit of defaulters.

Investigations set in train even before Burghley succeeded to the lord treasurership in 1572, and instigated because of one or two notorious scandals, brought matters to a head, but both scandals and efforts to deal with the underlying trouble had occurred before. A comprehensive act passed in Edward VI's last Parliament attempted to bring order out of chaos, but it confined itself to the administrators of Crown lands and did not touch the worst offenders, the tellers of the Exchequer.[80] Their powerful influence made itself felt in 1557 when a bill dealing with all who handled Crown money passed the Commons but was at once stopped in the Lords by Queen Mary, on the specious grounds that its terms would embrace some people whose accounts had already been settled.[81] The first effort made in Elizabeth's reign went wrong in the opposite direction: introduced in the Lords (therefore probably on the Council's initiative), the bill lapsed in the Commons after being read twice.[82] In 1566, Cecil moved in the Commons, but the organized interest there, which had succeeded in 1559, was still too strong; the bill vanished in committee, even though at that stage there remained nearly three months of the session.[83] The year 1571 at least produced positive action, very probably because those recent scandals gave Burghley the chance of overcoming vested interests, but the making of the act (13 Eliz. I c. 4) involved an unexpectedly complex history behind which moves and countermoves can be dimly discerned.[84]

[80] 7 Edward VI c. 1.

[81] *CJ* 1, 48, 50; *LJ* 1, 521.

[82] Ibid. 590–1; *CJ* 1, 57, 59.

[83] Ibid. 73.

[84] This reconstruction rests in the main on the evidence of the Journals: ibid. 84–5, 91, 93; *LJ* 1, 669, 671–3, 684, 689–91, 699, 701. But cf. also the parchment provisos attached to the OA for evidence touching amendments.

Although the problem made its appearance among the 'grievances' put forward on the initiation of supply (introduced there by that good Cecilian, John Popham), legislative moves started in the Lords where Burghley could keep an eye on them. Even so the bill did not have a straightforward passage. Two things were strange about it. It was committed twice, to a body from which Burghley was excluded, and its terms were extraordinarily severe, for it made failure to pay over all receipts within two months of a warning into felony (carrying, that is, the death penalty), only officers whose receipts did not reach £300 being exempt. By way of a charitable concession it provided that the consequences of a conviction should not affect the rights of widows and children.[85] These facts, it seems to me, can be read in one of two ways: either we have here an essentially unofficial attempt to deal with the grievance – the product of enthusiastic amateurs – or the bill formed part of a tactical plan of Burghley's, intended to soften up the threatened revenue officers before the real bill was moved against them. The second possibility may sound far-fetched, but, as shall be seen, it fits the outcome better.

Rather surprisingly, this savage measure got through the Lords and was sent to the Commons on 12 April where predictably it led to 'long arguments' and a committee (largely of experts and dominated by the men of business) which was instructed 'either to alter or add unto the bill or else to make new provisos at their discretion'. So reformed the bill returned to the House on 9 May and then (the record is deficient) appears to have passed, but all in vain because meanwhile strange things had been happening in the Lords. On 12 April, the very day that the Upper House sent down the bill, it gave a first reading to another one dealing with the same grievances, and – as the title employed by the clerk in his Journal indicates – it was this that became the act of the session. Insofar as these provisional titles offer guidance as to contents, we may conclude that only the second bill dealt with the tellers, the first having in effect been no more than a severe sharpening of the Edwardian act. Burghley's presence, so ostentatiously missing from the history of the first bill, is well vouched for in the story of the second, and there can really be no doubt about the second bill's official origin, whatever may be thought about the first.[86] Burghley now sat on the bill committee which not only reviewed the measure but also resolved on a conference with the Commons. This made sense in that their lordships were thus able to forewarn the Lower House about the change of course; it perhaps

[85] *Proc.* 247.

[86] We do not know the form of the first bill; the second employed the long enacting clause, but since it was redrafted in the Lords committee this offers no conclusive proof.

makes better sense still if the conference was intended to reveal the tactics of the two-pronged attack, to give the threatened interest the hope of a lesser evil, and to prevent the Commons from getting stuck on a measure which added to the felonies known to the law.

On 22 May, after the Lords had passed the new bill, the Commons received what their clerk described as a bill 'newly written and truly examined by the former book lately passed this House, to the end the same may likewise be examined by the House and so there pass accordingly'. The entry, pretending that bill no. 2 was only a revision of bill no. 1, covered up the way the Lords had used (deceived?) the Lower House. Bill no. 1 now vanished at once, and the new bill swiftly passed through all stages. It differed from the earlier proposal in two essential respects: it embraced tellers as well as receivers, and for the penalties of felony it substituted confiscation and sale of a defaulter's lands, to the extent of the Queen's claims upon him.[87] The £300 limit continued to stand. The Commons committee proposed three provisos accepted by the House, which exempted sheriffs and bailiffs (receivers of unimportant revenues), protected lands bought in good faith from a defaulting accountant against confiscation in satisfaction of his debt, and secured the discharge of an accountant's sureties once the Queen's claims had been met. A fourth proviso moved in committee gave general exemption to non-profit-making farmers and lessees of customs duties; this was struck out in the House. The Lords raised no objections to the Commons' amendments (which in no way weakened the bill) but took the opportunity to add one of their own which took care of two men who had evidently been behind that failed proviso in the Commons – Henry Golding and Thomas Neale, two customs farmers and the second an Exchequer auditor.

This victory of administrative honesty over peculation – victory of a sort – survived an attempt of Thomas Norton's in the next Parliament to modify it by an explanatory (that is, revising) statute. He had discovered an ambiguity in the clause protecting *bona fide* purchasers of tellers' lands because it would also exempt from confiscation for debt any supposedly *bona fide* acquisitions by revenue officers themselves – 'which were not reason'. However, though the bill, introduced in the Commons at the earliest opportunity, reached the committee stage, it was there dropped.[88] The act failed to carry in its wake an attempt to extend its provisions to collectors of clerical taxation; the bill passed the Commons

[87] This penalty had been suggested in the Commons during the debate on the first reading of bill no. 1 (*Proc.* 218).

[88] *CJ* I, 94–5 (12 and 14 May 1572); *Proc.* 342. It was no longer on the active list of bills sent to Burghley in June (SP 12/88, fos. 76–80).

but reached the Lords too late in the session to get further than second reading.[89] That this was the sole reason for its failure in 1571 appears from the manner in which the measure went through on the nod in the next Parliament when it was reintroduced on the initiative of John Parkhurst, bishop of Norwich, who was hunting a defaulting collector in his own diocese.[90] It must be added that the penal statute of 1571, achieved after so much endeavour, did little good; troubles especially with the tellers continued to beset the administration. Perhaps predictably, the tellers' gambling instincts tended to write off the dangers of the act until it was too late. What might have happened if instead of their lands their heads had been at risk hardly bears thinking about.

[89] *CJ* I, 89–90; *LJ* I, 686, 688, 692.

[90] 14 Eliz. I c. 7, an official bill introduced in the Commons and through all its stages in seven days: *CJ* I, 95–6; *LJ* I, 710–11. Cf. *The Letter Book of John Parkhurst, Bishop of Norwich*, ed. R. A. Houlbrooke (Norfolk Record Society, 1974 & 1975), 69.

8

Queen and state

THE SAFETY OF THE REALM

At the head of all bills enacted, convention and propriety placed measures concerning the monarch. The point was well expressed in 1581 when the Commons appointed a committee to prepare a bill for the protection of the Queen and articles for a subsidy. The clerk called it the committee 'for the great causes'.[1] Great causes were the causes touching the Queen. While supply has already been discussed, the further review of the Parliament's legislative achievement must begin, as the sessional statute always did, with the acts that touched her and her government.

In 1559, two acts, both started in the Lords, clarified Elizabeth's claim to the crown. They took the form of petitions from both Houses, as was only proper in view of their contents. The first declared Elizabeth and her heirs to be the lawful rulers of England on the grounds of her descent, affirmed the nation's intent to serve her loyally, and rendered void anything said to the contrary anywhere, including earlier acts of Parliament repugnant to this declaration.[2] It is worth noting that this pronouncement rested explicitly on the provisions of Henry VIII's last succession act of 1543.[3] Even though the statute took care to declare rather than enact the Queen's true claims, it thus recognized a species of parliamentary title. In this the act differed altogether from that passed for Mary which had rested her claims on her descent only, for which purpose it had had to undo Henry VIII's first divorce and repeal all the legislation that had accepted it.[4] In 1559 nothing was said about the second divorce, the condemnation of Anne Boleyn, or the attainder which had confirmed it: the statute of 1543 sufficed to override those unfortunate events. Nor was Henry's will referred to which, also by authority of Parliament, produced the same effect as the succession act. In short, the

[1] *CJ* I, 119, 123.
[2] 1 Eliz. I c. 3.
[3] 35 Henry VIII c. 1.
[4] 1 Mary I st. 1, c. 1.

obstacles to Elizabeth's succession which the upheavals of Henry's reign had created were simply ignored by the use of Parliament's legislative sovereignty, and all the lavish language about a hereditary right acknowledged by the loyal Lords and Commons could not really disguise this. Her grandfather's title had only been declared in Parliament, with no reference to that body's authority then or earlier over such high matters;[5] Elizabeth's title, however determined she was to regard it as vested in herself by God and inheritance, did owe its confirmation in law to a previous statute. Much of the history of Parliament since 1485 is exemplified in the difference.

Treating Anne Boleyn's attainder and Elizabeth's consequent bastardization as rendered irrelevant by an act of Parliament formed an obvious way out of an awkward dilemma, but – as it turned out – the device would not quite suffice. The act of 1543 had not restored Elizabeth's legitimate birth, and an illegitimate person, even when recognized as queen, could not by the rules of the common law own land. This difficulty was therefore removed by a very short act which claimed to restore the Queen in blood and declared her 'inheritable... to the late Queen Anne your mother, and to all other your majesty's ancestors and cousins of the part of your said mother'.[6] The act did not restore the mother but only the daughter to her rights at law, once again passing in silence over the disaster of 1536, and by a saving clause barred all actions against anyone who had lawfully acquired Boleyn property in the intervening twenty-two years. Not surprisingly, perhaps, the act, not printed in the sessional statute, was treated as private, but Cecil at once acquired a proper copy of it; as the Queen's agent in matters concerning her estate he might have need of it.[7] Both these statutes, clearing up the Queen's personal position, passed at speed, as might have been expected.

Thus Elizabeth was set on her throne. It remained to make sure that she would not be cast off it. The law could provide for this by defining and punishing two offences either of which would threaten her security and with her the security of the state – treason and sedition. These problems were greatly complicated by the Queen's position in the Church, for the chief threat to her came not from attacks on her claim to the Crown but from resistance to her claims as ruler of the Church, re-affirmed in the act of supremacy of 1559.[8] Though the problems of Church and religion, as they arose in Parliament, shall be separately considered in the next chapter, the treason law, even if most of it

[5] *Tudor Constitution*, 4.

[6] 1 Eliz. I c. 23.

[7] HMC, *Hatfield MSS* 1, no. 564.

[8] 1 Eliz. I c. 1. The making of this act has been thoroughly explained in Norman L. Jones, *Faith by Statute* (London, 1982).

concerned the consequences of her spiritual governorship, must be treated here.[9]

After the frequent enactments, repeals and reenactments of treasons, ever since 1534 when Thomas Cromwell had tried to bring order into the law,[10] Elizabeth's government started on a very cautious note. The act of supremacy made it treason to maintain any foreign (read, papal) jurisdiction in the realm only on the third occasion of doing so; it can fairly be said that this provision avoided backing the restoration of the royal supremacy in the Church with the full force of the treason law.[11] The particular treason act of 1559 dealt in effect only with attacks on Elizabeth's title to the crown by words ('open preaching, express words or sayings') and in writing; offences by words were to incur the penalties of praemunire (life imprisonment and forfeiture of property) on a first offence, of high treason upon the second, while those who put their attacks in writing were declared traitors from the first.[12] The same penalties applied to abettors. This act therefore really assumed the continued force of the original treason act of 1352 but extended its demand for an open deed (killing the king, raising war, and so forth) to the speaking and writing of treason, the problems which had first been recognized in 1534. The bill, officially sponsored, started in the Lords where it acquired several amendments before engrossment, all of them modifying its rigour. Particularly, the penalty for concealing a treason, which constituted abetting, was reduced to that traditionally applied to the offence known as misprision of treason; the punishment for this was not defined, which, since no one now seems clear what it supposedly was, must be called unfortunate. As they did in all subsequent acts for treason and sedition, the Lords made sure that peers should be tried by their peers in the lord steward's court; they also limited prosecution for treasonable words to six months after the date of the offence alleged. One of their provisos, now erased on the bill, displeased the Commons whose suggested alternative did not satisfy the Upper House who called for a conference. This produced the proviso now attached on a separate schedule: it called for two witnesses in all cases of treason and thus once again made statutory what had become usual practice.[13] The bill, which originally had passed the Lords in three days, ultimately lay in the Parliament for just about six weeks, but the delays resulted from urgent other business rather than from problems in the bill itself.

[9] The Elizabethan treason laws, their implications and enforcements are being studied by Dr Leslie Ward, a fact which renders full discussion unnecessary here. I shall confine myself to events in Parliament.

[10] G. R. Elton, *Policy and Police* (Cambridge, 1972), ch. 6.

[11] 1 Eliz. I c. 1, sect. 14.

[12] 1 Eliz. I c. 5.

[13] *LJ* I, 546–8, 555, 557, 562; *CJ* I, 54–8.

This half-hearted treason law, which really only repeated on Elizabeth's behalf her sister's act against slanderers of the Crown,[14] was backed up by two similar continuations of acts from the previous reign. The brief act against seditious words and rumours started in the Lords and passed both Houses without difficulty; the month's delay before the third reading in the Lower House again sprang from the general problems of the session.[15] But the fortunes of the bill 'to continue the act made against rebellious assemblies' are less clear-cut. It was a very brief measure which, after referring to the massive and time-limited act of the previous reign, simply continued it for the present Parliament and until the end of the next.[16] Starting in the Commons it reached the Lords on 22 March where it was at once committed.[17] There is then a gap in our information, extending over the notorious Easter recess of that session, but on 13 April a new bill received a first reading in the Lower House. It passed smartly enough and was accepted without comment by the Lords.[18] It thus looks as though the Lords had refused to have anything to do with the first bill but instead of replacing it with one of their own had asked the Commons to think again. All these bills for the protection of public order came from the Council: what had caused the demand for a *nova billa*? Of course, we cannot tell, but considering the bill which the Lords accepted one may suspect some defect in the law rather than the abandonment of a major reform. In 1566 the Lords twice read a true reforming bill 'for punishment of riots, routs and unlawful assemblies', but it vanished in committee.[19]

Moderate measures for the protection of the Crown against papist sympathisers illustrate the relatively conciliatory policy which Queen and Council managed to pursue throughout the first decade of the reign. Yet in 1563 a further act sharpened the law by extending the duty to take the oath of supremacy to every ordained minister, university graduate and lawyer, a first refusal being punished by imprisonment for life and loss of property whereas a second constituted treason.[20] The making of this act has remained a subject for debate. The original bill, introduced in the Commons, was committed (Sir Francis Knollys, protestant hardliner but also vice-chamberlain, in the chair), and the committee produced a new bill which, after travelling twice between the Houses, was passed with four provisos added by the Lords and a late one added by the Commons. The bill certainly proved contentious, its passage in

[14] 1 & 2 Philip & Mary c. 10.

[15] 1 Eliz. I c. 6; *LJ* I, 546–8, 565; *CJ* 54, 58. The Council of the North took special care to have the act enforced: *YCR*, VI, 42 (25 July 1562).

[16] 1 Eliz. I c. 16.

[17] *CJ* I, 58; *LJ* I, 568.

[18] *CJ* I, 59–60; *LJ/EHR*, 538–9.

[19] *LJ* I, 657–8.

[20] 5 Eliz. I c. 1.

the Lower House requiring a division (186 for and 83 against).[21] Sir John Neale predictably interpreted its history as showing his puritan extremists at work in sharpening a milder government measure.[22] Against this, Norman Jones has argued for some weakening of its provisions in the course of passage, a retreat which he ascribed to fear that in its original form it would never pass the Lords.[23] Jones found support for his view in the reports of the Spanish ambassador and some speeches in the Upper House, whereas Neale was relying on conjecture derived from his convictions about the existence of a puritan opposition. Even Jones, however, did not look at the Original Act with sufficient care, and both missed the crucial point: it does not look as though the original bill was backed by a united Council.

Soon after the revised bill had passed the Commons, Cecil reported to Thomas Smith, abroad on embassy, that 'a law is passed for sharpening laws against papists wherein some difficulty hath been because they be made very penal, but such be the humours of the Common House as they think nothing sharp enough against papists'.[24] In the first place, this plainly says that difficulties in passage were caused by those who thought the law too severe, not (as Neale argued) by ardent men seeking to make the government bill more stringent. Moreover, it suggests that the proposal did not originate with Cecil or the Council, the more so because later in the letter he expressly took personal responsibility for the bill prohibiting the sale of apparel on credit.[25] We know that the Queen disliked the act sufficiently to evade its effect by later ordering that the oath was never to be tendered a second time.[26] The act employs the long enacting clause, though this, of course, could have been introduced for the *nova billa*; still, the fact strengthens the case for an unofficial initiative. The Council showed itself divided over this measure. Francis Knollys chaired the committee which produced it, but even before the Parliament met, the lord treasurer, the marquess of Winchester, had expressed his hostility to harsher laws he understood were likely to be promoted. Cecil's remarks have been read as signifying some unease about that harshness, but he does not really say that he would have much preferred a less severe approach; if the Spanish ambassador, at this time well informed, can be believed, Cecil supported the need for the bill that passed in the crucial debate in the Commons when he talked down

[21] *CJ* I, 65–8; *LJ* I, 593, 595–8, 602, 604.

[22] Neale, *EP* I, 116–20.

[23] Jones, *Faith by Statute*, 171–5.

[24] BL, Lansdowne MS 102, fo. 24v.

[25] Ibid: 'I have been author of a short law...'

[26] Neale, *EP* I, 121. In the lord keeper's closing speech of the session (*Proc.* 111) the Queen was diplomatically made to thank the Parliament for its wise measure 'for the abolishing of the Romish power, the common enemy of this realm'.

opposition by pointing out the dangers with which international catholicism threatened Queen and nation. There is really no support for thinking that this act stemmed from the government; rather it looks as though ardent protestants, no doubt apprehensive, after Elizabeth's recent illness, about their Queen's chances of survival, talked the Commons into promoting a bill prepared in committee.

The indications are, therefore, that the initiative behind the original bill was unofficial, but the intention was probably known to members of the Council beforehand and in due course received some patchy Council support. Apparently the rumour went that the bill as planned would make a first refusal of the oath into treason, for that is what the earl of Northumberland thought it would do before the bill had even been read a first time in the Commons.[27] However, the Spanish ambassador, writing when only the first bill existed, already knew of the two different penalties: evidently they were in the bill as first drawn in committee. This means that the *nova* almost certainly did not differ in essentials from its predecessor, a probability also supported by the fact that it was brought in on the day after the committal of the first bill. This implies that the bill committee did sufficient detailed revising to necessitate a new draft but that they left the substance untouched: what we have now mended the presumably amateur drafting put before the House but kept intact the purpose first intended. This new bill was debated on second, or more probably on third, reading, leading to the exceptional use of a division, and the kind of difficulties Cecil mentioned are illustrated by the surviving speech of Robert Atkinson.[28] Atkinson, a lawyer of conservative, possibly even recusant views, who never sat in Parliament again, used both common law and Scripture to deny the need for such extreme steps: the act of supremacy, he maintained, sufficed to repress and punish disaffection. He also argued that anyone really hostile to the settlement of the protestant Church would have no difficulty in taking an oath which he would regard as invalid because it was demanded by heretics. It was this line of argument that Cecil blocked by outlining the threats from abroad; and in this he clearly, as the division was to show, followed 'the humours of the Common House'. Even so, nearly a third of the members present supported Atkinson.

The opposition to the bill in the Upper House coordinated things with that in the Lower. One point made by Atkinson drew attention to the

[27] Jones, *Faith by Statute*, 175.

[28] *Proc.* 96–102. The date – March 1563 – given on the copy of the speech used in *Proc.* must be wrong. The second and third readings took place on 17 and 20 February, after which there were no more proceedings in the Commons except for the agreement to the Lords amendments on 11 March.

fear that the differentiated penalties in the bill might be meaningless: being in the praemunire, he suggested, might not save a man's life since it was far from clear that he might not be 'out of the protection of the king and the law' – that is to say, could be killed with impunity. The point was taken up in the Lords, one of whose amending provisos (sect. 18) expressly declared such killing unlawful. Contact between the opposers in both Houses was further indicated by the speech made in the Lords by Viscount Montague who in a forcefully anti-protestant discourse repeated some of Atkinson's points.[29] The other three Lords provisos, all four being engrossed on one schedule, emphasized trial by peers for peers and tried to protect persons accused against fanatics, but the one prohibiting the killing of persons in the praemunire drew a further amendment from the Commons, attached on a separate schedule. The Lords proviso stood but it was not to prevent the execution of people lawfully sentenced to death nor to protect against punishment already provided anyone who brought into the realm papal sentences or exhortations.

Thus this much debated act represents not government policy but the desires of strong protestants in the Commons, much perturbed by threats of papal reaction from abroad, by the uncertainty of the Queen's life, and by fears for the future of the true religion in an England still supposedly (and actually) swarming with unrepentant catholics reckoned to be papists. It was not well thought out or very competently drawn. Nor was it 'sharpened' during passage, but neither did the modifications counselled by prudence have much significance, as indeed was to be true of the whole act because it came to be used so rarely in the battle against recusancy. Though the Queen's protestant councillors welcomed this addition to the Queen's protective armour, they did not originally promote it; the act underlines the possibilities open to private initiatives in the Parliament, but also the futility of such initiatives in matters of high policy unless care had been taken to involve the Council and especially the Queen beforehand.

If in 1563 the government had not thought it necessary to add to the laws protecting the Queen and the Anglican Settlement, the upheavals of 1569 and 1570 – the rebellion of the northern earls, the papal bull excommunicating and deposing Elizabeth, and the machinations of the duke of Norfolk and the Queen of Scots – altered the situation drastically. Thus the Council prepared two bills for the session of 1571. One in effect revived the law of 1534 which had made it treason at the first offence to deny the monarch's lawful title by word, writing or deed, thus ending

[29] John Strype, *Annals of the Reformation* (Oxford, 1824), I, i, 442–6.

the hesitations of 1559.[30] The other declared it treason to bring into the country or there spread around any papal bulls; concealing knowledge of such deeds became misprision of treason.[31] The official origin of the latter bill, which after revision carried the long enacting clause, is proved by the royal proclamations preceding it, the second of which contained a broad hint that distributing bills would be considered treason.[32] The Queen told the Parliament at the end of the session that she had from the first disliked the treason bill, thinking herself perfectly well protected by the law as it stood, but had given in to her Council.[33] She had been right to foresee trouble – trouble caused by loyal men's excessive fear for her.

Both bills were introduced on 9 April, one week after the start of the session, the one for treasons in the Commons and the one for bulls in the Lords. Neither had a simple passage. The Lords committed their bill at first reading and thus got a bill 'nova reformata'. What changes this produced we do not know, though we may suspect that the lengthy preamble and long enacting clause replaced simpler phrases in the official bill. In its new form the bill passed the Lords on 21 April. The Commons, busy enough on other matters, despite the Lords' express request that they might read and pass it quickly, took a little time over it. However, in the end they produced only a few verbal amendments one of which made the act retrospective by adding bulls obtained since 1559 to bulls to be obtained in future: before this change, the crucial bull of excommunication would seem to have been exempt from the act's provisions. Rather surprisingly, since only the amendment made the measure usable, the Lords asked for a conference but to all appearance allowed themselves to be persuaded.[34]

The treason bill became contentious because on its first reading that well known member of the Lower House, Thomas Norton, rose to propose major additions. He came prepared with a draft bill. Since he was in Burghley's confidence he will have known of the forthcoming official bill in advance and had clearly planned his intervention well; since he was not, as Neale thought, a leader of puritan opposition but rather one of the Council's trusted men of business in the Commons,[35] he is quite likely to have coordinated his move with those on the Council who

[30] 13 Eliz. I c. 1; *Proc.* 203 for the original terms of the bill, and 214 for its official origin. Neale, *EP* I, 226, rightly notes the relationship to the act of 1534.

[31] 13 Eliz. I c. 2.

[32] *TRP* II, 341–3 (1 July 1579) and 347–8 (14 Nov. 1570). A proclamation could not properly create new felonies or treasons, and the phrasing is therefore ambiguous.

[33] *Proc.* 257.

[34] *LJ* I, 671–3, 675–6, 685, 688: *CJ* I, 86–6, 88, 90.

[35] M. A. R. Graves, 'Thomas Norton the Parliament Man', *HJ* 23 (1980), 17–35.

shared his hatred of popery and fear for the uncertain state of the succession, with the Queen of Scots waiting in the wings – a fear which had driven the Council into covert agitation in the previous session.[36] For the purpose of Norton's draft was to bar from the throne as traitors any person, as well as his or her heirs, who had ever during Elizabeth's lifetime laid claim to the Crown of England; in addition, it was to be treason to deny the right of Parliament to legislate for the title to the Crown. Norton wished his proposals to be incorporated in the proposed act.[37] This led to a debate which there is no reason to rehearse here since Neale did so at length.[38] Some members denied the need for a new treason law, but the main argument turned on the question whether Norton's bill should be joined to the official bill or proceeded with separately. The leadership – Sir Francis Knollys assisted by Recorder Fleetwood – turned cautious and advised separate proceedings. Both bills were thus read separately on 12 April, with a still longer debate ensuing; official advice dithered between keeping the bills separate and consulting the Queen's legal counsel over the resolution of certain obscurities and doubts challenged by members. Knollys revealed that Queen and Council had given some time to Norton's additions and that the former at least was not pleased.[39]

However, both bills were jointly committed and the committee accepted the instruction that its lawyer members should confer with the Queen's legal counsel. When on the 26th the bills came out of committee still separate, the House divided and by a majority of over thirty ordered them to be conjoined.[40] And so they remained, though the Lords' amendments removed the most objectionable of Norton's proposals by taking out the heirs of any traitorous claimants from the ban upon inheritance of the crown. This must be inferred from the terms of the act because the Original Act is innocent of any corrections, having been written out anew in the Lords at the Commons' request, on account of the messy state into which it had got.[41] As passed, the act consists of eleven sections. Only the first two constitute the original government bill; sections 3–5, depriving claimants and asserting the authority of the Queen-in-Parliament in the settling of the Crown, represent Norton's addition; the last six are provisos, almost certainly the work of the Lords, which protect the interests of persons accused, to the point of guarding the charitable care of prisoners with food and bedding against all

[36] Below, pp. 365–74.

[37] *Proc.* 204.

[38] *EP* I, 226–31, based on *Proc.* 204–7.

[39] Ibid. 215–18.

[40] *CJ* I, 86 speaks of a majority of 36; Hooker's journal (*Proc.* 249) gives the figures as 170 to 138.

[41] *LJ* I, 692: the Lords appointed three peers and three bishops to check the accuracy of the copy.

punishment. The Queen, as she made plain at the end, had never much liked the whole business but had to be satisfied with the removal of her rival's heir from the proscription first intended; if that had been carried she would have had to do something about the succession since there would have been no legitimate successor left at all. The story of the bill testifies to the fears and passions of a House much exercised over the papal menace, though, as the division shows, there were plenty of men there who opposed Norton's move, but the behaviour of Knollys and Fleetwood suggests rather that they were torn between a desire to support Norton and awareness of the Queen's displeasure. It really cannot be supposed that Norton's move attracted no support from at least part of the Council. Whether one should suspect that he was put up by councillors to enlarge a measure the first version of which had sufficiently annoyed Elizabeth must remain debatable: considering how often a Council faction used the Commons to push matters against the Queen's wishes, I think it more likely than the notion that the initiative had been Norton's alone.

The aftermath of the crisis of plot and rebellion left two further marks on the statute book of 1571. One was the act of attainder which confirmed the sentences passed on the northern rebels – death for those caught and outlawry for those who had escaped. Cast in the form of a petition from both Houses, it was treated as a private (personal) act, being assented to *soit fait*.[42] Introduced in the Lords, it apparently restarted there after a first false attempt,[43] but the real work on it was done in the Commons. Here Sir Henry Percy, innocent brother to the guilty earl of Northumberland, appearing with counsel, secured a clause saving him harmless, and various relatives of the condemned men obtained a proviso protecting them. The other product of the aftermath was the act 'against fugitives over the sea'; it prohibited anyone from leaving the country without a royal licence and deprived those who refused to return of all their lands.[44] It looks to have been an unofficial bill started in the Commons which needed a good deal of improvement in the course of passage. The Lower House added the clauses safe-guarding the interests of the wives and children of fugitives, restoring penitent homecomers to their lands after a year's wait, exempting Lady Jane Dormer and her granddaughter, the duchess of Feria, from the act, and (this at the request of the Lords) limiting the act to the Queen's life. The Upper House further protected the interests of peers. They also made a number of

[42] 13 Eliz. I. c. 16 (not printed in the sessional statute).

[43] The first reference to it in *LJ* I, 672 notes the first reading as 'de novo'. Other references: ibid. 676–7, 686–7; *CJ* I, 86–90.

[44] 13 Eliz. I c. 3; *CJ* I, 85–7, 92–3; *LJ* I, 679, 690. For the amendments see OA; for the time-limitation cf. above, p. 135.

telling verbal changes to emphasize the limitation to Elizabeth's lifetime, to confine forfeitures to the offenders after whose deaths heirs would be able to inherit, and to improve the treatment of fugitives' dependents. It was not a good piece of drafting and its execution was to prove troublesome. To judge from its provisions, its makers were less worried about the self-removal of potential troublemakers than over the fact that such people would live abroad on the proceeds of properties in England. This appears also from an abortive attempt made in 1581 to prevent any money from reaching persistent fugitives by bills of exchange or upon bonds made to their benefit. What rankled, typically enough, was the thought that such nasty people might escape destitution.[45]

Within a few months of this Parliament's dissolution another was called in 1572, chiefly to consider the problems of the duke of Norfolk and the Queen of Scots,[46] but the Council took the opportunity to improve the protection offered to Elizabeth by the law. It introduced two short bills into the Lords, both limited to the Queen's life. One concerned itself with attempts to capture or destroy any royal castles, making it felony to plot such action and treason to carry it out: but that treason had existed since 1352.[47] The bill received extensive amendments first from the Commons and then, when they saw the Lower House's suggestions, from the Lords as well; it seems to have been drafted in ill-advised haste. The other bill attended to a somewhat novel problem in the history of sixteenth-century England: the existence of large numbers of prisoners for political (including religious) reasons who were not going to be either released or executed and thus might provoke attempts at rescue. The punishments for such endeavours were graded according to the stage in the prisoner's fortunes: whether he was waiting to be indicted (misprision of treason), had been arraigned (felony), or had been sentenced (treason). A tribute to legal ingenuity, the bill passed without difficulty.[48] It seems also to have been superfluous; at least, I know of no one tried under it.

Treason and the safety of Queen and Church did not trouble the session of 1576, but the new vigour infused into English catholicism by the opening of the Jesuit campaign made these issues one of the chief reasons for the recall of Parliament in 1581. Burghley considered what was necessary to sharpen the measures against catholics and decided on 'new provisions against offenders' which, however, would allow for mercy to the repentant. They should be able to secure 'remission upon submitting and reconciling themselves, except in treason which is left to

[45] *CJ* I, 124.

[46] Below, pp. 374–7.

[47] 14 Eliz. I c. 1. *LJ* I, 710–12, 718–20; *CJ* I, 97–101. A long paper sheet of amendments is filed with the OA.

[48] 14 Eliz. I c. 2; *LJ* I, 711–12, 717; *CJ* I, 97, 99, 100.

her majesty's mercy'.[49] What emerged was less conciliatory; even during the preparatory labours, the two essential articles to be promoted spoke only of making it treason to persuade any of the Queen's subjects to leave the religion established by law as well as to allow oneself to be so persuaded.[50] Two bills were in fact prepared, one for tightening up the law of treason against the catholic mission and the other against seditious words and rumours. Both originated with the Council, and both had a difficult passage in Parliament.

The act 'to retain the Queen's majesty's subjects in their due obedience'[51] began in the Commons where on the ninth day of the session Sir Walter Mildmay moved for consideration of the laws against papists and was backed up by Norton – a prepared Council manoeuvre. The committee appointed produced a bill brought in on 7 or 8 February by Sir Francis Knollys, again demonstrating the lead taken by strongly protestant councillors. At this point some confusion was caused by Sir Christopher Hatton who reported that the Lords had a similar bill before them and suggested a meeting: the Council were not united.[52] There followed a medley of debate and two conferences with the Lords, the second meeting on 27 February.[53] Out of this came a new bill drafted by Burghley,[54] and it was in effect this bill which, after some revision, appeared in the Commons as a *nova*, being twice read on 4 March. Thereafter it passed both Houses in a few days.[55]

The results of all these deliberations throw some doubtful light on the notion that the Lower House always wanted severer measures against catholics than Queen and government favoured.[56] One thing is certain: the act that passed had been weakened in many ways from the bill first introduced. Cromwell's diary, which gives a careful analysis of the

[49] SP 12/147, fos. 92–9, two separate notes seeking the Queen's views as to the degree of mercy to be shown.

[50] Ibid. fo. 91.

[51] 23 Eliz. I c. 1.

[52] *CJ* I, 123 has the bill reported on 7 Feb.; Cromwell's diary (*Proc.* 533) lists it on the 8th. As Neale says (*EP* I, 386), the bill Hatton mentioned was a minor and pointless attempt to sharpen the act for church attendance – a long way from a treason act.

[53] *CJ* I, 123, 130.

[54] SP 12/148, fos. 10–18, 37–71, two drafts in the hand of Burghley's clerk and plentifully corrected by Burghley. An endorsement on the first draft dates it to 2 March, between the conference and the next stage in the Commons.

[55] *CJ* I, 131; *LJ* II, 44, 46–8.

[56] Neale, *EP* I, 386–91, ascribes the considerable modifications in the bill to the Queen's intervention. There is no positive evidence for this, and his view forces him to call the treatment of the bill against rumours 'a rather droll reversal of roles' (ibid. 393). Much depends on one's interpretation of surviving pieces of drafting. What seem to me very plainly products of pre-parliamentary planning (reciting earlier acts and considering what was needed in addition) Neale read as the product of revision in the course of passage, under the Queen's instruction. The notes manifestly contemplate approaching the Queen and do not hint that they are already responding to her expression of views.

original proposal, shows it to have been much more savage and far-reaching.[57] The changes made achieved two ends: penalties for all the offences created, except the punishment of treason for persuading people away from their allegiance, were considerably reduced, and while schoolmasters remained subject to strict control the attempts to extend the same supervision to catholics among practising lawyers were abandoned. We remember that the Council pondered the need for legislation before the session opened and that the bill was introduced in the Commons by a Council party. We recall that Burghley had during the preparatory stages tried to insert some conciliatory purposes into the bill and that it was he who drafted the act which actually passed, using an exceptional second conference to impose it on the Commons. We note that even the first conference with the Lords produced a touch of softening – a minor modification which reduced the penalty for recusants' wives from imprisonment to a £20 fine.[58] All this could support Neale's view that Burghley and the Lords worked under instructions from the Queen. But it makes no sense at all to ascribe the removal of the lawyers from the bill to the Queen's intervention, whereas provisions which would have barred catholics from practising at law would have caused consternation at the Inns of Court. As has been said, Hatton's intervention, which tried to hold things up by mentioning an irrelevant bill and to get the Commons into touch with the Lords, strongly suggests that there were two opinions on the Council about the savagery of the measure, while the business over the lawyers is quite adequate to account for the delays in the Lower House. It need not be denied that the second bill may well have suited the Queen better than the first – if she wanted a treason act at all – but the indications are that the moderates on the Council took the initiative in the victory of restraint. So far as the evidence goes, the act was Burghley's and not the Queen's; he had thought along relatively conciliatory lines since before the appearance of the first bill (which may well have been the reason why the bill had to be moved in the Commons by the transparent device of a drafting committee); and the decision to make the crucial issue explicitly political rather than religious followed from his customary policy in these matters.[59]

[57] *Proc.* 533–4. Neale's description of the modifications is sound, even if his interpretation of them must be said to be doubtful.

[58] Ibid. 537.

[59] Neale, *EP* I, 388–9, rightly draws attention to the effect achieved by the insertion of three words which made it treason to convert Englishmen to Rome solely with the intention of making them withdraw their political allegiance to the Crown. He is wrong, however, in alleging that both Houses had first backed a bill that seemed to emphasize a treason derived from purely religious activities: the Lords did not see the first bill till the conference at which they called for modifications.

The second political measure of the session replaced the old Marian statute against seditious rumours renewed in 1559 for Elizabeth,[60] by a more extensive and severer act.[61] This, too, underwent a difficult and somewhat bewildering history with disagreements between the two Houses; these have been interpreted as springing from the Commons' efforts to prevent the act from operating against loyal critics of a puritan hue as well as against wicked catholics.[62] Like the treason act, this measure came from the Council, but a Council seemingly undivided over it; it introduced it in the Lords because, when two major bills were to be moved, they usually introduced them more or less simultaneously in the two Houses. The Lords passed what was a very severe act against any who spoke or wrote to the slander of the Queen, or who repeated such stories. At second reading the Lords removed the penalty of loss of goods from slanderers (who after pillory and loss of both ears were to be imprisoned at pleasure) but extended the punishment for repeaters of tales (pillory and loss of one ear) from one year's imprisonment to three.[63] In the Commons the bill passed with amendments and the addition of clauses proposed by Thomas Norton which made it a 'seditious rumour' to call the Church of England 'heretical or schismatical', words borrowed from the Henrician treason legislation.[64]

From this point the bill became a football in the game of self-importance which both Houses played in this session. The Lords, not liking the proposed changes, asked for a conference but then would not receive the bill back again because the Commons clerk had forgotten to put the bail (transfer clause) on the paper of amendments. This being remedied, the Lords demanded further amendments to undo the earlier amendments. The Commons had altered 'tending to the slander...' into 'intending the slander', a revision which put the onus of defining the alleged deed as offensive on the notoriously disputable assessment of what the accused had intended rather than on the court's judgment as to the effect of his words. There were good reasons for resisting a change which just possibly may have tried to prevent loyal criticism from being punished[65] but was sure to make the enforcement of the act very difficult. Other points stood also in dispute, especially the repeal of the old acts against rumours, though why this should have been thought necessary by

[60] Above, p. 178.

[61] 23 Eliz. I c. 2.

[62] Neale, *EP* I, 393–8, which gives most of the details. I do not find his interpretation as obvious as he did, and he certainly misread the origin of amendments on the OA.

[63] *LJ* II, 22–3, 25–6, 30. The paper bill, marked for engrossment, survives: SP 12/147, fos. 37–54.

[64] *CJ* I, 120–1, 128; *Proc.* 538.

[65] As Neale suggests: *EP* I, 315. He makes the amendment an insertion rather than a change of words already in the bill and thus ignores the legal problems it deals with.

anybody – ardent puritan or not – remains mysterious. The Commons took the line that they could not undo changes they had specifically made (in which, despite irrelevant precedents cited, they were wrong),[66] and they therefore returned the bill to the Lords as one 'that this House cannot deal withal'; in return, their lordships, declaring through the lord chancellor that they could not 'take knowledge' of the Commons' opinion 'touching the state of the said bill', would not receive it.[67] In this interplay of procedural high-horsemanship, the bill looked like dying in the keeping of the Commons clerk, until Christopher Hatton, in a skilful speech on the virtues of loyalty and the need to protect the Queen, got the House to appoint a committee for a new bill. This bill, produced within twenty-four hours, led to yet another clash with the Lords, but in the end it passed: the Commons insisted on the repeal of the earlier acts but conceded the particular amendments demanded.[68]

The compromise arrived at really favoured the original drafters of the bill and not perhaps a triumphant House of Commons. The speed with which the last committee produced a new bill indicates that the product differed little from the first proposals which the Lords had sent down. Norton's amendment, especially offensive to the Queen who at the assent rather contemptuously declared the whole act to be superfluous,[69] was dropped. The Commons succeeded in their desire to be rid of the old acts, a success which could have proved awkward because the present act had been framed as an extension, not as a replacement. The Commons' revision reduced most of the penalties to be inflicted: it was they who introduced the alternative of a heavy money fine in place of the pillory and the loss of ears, but it was the Lords who gave the choice between the alternatives to the offender, an insertion which remedied yet another potential defect in the conduct of any trial under the act. For the rest, all the original details – including the creation of certain felonies, the handling of offences committed outside the realm, and the limitation of the act to the Queen's life – stood as originally proposed. If Neale had been right in sensing here a triumph for 'the Commons' we should have to think that they safeguarded puritan criticism and also generously modified the punishment of catholics: which makes little

66 *Proc.* 544.

67 *CJ* I, 133.

68 Ibid. 134–5, *LJ* II, 52–3. Neale (*EP* I, 397, n. 2) ascribes some changes on the parchment bill to the Commons, but this is wrong. He did so because he took the points mentioned in *CJ* I, 135 as covering all the Lords' suggested amendments, whereas the text clearly states them to be only part of what the Upper House wanted done. Amendments on this OA, as was nearly always the case, were made in the second House to see it, though of course written in by the clerk of the first House.

69 *Proc.* 547: among those of the Lower House whom she excluded from her thanks because they had 'forgot themselves' was Norton (Neale, *EP* I, 395).

sense. One might speak of two possible triumphs. On the one hand, an act the Queen disliked and thought absurd was put on the statute book: but it had been her councillors in the Lords who had worked for it. On the other hand, the act finished up less savage than when it started: but that touch of moderate good sense resulted from the work of a committee appointed on Council initiative. The appearance of a quarrel between the Houses sprang from procedural technicalities, exploited by people who meant to stand on their dignity rather than wished to save puritan ears. The end-product, the act as passed, does not seem to have had major consequences in the courts.

We may, finally, note two minor issues linked to the story of the treason legislation. In the first place, there was the possibility that the life and reputation of the monarch, as well as the safety of the realm, might be threatened by occult practices. The 1581 act against rumours also made it felony to employ the wizard's art (astrology, divination and prophecy were especially mentioned) to forecast the Queen's death. Two acts of 1563, it will be recalled, had punished pretended prophecies by imprisonment and forefeiture of goods, witchcraft and sorcery by death: and both had been Council bills taking over from unmanageable measures privately promoted.[70] Neither act had caused any difficulties in Parliament, though failed later attempts to legislate against those dreaded forms of magic suggest that not everybody was satisfied with the law as it stood.[71] In view of the role which witchcraft and incantations had played from the first in rumours and spells against the Crown's schismatical policy in the Church,[72] it is surprising that Elizabeth's reign was half over before these apprehensions entered the law for the protection of the Queen. But fear of witches was increasing, and the act of 1581 testified to it. The other aspect of treason which received some attention concerned offences against the coinage, always regarded as very much within the personal prerogative of the Crown. An act of Henry V's having been accidentally voided in Mary's statute of repeal, an official bill of 1563 recreated the treason committed by 'clipping, washing, rounding or filing' coins, and in 1576 a follow-up statute, also of official origin, took care of the fact that the criminals in question had found new ways, not yet provided against, for profitably damaging the coinage.[73]

The first half of Elizabeth's reign witnessed a fairly constant concern to adjust the law protecting the state to meet new situations created by the continuing refusal of allegiance from catholics within the realm, and

[70] 5 Eliz. I cc. 15, 16. See above, pp. 110–11.

[71] *CJ* I, 74 (1566), 90 (1571).

[72] Elton, *Policy and Police*, esp. ch. 2.

[73] 5 Eliz. I c. 11; 18 Eliz. I c. 1. A failed bill of 1576 tried to improve the working of the mint; 'coiners' here meant those entitled to make coins (*CJ* I, 109–11; *Proc.* 485).

by the steady increase of pressure from catholics outside. In all these measures the government took the lead, several times against the Queen's own preferences and at other times in a divided state touching the need for greater severity. Only the peculiar treason act of 1563 would seem to have come as a surprise to the Council. Divisions within it provided the occasions for what could too easily be seen as non-official initiatives managed by supposedly puritan groups, but this interpretation will not stand up and more especially is not supported by the history of the acts in question in the Parliament. At the same time, it is certainly true that many members of the Commons dreaded the 'catholic threat' far more than the better informed Queen and her less passionately protestant councillors did, but it was not those extremists who shaped the acts. The Lords' chief contribution would seem to have lain in improving legal details in the acts and thus making them better enforceable, though in actual fact both substantive and procedural provisions too often burdened the use of them to the point where the Crown, as it did in Edmund Campion's case, preferred to fall back on the fourteenth-century statute. This piecemeal, reluctant and government-inspired legislation for treason testifies more to a reluctance to be driven into persecution than it speaks for the energy and determination of the Queen's councillors; but many who opposed the Queen's rule in the Church had cause to be grateful for these hesitations.

THE GOVERNMENT OF THE REALM

The legislation so far discussed directly and inescapably concerned the person and prerogative of the Queen; its common theme was protection for the head of the state, and its common purport revolved around the law of treason. However, some other matters directly affecting the Queen's conduct of government rather than her person also made their appearance in Parliament and shall be briefly considered here; they all constitute successful or unsuccessful efforts to assist the monarch by subjecting her actions to the supremacy of parliamentary statute.

One ancient grievance received attention in the 1563 session when three bills were introduced to control the royal prerogative of purveyance – the right to buy supplies for the royal household at prices fixed below market level.[74] The least important of them ordered purveyors to mark with pitch any cattle acquired for the Queen, so as to prevent

[74] Cf. Allegra Woodworth, *Purveyance for the Royal Household in the Reign of Elizabeth* (Philadelphia, 1945). This remains a sound account of its real subject, but some allegations concerning actions by the Commons, written under the influence of Neale and Conyers Read, cannot be substantiated in the sources.

illicit trading in meat diverted from its proper purpose. Though the bill passed the Commons it never got to the Lords; the session was nearly over, and the messenger – Cecil – may have taken care to bury a bill which, since it touched the prerogative, would have proved objectionable to Elizabeth.[75] The other two bills, introduced into the Commons on the same day and evidently the product of private initiatives, were quickly amalgamated into one. This passed all stages and had to be vetoed in order to prevent a more drastic invasion of the prerogative. The clerk's description of it, while uninformative as to detail, nevertheless indicates its tenor: 'against such as buy things purveyed for the Queen'. Probably it wished only to remedy the often complained of misbehaviour of purveyors who extended the privilege for private profit by dealing in foodstuffs bought cheap and sold dear; but since it meant to make such actions felony it is surprising that it was not stopped at an earlier stage.[76] It plainly was nothing like so adventurous as a plan found in Sir Thomas Smith's papers which would have abolished purveyance altogether, in return for an annual tax of a fifteenth on movables plus a surcharge of 6*d* on every tod of wool, this last 'being farmed of her majesty at £40,000 per annum'.[77] None of these unofficial attempts to control or convert purveyance got anywhere in the face of Elizabeth's unimaginative determination to keep her prerogatives intact, and the only act to pass touching purveyance was an official move to limit an exemption already in existence. An act of 1555 had excluded purveyors from five-mile circles around Cambridge and Oxford, in order to ease life for poor scholars.[78] This had apparently led to abuses as the inhabitants of villages in the neighbourhood of the two University towns took advantage of what had not been intended for them. Therefore a Council bill in the Lords declared that purveyors could invade the sacred circles if licensed to do so by the respective University.[79] The bill, which passed easily, acquired a modest renown because of a technical slip at the third reading in the Commons when, the question being put, it was found that certain amendments had so far been read only once. The third reading had therefore to be repeated after the amendments were first read twice. Since these included the section limiting the act to the end of the next

[75] *CJ* I, 68, 71–2.

[76] Ibid. 67–8, 71–2; *LJ* I, 616–18.

[77] BL, Harl. MS 4243, fos. 7v–8. Later in the reign, as Woodworth shows, compositions arranged with individual counties reduced the activities and misdeeds of purveyors.

[78] 2 & 3 Philip & Mary c. 15.

[79] 13 Eliz. I c. 21. Some seven years earlier, the Council had suggested to the University of Cambridge that they might consider what amendment they wished to see made of the earlier act concerning the matter (Cambridge University Library, MS Lett. 9, p. 80: 11 Oct. 1564); thus the act of 1571 was presumably drafted on the advice of the Universities.

Parliament a matter of some substance was involved, but what the slip really showed was that a bill which extended the powers of the Universities over their towns and environs had been passed without much attention.[80]

Other financial officers of the Crown also came under review. The story of the attempt to discipline all who handled the Queen's revenues has already been told;[81] we may note that the inadequacies of the resultant act did not prevent its principles from being extended to the collectors of the clerical tenth and the subsidies of the clergy. The relevant, very brief, bill got to the Lords too late for passage in 1571 but passed smoothly in 1572, to testify to the fact that no one in the Lower House greatly cared about protecting bishops and their agents.[82]

Of all the Queen's officers, the sheriffs and their deputies took up most time in Parliament. They made their existence felt in three different ways, though most of the bills devised for them failed. The first concern, which touched the Crown's revenue because it would have reduced the income from sheriffs' proffers, has already been discussed.[83] The two attempts made for this purpose stemmed from private initiatives, whereas the repeated and fruitless efforts to prevent abuses by sheriffs and their underlings came from the government. The first such bill emerged from the Council's pre-parliamentary planning in 1566.[84] It started in the Lords, was revised in the Commons, but then failed there at third reading.[85] Another attempt was made in 1576, and although this time the bill began in the Commons the fact that the Upper House, waiting for business, included it among those that it specially 'recommended to be expedited' indicates that once again the Council stood behind the move. It did no good: twice replaced by a *nova*, the bill disappeared after the third first reading, with two weeks of the session still remaining.[86] The Council tried once more in 1581. Its own bill, introduced in the Lords, pushed aside what must have been a private proposal in the Commons. Special care was taken, no doubt with an eye to learning from experience; the first bill was replaced even in the Lords; but the Lower House remained unpersuaded and after much amending the bill it finally voted it down on third reading.[87] The reason for this resistance to a reform of practices which were liable to be burdensome to the subject can be conjectured. We do know what the bills tried to do: malpractices connected with the return of writs and the empanelling of juries – that

[80] *CJ* I, 92; *Proc.* 383.
[81] Above, pp. 170–4.
[82] *CJ* I, 89–90; *LJ* I, 686, 692. – 14 Eliz. I c. 7.
[83] Above, pp. 169–70.
[84] SP 12/107, fo. 146.
[85] *LJ* I, 632, 634; *CJ* I, 75, 81.
[86] Ibid. 105–6, 108–9.
[87] *LJ* II, 21–2, 25, 27–8; *CJ* I, 120–2, 129, 133–4; SP 12/107, fos. 144–5.

is to say, with improper favours shown to men of local influence – were to be prevented by the imposition of a more stringent oath of office on various officers in local government.[88] The probability that knights and burgesses had their instructions to protect the interests of local worthies is supported by an entry in the records of Lincoln. On 23 March 1571, the city council resolved to procure an act 'discharging all penalties against the undersheriffs and their clerks', presumably on the assumption that the failed bill of 1566 would pass in the forthcoming Parliament.[89] Thus local interests three times blocked a reform of local government which the Council thought very desirable.

The third body of bills touching sheriffs throws further light on the relations between the centre and the shires. Among the government's plans for measures of reform drawn up at the beginning of the reign was one for appointing single sheriffs for every county and so to end the practice of pairing certain counties under one sheriff.[90] In 1566, an act to this effect was passed.[91] It claimed that in times past some counties had been too ill provided with worthy gentlemen fit to exercise the office, so that pairing had become necessary; nowadays, however, an increase in population had made such double charges too burdensome, while enough men competent to hold the office now existed. The desire for separation had, it was stated, been expressed by the gentlemen of those shires. The bill, an official measure introduced in the Commons, therefore divided the sheriffwicks of Surrey and Sussex, Essex and Hertfordshire, Somerset and Dorset, Warwickshire and Leicestershire, and Nottinghamshire and Derbyshire.[92] These, no doubt, were the counties from which the relevant requests had been received, for there were other pairs. Just as the bill was about to be concluded in the Commons, the gentlemen of Oxfordshire and Berkshire heard what was going on and put in a bill to do the same for their two counties.[93] The Lords incorporated this latecomer in the main bill which they much amended in detail; and so it passed.[94]

However, while the government might, as the preamble explained, expect better local administration from entrusting every county to its own

88 Indications of purpose are found scattered in the Journals (e.g. *LJ* I, 632) and especially for 1581 in Cromwell's diary (*Proc.* 530–1, 539). A surviving paper bill in HLRO (Papers Supplementary 1576–93) is most likely the first bill in the Lords in 1581; it is marked as twice read (which fits) and some of the corrections are in Burghley's hand. Its terms agree well enough with what Cromwell says came down from the Lords, though of course the bill had meanwhile been replaced by a *nova*.

89 HMC, *14th Report*, App. VIII (Lincoln), 65.

90 *TED* I, 329.

91 8 Eliz. I c. 16.

92 *CJ* I, 74–5, 77.

93 Ibid. 76, 78.

94 *LJ* I, 646–7, 653, 658–60. The Lords' amendments appear in the OA where every mention of Oxon. and Berks. is an insertion made at this stage.

sheriff, and while apparently in some counties there were enough people to aspire to the burdensome honour of the office, opinions differed elsewhere. When the act, a probationer, came up for renewal in 1571, Surrey and Sussex broke ranks by getting themselves taken out of it at a late stage in the Lords.[95] That this represented the view of one faction was confirmed in 1572 when a bill to renew the division (moved, presumably, by the side which won in 1566 and lost in 1571) passed the Commons but ran out of time in the Lords. Similar disagreements affected other paired counties which had not joined the original bill in 1566.[96] In that year, Buckinghamshire and Bedfordshire did produce a bill of their own, too late for the Lords' proceedings over the main bill; nevertheless, the two shires got theirs through both Houses, only to see it vetoed.[97] They did not give up: in 1571 they once again foundered on the veto, and in 1572 they reached the Upper House too late to get through.[98] Much the same fate befell Cambridgeshire and Huntingdonshire, even though they tried to speed things up by starting in the Lords; bills of separation passed both Houses in 1571 and 1572, and both were vetoed.[99] In these counties, therefore, opposition to the division, seemingly taken by surprise by late starts in the Lords, blocked the move by protesting in time to the Council to have the Queen postpone the decision until the proposers gave up. Things were settled more expeditiously in Norfolk and Suffolk: the one attempt to divide their sheriffwicks was defeated on a division in the Commons in 1571.[100] Clearly, East Anglian opponents to the East Anglian promoters were well established in the Lower House.

A last administrative problem which evidently plagued the Queen's government is a little surprising. It would appear that too many deeds, both such as conveyed lands or money to the Queen and letters patent of grants by the Queen, had been so ill drafted as to encourage tiresome doubts and dubious litigation. Right through the years here under review attempts were made to clean up a somewhat unnecessary situation produced by draftsmen's laxity. Both in 1563 and 1566 bills to confirm all letters patent issued since the first day of the reign, despite any technical errors they might contain, failed for lack of time, and it was not until 1576 that the desired act passed.[101] To judge from its terms,

[95] 13 Eliz. I c. 22, a short act which in its main clause left the two counties in. The exemption later in the act was inserted in the Lords' revisions (OA). This amendment produced a conference after which the Commons agreed to this omission.

[96] *CJ* I, 100–2; *LJ* I, 720, 723.

[97] *CJ* I, 78, 80; *LJ* I, 660, 662.

[98] *CJ* I, 89, 91–2, 102–3; *LJ* I, 692–6, 698, 723.

[99] Ibid. 682, 684–5, 713–14, 720; *CJ* I, 89–92, 100, 102.

[100] Ibid. 88–90.

[101] 1563: *CJ* I, 63, 71. 1566: ibid. 77–8, 80; *LJ* I, 662–3. 1576: 18 Eliz. I c. 2.

the chief problem had lain in failure to reserve the Queen's rights at law in leases of Crown lands. In addition lands had been let at rents below the customary level, and the beneficiaries of such official negligence were now to compound for the Crown's losses. No doubt such difficulties were aggravated by the prevalence of forged deeds against which a privately promoted act of 1563 had fixed severe penalties;[102] surprisingly, a Commons bill of 1581, which would have extended the punishment to any who altered or forged only part of a deed, was lost in the Lords because in the division the sides were equal.[103]

Cognate to the problem of questionable title deeds was the uncertainty whether properly certified copies should carry as much weight as the originals; a brief act of 1571 cleared this up back to the last day of the Reformation Parliament (4 February 1536).[104] Elizabeth's parsimonious preference for a lord keeper of the great seal instead of a lord chancellor necessitated an act of 1563 to confirm that the former had the same authority as the latter.[105] The checkered fortunes of cathedrals, collegiate churches and various schools in the ups and downs of the Reformation before 1558 led to the act of 1559 which equipped the Queen with power to give them much needed statutes and ordinances; though a Council measure, this was treated as a private (local) act, and it seems to have caused sufficient unease for an amending bill to be introduced in the next session; this received only one reading.[106] Forgery could extend to documents not formally issued by the Queen herself, and in 1581 a much disputed bill protecting the seals of privy councillors, other officers and town corporations passed the Commons only to be unanimously rejected by the Lords; perhaps they liked the proposed penalties even less than did those in the Lower House who had protested against making such offences felony, or they simply objected to a bill which because of its much disputed terms and many revisions must have been something of a dog's breakfast.[107] The point of all these bills and acts lies in this: matters of government, strictly by the rules within the powers of action enjoyed by Queen and Council, were nevertheless raised in Parliament, most usually on official initiative, because only in that way could offenders be brought to answer at law.

[102] 5 Eliz. I c. 14 started in the Lords; Commons provisos protected those who had unknowingly used forged documents, especially lawyers pleading such instruments in court.

[103] *CJ* I, 121, 124, 128; *LJ* II, 34, 38, 40; *Proc.* 531, 535. The petition behind the bill (SP 12/147, fos. 75–81) lists the kinds of fraud against which action was needed, the chief problem being that people in all good faith bought lands which the vendor had no legal right to sell though his forgeries pretended that he had.

[104] 13 Eliz. I c. 6.

[105] 5 Eliz. I c. 18.

[106] 1 Eliz. I c. 22; *CJ* I, 68.

[107] Ibid. 118, 120–1, 124, 127–8; *LJ* II, 36, 38, 41; *Proc.* esp. 531, 535, 537.

The tally of bills to reform details of government is thus not large, even though a little larger than conventional notions concerning the role of Parliament might lead one to suppose. Both official and private interests moved for a variety of improvements, but unlike the Council's labours for the protection of the Queen and state they achieved much less than they attempted. Yet it must be remembered that failed bills also took up parliamentary time, and sometimes a lot of it.

9

Church and religion

As the discussion of the treason laws has already made plain, problems of religion occupied much parliamentary time. The fact is familiar, and in the age of the Reformation, which in England had taken the form of statute-based changes in faith, administration and law, anything else would be very surprising. At the same time, the Queen regarded the Church and its affairs as her personal responsibility: she would decide whether she needed parliamentary assistance, and if she did not so decide Parliament had no occasion to intervene. All these matters have been several times discussed even in the recent literature, so that a really full treatment is superfluous here.[1] Nevertheless events in Parliament remain sufficiently obscure and current explanations – especially Neale's, which rested on the unproven assumption of the presence of a coherent puritan pressure group in the Commons – remain questionable, so that the whole body of the acts and the far more numerous failed bills need once more to be taken under review. The issues arising in Parliament resolve into six groups: the making of the Settlement and subsequent attempts to modify it, legal problems in the running of the Church, proposals touching the faith and its observance, the manners and fortunes of the clergy, the Church's possessions and the question of tithe, and a few miscellaneous points. They cannot be kept entirely separate – there are too many overlaps – but they do constitute the themes of this chapter.

It should be said at once that Neale's concentration on supposedly puritan manoeuvres, while demonstrably overdone and in great part a flight of fancy,[2] contains nevertheless an element of truth. Parliament became one of the arenas where protestants dissatisfied with the condition

[1] See esp. Neale, *EP* I and W. P. Haugaard, *Elizabeth and the English Reformation* (Cambridge, 1968), as more or less representing the traditional view; Jones, *Faith by Statute* and M. A. R. Graves and R. H. Silcock, *Revolution, Reaction and the Triumph of Conservatism: English History 1558–1700* (Auckland, N. Z., 1984), ch. 6, for the new approach.

[2] Below, pp. 350–3.

of the Church tried to promote reform. It was not the most important arena: Convocation (as intermittent), the printing press and the parish pulpit (always open) mattered more. However, Parliament's decisions had a universal and permanent import that other means of reform lacked. It is also true that in consequence Elizabeth, anxious to avoid change and determined to preserve her rule in the Church to herself, assisted by the bishops, came to dislike parliamentary meetings for giving those ardent spirits an opportunity. That truth was known at the time. In the mid-seventies, when the extravagant sect called the Family of Love was making progress in East Anglia, Sir Nathaniel Bacon learned from his brother Edward in London that 'the Queen is informed of many strange heresies lately sprung up, and I think rather to incense her against the Parliament than otherwise'.[3] Yet, as we shall see, many of the initiatives she resented came not from 'puritans' but from bishops and councillors; too often she found herself singlehandedly opposing what even her closest advisers desired. When one considers the much debated question who the puritans were, if often seems that there is only one definition which really works: the puritans were all those people whom the Queen disliked.

FRAMEWORK OF THE CHURCH

The English Church, reformed, de-reformed and re-reformed, came to rest on the two famous acts of 1559 for supremacy and uniformity.[4] They established it as a comprehensive national Church, ruled by the Queen as supreme governor, through a disciplinary structure of episcopal institutions (courts) assisted by royally appointed ecclesiastical commissioners for particular dioceses or either of the two provinces. It practised a protestant form of the Christian religion embodied in the revised Book of Common Prayer (1559) and the Thirty-Nine Articles of the Faith, accepted by the Convocations of the Church in 1563. The making of this settlement proved complex and difficult, opposition coming mainly from the Marian bishops and catholic peers in the Upper House; its maintenance came to be threatened both by irreconcilable catholics and later by protestants who did not regard it as final but wished to see further reform, mainly the removal of traditional elements still embedded in it. Those more radical or zealous protestants who supported such ambitions formed what used to be called the puritan movement – which has turned out to be less a movement than a confusion. Protestant zeal could be found in any corner of the Church, among laity and clergy, among bishops and deans as well as parsons and university students. The

[3] *The Papers of Sir Nathaniel Bacon*, 191.

[4] 1 Eliz. I cc. 1, 2.

changes looked for concerned matters as diverse as the vestments prescribed for the ministers of the Church, doctrinal doubts over ceremonies used, fundamentals of the faith, and in the extreme case of the presbyterian platform of the 1570s and 1580s the institution of episcopacy.[5] Not all of this penetrated into Parliament, but enough of it did. The making of the foundation acts has been very thoroughly analysed and shall here be taken as read.[6] It has now been established that the Settlement in the end looked pretty much like what Queen and Council – especially Cecil – had wanted from the first; the supposed success of radical protestant demands has turned out to be the product of a historian's oversubtle imagination. In 1559, all protestants and indeed most catholics rallied behind Elizabeth as Queen and therefore as the person entitled to decide the fate of the Church; but it would not be false to add that in 1559 only the Queen supposed that the Settlement would stand unaltered forever. Catholics hoped that it might yet be undone; most protestants felt sure that it provided but a start for a truly reformed Church.

In the seven sessions with which we are concerned no attack was mounted against the basic structure of this Church, though there were some attempts to modify it here or there. In the battles of 1559 not everybody overlooked the fact that Mary's repeal of Edward VI's act for a protestant ordinal left the Church without a lawful system for making bishops. A bill, poorly described in the Commons Journal as empowering the Queen to appoint bishops to vacant sees (a power she effectively enjoyed under the act of supremacy anyway) and better defined in the Lords as being 'for the admitting and consecrating of archbishops and bishops', passed the Commons that year but expired in the Lords after one reading: another success for the Marian bishops. Reintroduced in 1563 it got engrossed in the Commons before vanishing once more: protestants beginning to wonder about rites.[7] It was almost certainly an official bill, for the matter in the end received proper attention in 1566 in an act which was drafted by the attorney general.[8] This passed the Commons quickly, with one proviso of unknown purport annexed; in the Lords there was much opposition, with eleven catholic peers voting against the third reading, and the Commons proviso was replaced by another. This the Commons would not accept; the disputed proviso was changed once more, and so the act passed.[9] That is the story told by the

[5] The best general account of protestant protest remains P. Collinson, *The Elizabethan Puritan Movement* (London, 1967), but see also P. Lake, *Moderate Puritans and the Elizabethan Church* (Cambridge, 1982).

[6] Jones, *Faith by Statute*.

[7] *CJ* I, 58, 68; *LJ* I, 566.

[8] 8 Eliz. I c. 1; SP 12/107, fo. 146.

[9] *CJ* I, 74–6, 78; *LJ* I, 636, 638–9, 641, 651.

Journals, but the Original Act shows that the proviso finally agreed originated in the Lords. The confusion is probably best resolved by accepting that the extant proviso was essentially that drafted in the Lords and had only been modified in the Commons. The point matters. The body of the act simply, though at some length, cleaned up the current situation regarding clerical orders, confirming every parson and bishop already ordained. The proviso is a tack irrelevant to the purpose of the act; it in effect did away with every attempt made since the passage of the 1563 act to enforce the oath of supremacy.[10] In this it reflected, of course, the Queen's unwillingness to have the act applied, though it did not hinder future uses of it; it also backed those clerics, including Marian survivors, who had retained their doubts about the protestant settlement. Both the Journals say that in its final form it came from the Commons – the supposedly violently anti-catholic and puritan Commons of 1566.

The only other bill which directly affected the structure and power of the Church appeared first in 1571; it proposed to equip the ecclesiastical authorities with power to compel everybody's attendance at church once a quarter and the taking of the communion by the anglican rite once a year. Introduced in the Commons, it started a war of confusion and misapprehension.[11] A Commons committee immediately brought in a revised bill, but members of the committee offered conflicting advice to the House: some wished to consult the bishops (the counsel of Sir Thomas Smith, secretary of state), while others suggested an immediate further committal, as Recorder Fleetwood preferred on the grounds that the bishops would cause delays. For this, as he later told the House, he received a rebuke from the Council – but, as it turned out, this was because he had misjudged the bishops' interest and not because he had prevented them from killing the bill. It is evident that members of the Lower House thought they were dealing with an unofficial bill: later in the proceedings they even had to resolve that the bill was to be treated as general, which is very strange because from the first there was nothing local or private about it. In actual fact the first proposals leading to the bill had been drafted by Edmund Grindal, bishop of London, as Strype tells us who printed the draft (now lost) and recognized the hand.[12] The Council, which had clearly intended Smith to move for collaboration with the bishops, manifestly knew that that was no wrecking move. The long debates in the Lower House displayed much learning and ingenuity.

[10] See above, pp. 178–81.

[11] For the history of the bill in Parliament see *CJ* I, 82–3, 85–8, 91–2; *LJ* I, 681–3, 658, 695–7; for the terms of bill and debate see *Proc.* 201–2, 205–8.

[12] Strype, *Annals* I, i, 460–1; *A history of... Edmund Grindal* (Oxford, 1821), 478–81. The draft is not for either of the bills summarized in *Proc.* 201 and 205, but it shows the strong episcopal demand for more regular attendance at church.

It was argued that to compel people to attend services which might break the law by not obeying the act of uniformity would be to force worshippers into illegality; this drew the reply that if the service went counter to the law it would, by being no service, free the parishioners from attending. Edward Aglionby, burgess for Warwick, cited Plato and Cicero in his objections to exemptions granted to the private chaplains of gentlemen. Robert Snagge, a good protestant, mentioned the need to do something about non-observance at the Universities, by private schoolmasters in gentlemen's houses, and at the Inns of Court, all suspect refuges for catholic recusancy.

However, the bill passed the Commons in effect unaltered, putting heavy money fines on the disobedient and providing effective machinery for enforcement by the ecclesiastical authorities. In the course of passage, another bill which protected persons going to church from being arrested for debt, when they thus exposed themselves to the sheriffs' officers, was joined to the main bill.[13] The Lords gave it to a committee of twelve in which sat four bishops and four privy councillors, including Burghley. They seem to have made some amendments which led to a conference of both Houses, but the bill passed much as it had left the Commons. The Queen vetoed it. She knew that the bishops had been behind it, though no doubt the Commons' independent zeal added to her annoyance.[14] Her reasons for disliking the bill can only be conjectured. She may simply have wanted no statutes forcing a particular behaviour in religion upon her subjects, or she may not have wanted to exacerbate the divisions which the act's enforcement would have brought into the open. Or she may just have generally disliked bills for religion she had not at first agreed to.

The bishops' original initiative soon proved itself. In June 1572, Grindal, now archbishop of York, with several of his colleagues on the bench, had an interview with Elizabeth at which they tried to persuade her to withdraw her objections and presented her with a summary of the bill in articles. Elizabeth referred them to Burghley.[15] The lord treasurer received and digested this document (which can hardly have been new to him)[16] with the result that the bill was indeed reintroduced in the next session (1576) in the Upper House. Committal produced a *nova*, but its disappearance after a single reading suggests an outburst from the palace: that had not been the idea when the Queen deflected

[13] *CJ* I, 84, 86; *Proc.* 208.

[14] *Studies* III, 177–8.

[15] SP 12/88, fo. 7.

[16] SP 12/147, fos. 121–2 (misdated). The exception for gentlemen had disappeared; a new proviso permitting bishops to license abstention from communion to any persons whose refusal arose from scruples of conscience reflects another objection raised in the Commons' debates; the protection against arrest reappeared.

the bishops onto her councillor.[17] Nothing daunted, the bishops tried once more in 1581, with the same result.[18] On the other hand, no one in the Lower House ever tried to revive the idea of statutory control over attendance at church. Plainly, the notion came from the bishops responsible for a uniformly protestant body of Englishmen and women; they had got the Privy Council to support them, and their joint desires backed by a godly majority in the Commons foundered solely on the Queen.

Apart from these larger problems a number of matters concerning the running of the Church made their appearance in Parliament. None succeeded and few ever got beyond a first reading; all look like coming from unofficial initiatives; perhaps they signify little but they do indicate the concerns that attracted attention. Two topics refer to the structure of the Church: in 1566 the Lords took a bill for the confirmation of recently created deaneries (presumably the conversion of monastic cathedral priories into secular chapters) as far as the committee stage,[19] and in 1563 and 1572 very shortlived bills tried to transfer the county of Dorset from the diocese of Bristol to that of Salisbury to which it had belonged before the new see of Bristol was created in 1542.[20] However, most of the bills in this category attended to legal problems in the Church courts. In 1559 the old problem of a canon law suitable for protestant England was revived with a bill to appoint a commission of thirty-two experts to investigate; though this passed the Commons it did not get beyond a first reading in the Lords where more knowledgeable opinion prevailed.[21] The plans for such a commission went back to the submission of the clergy of 1532, but since then the work had been done by such commissioners in the reign of Edward VI, a point at last remembered in 1571.[22] Somebody decided to enact a law for the qualifications of judges in the Church courts: they were to be graduates of Oxford or Cambridge. In 1563 the bill passed in the Lower House and lapsed in the Upper after second reading; in 1566 even the Commons read it but once.[23] Old resentments manifested themselves against the privilege known as benefit of clergy – a claim to clerical status which transferred a convicted criminal for punishment to the bishop's court where clerks convict got off by various devices (including, though the bill does not seem to have thought of that, escape from prison which was exceptionally easy). In 1566 Norton brought in a bill which wished to abolish the usual means for defeating those courts which was compurgation (proving oneself innocent by the oaths of a stated number of helpers), and after

[17] *LJ* I, 731–2, 740. [18] Ibid. II, 29. [19] Ibid. I, 651, 657.
[20] Ibid. 613, 709. [21] *CJ* I, 55–6, 58; *LJ* I, 566, 568.
[22] Below, p. 208. [23] *CJ* I, 68–71, 76; *LJ* I, 611.

this failed to progress beyond first reading he raised the issue in 1571. His passionate denunciation of the perjuries thus committed, backed by a good protestant attack on Thomas Beckett's responsibility for the exemption of criminous clerks from the hangman's attention, persuaded the House 'to have care for a redress'. Four weeks later Norton found time to dig out his old bill and present it; it passed in three days, but it was too late to get it past a second reading in the Lords.[24] Norton's choice of a grievance and his mention of Beckett link him to that body of common lawyers who had testified to their hostility to ecclesiastical courts and benefit of clergy in the days of Thomas Cromwell.[25] In that same session of 1571 someone else tried to prevent ecclesiastical judges from commuting penances for money payments unless they had obtained the approval of two J.P.s, a striking manifestation of puritan trust in the magistrate; this bill, after rushing through the Commons, died in committee in the Lords.[26]

Of all these protests against clerical laxness one bill, though it too failed, left a slightly bigger impact. In 1571 George Carleton, who fairly deserved the name of puritan, proposed to repeal the act of 25 Henry VIII c. 21 insofar as it granted powers of issuing licences and dispensations to the archbishop of Canterbury (the act which had led to the erection of the Canterbury Office for Faculties). This, Carleton asserted, made that prelate 'as it were a pope'; it had been 'procured by the bishops of that time'; protestant bishops should not wish to follow their popish predecessors' practices. Actually, the dispensations act was entirely the work of Thomas Cromwell, and it reserved the more important licences to the court of Chancery. The preamble of Carleton's bill spoke highly of Archbishop Cranmer and conceded some goodness in Archbishop Parker, but thought it unlikely that all future holders of the office would be as worthy. For which reason the bill prohibited all archiepiscopal licences which went counter to the Word of God, the laws of the realm or edicts of Convocation, or were prejudicial to the Queen's 'crown and dignity, or to the due allegiance' owed by all subjects, a comprehensive catalogue which could have provided endless and profitable litigation in efforts to define its meaning.[27] The bill did not do well in the debate where it was shown to be both vague (what particular grievances was it supposed to remedy?) and superfluous (bishops, said James Dalton perhaps ironically, 'can do nothing contrary to the Word of God'). Fleetwood took the opportunity for one of his meandering

[24] *CJ* I, 75, 89–90; *LJ* I, 686, 688, 691; *Proc.* 224, 252. Cf. also below, pp. 301–2.

[25] G. R. Elton, *Reform and Renewal: Thomas Cromwell and the Common Weal* (Cambridge, 1973), 129–36.

[26] *CJ* I, 88–90; *LJ* I, 686, 689, 692; *Proc.* 253.

[27] SP 12/27, fos. 221–5 (misdated).

discourses, ranging over the etymology of the word 'discretion', trying to make a history for the word 'faculty', and getting his own back on an unnamed judge who had offended him. The reporter noted that he spoke 'learnedly and withal pleasantly', which helps to remind one of changing standards in such matters, for in effect Fleetwood as so often contributed nothing of substance.[28] However, Carleton's bill proceeded, though committal produced a *nova*. This reached the Lords, but since they appointed a committee including four lords spiritual (one of them Parker), it is no wonder that the bill never emerged from it.[29] Altogether the Parliament proved to be poor ground on which to reform the government of the Church – if indeed that government needed reforming.

REFORMATION

Not surprisingly, the Parliament turned out to be even less successful as an instrument for improving the moral and spiritual welfare of a nation most of whom (including the Queen) were not ardent protestants. On the other hand, a number of such protestants got elected to the House of Commons, and in consequence talk occurred of such 'puritan' ends – talk plus a bit of action which Neale took to prove the existence of a coherent puritan pressure group. In reviewing the bills for reform in religion it is therefore, unfortunately, necessary to keep his interpretation in mind and to trouble ourselves with assessing how far it might prove acceptable; for even though his construction of a puritan 'choir' will not persuade, he could still be right about the individual instances of reform proposals. Not all of these were as absurd and futile as the bill of 1566 'for offenders in swearing, drunkenness &c' which after a long moralising preamble wished to prohibit all taking of oaths except in proper courts and in private matters of weight 'where it may lead to the glory of Almighty God'. Even Sir Frances Knollys, chairman of the bill committee, who had often testified to his sincere and austere protestantism, could do no more with it than bury it.[30]

Six other bills for religion appeared in 1566. They were tagged A to F by the clerk (and therefore alphabet bills by Neale); they were all introduced in the Commons on two successive days; they therefore looked to Neale like 'a whole code, all unofficial bills! It would take a simpleton not to suspect a planned drive.'[31] There is something to be said for restoring the simple mind to this problem. We do not know who promoted the bills; the conviction that they were all unofficial rests only

[28] *Proc.* 222–3.
[29] *CJ* I, 84, 87–8; *LJ* I, 684–5.
[30] *CJ* I, 78–9; BM, Lansdowne MS 105, fos. 199–200.
[31] Neale, *EP* I, 166. Better a simpleton than a bully.

on belief. We are far from well informed about their contents, but we can be sure that they tackled widely differing questions; the word 'code' seems quite wrong for them. Bill A, which proposed to give statutory authority to the Thirty-Nine Articles approved by Convocation in 1563, alone dealt with an aspect of the faith; and the supposition that it was a 'puritan' measure somewhat conflicts with the later argument that in the renewed debates of 1571 everything turned on the puritan desire to avoid legal compulsion to subscribe to all the Articles.[32] It is, in fact, the only 'alphabet bill' of 1566 about whose background we know anything. It passed the Commons in short order, though the late introduction on 5 December meant arrival in the Lords ten days before Christmas, not a propitious time unless there was no opposition to be encountered. Since the Queen totally rejected the bill, it proceeded no further in the Upper House than a first reading: she had expressly ordered the Lords to stop.[33] This produced a formal and solemn appeal, written on parchment, from fifteen bishops headed by the two archbishops, 'that the said bill by order of your majesty may be read, examined and judged by your highness' said Upper House with all expedition; and that if it be allowed of and do pass by order there it would please your majesty to give your royal assent thereto'.[34] The bishops pointed out that the bill touched God and salvation, that the Articles comprised the faith of the Church of England and had been set forth by the Queen's own authority, and that their enforcement would assist the uniformity everybody wanted. At the end of the session Cecil much regretted Elizabeth's successful stand against it.[35] It seems rash to suppose that a bill supported by the secretary of state and the episcopal hierarchy originated in a purely private initiative; and since, as the bishops pointed out, it in no way innovated, the promoters had every reason to expect its passage. If those promoters included official elements they also had every reason to know about Elizabeth's likely reaction and to disguise their initiative, not for the first or last time. At any rate, Bill A was not part of a drive planned by puritan zealots. The Queen well knew that there had been mitred backing; she accused some of the bishops of having put the bill into the Commons, and though Parker himself claimed not to have known about this nor even to have heard the single reading in the Lords, she was most probably right. According to Parker she objected not to the bill as such and certainly not to the Articles, but to the hugger-mugger way in which it

[32] Ibid. 204–7.
[33] *CJ* I, 79–80; *LJ* I, 658.
[34] SP 12/41 fos. 100–101 (printed in Matthew Parker, *Correspondence* [London, 1853], 291–4).
[35] SP 12/41, fo. 76.

had been started, in an effort, she implied, to outflank her unwillingness to have the Parliament legislate for the Church.[36]

The remaining five bills for religion were all read once in the Lower House on 6 December and not heard of again, though the session resumed after Christmas and did not end until 2 January.[37] The concerted drive seems to have lacked steam. More to the point still, except for B, which professed to be 'for the order of ministers' and when revived in 1571 was described as securing the clergy's adherence to uniformity in their preaching and behaviour,[38] none of them touched a matter of doctrinal belief. All of them were designed to remedy supposed defects in the behaviour of the clergy of the sort that anti-clerical laymen had complained of since before the Reformation – nonresidence, corrupt presentations to livings, dubious leases and more doubtful pensions out of benefices. Bill B, with its intention to control preaching, meant to impose the sort of obedient conformity which, we are told, puritans stood opposed to; its terms, which permitted deprivation at the pleasure of the diocesan bishop, again suggest an episcopal initiative. The bills against abuses, too, reflect the concerns of reforming and active bishops (most of them products of the Marian exile) at least as well as those of the laity or the lower and supposedly radical clergy. The tactical error, perhaps forced by the parliamentary time-table in 1566, which started all six bills at so late a stage in the session, might also hint that the promoters did not sit in the Lower House. So far as the inadequate evidence goes, it supports the conclusions that if there was an offensive mounted in 1566 it came from the hierarchy, and in its mixture of targets is unlikely to have constituted a proper programme (let alone a code) – certainly not one prepared by an 'opposition'. Most likely the bills stemmed from various minds and people; the production of such a set of reforming bills recalls the methods used by the Council when it picked up ideas promoted in earlier sessions or around the country and then assigned various officers to draft suitable bills.[39]

Such conclusions must, of course, influence our interpretation of the 1571 session when religion again (and effectively for the last time in our period) became a major concern in the House of Commons. The modest turmoil began with a speech by William Strickland on the need for

[36] Parker to Cecil, 22 Dec. 1566: SP 12/41, fo. 121. The bishops were not agreed on all points: Edmund Gheast of Rochester knew that Richard Cheney of Gloucester objected to the drafting of the article on the Lord's Supper which, Cheney claimed, took away the corporeal presence. If the bill had proceeded, Gheast would have insisted on debating the question in the House (ibid. fo. 135).

[37] *CJ* I, 79.

[38] *Proc.* 208, 246.

[39] Above, pp. 71–2.

further reform, in the course of which he called Norton in aid.[40] Strickland certainly was a genuine puritan and probably a follower of Thomas Cartwright; the bulk of his speech insisted on the need to reform the Prayer Book along lines familiar since the Vestiarian Controversy. 'Although (God be praised),' he said, 'it is drawn very near to the sincerity of the truth, yet are some things inserted more superstitious and erroneous than in so high matters be tolerable'; and he specified the standard objections to the sign of the cross in baptism, and the right of women in emergencies to administer the sacrament. But his appeal to Norton concerned the code of the spiritual law prepared in Edward's reign and entitled *Reformatio Legum Ecclesiasticarum*, recently put out in print by John Foxe. Strickland knew that Norton had a copy which he could produce; he does not seem to have known of the printing which would have enabled him to bring his own copy. Nor was he apparently aware that the code, if enforced by statute, would not have pleased deviationists appearing before the Church courts. He added rather grimy grievances concerning papists who remained in valuable livings while 'honest, godly and learned protestants' went begging, about boys under the canonical age and other unqualified persons getting licences to hold benefices, about pluralists. When these topics are mentioned, as often they were, one is never quite sure whether the speaker wishes to provide better pastors for neglected souls or better livings for neglected pastors. However, what Strickland after all this lamenting actually called for was a committee to confer with the bishops about possible reforms. Norton responded by agreeing that he had a copy of the *Reformatio* but confined himself to a pedantic correction of Strickland's recital of its supposed authors: the point mattered because Strickland had poured praise on well known radical protestants from abroad who had been in England in the 1550s, whereas in truth (as Norton quite correctly pointed out) the code had been the work of English divines of moderate views. For the rest he wished to support the prohibition of simoniacal practices in appointments to livings.[41] No more was to be heard of the reform of the canon law which the bishops certainly did not wish to receive at the hands of Parliament.

Neale spoke of Strickland's proposals as equalling the complete puritan programme of the 1560s. 'To assume that it sprang from Strickland's mind alone would be childish', and he divined 'party organization' behind it, speculating whom that party might have included.[42] But even if Strickland represented views agreed with some

[40] Cf. Neale, *EP* I, 193–6. His account is affected by his erroneous conviction that Thomas Norton was a leader of opposition. He also misdates Strickland's intervention to 5 April (p. 193); the tacit switch to the 6th (p. 195) is correct.

[41] *Proc.* 200–1.

[42] *EP* I, 195.

'radical clergy', he seems to have lacked a party in the House. Norton's cool reaction suggested as much, and so did the subsequent work on the bills for religion that emerged from the committee promptly appointed.[43] These amounted to a revival of five bills from the previous session produced by Norton who, acting for the Council, had retained the alphabet bills in 1566. However, there was one new bill apparently not referred to the committee: that for 'the reformation of the Book of Common Prayer', introduced by Strickland on 14 April and embodying the objections to ceremonies licensed in the Book which he had mentioned in his speech. It was in fact the only audacious, and from the official point of view outrageous, bill of the session, and Strickland stood alone in backing it. The Commons read it once. Two privy councillors immediately opposed it, advising that, while matters of heresy might be properly handled in an act of Parliament, matters of ceremony should be referred to the Queen 'who has authority as chief of the Church to deal therein'. Two members offered Strickland some very hesitant support in speeches that avoided touching on the substance of the bill, and the House resolved to petition the Queen for permission to proceed.[44] This avoided infuriating the extremists but made sure that the bill would sink; it is noted as 'stricken' from a list of bills produced towards the end of the month.[45]

We return to the work of the committee on religion. Five of the 1566 bills were revived and two passed, though in an amended state. One was the bill against simony (the old bill E), the only one to which Norton had from the first given his backing. We may therefore say with confidence that it was agreeable to the Council.[46] A very short bill, using the short enacting clause, it prohibited the subletting of livings by absentee or pluralist incumbents; as Hooker put it, 'beneficed men shall not appoint their benefices to any evil or simoniacal uses'.[47] Despite its official origin it had been much amended in the Lords, as the Original Act shows. The Upper House removed the only express mention of simony by deleting a whole clause declaring void all contracts and agreements that might be so termed; and they took out the one bit of puritanism left in the Common's bill when they altered an exception for

[43] Above, pp. 99–100. The summary account given there will here be enlarged in some details from the point of view of legislative intention and initiative.

[44] *CJ* I, 84; *Proc.* 200–2, 247.

[45] SP 12/77, fo. 111. Strickland's bill had been the occasion of his so-called arrest (i.e. he was ordered to attend upon the Council and meanwhile stay away from Parliament): *Proc.* 225. Neale's bewildering remark (*EP* I, 200) that this and other matters are noted 'in the part of the diary that is lost' is explained by the fact that the note is in the part of the diary that survives.

[46] 13 Eliz. I c. 20.

[47] *Proc.* 250.

'preachers using preaching and by reason thereof allowed to have two benefices' to 'persons by the laws of this realm allowed to have two benefices'.[48] The point signified, for a bill concerning pluralism, non-residence and the proper preaching of sermons (another left-over from 1566) was dropped by the Lords after one reading, the session being nearly ended.[49] Thus the only law governing pluralism remained the act of 1529 (21 Henry VIII c. 13) which permitted pluralism more readily than did the intention enshrined in the Commons' version of the clause.

The bill to confirm the Thirty-Nine Articles was also revived under the somewhat obscure title 'for conservation of order and uniformity in the Church'; the Commons shot it through in two days but on 1 May the Queen stopped it after one reading in the Upper House.[50] The outcome must have been disappointing to people in both Houses who had shown some eagerness to cooperate. The Commons, as we have seen, had immediately endorsed Strickland's motion for a general reference of reform bills to the bishops. On 10 April it was reported that the bishops would like the Commons to ask the Lords for a conference on the bill of Articles, and this was at once agreed to;[51] next day, Sir James Croft (comptroller of the Household and chairman of the deputation) asked whether this meant a genuine conference or the seeking of instructions from the bishops. Norton's compromising advice, which was accepted, indicated some differences of views: he suggested calling the meeting a suit (that is, a request for assistance) but that nonetheless the Commons committee should 'confer' and accept the bishops' directions no 'further than their consciences should be satisfied'.[52] Something turns on the (unknown) provisions of the revived bill A. The 1566 bill had certainly meant to enact all the Thirty-Nine Articles, and the title of the new bill referred to 'uniformity in the Church', which does not sound like reservations concerning some part of the Thirty-Nine. When the Queen came to block the bill she explicitly approved its terms and only declared that she preferred to enforce the Articles 'by her royal authority of supremacy of the Church of England and not to have the same dealt in by Parliament'.[53] Yet Neale persuaded himself that the bill meant to limit the number of Articles confirmed, for which conclusion there is certainly no straightforward evidence.[54]

48 OA; *CJ* I, 84, 87–8, 91; *LJ* I, 684, 686, 689, 692.

49 *CJ* I, 89–90; *LJ* I, 668. To judge only by the titles of bills (which is all we know), it probably combined the old bill C (for the residence of pastors) with an earlier bill of 1566 'to avoid pluralities of benefices' which had stayed in a committee chaired by Cecil (*CJ* I, 76–7).

50 *CJ* I, 86 (two readings on one day, the third on the next); *LJ* I, 678.

51 *CJ* I, 84.

52 *Proc.* 208. Neale (*EP* I, 198) misinterprets the meaning of 'suit' as a seeking to retain freedom of action, which is contrary to Tudor usage.

53 *CJ* I, 87; *Proc.* 250.

54 Neale, *EP* I, 203. 'As we have already noted', he says, but I cannot find where we have done so.

However, evidence of an indirect kind does exist, creating doubt and confusion. The suggestion that not all the Articles would become statutory appeared in the bill 'to reform certain disorders touching ministers of the Church' (ex-bill B, discussed in a moment) which in its original form had allowed for the possibility that the present session of Parliament or Convocation would alter the tally of Articles. In addition, there is Peter Wentworth's account, given four years later, of a meeting with Archbishop Parker. On 25 April, the day before the bill of Articles was read in the House, a committee of six including Wentworth was appointed to attend upon Parker and answer his questions on 'matters of religion'.[55] According to Wentworth's long-distance recollection, Parker had asked why some things had been left out of the book of Articles. He was told that the Commons had not had time to examine the doctrinal purity of all the Thirty-Nine. Not surprisingly Parker had protested that the Articles had been agreed by all the clergy: surely the Commons would accept their guidance on this. Whereupon gallant Peter testified to his faith with ringing words about not making bishops into popes.[56] So much is famous, but no one has ever asked what it was that the Commons supposedly wished to omit. Wentworth has Parker refer to 'the homilies consecrating the bishops and such like', which makes sense only if a comma is inserted after 'homilies'. In that case we are talking about Articles 35 and 36, right near the end; the remaining ones deal with the powers of the civil magistrates, condemn the Anabaptist doctrine of communism, and approve the proper use of an oath. The puritan objections to ceremonies, the issues prominent in the 1560s and in Strickland's bill, do not at all arise here. If we can trust Wentworth's direct-speech report at all, it looks as though he may have spoken something like the truth: the Commons had not managed to get to the end of the book and wished to confirm only as far as they had studied. This would signify dumb insolence rather than a design to save puritans from having to subscribe to Articles they disliked, for those last Articles hardly belonged in that category.

Anyway, it was the Queen who terminated the bill of Articles and not the bishops, and she, as has been said, appears to have seen nothing objectionable in its contents; it is really very hard to believe that the bill contained a selective list of articles to be approved, though an incomplete or selective list may have been attached to it. That leaves us with the second bill to pass, that intended 'to reform certain disorders touching ministers of the Church'.[57] It aimed to prevent inadequate men serving cures of souls, and Neale argued that it represented a half-hidden puritan triumph.[58] The case is less clear-cut than he made out. The original bill

[55] *CJ* I, 86.
[56] *Proc.* 432.
[57] 13 Eliz. I c. 12.
[58] *EP* I, 206–7.

in effect included three provisions.[59] All holders of benefices were to subscribe to the Thirty-Nine Articles and publish them in the parish church: 'on pain to be deprived *ipso facto*' (without further proceedings); anyone preaching against this was to be deprived at his bishop's pleasure; all incumbents on institution must have passed twenty-two years of age, nor could anyone hold a living unless 'he can render an account of his belief in Latin or has the gift of preaching'. With some stretching the last point, confining livings to the learned but allowing the presence of possibly inspired though untutored preachers, may be ascribed to a radical initiative; but the rest of the bill imposed full conformity and control by the hierarchy. Once again we find a bill for religion to which the bishops and the Council had as good reason to extend their favour as anyone. The act as passed added a few points the only significant one of which confined livings worth £30 a year to bachelors of divinity and preachers licensed by the bishops or the Universities. That is to say, it remained a bill attractive to anyone concerned to create a learned and proper and conforming ministry in England. Many bishops had for years been protesting about the unfit people that were presented for induction. Nor does the passage of the bill indicate much trouble.[60] It was committed in the Lower House but no change is known to have come of that; however, on third reading it was not approved, being further debated and read a fourth time for passage. The reason for this, as Hooker tells us, was 'much ado concerning the words minister and priest as also very sharp talk touching private men'.[61] The second doubt, a revival of the fear that popish gentlemen's chaplains would escape the control of the act, left no mark upon it, but where it occurred the word 'priest' was erased on the parchment bill.

However, one larger change was made on the parchment bill, and this to Neale constituted the visible proof of a puritan victory. The Articles of Religion to be subscribed had originally been identified in a double formula:

> Confession of the true faith of Christ agreed upon by the archbishops and bishops of both the provinces and the whole clergy in the Convocation holden at London in the year of our Lord God 1562 [i.e. 1563] and published according to the order appointed by the Queen's majesty's injunctions, or so much of the said Articles as be or shall be allowed or confirmed in this present session of Parliament or in Convocation.

This had therefore allowed for the possibility that a bill reducing the number of binding Articles might pass, but the Queen had put a stop to that. Therefore the phrase was amended on the Original Act to read

[59] *Proc.* 208.

[60] *CJ* I, 84, 86–7, 91; *LJ* I, 682, 684, 691, 694.

[61] *Proc.* 249.

'which concern only the confession of the true Christian faith', followed by slightly altered phrases about the 1563 Convocation and the Queen's injunctions. Neale, very possibly deriving his case from the fact that some puritans later tried to choose which Articles they would agree to, on the grounds that the act compelled subscription 'only' to what concerned doctrine,[62] claimed to see a puritan triumph in the phrasing which could be read as not demanding obedience to non-doctrinal Articles. But since the Thirty-Nine Articles were a statement of doctrine it is hard to see which Articles had thereby been made optional, and if all that was in question were the three allegedly mentioned by Parker to Wentworth the gain was nil. To me that word, 'only', reads much more like a justification of the demand for subscription: it implied that it was right to ask for compliance because the sole purpose of the Articles was to define the true faith as agreed to by the Church of England.[63]

Furthermore, it is by no means certain that the change was made in the House of Commons, as Neale assumed. The Lords Journal tells us that the bill was at the last amended in the Upper House, being then sent down and returned on the same day; the Commons had at once agreed to the Lords' amendments. Yet the only passage in the parchment which fits this account is this altered definition of the Articles, an alteration which therefore looks much more likely to have been made in the Lords.[64] One can see why. The bill as they received it included an option which the Queen's prohibition had three days earlier rendered out of date; it

[62] M. M. Knappen, *Tudor Puritanism* (Chicago, 1939), 266–7. The evidence he cites belongs to the mid-eighties but it suggests that Art. 36, for the consecration of bishops, proved objectionable to presbyterian puritans. The zealots of 1571 did not much like bishops but were raising no objection to the institution of episcopacy.

[63] I am no theologian but I find it hard to discover an Article among the Thirty-Nine that is truthfully not concerned with 'the confession of the true Christian faith'. Art. 20, affirming the Church's right to decree rites and ceremonies, expressly condemns any such as are contrary to Scripture, in view of which anybody who objected to anglican ceremonies as unscriptural could presumably subscribe quite cheerfully. Doctrine inevitably enters into every Article. Art. 35, confirming the Homilies which some puritans found objectionable, does so on the grounds that they contain 'a godly and wholesome' doctrine.

[64] In his article which supposedly provided the learned foundation for the story as he told it ('Parliament and the Articles of Religion, 1571,' *EHR* 57 [1952], 510–17) Neale speaks of three kinds of corrections on the OA. One is the elimination of the word 'priest': we have seen that there is supporting evidence for this being done by the Commons. Secondly there are some very minor verbal changes: these he ascribes to the Lords. The third is the big change in the description of the Articles: was this done by the Commons or the Lords? Although we have a diary reference to the debate on fourth reading when the commons altered the bill, and although this mentions the objection to 'priests', it says nothing of the much bigger amendment. Neale worries about the clerks' hands on the parchment bill, but of course all amendments on an engrossed bill had to be made by the clerk of the House of initiation: the same hand would have inserted the new words whether Lords or Commons had asked for them.

is entirely probable that this last-minute introduction of reality arose from the usual practice of the Upper House to have the judges look at the thing. Neale's theory would suppose either that no one except the victorious puritans in the Lower House realized the meaning of the rephrasing, or that the Lords passed and the Queen assented to an act which allowed sensitive consciences to choose what they would subscribe to. On balance it seems a great deal more likely that at the time no one read that secret meaning into the words.

Like the rest of the session's bills, the act for subscribing to the Articles thus demonstrates what really happened. Good protestants in both Houses wished to tighten the hold of the law on the clergy by preventing crypto-papists (especially Marian survivors) and ill qualified persons from serving cures. The lead was taken by the bishops in the Upper House and the Council's men in the Lower. Anything that overstepped that precise line got short shrift – Strickland's general reform of the Prayer Book, the attempt to distinguish among the Articles, and legislation against pluralism which, since the necessary laws already existed, the Queen thought to be a matter for the bishops. The session testified to protestant zeal and apprehensions, but not to a concerted and antiepiscopal puritan programme which managed to score some victorious points. Hindsight is not relevant. What Peter Wentworth later told is like the soldier's evidence, and what puritan casuists later tried to make (unsuccessfully) of the 'only' phrase says nothing about the intentions of the statute when it was made.

This reconstruction is really supported by the only further attempt in the remaining three sessions to bring about reform by statute. In 1572 a bill entitled 'concerning dispensations for rites and ceremonies' was introduced on 17 May, halfway through a session preoccupied with the Queen of Scots and the duke of Norfolk.[65] On this occasion, the extant text of the bill and the provable coordination with the authors of the contemporaneous *Second Admonition to the Parliament* (such firebrands as John Field) do testify to an unmistakably puritan manoeuvre. The bill spoke plainly, even blatantly, especially in its interminable preamble. The act of uniformity had, we are told, had some virtue, but because the previous reign had caused much 'backsliding...from true religion to superstition' the act had permitted the retention of too many false ceremonies. Since that time the progress of good preaching of the gospel

[65] The story is told at length by Neale, *EP* I, 297–304, for once pretty accurately. For the evidence see *CJ* I, 95–7; *Proc.* 330–1, 362–3, 368–9. The original bill and that replacing it, as well as the Speaker's letter to Burghley of 20 May (SP 12/198–9, 204, 206–15) are printed in *Puritan Manifestoes*, ed. W. H. Frere and C. E. Douglas (London, 1954), 149–52.

had produced many congregations eager to attain 'some further form' than was prescribed in the Prayer Book, as well as many learned and zealous ministers who, with the permission 'of some godly bishops', had endeavoured to meet the demand by varying the services from those technically established by law. The preamble praised the exercises known as prophesyings by which the return to the primitive Church of the Apostles and approximation to the best reformed Churches of the present day had been much advanced. But such godly ministers had enemies who used the most trivial departure from the Prayer Book to get them into trouble at the assizes. The proposed bill, in form a petition to the Queen, would therefore preserve the act of uniformity in force against any users of 'papistical service rites and ceremonies' but would except ministers suitably licensed by their bishops from adherence to the Prayer Book, with special permission to borrow from the stranger Churches in London which used Huguenot and Dutch forms of worship. If this bill had passed the puritan desire to teach and preach in defiance of the Prayer Book would have become the law of the land: the purpose of Strickland's bill of the year before would have been achieved indirectly.

There was never any prospect of this happening, though the bill received some support in debate. It was engrossed without opposition on second reading, but then the champions of common sense gathered their wits, and the third reading, instead of passing the bill, committed it. At this point, on 20 May, Speaker Bell received a note from Burghley, asking what exactly was going on. In reply Bell reported the substance of the bill and emphasized that the grievance most complained of concerned malicious prosecutions of nonconforming ministers for often very minor infringements of the Prayer Book, such as reading a chapter of the Bible on some other day than that appointed in the Book. He also reported the naming of the revising committee and expressed his opinion that with Mr Treasurer (Sir Francis Knollys) in the chair it would make sure that the bill was 'not like to take any effect'. As for the promoters of the offensive proposal, he preferred to put nothing in writing but would tell Burghley by word of mouth 'as much as shall become me on that behalf'. He erred about Knollys's intentions: the committee produced a *nova* which diligently toned down the offensive preamble but left the substance untouched.[66] The Queen exploded. By her command, received on 23 May, both bills were sent to her – a breach of parliamentary privilege inasmuch as the proceedings of the House were not to be divulged outside it, but then the larger part of the House opposed this

[66] The parchment bill was endorsed with the committee list, headed by Sir Francis Knollys; it is marked 'vacat quia nova'.

brash attempt to license puritan nonconformity. The next day Knollys reported Elizabeth's total disapproval of the bill, its promoters and the Commons (for accepting the bill). At the same time she had clearly taken trouble to reassure both Knollys and Thomas Wilson (master of Requests), who both put their defence of the House in the best possible light, that she loved her loyal Commons and had no desire to oppose genuine measures for the protection of the realm against papistical subversion. More to the point, she asked the unanswerable question: she wanted proof by example that the charges of malicious indictments were true.

That ended the episode, and the House, without a murmur, accepted a direction from on high that in future no more bills for religion should be read there unless they had first been discussed with the bishops and their permission had been obtained. As the anonymous diarist remarked, this 'seemed much to impugn the liberty of the House', but, as he somewhat sadly commented, 'nothing was said unto it'.[67] The reformers of religion had overreached themselves by trying for the jackpot, and the House accepted the Queen's point of view because it had never, in fact, been dominated by the extremer elements. There were to be no more bills, either, for the reform of the ministry, though doubts about clerical abuses continued to surface. The petition concerning objectionable practices presented in 1576, and the reminder sent up in 1581, were not intended to lead to legislation in Parliament; they displayed obedience to Elizabeth's instructions by doing no more than invite her to do as she had said she would, that is, to see to reform through the bishops. And this she did in response to the petition: she conferred with the bishops and secured the passage of reforming canons in Convocation.[68] Thus she preserved a firm separation of Church and state, ruling both but through different channels of administration. It should be said that her policy went far beyond that which her father and brother had practised in whose reigns the subjection of the national Church to parliamentary statute had been quite manifest and fully accepted by the Crown. It may well be that she took her stringent line because she did not want the radicals in Parliament, some of whom should indeed be called puritans, to exercise effective influence. But she succeeded in imposing her policy with such ease because those radicals had always been few and had never come within sight of organizing the Commons into an opposition. Management of the House sometimes faltered but never lost. There was no concerted puritan programme moved in Parliament by a coherent party; improvement of Church and clergy succeeded when it was put forward by the official leadership, especially the bishops; and extremer effort, trespassing on the supreme governor's announced preserve, invariably failed.

[67] *Proc.* 331.

[68] Neale *EP* I, 349–53, 398–404.

PROPERTY

A considerable number of doctrinally uncontentious bills were put up, nearly always in the Commons, concerning matters touching the clergy; more especially, the first session of 1559 witnessed efforts to sort out the confusion of titles to bishops' lands and their disposal during the changing occupations of Edward's and Mary's reigns, and to seek the restoration of beneficed clergy deprived by Elizabeth's predecessor.[69] But of all the issues raised in these seven sessions only one made it all the way to the statute book, with another act in explanation of the first to follow. That was the bill of 1571 against misdemeanours committed by incumbents, from archbishops to village parsons, who allowed the endowment of their living to decay by dilapidations and by long leases, thus depriving their successors of sufficient income.[70] Such behaviour was treated as fraudulent and subsequent incumbents received the right to sue their predecessor for compensation. The act, promoted it would seem by unofficial interests, passed without difficulties, though in 1576 it became necessary to revise the bill in order to protect the interests of Sir Thomas White who had just founded St John's College at Oxford and wished to preserve the leases he had taken out on the lands with which he had endowed the College.[71] Dilapidations and burdensome leases, the latter especially damaging in an age of inflation, affected the viability even of episcopal sees and led to much litigation.[72] The acts were intended to clarify dubious legal positions but do not on the whole seem to have been very helpful. The problems of clerical poverty, often urged by bishops and pamphleteers alike, did engage attention several times. In 1563 it was proposed to allow bishops to unite livings up to a joint value of £24 a year, quite a reasonable income for a parson except that it marked the upper limit permitted and said nothing about what might actually be provided by such unitings. The bill, which started in the Lords, was replaced by a new one in the Commons who wished to limit the operation to benefices individually worth under twenty marks (£13 13*s* 4*d*); but the *nova* was read the first time the day before the close of the session, so that was that.[73]

Combining livings had the unfortunate effect of reducing the number of opportunities for the clergy, a point of less importance early in the

[69] Cf. Jones, *Faith by Statute*, 104–13.

[70] 13 Eliz. I c. 10, amended by 18 Eliz. I c. 11.

[71] *LJ* I, 642, 680, 694, 745–6, 748: *CJ* I, 91, 108, 111–13; *Proc.* 254, 483.

[72] F. Heal, *Of Prelates and Princes: a Study of the Economic and Social Position of the Tudor Episcopate* (Cambridge, 1980), 299–303.

[73] *LJ* I, 600, 602–5; *CJ* I, 69, 72. In the same session a private bill for the uniting of churches at Winchester got to a second reading, possibly being merged thereafter with the general bill (*LJ* I, 597–8).

reign when the bishops were liable to complain about the lack of suitable ordinands; it might also complicate the lives of the parishioners. The fundamental problem lay in impropriation, the acquisition of the rectorial rights (always the greater tithe and often the glebe lands as well) by outsiders (mostly laymen) who then paid an inadequate stipend to the vicars they appointed to serve the cure; but drastic moves against impropriators who included many landowners and lawyers stood little chance in the House of Commons. Nevertheless, several bills tried to augment the income of poverty-stricken parsons by persuading, if not compelling, impropriators to restore to the incumbent some of the income at least that they had engrossed. It was a project close to William Cecil's heart, and he tried four times, always in vain.[74] In 1563 he prepared a bill which encouraged complaints from ministers in towns to the lord chancellor who was then to appoint a mixed commission of laymen and clergy to investigate. They were to assess the value of the living, the pay of the vicar, and the size of the congregation; on the basis of those calculations they were to assign a portion of the tithe to the complainant, but such benefits were to be conditional upon residence in the living. Introduced in the Lords, the bill ran into trouble in a Lower House full of impropriators and got no further than the first reading of a replacement bill.[75]

Nothing daunted, Cecil tried again in 1566 when he hoped to extend the relief offered from town livings to all the Church. He gave a lot of attention to the drafting, beginning with a set of articles which he revised several times and finally turned into a proper bill.[76] This made impropriators responsible for voluntarily augmenting the incomes of their vicars by endowing them with the impropriated income by deed enrolled in a court of record or in the presence of a body of clerical witnesses – the ordinary of the diocese, three persons beneficed in the same diocese, and a notary public. The impropriator could compensate for his loss by reserving to himself and his heirs whatever rents he wished to retain. The Queen was empowered to carry out the same good deed by letters patent. Careful and detailed clauses controlled what in effect amounted to a return of its proper endowment to the Church on fixed and lasting leases, anticipating by three-quarters of a century the ambitions of William Laud. It causes no surprise to find that this

[74] Briefly touched on above (pp. 69–70), Cecil's concern is indicated by his work on draft bills.
[75] SP 12/28, fos. 7–11; *LJ* I 610; *CJ* I, 71.
[76] In drafting sequence: SP 12/107, fos. 160–9 and fos. 128–41; 88, fos. 98–103; 77, fos. 177–83; 107, fos. 148–59. The drafts do seem to belong to a single sequence and one occasion. I assume that they represent the work done towards the first appropriate bill mentioned in the Journals; besides, the diary description of the bill for 1576 makes it even more likely that these drafts belong to 1566.

potentially very enlightened measure received just one reading late in that over-busy session.[77]

The next attempt, in 1576, therefore tried for rather less: it confined the transfer of impropriated incomes to such livings as had been acquired by an ecclesiastical but nonresident rector. (There were quite a number of these because post-Reformation impropriations descended from monastic appropriations: after the Dissolution, the new owners took those rights over, and while this brought in many laymen it also meant that bishoprics and colleges endowed with monastic lands held many impropriations). This proposal therefore amounted to a redistribution of income within the Church. The Lords passed the bill speedily, but rather surprisingly it died in committee in the Commons.[78] Perhaps lay impropriators feared that their turn might come next if they agreed to doing away with impropriation by churchmen. So in 1581 yet another attempt introduced a revised form of the bill of 1566, asking impropriators to assign to the incumbent a portion of the rectorial income or a rent thereon, with a special injunction to ecclesiastics to bring the livings up to £20 a year, but this fared no better – one reading in the Commons.[79]

Helping the economic condition of the Church by returning the tithe, or even a part thereof, to where it belonged turned out to be a hopeless enterprise, even with Cecil pushing it. On the other hand, clerical claims for tithe payable to nonimpropriated livings caused the familiar complaints from tithe-payers and also led to failure. A general bill, 'touching the payment of tithes' or 'for ordering of the tithe', was rejected in 1571 at first reading in the Commons; most likely it was promoted by the clergy and tried to enforce regular payment upon reluctant parishioners.[80] To balance things, a bill of 1576 to abolish tithe on woods of more than thirty years' growth also vanished after one reading.[81] In the same session two local bills concerned themselves with tithe. The town of Reading desired a settlement like that authorized for London by an act of 1545 (37 Henry VIII c. 12) and got the bill through both Houses, but the Queen's veto indicates that local differences of opinion had not been reconciled in advance.[82] Halifax did better. A private act introduced in the Lords recited a history of trouble reaching back into the 1530s; there had been an archiepiscopal decree, actions in courts, and finally a Star Chamber decree which with the consent of the

[77] *CJ* I, 79.

[78] *LJ* I, 747–8; *CJ* I, 114–5; *Proc.* 491 – 'for parsonages impropriate being in spiritual persons' hands to be demised to vicars'.

[79] *CJ* I, 132; *Proc.* 543.

[80] *CJ* I, 89; *Proc.* 252.

[81] *CJ* I, 110; *Proc.* 487.

[82] *CJ* I, 107–10; *LJ* I, 740, 744, 745; *Proc.* 483. For the tithe settlement in London cf. Susan Brigden, 'Tithe controversy in Reformation London,' *J. of Eccl. History* 32 (1981), 285–301.

parties ordered an arbitration by the earls of Sussex and Leicester, with by way of a follow-up a final assessment of disputed points by two members of the Council of the North. All this having been done, the bill confirmed the settlement and ordered all relevant documents to be enrolled in the Chancery by the opening day of the Michaelmas term 1577.[83] Halifax proved the wisdom of lengthy preparatory negotiations if one wished to avoid seeing a bill killed at a late stage.

Another issue over ecclesiastical property sprang from abuses alleged against collegiate bodies that had benefited from the dissolution of the monasteries and chantries earlier in the century. The available information is so inadequate that any reconstruction must be doubtful. A bill of 1566 tried to penalize 'masters of Colleges' (probably at the two Universities) for transactions in chantry lands carried out since the death of Henry VIII, but the Lords read it only once after the Commons had passed it.[84] In the seventies the attack turned upon corporate owners of ex-monastic property, by means of bills ostensibly 'explaining' a clause in the act of 1539 which had allowed ex-monks to purchase lands but barred them from acquiring such property by inheritance (31 Henry VIII c. 6, sect. 2). In 1571 the bill designed 'to meet with subtle practices of such corporations of cathedral churches as shall surrender their houses into her majesty's hands and to take the same again' in order to void leases recently made out of the endowment – though how 'explaining' that earlier clause would affect the issue remains mysterious in the absence of more detailed knowledge. One reading in the Commons was all that the bill achieved.[85] This trial balloon seems, however, to have encouraged the promoters to try once more, and the bill, a public one,[86] came back in 1576. Its general scope appears to have become enlarged. It would seem so to have explained the contentious clause that any ex-monastic lands held by Colleges and other spiritual corporations must have been acquired by purchase and by no other means; this would have ruined all new foundations not in existence when the lands were sold and blessed thereafter with donor's gifts. The bill passed both Houses but with an exemption clause for the Colleges of the two Universities and for Eton and Winchester, an amendment inserted in the Commons at the request of the Lords who would seem to have sent down an exempting bill received in their House.[87] Apparently this wrecked the intentions of the main bill's promoters who protested to Burghley a few days after the passage of the bill but a fortnight before the assent. The Colleges involved apprehended that the 'explaining' act threatened the title of the

[83] 18 Eliz. I, OA 29; *LJ* I, 735, 738–9, 741; *CJ* I, 109–10.
[84] *CJ* I, 75, 78–9; *LJ* I, 658.
[85] *CJ* I, 84; *Proc.* 208.
[86] SP 12/107, fo. 144.
[87] *CJ* I, 106–8; *LJ* I, 735–7.

Crown to some monastic properties and therewith their own title to lands obtained by royal grant. To this the bill's sponsors replied that the Henrician act had never meant to affect the Colleges and that the explanation therefore altered nothing, while the royal title as well as the rights of the Colleges had long since been fully established in law. They therefore asked that the dispute be referred to a committee of eminent lawyers.[88] The session ended before the problem had been clarified, and the bill therefore lapsed, being either vetoed or never presented for the assent. The episode well illustrates how bills finished in both Houses could still be stopped from passing. However, the only thing really clear about it all is that the purpose of the bill and the causes of dispute remain intensely unclear.

A few other bills, none of which passed, may be listed to show the sort of issues touching the clergy that raised a potential legislative concern in Parliament. One bill of 1576, demanding that patrons of livings should be informed of any vacancy occurring 'ipso facto by force of any statute' within six months of this happening, to prevent them from losing their rights of presentation, did get through but was vetoed, possibly because failure to present transferred the right to do so to the Crown.[89] Corrupt presentations – that is, simony – received brief attention in the Lords in 1572; did someone wish to revise the act of the previous session?[90] One could wish that the establishment of a depository for parish registers, twice attempted (in 1563 and 1576), had come to fruition: historical demographers and genealogists would both today be grateful for so early and sensible a care for their sources.[91]

This chapter on the Parliament's involvement with the Church and the faith may suitably conclude with a story of characteristic intolerance properly done down. The Dutch sect called the Family of Love had established itself in England in the 1570s, only to be outlawed by a proclamation of 1580 which ordered its writings to be burned and its practitioners imprisoned 'and to receive such bodily punishment and other mulct as fathers of damnable heresies'.[92] This was not enough for some earnest members of the Commons who in the next session of Parliament (1581) brought in a bill of pains: members of the sect were to be whipped for a first offence, branded with the letters H.N.[93] for a second, and executed as felons for a third. The second reading debate led to a long argument, extending over two days, 'whether pains of death might be inflicted on a heretic'. The result was a second new bill which

[88] SP 12/107, fos. 110–13.
[89] *CJ* I, 106–7, 110–12; *LJ* I, 736, 740, 744; *Proc.* 480.
[90] *LJ* I, 707, 709, 711, 715.
[91] *CJ* I, 68, 105–6.
[92] *TRP* II, 474–5.
[93] Hendrik Niklas, founder of the sect.

died in committee.[94] The whole of that session lasted barely five weeks, but for the persecution of harmless sectaries even those 'puritan' Commons readily took time off from the urgent business of passing bills that mattered. On the other hand, it must be conceded that the tone of the royal proclamation was savage, and if Edward Bacon was right that news of the sect was being spread in order to turn the Queen against the Parliament there may have been a need to demonstrate the difference between heretical sectaries and zealous but loyal protestants.

[94] *CJ* I, 127–30; *Proc.* 536, 538, 540.

10

The common weal

GENERAL

Far and away the largest number of bills put into the Parliament concerned themselves with the common weal for which, in the Queen's view, it was the proper function of members of either House to propose action of one kind and another. In principle, nothing that touched the inhabitants of the realm in their daily lives stood outside the reforming, restricting or promoting powers of the Parliament, and in practice this principle was pretty consistently obeyed. The range of topics touched upon is remarkable, even if a majority of bills failed to get through, and some things thought of might amaze; indeed, the range is too wide to be fully recited here without burdening attention well beyond what it should be asked to bear. Acts did not often result from the more extravagant moves, few of which look likely to have been initiated by the government, but that does not diminish the interest of some initiatives. One bill that did pass in 1563 completed the sixteenth-century code against gypsies which had been officially begun in 1531 and elaborated in 1554.[1] These alien 'vagabonds' caused fear and hatred, and typically enough each act got more savage. That of Henry VIII had attacked them for thieving and proposed to expel them, while the next one made it felony to be a wandering Egyptian. The act of 1563 worried about the Englishmen who dressed as gypsies in order to pursue a life of crime and added them to the tally, providing only that any native-born person found in such company could not be expelled from the realm. Cecil included the measure among the good acts passed in the session, but the earl of Arundel voted against it.[2]

Why in 1559 artificers and husbandmen were specially singled out as

[1] 22 Henry VIII c. 10; 1 & 2 Philip & Mary c. 4; 5 Eliz. I c. 20. See A. L. Beier, *Masterless Men: the Vagrancy Problem in England, 1540–1640* (London, 1985), esp. 57–62.

[2] *CJ* 1, 66–7; *LJ* 1, 596–9; BL, Lansdowne MS 102, fo. 25.

persons who should not eat meat on Wednesdays, or whom a bill of 1571 had in mind as potential 'seducers and corrupters of youth', must in the absence of further evidence remain mysterious.[3] There is no mystery about the attempts of one Giles Lambert to set up a monopoly of oil-making out of vegetable seeds.[4] He tried first in 1572, with a petition to the Parliament. This pointed out that foreign (especially Spanish) oil was essential in the cloth industry but that the suppliers had pushed the price up till it put an extra 5*s*. on every shortcloth and 3*s*. on every broadcloth. It was wrong that an essential English industry should depend 'upon the wavering will of foreign potestates [sic]', and the petitioner claimed to have 'brought to light a most necessary and fruitful secret' for making such oil in England. But he needed capital to finance the exploitation of his discovery and therefore asked for an act which would give him and his associates for thirty years a rake-off called 'oil-silver' (one penny on every broadcloth made and a halfpenny on every kersey) so long as foreign oil remained at or below £24 the ton. Presumably, if it rose above that he expected to be able to undercut the Spaniard. The consequent trial bill was not pressed beyond a first reading in the Commons, and when reintroduced in 1576 was dashed at that stage: one would not expect the clothing interests to tolerate such an impost for the benefit of a secret and unproven invention.[5] Lambert's device was in any case rivalled by another, put forward in March 1576 by Lawrence Cookson who similarly petitioned for an act granting him large plots of land for the growing of hemp-seed from which oil would be extracted; though Cookson prepared the necessary bill it does not seem to have been put into the Parliament.[6] Yet Cookson already held a patent of monopoly; all he lost was the confirmatory act. Lambert got nothing.

A bill to confirm all existing weights and measures used in the realm – that is to say, for keeping confusion confused – and to reform misbehaviour on the part of clerks of markets deserves attention less for its own sake than for the fact that details of debates were recorded on the second readings of both the original bill and the *nova* produced in committee: a useful reminder that matters regarded as of very little moment by historians could attract serious concern from both burgesses and diarists. The lieutenant of the Tower hoped that poor men receiving

[3] *CJ* I, 60, 88. [4] SP 12/86, fos. 191–2.

[5] *CJ* I, 95, 111 (2^a there is a scribe's error); *Proc.* 362, 487–8.

[6] SP 12/86, fos. 185–90 (misdated); 107, fos. 116–7, 119–20. In his petition Cookson referred to an act of 1566, about to expire, but I cannot identify an act that fits. Cromwell's diary makes certain that the bills put in in 1572 and 1576 were Lambert's. Other people tried for privileges in the making of rapeseed or coleseed oil without going to Parliament: Joan Thirsk, *Economic Policy and Projects* (Oxford, 1978), 68–9.

doles of corn might have them measured by the largest bushel in use; Richard Galles thought the bill unnecessary and indeed unfortunate in that it allowed justices of the peace to interfere in boroughs; Edward Grimston elaborated on the bad behaviour of clerks of the market who sublet their offices to 'divers evil persons' and exacted fees for inspecting measures long since agreed as approved. The House agreed with Galles and dropped the bill.[7]

Markets attracted the attention of the devout. In 1566 two bills, one called by the clerk 'general' and the other 'little', moved against the holding of markets and fairs on Sundays; the general bill returned in 1571; each bill got just one reading. Their promoters might have done better if they had followed the example set by the manor of Battle in Sussex. There the lord of the manor, Viscount Montague (a well known catholic), in 1566 promoted a private bill to transfer the weekly market from Sundays to Thursdays, on the grounds 'that it is more convenient' for the inhabitants to attend divine service on Sundays. Being a private bill, it passed unaltered.[8]

Lastly, at this point, two very special interests. The humanist passion for education and the Church's need for a large supply of trained ministers made the sixteenth century one of the great ages for the Universities – the century in which Cambridge caught up with Oxford. Among the favourers of good letters were the highly educated Queen herself as well as among those close to her the two chancellors, Leicester (Oxford) and Burghley (Cambridge). Not all their motives may be thought pure as snow; there was also the desire to keep the Universities under control and prevent them from becoming even more than already they were the breeding grounds for radical views in Church and religion. Out of this mixture of concerns came two successful bills in their favour and one unsuccessful bill to their detriment. The most important of the acts passed in 1571: it incorporated both Universities in the name of the chancellor, masters and scholars, giving them a legal personality which enabled them fully to govern themselves.[9] Their present structure still derives from that act which was private and not printed till about a century later,[10] but it originated in government circles and used the short enacting formula. Even though it was not framed as a petition it carried the sign manual, the only non-petitionary bill of this era to do so, and by so signing it the Queen testified that its opening words were sincere: 'For the great love and favour that the Queen's most excellent majesty

[7] *CJ* I, 95, 97, 102–2; *Proc.* 378, 403.

[8] 8 Eliz. I, OA 34; *CJ* I, 78–9; *LJ* I, 664.

[9] 13 Eliz. I c. 29.

[10] A copy survives, marked up for printing: SP 12/78, fos. 127–68. The handwriting places it not earlier than ca. 1700.

beareth towards her highness' Universities... '. Introduced in the Lords only five days before the dissolution, it passed at record speed; against all the rules, the Commons read it three times in one day but managed to add a proviso to protect the rights of the two University towns. One odd bit of by-play occurred in the drafting. Originally the last clause had saved the rights of existing lessees and others with lawful claims against the Universities listed in the order Oxford–Cambridge; looking this over, Burghley reversed the order, and so the clause stood.[11] The late date of introduction was probably unintended; the bill as planned raised some predictable objections from other interests, and answering them took some careful drafting.[12] Even so, the doubters secured the Commons' proviso.

Five years later it was the Colleges that received attention, in an act safeguarding their incomes.[13] The bill was public but the initiative private: a strong tradition maintains that it was sponsored by Sir Thomas Smith, secretary of state and lately Regius professor of civil law at Cambridge.[14] He did well for the cause. A short and simple act, it provided that in all future College leases two-thirds of the rent should be set in cash, the remainder being payable in kind – either corn or malt. Smith, author of that excellent economic treatise of 1549, 'The Discourse of the Common Weal', and benefactor to Queens' College, thus built into College incomes a very useful hedge against inflation, and his name remained revered for a reason even better than his intellectual career. But not everybody loved the Colleges. Another bill of 1576 attacked the alleged practice of selling places – fellowships and scholarships – in the Colleges and Halls of the Universities, but also of prebends and places in hospitals and deaneries. A public bill introduced into the Lower House, it passed with no difficulty at all until it reached the assent when the Queen vetoed it, perhaps because it meddled with the administration of the Church but quite probably also because it harassed institutions for which she entertained a great love.[15]

The Universities had their friends at court; members of the Lower House seem to have been less fortunate. Both the bills introduced to

[11] SP 12/78, fos. 169–70.

[12] Ibid. fos. 171–4. The act owed something to initiatives on the part of the beneficiaries. In June, the public orator of Cambridge wrote letters of thanks for their assistance in Parliament to three peers, the lord keeper, the Speaker, the attorney general, and six members of the Commons (Cambridge University Library, MS Lett. 2, 408–18).

[13] 18 Eliz. I c. 6.

[14] Mary Dewar, *Sir Thomas Smith: a Tudor Intellectual in Office* (London, 1964), 185–6. The tradition is supported by a letter of thanks from the University of Cambridge which calls Smith the first mover of the bill for the Colleges (above, n. 12, p. 410).

[15] *CJ* I, 110, 112; *LJ* I, 743, 745–6; SP 12/107, fo. 144.

improve their standing failed. In 1559 one reading disposed of a bill 'touching knights and burgesses, for attendance in the Parliament', but since this would have attacked the notorious willingness of members to absent themselves from the House for more interesting or profitable pastimes it is no wonder that it failed.[16] In 1571, someone tried to bring appearance into line with reality in yet another way. The bill was aimed to repeal the Lancastrian acts concerning burgesses' residential qualifications and openly to permit what in any case was constantly happening – the election of burgesses in no real sense resident in the borough they represented. This led to an interesting debate: interesting because it shows how anciently established humbug and pomposity are in the Commons.[17] After some ineffectual contributions, James Warnecombe, an oldish parliamentary hand, warned burgesses present that the bill 'may touch and overreach their whole liberties' because if local links were to be severed 'lords' letters shall from henceforth bear all the sway': nomination by patrons alone would in future elect members. He himself had once sat for Herefordshire and three times for different boroughs there and in Shropshire. Thomas Norton tried to justify the bill (which suggests Council origin or at least approval): it would prevent unsuitable representatives being sent by places too small to exercise a proper choice, and besides nonresidents were often returned as things stood. 'He argued that the whole body of the realm and good service of the same was rather to be respected than the private regard of place or privilege of any person.' Evidently he thought that support for the existing law came from unimportant people in unimportant places who saw no chance of preening themselves in Parliament if the residence qualifications were abolished.

That seemed to conclude the debate, and the Speaker put the question for engrossing; the ayes had it. But Speaker Wray again showed his weakness in the chair, for instead of passing on to the next business he allowed a member to rise and address the House. This member, as the anonymous diarist noted, 'said thus as far as my memory may serve to report'. The speech fills four large pages in the printed edition, with many Latin quotations and obscure allusions. It is the longest speech in the diary and the only one reported with neither summaries nor paraphrases; the diarist cannot have worked from memory but must have had the text before him, and the chances are that he was himself the orator in question. Unfortunately he also for once did not give the speaker's name. His speech attacked the bill. The House needed local men as local experts: 'we who neither have seen Berwick or St Michael's

[16] *CJ* I, 60. [17] Ibid. 84–5; *Proc.* 225–31.

Mount can but blindly guess at them, albeit we look on the maps that come from thence.' He told some history, citing approvingly the example of boroughs who had refused to act as instructed by letters from dukes or even the Council.[18] Countries without a proper House of Commons all suffered the consequences, from the absolutism of kings in Spain and Portugal to 'the monstrous governments of the common people in some parts of Germany'. Even he began to realize that he was trying the patience of the House: 'I stand too long hereon and abundance of matter occasioneth confusion.' So his final message (admittedly followed by a long peroration) was plain: 'It was meant at the first, and first institution of Parliaments, that men of every quarter and all sorts should come to this court; that they shall be freely chosen; this in every age hitherto hath seemed best.' And so, shutting his and everybody's eyes to the real world of borough elections, he won the day. Robert Bell, another of the Council's men of business, pointed out that some constituencies simply had to look outside for suitable candidates, and Francis Alford offered the compromise proposal that at every election one of the men returned should be a local man, for his inside knowledge, and the other a capable speaker to give voice to that knowledge. It was too late. The vote for engrossing was ignored and changed to committal; and the committee let the bill die.[19]

[18] 'In Queen Mary's time a Council of this realm (not the Queen's Privy Council)': what did he mean?

[19] Do the names of the committees provide a clue to the identity of the anonymous diarist? It was certainly usual to put members who had shown a serious interest onto bill committees, and the nameless speaker had done that. Of the other contributors to the debate Bell, Warnecombe and Alford sat on the committee. So did Fleetwood, but his contributions to debates always mention his name. We are left with five names. The chairman was Sir William Hilton (*CJ* by mistake calls him Thomas), knight for Northumberland; this was his only Parliament, and he is in any case a very unlikely candidate. Robert Guynes sat only in 1571, which excludes him since the diary resumed in 1572. Richard Bedell and Thomas Atkins fit the dates of membership but pose problems. Bedell, a common lawyer of strong protestant views, died in 1572, which might explain why the diary did not continue thereafter; however, he was a manifest and regular carpetbagger. Atkins, on the other hand, who sat for Gloucester in every Parliament from 1571 to 1593, possessed an independent cast of mind which fits the argument of the anonymous speech; also at least one other speech recorded against his name (*Proc.* 331, 376) reads, with its pompous Latin quotations, rather like this speech. But Atkins like Bedell is mentioned by name elsewhere in the anonymous diary (ibid. 232, 238), which weakens the case for their not being named on this occasion. Both also were newcomers to this Parliament and might have hesitated to deliver a lecture on ancient parliamentary history and practices. That leaves Robert Bowes, a member in every Parliament from 1563 to 1589 who in this one sat for Carlisle, supposedly as a client of Lord Scrope's. Member of a well-known Yorkshire family with a Cambridge education, from 1576 treasurer of Berwick and thenceforth very busy in the service of the Crown, a man whose protestant loyalties had saved him from getting involved in the 1569 rebellion, he does fit the profile in several ways. The anonymous diary never mentions him but neither does Cromwell's. The case must rest unproven.

So much for eccentricities and oddities of legislative initiatives. The main body of bills for the common weal was both more serious and duller, being often the product of particular local concerns, though at times it suggested that the reforming zeal that had been at work in Parliament since 1529 had not yet exhausted itself. The material in question falls naturally in four sections: agrarian affairs, manufacture, trade and shipping, and social problems. They shall be reviewed in turn.

AGRARIAN MATTERS

The agrarian history of the earlier sixteenth century had been stormy, but throughout most of Elizabeth's reign, until the 1590s, the rural scene enjoyed a species of sunshine. One consequence of this was the absence of major legislation in the years 1559–81. Government did not feel called upon to interfere, and private and local interests saw little need to call attention to the applecart. The only tillage act usefully demonstrated the reason why. Passed without much difficulty in 1563, it in effect summarized and confirmed the laws against enclosure, the engrossing of holdings, and the decay of houses and husbandry which had been made in the exciting days of the enclosure movement between 1489 and 1536.[20] It also repealed earlier summarising statutes passed in the previous two reigns. A very long act, it carefully set out rules for keeping lands under tillage, defined lawful conversion to pasture, and specified exceptions. In terms of agrarian practice it was out of date when passed. In effect a code for farming, it fell in with the code-making habit in matters economic which had been rampant under Edward and Mary; it also continued the earlier addiction to making such codes time-limited. One way and another it has the air of a Council measure, but the air misleads. At least there are odd aspects that cast doubts.

The act carries a peculiar enacting formula: after a short preamble recalling the legislation of Henry VIII's day, this states that 'it is therefore ordained' by the Queen with the assent of both Houses and by the authority of Parliament, and so forth. This suggests that it originated in a set of articles presented to the draftsmen to which prefatory matter had to be added. Such a genesis is not unusual, but Council bills commonly reformulated the draft so as to hide the article form. The bill was introduced into the Lords and after sitting around for twelve days handed to the learned counsel assistant in that House, which may diminish the chance that the Privy Council had planned it. Cecil's brief reference to it in a letter to Thomas Smith points two ways.[21]

[20] 5 Eliz. I c. 2.

[21] BL, Lansdowne. MS 102, fo. 25 (27 Feb. 1563).

After listing bills that had passed the Commons he spoke of two more bills, the one against gypsies and 'another to remedy the defrauding of statutes for tillage', as though the proposal was news to him. Yet on the day he wrote the bill had not even been introduced in the Lords. His foreknowledge argues for a Council initiative which so much else about the bill calls in question. Most probably the private promoters of the measure had cleared things with the principal secretary before the session, though they then produced a bill which needed expert advice. Perhaps that promoter was Richard, Lord Rich, lord chancellor during the duke of Somerset's reforming administration and now the only peer to be joined with the lawyers for revising the bill. It would be pleasant to think that the man who allegedly swore away Sir Thomas More's life should towards the end of his days have helped to remedy the chief agrarian problem identified in *Utopia*.

If tillage was to flourish the trade in corn needed to be encouraged. In this respect Tudor governments always faced a dilemma. On the one hand, their first concern was to ensure a sufficient and not too expensive supply for the people of England, which meant the restriction of exports; on the other hand, good prices for grain encouraged landowners to keep their lands under tillage.[22] In 1559 a bill permitting the export of grain (wheat, barley, beans, rye, oats) as long as their prices did not rise above limits stated was dashed at third reading in the Commons.[23] Most probably it was unofficial because when it was reintroduced in 1571 Cecil had put in a lot of work into converting it into the bill the government wanted. This bill started in the Commons, but the Lords decided on detailed revisions so considerable that they felt obliged to replace it, which necessitated a conference.[24] This sort of thing shows how inadequate views of the Upper House are which treat it simply as the Council's rubber stamp. The new bill had the short enacting clause, taken from its predecessor. It set up machinery for the licensing of exports which, in characteristic Tudor fashion, called upon the localities to investigate the state of harvests and prices before permitting trade outside the realm (in English-owned vessels only), but also insisted that any stop should first be cleared with Queen and Council. Although the body of the bill provided for all sorts of complicated safeguards, involving local government agencies, the Councils of the North and the

[22] On exports cf. *The Agrarian History of England and Wales, IV: 1500–1640*, ed. Joan Thirsk (Cambridge, 1967), 524–6. [23] *CJ* I, 60–1.

[24] 13 Eliz. I c. 13; *CJ* I, 87–8, 91–3: *LJ* I, 689, 695–6, 699. The engrossed Commons' bill is SP 12/28, fo. 63 (which bears the bail but not the Lords' assent); its replacement, the OA in HLRO, started in the Lords. Burghley's work on the first bill, so extensive as to call for replacement, is SP 12/28, fo. 64.

Marches of Wales, and the justices of assize, Burghley was still not satisfied; he drafted a proviso enabling the government at any time by proclamation to arrest exports either generally in the realm or from particular ports named.[25] That proviso, barely altered from the draft, appears as section 4 of the act. The Commons made a number of minor amendments.[26] The act claimed to benefit both tillage and shipping, and in the favourable conditions of the 1570s it probably did.

Internal trade in corn also had its problems. London's food supply always presented the biggest headache, but a bill promoted by the city in 1563 to allow import of foreign corn with no customs duties paid lapsed after second reading, even though it was followed by two of its influential men in the Commons – Alderman Sir William Chester and the recorder, Ralph Cholmeley.[27] Duty-free import by foreigners as well as natives was expecting too much, and since no further attempt was made it may be supposed that this proposal, clearly influenced by the unhappy experiences of the 1550s, disappeared as better conditions allowed London to be fed from English grain stocks. That internal trade was in the hands of corn-badgers whose operations together with those of cattle-drovers were controlled by licences issued under an act of 1551 for the suppression of engrossing and forestalling.[28] A privately promoted act of 1563 complained that too many unfit persons, eager to live easy lives, had wangled themselves such licences; it imposed tighter controls and committed enforcement to the justices of the peace. The bill committee, chaired by the recorder of London, produced a *nova* which slid quickly through both Houses.[29] The act is held to have assisted the expansion of internal trading in grain because the licensing system helped merchants to build up their organization,[30] but there were moments when it was thought that too many licences were issued too easily. In October 1574 the Privy Council warned the justices of Northamptonshire to exercise restraint: too many badgers in the trade were by their competition driving the price of grain too high.[31]

In this period agriculture was certainly experiencing some degree of transformation, whether one should speak of the beginnings of the agricultural revolution or not,[32] and understandably plans for improve-

[25] SP 12/41, fo. 196, a collection of notes for parliamentary business which thanks to this item can be placed in 1571, not 1566 as in the *Calendar*.

[26] Paper filed with OA.

[27] *CJ* I, 65; CLRO, Rep. 15, fo. 189.

[28] 5 & 6 Edward VI c. 14.

[29] 5 Eliz, I c. 12; *CJ* I, 64–7; *LJ* I, 600–2.

[30] *Agrarian History*, IV, 580.

[31] HMC, *Buccleuch III* (*Montague Papers, Second Series*), 13.

[32] The battle over this issue between *Agrarian History*, IV, and E. Kerridge's *The Agricultural Revolution* (London, 1967) has never been decided. Common opinion seems to have turned against the second, but I find much of it very persuasive.

ments left their mark in the Journals. The form of land improvement which really needed legislation was drainage. Individuals could turn to up-and-down husbandry or marl their fields without laws, but drainage needed money which there were only two ways of raising: either by the imposition of a local rate, which had to be authorized by act, or by obtaining rights for a syndicate of investors, which were best confirmed by act. The second was the method used for the draining of Plumstead marshes in Kent, a hardy perennial in the parliamentary calendar. In 1563, an Italian entrepreneur, Jacobus Accontius, obtained a private act granting him the necessary rights for four years ending in March 1567, under stringent conditions compelling the allocation of half the drained lands to existing local owners.[33] After some work done, Accontius got discouraged and conveyed his rights to a London syndicate which included a groom of the Chamber (also an Italian), a mercer, two grocers and two drapers. At the cost of £5000 they cleared about 600 acres and wished to continue. For this they promoted a private act in 1566 which confirmed the transfer and extended the rights until March 1576, as well as giving four years' exemption from tithe to help cover the costs.[34] In the next few years there were some changes in the syndicate, while the work was held up because 'during the time of restraint between this realm and the Low Countries workmen most fit for that purpose could not be had'. Another act in 1572 therefore extended the concession until June 1581.[35] So in 1581, the syndicate, once more changed and somewhat enlarged, came back to Parliament. This time they wanted only a two-year extension of rights and obtained some notable concessions: the drained lands were now reserved for the syndicate, to be held of the Queen in free socage at a rent of one penny an acre ('as of our manor of Greenwich')[36] and the exemption from tithe was prolonged to seven years.[37] Moreover, as has already been said,[38] as a special favour the act was made public and printed, one feels in order that it might stand and free Parliament from further bills about Plumstead marshes.

Unlike Accontius & Co., the Huntingdonshire entrepreneurs who planned to drain inundated land near Godmanchester did not press the matter, while a bill against draining salt marshes (allegedly a threat to

[33] 5 Eliz. I, OA 36; *CJ* I, 66–7, 69; *LJ* I, 603, 605, 608, 610, 612. Accontius claimed that the interested parties were too many to make individual consents possible.

[34] 8 Eliz. I, OA 25; *CJ* I, 75, 80; *LJ* I, 663–4.

[35] 14 Eliz. I, OA 14; *CJ* I, 97, 99, 100; *LJ* I, 717–19, 723.

[36] Cf. J. Hurstfield, 'The Greenwich Tenures of the Reign of Edward VI', *Econ. Hist. Rev.*, 2nd ser. 8 (1949), 72–81.

[37] 23 Eliz. I c. 13; *CJ* I, 132–3; *LJ* II, 29, 33, 49. The Lords delayed the bill 'till the parties have brought in their several bonds' guaranteeing performance.

[38] Above, p. 46.

harbour facilities) died in committee.[39] Linked to the problem of drainage were the activities of commissioners of sewers, responsible for the control of rivers and coastal erosion, who had been organized by an act of 1532; when this act was made permanent in 1550 such commissions were limited to five years.[40] By 1571 it seemed that this did not give the commissioners sufficient scope, and a privately promoted act, twice replaced during passage by new bills, extended the time to ten years.[41] The same session witnessed one somewhat prophetic drainage act 'for making the river Welland navigable'. It was petitioned for by the town of Stamford (Burghley's town) and passed smoothly;[42] no one will have thought that here lay one of the first moves towards the draining of the Fens.

Bills came before Parliament concerning various aspects of agrarian improvement; most of them flopped but even so they illustrate local ambitions. Some tried to offer encouragement to the growers of hops, notoriously a novel cash crop introduced in that century, with a bill brought forward in both 1571 and 1572.[43] In 1581, a bill to protect the realm from fraud by insisting that imported hops should be 'truly packed without mixture of dross, sand or leaves' passed both Houses in good time for the assent but failed to become law; one wonders who persuaded the Queen to assist corrupt importers – or whether native hop growers preferred to disillusion the purchasers of rival imports.[44] Farm animals were not forgotten. In 1572 somebody remembered earlier efforts to increase dairy cattle and proposed that everybody who reared livestock should be compelled to rear a calf for every five kids he had (we are talking of goats). It was pointed out that 'the nature of the soil' in some places would not support calves, and Sir Francis Knollys acknowledged that regions would have to obey their conditions. But though he welcomed the bill because cheese was 'necessary for the common weal for the furniture of ships', the bill did not reappear after a single reading.[45] Horses had better luck because with them the chief problem lay in preventing a depletion of numbers by exports for sale: military needs called for control. In 1559 a possibly official act (it started in the Lords) revived the Henrician statute prohibiting exports to the ancient enemy

[39] Both in 1576: *CJ* I, 107, 111. The second bill was earmarked for expedition by the Lords (SP 12/107, fo. 144), but that did it no good either.

[40] 23 Henry VIII c. 5; 3 & 4 Edward VI c. 8.

[41] 13 Eliz. I c. 9; *CJ* I, 84, 89–92; *LJ* I, 674–6, 680, 682, 685, 695. The replacement bills had the consequence that though the whole business started in the Lower House the bill as passed began in the Upper.

[42] 13 Eliz. I, OA 13; *CJ* I, 87–8, 91; *LJ* I, 684–5, 688, 692.

[43] *CJ* I, 89, 98.

[44] Ibid. 121, 130; *LJ* II, 41, 49–50; *Proc.* 531.

[45] *CJ* I, 100; *Proc.* 387.

in Scotland, and in 1563 the permission granted in 1547 to travellers to take horses abroad for personal use was revoked because it had been fraudulently abused.[46] On the other hand, a Commons bill of 1559 to inhibit excessive dealings in horses was dashed in the Lords on third reading.[47]

Desire to preserve the supposed English monopoly in the production of raw wool – already well out of date – produced the most savage preservation act of that age or perhaps any other, possibly too savage even for the animals' rights campaigners of the later twentieth century. A statute of 1566 prohibited the carrying of any live sheep out of the realm.[48] It seems to have been an official bill responding to 'sundry good causes and considerations moved in this high court of Parliament', and it was very brief. All persons involved in such a trade were, on first offence, to forfeit all their goods for ever (moieties to Queen and informer), be imprisoned for a year, and (if still alive) were to lose one hand which was to be nailed up in the market place. A second offence, presumably onehanded, constituted felony. The bill was twice replaced in committee but then passed in a flash.[49] Though special care was taken to commit enforcement to justices of oyer and terminer, of gaol delivery and of the peace, one can only hope that it was never activated by any informer.

Perhaps more interesting are the various efforts made to preserve wild animals useful to human consumers. Fish spawn received protection in the first Parliament of the reign, though the Lords added a proviso exempting uncontrollable rivers – Tweed, Usk and Wye.[50] A more comprehensive act tried to prevent 'the unlawful taking of fish, deer and hawks'; one in the long series of game laws, it confined itself to protecting properly licensed deer parks and passed after a good deal of dispute in the course of which rabbits, at first included, vanished from the bill, perhaps because Knollys attacked them for eating other men's corn.[51] The Thames fishermen persuaded the court of aldermen to assist them with a bill to remove unlawful nets in their river; when this got nowhere they tried again in 1566, only to have their bill rejected by three votes in a House of 127; just before this happened, the city authorities decided to take steps of their own by act of Common Council, an interesting

[46] 1 Eliz. I c. 7: the Queen's printer produced 500 copies of the act in broadsheet form for proclamation, for 22*s* 6*d* (BL, Add. MS 5756, fo. 121); 5 Eliz. I c. 19.

[47] *CJ* 1, 56, 58–60; *LJ*/*EHR*, 537–8.

[48] 8 Eliz. I c. 3.

[49] *CJ* 1, 74, 76, 78, 81; *LJ* 1, 663–4.

[50] 1 Eliz. I c. 17.

[51] 5 Eliz. I c. 21; *CJ* 1, 66–8; *LJ* 1, 602–3, 607–8, 610, 613. To be precise, the act punished the destruction of fish ponds and deer enclosures, as well as the taking of hawks' eggs from specially built eyries. A bill of the same session which also protected fish ponds and rabbit warrens was probably merged in committee with the main bill (*CJ* 1, 63–4).

example of the manner in which London bills unnecessarily absorbed parliamentary time.[52] Three attempts to protect rabbit warrens all failed. In 1571 the bill lapsed after first reading, but probably the same one was reintroduced in 1572: it punished disguised coney hunters with three months in gaol, indemnified keepers who might happen to kill such poachers, and gaoled for a full year any warrener in cahoots with the enemy. The Commons threw it out on first reading. The third bill (1581) imposed money fines as well as imprisonment but said nothing about lawful killing; it got to the motion for engrossing before being voted down.[53] Rabbits had few friends. Typically enough, the protectors of pheasants and partridges proved more successful with a bill against the taking of birds too young to eat and against hunting in corn-fields before the harvest was gatherred in, though they too needed three tries. In 1571 the bill was not followed; in 1576 the two Houses could not sort out their disagreements in time for the assent; and in 1581 the bill shot through.[54]

Not all birds, however, were protected. In 1559 and 1563 a bill was introduced to revive the Henrician law for the extermination of seed eaters – rooks and choughs. It passed both Houses on the second occasion, was vetoed, came back in 1566 (presumably suitably altered) and got through.[55] It was not a Council bill, and the documentation contains some mysteries. The vetoed second bill, engrossed on parchment, survives in the House of Lords; contrary to the evidence of both Journals, it claims to have started in the Lords.[56] The bill which passed was engrossed in a distinctly unofficial hand and shows that the time-limitation was added later, most likely on third reading in the Lower House where the bill had originated. It is hard to be sure of the parliamentary fortunes of this bill. Still, farming interests had won their battle against rooks and crows. They failed to stop hawkers using long-winged hawks, apparently another threat to seed-corn.[57]

MANUFACTURES

Manufacture and trade in its products provided the single largest group of bills submitted to Parliament, and an exceptionally high proportion of them got nowhere. These endeavours reflected the ambitions of well organized interests – town and companies – as well as of enterprising

[52] *CJ* I, 68, 71, 77–80; CLRO, Rep. 15, fo. 127 (20 Jan. 1563) and Rep. 16, fo. 147v (10 Dec. 1566).

[53] *CJ* I, 86, 90, 122, 124, 128; *Proc.* 371, 532.

[54] *CJ* I, 90, 108, 111, 113–14; *LJ* I, 745–6; 23 Eliz. I c. 10.

[55] *CJ* I, 57, 60, 69, 71–2, 78, 80; *LJ/EHR*, 537–8; *LJ* I, 617–18, 663–4; 8 Eliz. I c. 15.

[56] HLRO, Parchment Collection, Box 1.

[57] 1572: *LJ* I, 719.

individuals, and very little of this flood of proposals originated with the government. Older views which used to ascribe every controlling statute to Council policy have rightly been abandoned. The number of people involved was considerable, though its total still made them a minority in a nation mostly engaged in agrarian pursuits. However, the interrelation of cloth manufacture and wool production drew in interests with no urban background. Much of this mass of bills has already been discussed in the analysis of initiatives and elsewhere, and some of it justifies no comment, being too obscure or strictly ephemeral; for too many of these bills we know only the titles assigned by the clerks in their Journals. Nevertheless, if the work of Parliament is to be seen in the round, these somewhat unexciting issues cannot be ignored.

Nothing can be usefully said about the bill touching pewterers (1563), the bill for the true making of soap and vinegar (1566), or the two attempts to legislate 'for embroiderers' (1566, 1571), except that they probably demonstrate the existence of interested parties insufficiently organized to get anywhere.[58] The 1559 bill for the garbling of feathers (selling stuffing for bed and cushions) passed both Houses and was vetoed, presumably because it trod on the toes of manufacturers able to get a hearing at court.[59] Competent rivals did for a bill which would have granted the cutlers of London powers of search within a radius of three miles around the city, so as to establish a monopoly in the making of swords, rapiers, daggers and other weapons. Exhibited in Parliament on 25 October 1566, the bill drew an immediate protest from the cutlers of Westminster who asserted that it would infringe privileges they held by patent; the bill died at once.[60] On the other hand, one to prevent fraudulent practices by goldsmiths did get through in 1576, with such difficulties that knowledge of the original initiative has got lost. It was clearly not promoted by the company of goldsmiths who under it became liable to forfeitures and in the course of its passage were heard by counsel in the Commons, but neither did it begin as a government bill. Its history, starting in the Commons, involved two *novae* in that House and another in the Lords, this last, now framed by government draftsmen, becoming the act.[61] For so very brief an act this is really quite extraordinary; very possibly the final version had lost details offensive to the goldsmiths, whom one would normally expect to be able to defend themselves.

Another act to control an industry passed in 1581, 'for the true

[58] *LJ* I, 590; *CJ* I, 77; ibid. 77, 79, 90.
[59] Ibid. 54, 56, 61; *LJ* I, 577; *LJ/EHR*, 539–40.
[60] *CJ* I, 75; SP 12/36, fos. 79–80.
[61] 18 Eliz. I c. 15; *CJ* I, 107, 109, 111, 114–15; *LJ* I. 743, 746, 748, 750.

melting, making and working of wax'. Though it was twice so far amended in the Commons that *novae billae* had to be drawn, the final act bore the official enacting clause; nevertheless, like the goldsmiths' bill, it did not originate with the Council.[62] Its beginnings appear in a bill of 1572 which would have equipped the master and wardens of the London waxchandlers with powers to search out and destroy corrupt wax (admixture with rosin and other deplorable practices) within forty miles of London. The first reading drew immediate objections from a surprising threesome – one of the burgesses for Oxford (who may have been vague about the distance from London), Recorder Fleetwood (London) and Robert Snagge who sat for a Cornish borough. The waxchandlers do not seem to have prepared their ground very well. In consequence the bill was amended to restrict the circuit supervised to twenty miles, but also to include Stourbridge fair; in this form it was rejected on third reading. On this occasion a Cambridge member objected that the inclusion of the fair constituted 'an injury both to the University and the town'; Sir Roland Hayward, alderman of London, rather pointedly remarked that allowing unskilled men to exercise supervision would do only ill; and Snagge saw no reason why Londoners should obtain such jurisdiction. He also thought that supposedly bad wax should not be burned, which would destroy the evidence for a charge of poor workmanship; besides, there might be good wax there to be picked out for the poor.[63] However, the problem of ill-made and deceitful wax would not go away. The act sponsored by the Council therefore transferred the enforcement of control to the usual method of actions brought by informers.

Three bills dealt with licences granted to projectors. One of them caused no problem at all, for good reason. It covered the manufacture of salt for which one Francis Barty, an Antwerper denizised under Edward VI, had obtained a patent on 10 January 1566. This patent he had almost at once sold to a syndicate headed by the earls of Pembroke and Leicester, Lord Cobham, Sir Francis Knollys and Sir William Cecil, who in the next session put up a bill to protect their monopoly (which they proposed to exploit by licensing actual saltmakers). The bill and act were both private and passed with the speed to be expected in the circumstances; Knollys himself carried the bill to the Lords where two of his co-monopolists were waiting for it.[64] Without such influence the road of the projector could be much more difficult, as the fate of a bill put into the session of 1566 by one William Humfrey demonstrates; the story

[62] 23 Eliz. I c. 8; *CJ* I, 127–33; *LJ* II, 49–51.

[63] *CJ* I, 99–102; *Proc.* 313, 383, 385, 402.

[64] 8 Eliz. I, OA 33 (later printed as c. 22); *CJ* I, 80–1; *LJ* I, 663–4. On the relevant days, 23 and 24 Dec., Leicester and Cobham attended but Pembroke was absent.

also tells something about the handling of private legislation.[65] Humfrey, too, sought no more than statutory confirmation for a patent to mine metals and manufacture latten, the alloy of copper and zinc which, cheaper than pewter, was coming in as a material for pans and tankards. He explained his difficulties to Cecil.[66] For some reason he started the bill in the Lords where on second reading it was committed to twelve peers and one judge.[67] There arose 'so many doubtful opinions among the lords' and a demand for so many provisos 'that the whole bill might be thereby overthrown or made of very small effect'. Humfrey complained that the committee particularly objected to drafting faults though the trouble had arisen from the bill being 'divers times altered according to several opinions of lawyers' and also made in some haste, 'fearing a lack of time'. Thus, having learned 'which way best to deal', he had divided the bill and had had the part for the making of latten overseen by Richard Weston, J., a member of the bill committee, and Thomas Carus, Queen's serjeant and soon to be a judge. This new bill he had given to the duke of Norfolk, chairman of the committee. Such careful preparation also availed him nothing: when the new bill was read a first time some of the lords objected to any grant for the mining of metal ores, mainly on the grounds that projectors should first come to terms with the landowners affected. The bill lapsed.[68] Humfrey now proposed to bring in a bill for mining in general which would benefit from the parliamentary experience he had gained, but he seems to have abandoned the idea. That bill would never have stood much of a chance anyway because in the same session a private act confirmed a patent for digging alum and copperas which John Blount, Lord Mountjoy had acquired from the original patentee, one Cornelius de Vos. This bill, which was started in the Commons and reached the Lords the day after Humfrey's bill was committed, passed with some amendments;[69] a general privilege for mining metals would certainly have been in conflict with it, and Mountjoy sat on the committee which received Humfrey's proposal. Perhaps Humfrey came to take some consolation in the ruin which the search for alum and copperas brought to Mountjoy.[70]

The speed with which foreign entrepreneurs sold off their patents to the Queen's courtiers, while it says something about the greedy gullibility of the purchasers, also illustrates the problems that aliens faced in making

[65] For Humfrey, a goldsmith and prominent mining entrepreneur, see M. B. Donald, *Elizabethan Monopolies: the History of the Company of Mineral and Battery Works* (London, 1961), 6–18, 24–33.

[66] SP 12/41, fos. 98–9, 122–3.

[67] *LJ* I, 653.

[68] Ibid. 658.

[69] 8 Eliz. I, OA 24 (later printed as c. 21); *CJ* I, 75, 77–9; *LJ* I, 653–7.

[70] L. Stone, *The Crisis of the Aristocracy* (Oxford, 1965), 353–4.

a living in England. The existing laws troubled them quite sufficiently, limiting the trades they could enter and burdening them with heavier taxation, but that did not stop various people from trying to make things even worse for them. In 1563, a general bill for expelling all strangers 'not being here for religion' appeared in the Comons, but that was rejected and the bill torn (to prevent reintroduction) on second reading.[71] Another bill of the same session, to prevent merchants beyond the sea from marrying foreign wives, got the fate it deserved – one reading and disappearance.[72] In 1576 it was proposed that people born in the Queen's dominions both of whose parents were aliens should themselves be treated as aliens when it came to the payment of customs; this got as far as committal before it vanished.[73] The bill was promoted by the London aldermen's court who ordered Norton to draft it and wished Burghley to 'be made privy thereunto'; the court had been told that foreigners deliberately brought their pregnant wives to England to gain advantages for their children.[74] Revived in 1581 it roused much opposition as contrary to nature and equity, but it passed the Commons; the Lords let it drop.[75] In 1576 also anger at the consequences of disputes with foreign powers which led to the confiscation of English goods abroad spilled over in a bill to have foreign merchants in England treated 'in like sort as the same foreign princes treat her majesty's subjects', but this attempt to constrain the Queen's outward policies also did not get far.[76] There is a mystery about the 1571 session. The poor artisans of London in April that year secured the support of the mayor and aldermen for a bill against 'strangers artificers' and a promise that it should be 'preferred and followed' in the Commons, but no such bill appeared in the fortnight remaining of the session even though it had been ready. Perhaps the poor handicraftsmen jibbed at the cost.[77]

However, the underprivileged also could play this game, and in 1572 they made an effort which caused an uproar in the city. The bill the strangers got read on 24 May charged the city with imposing unjustified payments on aliens (a term which here included Englishmen outside London and especially the inhabitants of Southwark) and taxing them at their dwelling place instead of their place of work, the latter seemingly bringing certain advantages. Fleetwood at once denounced this as a slander on the city and maintained that if it were true London was

[71] *CJ* I, 63.
[72] Ibid. 68.
[73] Ibid. 107, 110.
[74] CLRO, Rep. 19, fo. 38v.
[75] *CJ* I, 118–9, 121–3, 127–8; *LJ* I, 34, 38; *Proc.* 528, 532–3, 537.
[76] *CJ* I, 107–8; *Proc.* 481.
[77] CLRO, Rep. 17, fo. 144. The bill for paving Tower Hill and improving the water supply there, approved on the same occasion, also did not get to the Parliament.

practising extortion which could be punished at law. Nevertheless, the bill was committed.[78] The first counterattack came from the wardens of the companies accused who on 5 June obtained permission to put in a bill legalizing the 'quarterage' which, so it would appear, they had been demanding of aliens.[79] But this line was not pursued because a fortnight later the wardens of eight craft companies appeared in the mayor's court to complain of the bill which not only accused them in particular 'of sundry exactions and injuries' but preferred general charges against all London companies. They were told to get learned counsel to prepare their separate cases in support for what they were doing; if they could not allege express law or grant they were to make a case in equity. The idea was to supply ammunition to London's men in the Commons who had been instructed to oppose the bill. The court also resolved that in future no company should charge aliens for the registration of their licences to practise – a quiet admission that the complaints were justified. It would be best, it was recorded, if the whole dispute were resolved by Common Council. To this the promoters of the aliens' bill agreed on the 20th; they abandoned their bill and heard the court promise to take good order in the matter.[80] As usual, nothing seems to have been done, and the aliens, led by Englishmen from Southwark, renewed their bill in 1576 when again it was committed on first reading and then disappeared.[81] Perhaps the reminder did bring about action by the Common Council.

Aliens played a part also in the bill the brewers lost in the Commons and despite mayoral advice did not put in again into the Lords;[82] the brewers wanted permission to employ more than the four Flemings and other foreigners that they were allowed to retain. Altogether, bills touching beer, one way and another, did not do well. The coopers admittedly succeeded in their endeavour to put up the price of barrels, a price which had been fixed by an act of 1532. Since that time, they claimed, their costs had just about trebled, 'to...the utter undoing of themselves, their wives, children and families, as is most evident'; they asked for the repeal of the relevant clause and that prices should in future be fixed by the city authorities. The bill lapsed in 1563 but passed in the next session.[83] The brewers' desire to prevent an increase in the price of malt by engrossers failed twice.[84] So, however, did attempts to restrain the trade: to put down brewhouses on the bank of the Thames below

[78] *CJ* I, 97; *Proc.* 380.

[79] CLRO, Rep. 17, fo. 323.

[80] Ibid. fos. 335, 337.

[81] *CJ* I, 110; that this was the same bill appears from its description in SP 12/107, fo. 132.

[82] Above, p. 78.

[83] *CJ* I, 68, 71; 8 Eliz. I c. 9 (private bill made into public act).

[84] 1566: *CJ* I, 75; 1576: ibid. 107, 110.

London Bridge (1566), to stop the making of extra-strong beer (1576), to control the number of innholders and the behaviour of tipplers (alehouse keepers: 1576), and to transfer the licensing of alehouses from J.P.s to the justices of assize (1581).[85] Drinkers of wine also formed a target in the Commons for reformers who had grown suspicious of wine-shops. Licences for retail outlets attracted a hostile but unsuccessful bill in 1559.[86] On the other hand, the bill to liberate the wine trade (import and retail), which in 1566 passed the Commons by thirty votes out of 160, was quashed ('quassata') by the Lords on third reading.[87] The bill came from the London Vintners' Company who had obtained the approval of the mayor's court; it had been agreed that 'the knights and burgesses of this city shall be specially moved for the furthering of the same'.[88] It proposed to repeal the highly restrictive act of 1553 (7 Edward VI c. 5) which had severely limited the number of taverns permitted in towns and had fixed prices. The Vintners were to have the right to sell wine anywhere, retail or gross, as also to supervise all tavern keepers throughout the realm not free of the company.[89] The bill drew Cecil's wrath, who prepared a paper of arguments against it.[90] Any increase in the importation of wine would worsen the balance of trade which was already adverse because of the trade in silk, wine and spices – luxury goods whose use should be restrained. 'Willingly to make a law to increase any of this is to consent to the robbery of the realm.' Wine was the worst offender for four reasons. 'It enriches France whose power England ought not to increase.' It had to be paid for in cash. The bill would augment the number of taverns, and with it disorder and trouble. Wine drinking reduced the consumption of ale and thereafter damaged tillage. The Vintners' argument that the Edwardian act, by restricting shipping, had helped to bring on the decay of port towns, Cecil refuted at some length. And though he failed to prevent passage in the Lower House he evidently was able to get the Lords to defeat the bill and prevent an explosion of wine-bibbing. As against this, the Commons in 1576 stopped what must have been a Council scheme for enlarging the Queen's income from the butlerage and prisage on wines.[91]

[85] Ibid. 75, 106, 110–12, 121. The two bills for 1576 were joined in committee; they and the bill of 1581 were all dashed in the Commons. Cromwell's diary mentions the bill for strong beer under 1572 (*Proc.* 387): most likely a copyist's error.

[86] *CJ* I. 54–5, 60.

[87] Ibid. 76–8; *LJ* I, 651–3. For Fleetwood's muddled memory of the occasion cf. above, p. 84, n.121.

[88] CLRO, Rep. 16, fo. 130.

[89] The version prepared for the mayor's court (SP 12/28, fos. 108–9) was redrawn in the proper form of a paper bill in Parliament (ibid. 41, fos. 68–71).

[90] Ibid. 41, fos. 151–2.

[91] *CJ* I, 106–7, 109–11, 113.

Armament manufacture formed another activity which produced bills for the Parliament. In 1559, the Commons rejected an extravaganza: no doubt from patriotic fervour at the start of the new reign someone wished to turn the Thames watermen into a sort of home guard by compelling them to acquire morions and hackbuts – helmets and guns.[92] More pointful bills divide between the defenders of the old and those fearful of the new. The bowyers of London in 1563 got a bill for the repeal of a Henrician price-fixing statute, so far as it affected them, through both Houses but met the veto; in the next session, the bill, perhaps revised, passed into law.[93] However, archery was not what it had been, and the profits of bowyers and fletchers had been falling off. General opinion blamed the cost of bows, but the bowyers in turn blamed the scarcity of bowstaves which, they held, could be remedied if old laws compelling all merchants (especially of the Hanse) trading to England to include a quantity of such staves in proportion to the value of other goods they were importing. In 1571 they therefore obtained a very short act which confirmed those earlier laws back to Edward IV's time, allowed half the profits from forfeitures to informers where previously the lot had gone to the Queen, and rather wistfully mentioned the need to enforce the old statutes against unlawful games which drew people away from practising their archery (and buying their expensive bows).[94] The bill caused no problem in Parliament but its structure suggests an unusual cobbling together of proposals. Each of the first two clauses has a separate preamble followed by the short enacting clause: two separate proposals, reframed by government draftsmen, were put in sequence. The third clause is an appeal to the Queen to do something, added as an afterthought. This was also the only part of the act to become effective: in March 1572 a proclamation appointed county commissioners to see to the enforcement of the laws against various games.[95] The absurd idea that foreign merchants could be forced to carry bowstaves along with wine or spices or indeed Baltic stores produced no action, a fact of which the London bowyers soon enough complained to the Privy Council.[96]

Of course, the bowyers' troubles really reflected the obsolescence of the bow and the arrival of firearms. Since the days of Henry VIII,[97] the law had shown much distrust of their spread, especially into private hands,

[92] Ibid. 60–1. In the division on third reading the noes had it by ten votes in a House of 114.

[93] 1563 (started in the Commons): *CJ* SI, 64, 66–7, 69; *LJ* I, 595, 597, 600, 603, 606. The Lords had added a proviso. 1566: 8 Eliz. I c. 10 (started in the Lords): ibid. 653, 655–6, 663; *CJ* I, 79–81.

[94] 13 Eliz. I c. 14.

[95] *TRP* II, 361–2.

[96] SP 15/21, fo. 245.

[97] Especially 33 Henry VIII c. 6 (1542).

but in 1571 a serious effort was made to accept facts and provide proper conditions for their use. A bill 'for shooting in handguns and arquebuses' introduced into the Lower House had behind it some very detailed and careful drafting by Burghley himself; it was backed up by a person surnamed Saul in a memorial addressed to the 'lords and burgesses of the high court of Parliament'.[98] Its purpose tended towards establishing sound standards for the equipment and a proper training in its uses, in the interests of national defence, but in that short session even Burghley could not get it through; it passed the Commons but reached the Lords on the day of the dissolution.[99] The bill brought into the 1572 session looks, as far as we can know the contents of either bill, to have been quite different from its predecessor, with the initiative coming from elsewhere – probably from the London armourers. This bill its promoters backed with a special set of articles 'concerning our bill put in for the service of the prince'.[100] The articles went to the committee appointed on first reading and produced a revised bill. At first the proposal had concentrated on prohibiting the import of firearms and quality control for those manufactured at home, the latter being committed to expert gunmakers. In the debate, Sir Francis Knollys welcomed the bill because 'most pieces which come from beyond the seas are falsely made', but he cast doubt upon the control clauses which 'tendeth to a monopoly'. Another speaker expressed some cynicism about the native capacity to produce the quality of weapons needed: 'promises very seldom performed'.[101] When the revised bill came up for second reading it was agreed (as proposed in the articles) that supervision should be entrusted to the Ordnance Office, and Sir William Winter, admiral and expert, contributed the opinion that smaller-bore weapons were preferable. They used less lead, the soldier could carry more ammunition, and smaller bullets 'will pierce better and fly as far'.[102] On third reading this line of specialized knowledge went further. One member preferred freedom to have weapons made to shoot bullets at either twenty or thirty to the pound of lead, to which Knollys replied that that would defeat the whole purpose of the measure which was intended to achieve standardization: soldiers could help each other out at need, and besides, the royal armoury stored the slightly larger bullet. Winter repeated himself. Though the bill passed the House it did not become law; most probably the gunmakers who did not wish to be controlled from London secured

[98] SP 12/78, fos. 225–31; SP 15/20, fos 53–60 (two similar discourses by the same man). Saul maintained that the existing ban on handguns was meant only to protect a few wildfowl.

[99] *CJ* I, 90, 93; *LJ* I, 701.

[100] SP 15/21, fo. 72.

[101] *Proc.* 372.

[102] Ibid. 385.

the veto.[103] Nor was it ever revived, and what looks like an enlightened measure supported by the Council dropped out of the programme.

One reason for this military backwardness lay in the continued fear of firearms in private hands. In 1576 a comprehensive bill made it a felony to carry a pistol with intent to kill; even wounding in the course of an assault either on the highway or in the victim's own house was to be felonious, and administration of poison 'to the intent to kill' was added for good measure. The bill vanished in committee.[104] A like bill was introduced in the Lords but immediately abandoned, presumably in hopes that the Lower House would deal with the matter.[105] Another bill of that session 'against the wearing and using of unlawful weapons' (perhaps with less severe penalties) got a bit further but in the end also failed.[106] So while in 1571–2 the new weaponry attracted official favour, in 1576 it came under multiple attack; both endeavours, however, ended in nothing being done. The same fortune attended bills dealing with the making of defensive armour. In 1566, Sir Henry Sidney, then abroad in Ireland as lord deputy, through shortage of time lost a bill to confirm a patent granted to a syndicate chaired by himself for the making of steel plates for body armour;[107] in 1581, a bill promoted by the London armourers to obtain monopolistic control over all armour brought for sale to London failed to progress beyond a first reading despite some of the most intensive lobbying vouched for in the reign.[108]

Armaments depended on the availability of iron and steel, and since at this time iron needed charcoal both to extract it from the ore and to convert it into steel the claims of the industry clashed with the need to preserve timber for fuel. Bills to preserve wood or increase it appeared in every session except 1572, but few came to anything. Usually the matter was raised early in the session, so that the preservation of timber showed signs of becoming the 'bill *pro forma*' – the one read at the opening of a Parliament immediately after the election and approval of the Speaker, by way of declaring that the Commons had become a House. In 1559 a bill against the felling of forest trees was the first one read, but it was not *pro forma* in the strict sense, progressing as far as the committal of a *nova*.[109] Late in the session there appeared a bill 'for increase of woods' which reappeared in 1566 as the opening bill; neither

[103] *CJ* I, 96, 99, 100; *LJ* I, 717–19, 723. In the last entry the clerk put 2ª by mistake for 3ª.

[104] *CJ* I, 106.

[105] *LJ* I, 739.

[106] *CJ*, 107, 110–11.

[107] Ibid. 77, 79–80; *LJ* I, 662.

[108] *CJ* I, 121; *Proc.* 530. The story of the armourers' lobbying is to be published by Mr Ian Archer to whom I am grateful for letting me know of it.

[109] *CJ* I, 53, 55, 57.

progressed beyond a first reading.[110] In 1571 it came second in the race; it had clearly been held in readiness but was beaten to the tape by the bill for coming to church, another sign that management was not doing so well in that session.[111] It is likely that this *pro forma* bill confined itself to timber in the neighbourhood of London, for in 1571 it was then 'enlarged and made general' because somebody started a debate on it;[112] seventeen days into the session three members (Fleetwood, Norton and Edward Fenner who represented Sussex iron interests)[113] were instructed to draw the general bill. The bill for London complained of the reckless cutting of young timber within a radius of twenty miles around London, which for quick profits endangered the city's fuel supply.[114] The reformed bill got as far as a Lords committee which asked for a conference; there things ended, with the end of the session six days away.[115] In 1572, with great affairs the business of the session, nothing was heard of timber, but the general bill of 1571 was revived in 1576, also to lapse after a single reading. It certainly tried to do more than could possibly be enforced: apart from protecting all trees against cutting until they were twelve inches square in section and had grown at least three feet high, it wished to compel the enclosure for timber of an acre of land for every acre cut.[116]

The Journals' laconic headings hide a more specific line of attack on the felling of timber around London for charcoal burning in the service of the iron industry. A general hostility to iron mills for driving up the price of wood appeared in the comprehensive programme of 1559,[117] but it was not the Council that went into action. A very short unofficial act of 1559 prohibited the making of charcoal within reach of the sea and of navigable rivers (without such transport the product would not be able to reach iron-smelting furnaces), Sussex being excepted; but clearly this proved ineffective.[118] In 1572 a bill, put in by London and described as being for the preservation of timber, in fact wished to stop ironmaking within twenty miles of London and the Thames;[119] revived in the Commons in 1581, it extended the limit to twenty-two miles and in that form passed, after a most laborious passage during which attempts were made to reduce the protected area to eighteen miles around London and

[110] Ibid. 59, 62.
[111] Ibid. 83.
[112] *Proc.* 202, 245.
[113] In 1563 a bill to preserve wood 'about the South Downs in Sussex' starting in the Lords, died after a second reading in the Commons (*LJ* I, 601, 605–6; *CJ* I. 70–1).
[114] SP 46/25, fos 22–5 (agrees with description in *Proc.* 202).
[115] *CJ* I, 85, 88–92; *LJ* I, 690–1.
[116] *CJ* I, 104; *Proc.* 477.
[117] *TED* I, 329.
[118] I Eliz. I c. 15.
[119] CLRO, Rep. 17, fo. 311v; *CJ* I, 96, 98; *LJ* I, 712–13, 719; *Proc.* 370.

eight from the river.[120] Exempting provisos for the properties of Moyle Finch esq. and Lady Judith Pelham (widow of Sir John), which the Lords wished to add, disappeared after a conference between the Houses. London was not the only community to object to the presence of wood-consuming iron mills. In 1563 Guildford promoted a bill for the destruction of such a mill at Shere, some seven miles from the town. Informed that the mill belonged to one Mr Elryngton, the House instructed the Speaker to invite him to defend his interest; he came to get a copy of the bill, appeared on a day given with two learned counsel (Plowden being one of them), and received a copy of a submission by Guildford. In the end the parties were referred to a committee of twelve which never reported.[121] Very probably Elryngton and Guildford came to terms, but meanwhile the House had spent quite a bit of time on this private matter. The larger issue – fuel against iron – was never resolved in the reign, but charcoal burning and the provisioning of London notoriously between them cut into the shipbuilding materials available in England. Yet iron production increased sufficiently for a bill to be twice attempted (1566, 1576) for the promotion of wire-making and against all imports of wire except for virginals and clavichords, presumably beyond the skill of English wire-drawers. It failed both times.[122]

Ironmaking was still a very minor industry in England whose chief manufactures were leather and textiles. Both came to Parliament. Privately promoted acts of 1559 tried to settle practice in the two branches of the leather industry – heavy leather men (tanners) and light leather men (curriers).[123] In the next session there passed a general code for the various trades involved in the making and use of leather which was to govern production until the later seventeenth century. Its making has been analysed by L. A. Clarkson who concluded that it stemmed from various privately promoted ideas and involved government only inasmuch as the Council in the Commons were responsible for putting this diversity into order.[124] Even this is doubtful; most probably, from

[120] 23 Eliz. I c. 5; *CJ* I, 120, 125, 128–9, 131–4, 136; *LJ* II, 51, 53.

[121] *CJ* I, 62–4.

[122] *CJ* I, 75, 107–9; *Proc.* 483. The second bill was promoted by the Company of Mineral and Battery Works to protect its new wire mill at Tintern which, it was claimed, could ultimately employ 10,000 people in making carding wire for wool; it would also enhance the value of iron from £11 13*s.* 4*d.* a ton in the raw state to £280 after manufacture, with much profit to the many hands through which the iron passed (SP 12/148, fos. 31–2). Thc Commons dashed the bill on second reading.

[123] 1 Eliz. I cc. 8, 9. For the structure of the industry cf. L. A. Clarkson, 'The Organization of the English Leather Industry in the Late Sixteenth and Seventeenth Centuries', *Econ. Hist. Rev.* 2nd ser. 13 (1960–1), 245–56.

[124] L. A. Clarkson, 'English Economic Policy in the Sixteenth and Seventeenth Centuries: the Case of the Leather Industry', *BIHR* 38 (1965), 149–62.

Clarkson's own description, the act grew out of private initiatives and compromises in committee, a point supported by the lack of realism in it.[125] Though it endured it had grave defects. Its prescriptions contravened necessary and indeed best practices in the tanning and currying of leather, and it worked only because tanners especially ignored it. All this was explained to Burghley in a long expert opinion, probably submitted in 1572.[126] In 1571, London had seriously contemplated an amending act, and in the next Parliament the relevant bill passed the Commons, too late to get through the Lords.[127] It was not brought back. Nor did any of the other bills concerned with leather achieve anything. In 1563 it was hoped to protect the bark of oak trees felled for timber, oak bark being the essential material for tanning; the bill failed at second reading and was torn up.[128] Neither tanners nor curriers obtained the right to buy rawhides and tanned leather respectively; that trade remained in the hands of the manufacturers, especially cordwainers (shoemakers).[129] The cordwainers had in fact won their battles with the curriers,[130] but two attempts to get their privileges confirmed by statute were dropped after one reading,[131] as was the attempt to prevent shoes from being made outside towns and their guild controls.[132] Three bills tried to introduce improving (restrictive?) practices into the tanning and working of leather – all in vain.[133]

The industry did secure one further act. In 1559 it was made felony to carry leather or any materials needed in its manufacture out of the country,[134] and when this act, a probationer, was by an oversight left out of the continuance act of 1571 it was quickly revived in 1572.[135] In actual fact it does not seem to have worked very well. At any rate, a little later 'the poor artificers and labourers not only of the city of London but of the whole realm of England' petitioned the Lower House.[136] The act passed, they said, to keep leather cheap and plentiful, instead of which the price had risen and leather was hard to come by. Although the Commons no doubt knew the reason better than 'we poor people of the rude and ignorant multitude', the petitioners put the trouble down to

[125] 5 Eliz. I c. 8.

[126] BL, Lansdowne MS 5, fos. 182–6.

[127] CLRO, Rep. 17, fo. 132v; *CJ* I, 102–3; *LJ* I, 723; *Proc.* 403.

[128] *CJ* I, 63.

[129] Ibid. 63–4.

[130] Clarkson, *BIHR* 38 (165), 153.

[131] *CJ* I, 76, 89.

[132] Ibid. 77.

[133] Ibid. 60 (hides four and a half years old to be reserved for shoesoles); 75, 77 (tanners not to cut womb leather); 106 ('for cutting and working tanned leather' – perhaps a reintroduction); 130, and *Proc.* 540 (no one to dress leather 'like to Spanish or buff leather' until he has been in the trade for seven years).

[134] 1 Eliz. I c. 10.

[135] 14 Eliz. I c. 4, a Lords' bill.

[136] SP 12/41, fo. 195: probably intended for the 1576 session.

the abuse of export licences granted by the Crown: 'underministers' of the licensees exported far more than the grant specified. They therefore begged that the Queen be informed and the licences revoked. The poor artificers had put their finger on the weakness of all this restrictive legislation, favoured by the manufacturing interests and pressed upon government. General acts were intended to be operated by judicious licensing, itself profitable to Queen, courtiers and entrepreneurs, and this opened the door to a wholesale evasion of statutory rules. It is unlikely that the revision of those rules in 1576, confirming some parts of the restrictions and relaxing others, solved the problem of the price rise.[137] A general bill to control licensed exporters, which also included the domestic trade in raw wool, disappeared without trace in the same year.[138] A particular prohibition of the export of fells and skins into Scotland from Carlisle and Berwick was taken seriously enough to get as far as a *nova* at which point it ceased.[139]

Of course, the trades affected by the inhibition or permission of exports were by no means necessarily of one mind, a point well illustrated by the case of sheepskins. In 1563 transporting sheepskins and buckskins overseas was prohibited.[140] Behind this act stood the skinners and furriers who in 1566 tried in vain for a more penal act which would extend the ban to fox and otter skins as well as stop tailors from practising as skinners.[141] Instead an official bill passed which favoured another set of people.[142] The export of skins having been allowed by the general proclamation for renewing the intercourse with the Low Countries (the ban was supposed to have helped harm those relations)[143] it was now again stopped because those fears had proved to be wrong; but the earlier act's prohibition of the export of parchment leather was revoked because that trade had turned out to be very profitable to English parchment-makers who had found a good market abroad. It ought to be added that Elizabethan government really did not command the number and quality of customs officials which these increasingly complicated controls required.[144]

The textile industries put far more bills into Parliament than anyone else, but also with very limited success. The manufacture of cloth in one way and another involved a large part of the population, from the

[137] 18 Eliz. I c. 9.
[138] *CJ* I, 112; *Proc.* 489. The bill is SP 12/107, fos. 133–7. It was fielded and buried by Sir James Croft, a privy councillor.
[139] *CJ* I, 128–31.
[140] 5 Eliz. I c. 22, privately promoted.
[141] *CJ* I. 77; the bill is in SP 12/41, fos. 35–6.
[142] 8 Eliz. I c. 14.
[143] *TRP* II, 259–60.
[144] The Tudor customs service needs a new and full-scale study.

production and spinning of the wool to the finishing processes and sale; highly organized, it revolved around the middleman, the clothier who acquired the yarn, employed the weavers on piecework, and either sold the product himself or passed it on to the exporting merchants. From about 1550 to the Restoration the cloth trade was usually depressed, a condition which succeeded to an exceptional and distinctly feverish boom, and which quite understandably turned all the parties concerned towards attempts at legislative assistance. The multiplicity of operations and people in part accounts for the proliferation of bills, while the conflicting interests – conflicts between the various crafts and conflicts between the various regions of production – helped to assure the failure of most of them.

One possible answer to the slump was to diversify by encouraging the production of linen cloth, though the chief purpose behind the campaign for growing flax and hemp lay in the shipwrights' need for cables. Thus in 1563 a clause in the navigation act revived the act of 1532 for the sowing of those plants, and the county of Hertford failed in 1581 to gain exemption from that law.[145] But early in the reign linen cloth also received attention. An act, promoted officially, attacked fraudulent practices in its manufacture: linen weavers were stretching the cloth and filling in with chalk and other substances, so that a few washings left the piece in tatters.[146] In 1563, two bills tried protection and encouragement. One wished to prohibit the import of dressed flax; the other wished to compel clothiers to produce one linen cloth twelve ells long for every four broadcloths or twelve kerseys they handled. Neither bill reached a reading in the Lords.[147] The real concern lay with woollen cloth.

Wool production and cloth manufacture were statutorily governed by two codifying statutes of Edwards VI's reign (1552). That for wool, designed to protect the fading prosperity of the Calais Staple, barred everybody except clothiers and staplers from buying wool from the producer, ostensibly in an effort to keep down prices which had allegedly been driven up by competition; it allowed sheep-farmers to store their wool unsold for only twelve months.[148] All efforts to break this monopoly, rendered even more depressive for the trade by the loss of Calais, failed in the seven sessions down to 1581. The wool-winders, forced to obtain

[145] 5 Eliz. I c. 5, sect. 19; *CJ* I, 127–9, 131. The clause in the 1563 act stemmed from a bill of 1559: ibid. 59. A bill for the better manufacture of cables from hemp, read twice in 1572, was formally dashed in 1576: ibid. 103, 106–7. For the bill see HLRO, Papers (Supplementary) 1575/6.

[146] 1 Eliz. I c. 12.

[147] *CJ* I, 64, 66, 72; 70, 72.

[148] 5 & 6 Edward VI c. 7. Cf. P. Bowden, *The Wool Trade in Tudor and Stuart England* (London, 1962), 106–25.

the material for their craft from middlemen, tried twice in vain,[149] and the same fate befell the worsted makers of East Anglia who wanted to buy long-staple wool locally.[150] This last bill was vetoed, to demonstrate the influence of licensed wool merchants in government circles. Better luck attended New Woodstock in Oxfordshire, a decaying town which in 1576 (after a failed bill in 1572) obtained special permission to restore its fortunes by setting up the buying and selling of wool at its town fair.[151] In the much coarser wools of the northern counties neither wool merchants nor clothmakers had much interest, but that made no difference. Two bills turned up in 1563 to free that trade. One was rejected at once, in order to allow the other to proceed;[152] designed to permit local J.P.s to issue licences to buy wool in Lancashire, Cheshire, Yorkshire, Durham, Westmorland and Cumberland for the making of 'cottons, rolls, rugs and other coarse cloth', it too was vetoed.[153] There were again two rival bills in 1566; they got nowhere.[154] On the other hand, bills further to restrict the trade in wool did no better. A general attack on wool-broggers got a first reading in 1563; a bill to prevent sheep-farmers from selling any wool not of their own production got into committee in 1581.[155] The regular middlemen, that is to say the clothiers, maintained their hold on the raw material.

The clothmaking act of 1552, an enormous and very detailed measure, fixed standards of quality and specified rules for the various cloths and clothmaking districts; it was amended and expanded in 1558.[156] The bulk of the cloth bills under Elizabeth tried to modify this massive code either in general or for a given region. It would be intolerably tedious to recite them all, especially as nearly all failed; by my count, twenty-eight bills fell into this category to which the four bills of the London clothworkers should be added.[157] Several bills refused to lie down at a first defeat. Wonersh in Surrey, trying for the right to manufacture cloth, flew a kite in the Commons in 1563; in 1566 they got their bill through the Lords but saw it dashed at the report stage in the Lower House where representatives sat for existing clothmaking districts.[158] Coggeshall and

[149] 1563 and 1571: *CJ* I, 65–6, 89. On the second occasion they had strong support from the city of London (CLRO, Rep. 17, fo. 134v).

[150] *CJ* I, 71–2; *LJ* I, 607, 615, 617.

[151] *CJ* I, 96, 101; *LJ* I, 721–3; 18 Eliz. I c. 21. The conversion into a public act proves special favour, which presumably also accounts for its passage.

[152] *CJ* I, 67.

[153] Ibid. 70, 72; *LJ* I, 615–16, 618.

[154] *CJ* I, 74, 77–9.

[155] Ibid. 78, 121, 125.

[156] 5 & 6 Edward VI c. 6; 4 & 5 Philip & Mary c. 5.

[157] Cf. above, pp. 83–4, for a discussion of several of these bills.

[158] *CJ* I, 69. – *LJ* I, 644, 646–7; *CJ* I, 77–8, 81.

Bocking, two of the four Essex towns whose right to produce cloth had been reaffirmed in 1559,[159] wished to proclaim their special skill by the use of a unique mark (a cock), but failed in both 1571 and 1572.[160] Somerset clothiers tried four times, always in vain, to obtain exemption from the statutory standards for the cloths called Tauntons and Bridgewaters.[161] It is plain that in 1576 and 1581, and possibly also in 1563, cloth bills were referred to a single committee where rival interests could cancel each other out. Of the nine bills so treated in 1581 only two were reported for further action; one of them was promptly dashed while the other died in the Lords.

All this eager activity produced only two acts. In 1576, certain clothiers of Wiltshire, Somerset and Gloucestershire put in a private bill licensing them to live out of corporate towns, contrary to the Marian act; that is to say, they sought to escape guild regulations. They put their backs into the promotion. A Gloucestershire worthy, Sir Henry Poole, agreed to prefer the bill from outside to the Lower House, and when the bill committee was due to meet the promoters circulated its members, humbly desiring their 'honourable presence and assistance by two of the clock', adding at the foot 'the committee is in the Star Chamber'.[162] Their labours paid off: not only did they get their act but they avoided fees to Speaker and clerk when it was made public.[163] The other successful bill was that of 1566 for the Shrewsbury drapers which two sessions later had to be repealed when the underhand tricks of its promoters were revealed to the Parliament.[164]

Bills to improve the clothmaking code could also come to grief, as one did 'for the true making of woollen cloth' in both 1576 and 1581; we do not know its import except that it tried to improve the authority of the sealers of cloth (ulnagers) with whom the enforcement of the code in effect lay.[165] There had been a plan to do something along these lines as early as 1559 when the long delays over the settlement of religion had

[159] 1 Eliz. I c. 14. A clause in the Marian clothmaking act had inadvertently threatened the livelihood of some established manufacturing towns.

[160] *CJ* I, 89, 98, 100–1; *LJ* I, 720, 723; *Proc.* 381.

[161] 1566: *CJ* I, 77. 1571: ibid. 90. 1572: ibid. 101. 1581: ibid. 120, 122, 130–1; *LJ* II, 44; *Proc.* 530, 532, 540.

[162] SP 12/107, fo. 109. According to HPT III, 232, Poole did not sit in 1576, and since he does not appear on the committee for the bill he had 'preferred' (*CJ* I, 106) we must conclude that this is true and that he had merely pressed the bill on the clerk. Those three counties altogether did well: in 1584–5 they secured an exemption from the code, at the same time as did the weavers of Devon and Cornwall who had tried in vain in 1581 (27 Eliz. I cc. 17, 18; *CJ* I, 121, 123, 132; *Proc.* 531–2).

[163] 18 Eliz. I c. 16; SP 12/107, fo. 144 shows that the bill started as a private one.

[164] 8 Eliz. I c. 7; 14 Eliz. I c. 12; cf. above pp. 131–2.

[165] *CJ* I, 109–10 (rejected), 124 (committed). A comprehensive revision of the code passed in 1601 (43 Eliz. I c. 10).

postponed the bill till it was too late to get it through.[166] The ulnager for Lancashire did better than his colleague for Worcester: after one abortive effort in 1563 his fees were settled by an act which also modified the code for the cloth produced in that country.[167] There was some apprehension that the crucial seals might be forged; in 1566 a Lords' bill, several times reformed, for ensuring that they should all be engraved at the Mint in the Tower ran out of time in the Commons.[168] It is not really clear who backed the successful bill limiting the length of kerseys to eighteen yards, but it was certainly not the Council, though the conference called by the Lords does not seem to have changed anything.[169]

Success also attended the bill against malpractices in the dyeing of cloth, but only after some vicissitudes. Tried first in 1566 it was rejected when the Speaker put the question for engrossing.[170] Its fate was no happier in 1572 when, however, we learn of its contents and the reason for rejection.[171] The bill's second half provided against the use of bad dyestuffs and poor workmanship, but the first half tried to prohibit the export of undyed cloth – the 'white', unfinished cloth for whose export the Merchant Adventurers of London held a monopoly. In the second-reading debate, John Marsh, a respected member for London and at the time governor of the Adventurers,[172] declared that it was an 'innovation so great and so perilous to the state'. He produced all the arguments which were to recur until the failure of Alderman Cockayne's disastrous scheme in the 1620s proved them right: the English finishing trades were not up to the task, and there was no sale abroad for finished cloth. John Hastings, member for Reading, took the other side and argued that 'the commodity of the whole realm' should be preferred to that of London. At the time he held a monopoly patent for the making of certain lesser finished cloths in a Dutch style. Sir Francis Knollys, in the middle as usual, admitted that finished cloth would bring much higher profits to England, but pointed out that the Merchant Adventurers had paid £1000 for their privileges, which they would not have done if there were any market for the dyed and dressed product. Thomas Atkins, representing Gloucester whose cloths went to the Adventurers for export, agreed and thought that the bill would serve well if its first part were removed. When reintroduced in 1581 the bill did precisely that and so passed, as a measure to control the dyeing of cloths for the domestic market but

[166] *CJ* I, 53, 56, 59–61; *LJ* I, 538.
[167] *CJ* I, 67–8, 70, 72; *LJ* I, 616; 8 Eliz. I c. 12. For Worcester see *CJ* I, 68.
[168] *LJ* I, 642–3, 648, 657–9; *CJ* I, 80–1.
[169] 14 Eliz. I c. 10; *CJ* I, 100–1, 103; *LJ* I, 723, 726.
[170] *CJ* I, 76, 80.
[171] Ibid. 95, 102; *Proc.* 343, 406–7. The breviate of the bill survives: SP 12/92, fo. 30.
[172] Cf. HPT II, 274.

leaving the export trade to be dominated by white cloths and the Adventurers.[173]

One last group of bills links to the problems of wool and cloth. They dealt with caps and hats, were mostly advanced by the London haberdashers, and complained of troubles which seem to have sprung from changes in fashion as well as inadequate workmanship. A bill against the thickening (felting) of caps with wrong materials and methods, complaining also of the expensive import of foreign felt to make hats, failed in 1559 and 1563 but got through in 1566; it had the support of the mayor and aldermen. The chances are that opposition was roused by the haberdashers' desire to control cap-making throughout the realm; in the end, a proviso exempting Norwich got the bill through.[174] This still did not satisfy the haberdashers who regarded the more profitable caps as the true English headgear and the newfangled hats as deplorably foreign things. So they twice tried to prevent the purchase of the foreign wools needed for hats,[175] and when that failed borrowed a notion from the Council's preoccupation with sumptuary laws. In 1566 a bill to compel people to wear caps and not hats on holidays was committed,[176] and in 1571 this extraordinary measure became law.[177] Making exceptions for women of standing and all men worth £13 13*s*. 4*d*. from land, but imposing the statutory penalty on the parents and guardians of hat-wearing children between the ages of six and twenty-one, it caused a division in the Commons but no hesitation in the Lords, content that their kind would not be affected. Still not satisfied, the makers of caps tried to strengthen the act of 1566 in 1576 by tightening the regulations for apprenticeship,[178] and in 1581 by making even more stringent rules for this as well as excluding aliens from the craft.[179] But Parliament had had enough of the haberdashers.

[173] 23 Eliz. I c. 9. It may be that the bill as introduced still looked like that of 1572 and that the dropping of the first part was done in committee from which indeed a *nova* emerged (*CJ* I, 130). The dyers had some cause to complain: after all an act of 1566 had already provided for the export of one 'wrought' cloth for every nine exported unfinished (above, p. 83).

[174] 1559 (starting in Commons): *CJ* I, 53–4, 56, 58. 1563 (starting in Lords and dashed in Commons): *LJ* I, 586, 598, 600; *CJ* I, 68–70; CLRO, Rep. 15, fo. 177v. 1566 (starting in Commons): 8 Eliz. I c. 11, amended in both Houses.

[175] *CJ* I, 68, 71–2, 77 (1563, 1566). [176] Ibid. 76–7.

[177] 13 Eliz. I c. 19. Thanks to the previous act, the promoters were now able to describe themselves as 'the fellowship and company of cappers of...England'.

[178] *CJ* I, 107–8, 111, 114; *Proc.* 482, 484, 486. This bill had the support of the city (CLRO, Rep. 19, fo. 45v).

[179] *CJ* I, 127, 129; *Proc.* 537.

TRADE AND SHIPPING

The bills dealing with trade often concerned themselves, for obvious reasons, also with aspects of manufacture, and some have therefore already been discussed. Keeping the two apart distorts the role of Parliament as legislator for the common weal, even if in the main it makes a clearer overview possible. A good many bills on trade and shipping came to the Parliament, though markedly fewer than those for industry; the proportion of successful bills is a little higher, and rather more of them stemmed from Council programmes.

The fundamental purpose of virtually all bills and acts for trade is summed up in two words: protectionist restriction. We have already seen that every effort was made to keep the raw materials and basic products of England's chief industries from reaching foreign competitors. The principle was applied, with some success, to leather and the materials used in its production but did not work so well for woollens because there the only successful trade relied on the export of unfinished cloth.[180] The further principle that favoured native-born traders over aliens, more particularly in the rates of customs paid on both imports and exports, not surprisingly led to the practice known as 'colouring' by which the foreigners employed Englishmen as fronts in their activities. Some held that the occupation of trading was brought into disrepute by such dishonesty, and in 1562 a bill was prepared which sought to provide a comprehensive remedy.[181] Merchanting had once, it stated, been an honourable profession, but the intrusion of all sorts of dubious participants had caused it to be despised. Inexperienced or deceitful men were pushing out the established traders from the leading towns. People who invested in the export trade just to employ their money (actually the mainstay of joint-stock companies!) knew nothing of business and opened the door to the unscrupulous. Idle young men preferred the sea to the learning of a proper occupation and caused havoc abroad. Smugglers abounded and professional gamblers. The bill therefore proposed to confine all overseas trading, in or out, to nineteen established port towns,[182] to force merchants without the qualification of apprenticeship to cease activities, to compel all qualified persons to move into one of the licensed towns, and to set up local registers of properly established merchants. By way of an afterthought the bill confined apprenticeship to the sons of the better off and (contrary to the

[180] Above, pp. 82–4. [181] SP 12/27, fos. 212–19.

[182] London, York, Norwich, Newcastle, Hull, Boston, Chichester, Southampton, Poole, Lyme, Dartmouth, Plymouth, Exeter, Bristol, Barnstaple, Westchester, Carmarthen, Haverford West and Tenby.

Adventurers' monopoly) opened the trade with Antwerp to all Londoners experienced in foreign trade. The resulting fines were to be divided equally between the Queen, the informer and the offender's town. The proposal echoes the code-building inclinations of the era, except that this code for overseas merchanting never appeared in Parliament. In 1572 a much milder measure, confining overseas trading to those who had undergone a seven-years' apprenticeship or had acquired twelve years of proper experience received a first reading; Fleetwood called it a monopoly, and it was immediately voted down.[183] Nor did it do better at a second attempt in 1581.[184] 'Colouring' certainly continued, to judge from the persistence of complaints.

We have seen that the haberdashers tried to destroy the competition of foreign imports;[185] they were not the only people to do so. A bill 'to avoid French wares and wines' got read once in 1559, but its purpose was not forgotten; almost five years later, during the quasi-war with France, a proclamation banned the import of French wine except those taken as prizes on the high seas.[186] A successful bill came from the small-craft specialists of London; in 1563 an act passed which prohibited the import of such things as gloves, girdles, knives, daggers, scabbards, pins and points. The Lords limited it till the next Parliament but since the act was regularly recontinued this did not matter.[187] A more general bill against imported wares failed in 1576 for lack of time.[188] In 1581 the Commons stayed at third reading a bill to empower the Queen to reply in kind to any country which put an embargo on English goods. Defended by Knollys, it was probably a Council bill, but the member for Liverpool manfully attacked it for being but an attempt to benefit the merchants of Hamburg – an obscure argument not clarified by the diary entry but persuasive enough to cause the government to withdraw it.[189] The State Papers contain other schemes against foreign imports which cannot be related to any action in Parliament. A draft proviso freed all retail trade in imported goods in Cornwall, Devon and Dorset as well as parts of Somerset and Gloucestershire;[190] a proper draft bill repealed the proviso in the 1571 continuance act which had exempted wine and spices

183 *CJ* I, 99; *Proc.* 384.
184 *CJ* I, 132.
185 Above, p. 253.
186 *CJ* I, 53; *TRP* II, 241–2 (8 January 1564). The mention of the matter in the Commons moved Lord Paget to enquire of Sir Thomas Parry how the Queen felt about his licence to import wine (HMC, *Hatfield*, I, no. 572).
187 5 Eliz. I c. 7. The bill was prepared by the beneficiaries (the hand that wrote it occurs nowhere else in the parliamentary archives); the time-limit, added in another hand, originated in the Lords, to judge from the bill's travels between the Houses: *CJ* I, 64, 66–7; *LJ* I, 599–603.
188 *CJ* I, 90–1; *LJ* I, 694.
189 *CJ* I, 100–1; *Proc.* 385, 387, 390. The stay was moved by the comptroller, Sir James Croft.
190 SP 12/147, fo. 67.

from the Edwardian act against regraters.[191] To a copy of this draft a list of price increases is appended which alleges (among other things) that free trade had doubled the price of French wines to £18 the tun and raised a hundred-weight of prunes from 9*s*. to 19*s*.

Another approach to the control of trade outside the realm tried to assure the honest payment of customs duties by insisting that imports must be landed during the hours of daylight and at places served by customs officers. In the session of 1559 an act passed to that effect which looks like a government bill framed as a petition from Lords and Commons.[192] A bill to do the same thing for outward bound merchandise got nowhere in 1563.[193] The same fate befell Burghley's attempt in 1576 to amend the 1559 act by permitting royal commissioners to designate suitable wharves and quays for the unloading of imports; passed easily in the Lords, it was after conference dashed on third reading in the Commons.[194] It appears to have been revived in 1581 when even the Lords would have none of it.[195] Opposition to delegated legislation manifested itself more than once in these Parliaments. In 1563, Southampton obtained an act to confirm the patent under the great seal which gave it a monopoly for the landing of malmsey and sweet wines, and in 1566 an attempt of the Venetian merchants to abolish that monopoly, in return for forty marks paid by them to the town for every ship discharged elsewhere, got no further than a first reading.[196] A somewhat obscure bill of 1563 to confiscate all goods imported indirectly – that is to say, taken on in entrepot towns abroad – had nearly passed both Houses; when the Lords insisted on amending it by excepting wine the Commons rejected what they had previously agreed to.[197]

As is sufficiently well known, one common way of controlling overseas trade employed chartered companies, but such charters did not necessarily require action by Parliament. The greatest of them all, the Merchant Adventurers of London trading to the Low Countries, never bothered to have theirs confirmed by statute, though when a bill of 1563 proposed that for a payment of ten marks any Englishman could become a member of the company and trade freely within the area of their

[191] Ibid. 107, fos. 174–7. Both copies of the draft bear the date 11 March 1576, but the notes are not contemporary. That date was a Sunday and thus cannot allude to action in Parliament; in any case, I cannot find a bill in that session that might represent the proposal. The proviso to be repealed was 13 Eliz. I c. 25, sect. 8.

[192] 1 Eliz. I c. 11; *CJ* I, 58–9, 61; *LJ/EHR*, 539–41.

[193] *CJ* I, 69.

[194] *LJ* I, 744; *CJ* I, 112–15; *Proc.* 491. The bill survives in Burghley's papers (BL, Lansdowne MS 105, fos. 207–14).

[195] *LJ* II, 27–8.

[196] 5 Eliz, I OA35; *CJ* I, 75.

[197] *CJ* I, 76, 79–81; *LJ* I, 662–4. The title referred to 'dunnage wares' which I take to mean cargo picked up during the voyage home to fill partly empty holds.

monopoly they hastened next year to get their patent of incorporation.[198] In 1576, the outport merchants attacked the London company for breaches of the 1497 act which had supposedly protected them against London's monopoly and exactions;[199] and in 1581 another effort was made to throw the company open to all comers, drawing a powerful defence from the monopolists;[200] all in vain. The sad story of the Bristol adventurers has already been mentioned: the act of 1566 making a patent of Edward VI's permanent had to be repealed in the next session when it turned out that a minority had obtained the first by devious means.[201] In fact, the only creditable act establishing a trading monopoly was that incorporating the Muscovy company in 1566.[202] The promoters supported their bill with a careful statement of needs and advantages which at the end displays a useful understanding of parliamentary procedure. 'If any of the Parliament House wish the bill to pass but for term of years or till the next Parliament', they pointed out that the patent carried no time-limit and that the activities of the company depended on its secure future existence. However, being recent and not yet famous, they had to accept three rather suspicious provisos added in the Commons. They could not export unfinished cloth to their area of operations, so as not to interfere with the trade route which brought English cloth finished at Antwerp to Danzig and Cracow; if voluntarily they ceased trading with Russia for three years in time of peace their monopoly was at an end; and any persons who during the ten years before December 1567 had traded with Russia from York, Newcastle, Hull and Boston were entitled to join if they invested the same amount as other subscribers did.

If trade was to be directed to specified landing places, England's harbours had to be kept in decent condition. The problem, especially of the Channel ports, received recognition, but little was attempted and less achieved. In 1566, bills for improving Hartland harbour in Devon, for setting up commissions to enquire into the general decay of landing facilities, and for the maintenance of Plymouth and Dartmouth failed at

[198] *CJ* I, 66. The bill is SP 12/41, fos. 102–21; articles attacking its preamble as untrue are ibid. 93, fos. 175–6. A modern note on the bill claims that it was read on 19 Dec. 1566 which is wrong; neither *CJ* nor D'Ewes mentions any such bill under that date. Perhaps the note misled George Unwin who spoke of two relevant bills in 1566 (*Studies in Economic History* [London, 1927], 170). He gave no reference, and I can find no bill in 1566 and only one in 1563. [199] *CJ* I, 111; *Proc.* 488.

[200] *CJ* I, 128, 130, 132. The terms of the bill appear not from *Proc.* 538 (rather misleading) but from the counterblast (SP 12/148, fos. 19–30) which explained why applicants for membership should be refused.

[201] 8 Eliz I., OA 22; 13 Eliz. I, OA 22. See above, pp. 131–2.

[202] 8 Eliz. I, OA 20. It does not mention an earlier charter but would seem to have confirmed that of 1555 (T. S. Willan, *The Early History of the Russia Company 1553–1603* [Manchester, 1956], 7). Willan does not mention the private act of 1566.

various stages.[203] The only port to receive serious attention was Dover, recognized as the most important place of refuge in a storm for London-bound traffic going up Channel, and notorious for centuries as a difficult port to keep clear.[204] In December 1565, the Privy Council, informed by Lord Cobham (as warden of the Cinque Ports) that the harbour was once again silting up, with its pier and fortifications well decayed, decided that the repairs required 'some general assistance' from the whole realm and resolved to take action in the forthcoming session of Parliament.[205] Cecil drew the bill which proposed to repair all the harbours between Portsmouth and the Thames by means of a quarterly levy upon every householder (1*d*.), every 'yeoman at husbandry having...a ploughland' (2*d*.), and every merchant of London or other corporate town (6*d*.), these payments to be collected for ten years. The bill organized the collection and administration of the money, the only thing left blank in the draft being the agency which would actually see to its application to the ultimate purpose.[206] An ambitious, not to say oppressive, scheme but not a successful one, despite the official initiative: introduced some five weeks after the start of the session, the bill was read once and then forgotten.[207] The problem, however, stayed in the memory, and an act specifically for financing repairs at Dover passed at last in 1581.[208] It, too, was a government measure, using the Queen's name who allegedly had shown a very special interest in providing for the safety of her ships. The over-hopeful idea of making the whole realm pay for repairs had been dropped; instead a tax of 3*d* per burden-ton was to be levied on every ship passing through the straits. In committee this was redrawn and the terms of the levy were changed. It was now to fall only on ships owned or part-owned by Englishmen; on the other hand, all seagoing vessels, wherever they plied, were subjected to it. The administrative sections provided for the collection of the money, delivery to the Exchequer, and assignment without further warrant to unnamed persons who would attend to the repairs.

Ships and shipping notoriously occupied a high place on the parliamentary agenda, producing several acts and hardly any failed bills. The government as well as commercial interests were concerned about maintaining an English merchant fleet, about giving English ships advantages over foreigners in the carrying trade, about a sufficiency of

[203] Hartland: *CJ* I, 76, 79, 80; *LJ* I, 569–61. Commissions: *CJ* I, 79, 81. Plymouth: ibid. 89–92; *LJ* I, 698–9.

[204] Work on Dover harbour occupied a high place in Thomas Cromwell's concerns in the 1530s when the port had been even more important as the northern end of the Channel 'bridge' to Calais.

[205] *APC* VII, 310–11.

[206] SP 12/41, fos. 16–22.

[207] *CJ* I, 76.

[208] 23 Eliz. I c. 6; *CJ* I, 128, 131–2; *LJ* II, 48–9; *Proc.* 538.

trained seamen, and about the protection of the realm against possible invasion. These considerations recur in the preambles of the various acts. Linked to these matters were the needs of the English fisheries, but there the ostensible concern with security hid disagreements between fishing ports and the London Fishmongers Company who looked for liberty to import Dutch catches at the expense of English fishermen. The battle over the herring was won by the port of Great Yarmouth in Norfolk, assisted by fishing ports all round the east and south coasts, in an act of 1581, though disputes continued actively thereafter.[209] The general history of acts for shipping and navigation is best followed chronologically.

The first Parliament of Elizabeth opened the litany with an officially sponsored act which repealed earlier legislation and tried to stop English merchants using foreign vessels; if they did so they would pay strangers' customs duties. One section banned small ships (hoys and plates) from trans-Channel traffic altogether. Exceptions were made for the regular wool and cloth fleets organized by the Merchant Staplers and Adventurers who had to use foreign ships to make up their necessarily large assemblies, and also for Bristol which of late had lost too many ships in Queen Mary's war.[210] The bill passed without difficulty, except that 47 out of 131 members of the Lower House voted against it on third reading, a minority no doubt well connected to the London Fishmongers who in February 1563 persuaded the court of aldermen to promote a bill of repeal in the next Parliament.[211] It is likely that those opposing the 1559 act objected more to the ban of hoys (used by those trading in fish) than to the prejudice against foreign vessels. In fact the bill carried a time limit which would have called for attention in the Parliament of 1571 when, nothing being done, it lapsed; it had meanwhile been superseded by the vastly more ambitious and important navigation act of 1563.

This act,[212] the product of much parliamentary labour, constituted one of those codifying statutes which characterized the work of government in the 1550s and the early 1560s, and like all such acts contained a variety of initiatives and purposes – including, no doubt, that favoured by the Fishmongers' proposed bill. As passed, the act carried the long enacting clause, and it does indeed seem not to have been part of a Council programme. The planning document of 1559 had said nothing about the needs of the navy; on the contrary, it had taken the line that English shipping was in so healthy a state that it needed no special protection.[213]

[209] 23 Eliz. I c. 7. For the story of the fisheries see my 'Piscatorial politics in the early Parliaments of Elizabeth I' (forthcoming).

[210] 1 Eliz. I, c. 13.

[211] *CJ* 1, 60; CLRO, Rep. 15, fo. 188.

[212] 5 Eliz. I c. 5.

[213] *TED* 1, 329–30.

The bill's career began on 6 February 1563, some four weeks into the session, with a motion by Sir William Winter, England's leading naval expert of the day, 'that this House have regard to some bill for the navy'; evidently no such bill was before the House nor could Winter produce it at once. It took another fortnight to get it into the pipeline, and when it appeared it aimed not only to strengthen the navy but also attended to the carrying trade in fish and wine.[214] The committee, chaired by Cecil, brought in a new bill which for the first time contained the contentious clause making Wednesday a compulsory fish day – contentious because, while Cecil meant to encourage fishery, protestant opinion in the House smelt something popish in this 'fast'.[215] The outcome was seen in repeated days devoted to long debates, until finally on 11 March the Wednesday clause was carried by 179 votes to 97.[216] In the course of passage the bill had acquired three provisos to which the Lords, who did not hold the bill up, added six more.[217]

Two documents survive which provide further evidence for the difficulties encountered. One is a set of notes in Cecil's hand which plainly registers changes made in the committee he chaired.[218] Apart from the painful drafting of the provision for the Wednesday fast, the committee was responsible for putting in the clause extending to mariners the fifteenth-century punishment for deserting soldiers (section 18), and at a late stage for that reviving the Henrician act for hemp and cables (section 19). Secondly we have Cecil's draft of a speech, delivered during the debates over the fast, in which he spelled out the problems affecting the maintenance of England's shipping when the Levant trade had declined because of the Turk's conquest of those regions, the spice trade was efficiently monopolized by Spain and Portugal, Baltic tolls were reducing trade there, and so forth. Cecil appears to have learned some realities since 1559. Much of this could not be helped, but the decline of fishing, he argued, could be by restoring consumption to the level it had attained in 1536 (before the dissolution of the monasteries!); and thus English ships could be kept in business. There is really no doubt what held the bill up, even if Cecil's arguments in the end persuaded a sizable majority.[219]

214 *CJ* I, 65–6.
215 Ibid. 66.
216 Ibid. 69.
217 *LJ* I, 604–5, 608, 611. The provisos appear on separate schedules attached to the OA – three schedules originating in the Commons with one proviso each, and two schedules from the Lords with respectively one and five provisos.
218 SP 12/78, fos. 232–3.
219 *Proc.* 103–7. A mysterious bill 'for the better abstinence from flesh upon the days thereunto appointed' was read once in the Commons on 22 March (*CJ* I. 70), a week after the navigation bill had passed the Lower House; was it intended to back up 'Cecil's fast' or to revive fears of popish practices?

The bill that emerged from all this drafting and redrafting bears the marks of its history. It positively lacks any character of a planned and thought-through enterprise, from the preamble (barely a sentence) to the confusion of its clauses. We start with various measures to protect English fisheries; we turn to confining the trade in French wines and Toulouse woad to English ships; we move on to the introduction of fish-days, with reassuring words about people who hold licences exempting them on health grounds; we find next a series of odds and ends including the clauses on deserters and hemp; this is followed by lengthy provisions for enforcement. It looks as though the bill that came from the committee on 26 February ended here, at section 21. On the first day of 'long arguments' (2 March) Cecil brought in a proviso (sections 22–4) which slightly modified the fast and especially included the remarkable clause which made it an offence to preach that the fast had any spiritual purpose or benefit: it was a purely 'political' measure.[220] The Commons Journal fails to tell us when the bill was engrossed, but it clearly had not yet been because the three provisos run on in the bill, as do the next clauses forbidding the impressment of mariners for military purposes and saving the rights of liberties and franchises. At this point (13 March) it must have been engrossed, for the remaining nine sections appear as separate provisos. The Commons read theirs on the 15th: these forbade the enlisting of fishermen as seagoing mariners, saved the rights of the Cinque Ports and of Yarmouth's herring fair (yet another interest intruding), and limited the act to ten years starting at Michaelmas 1564 and thereafter to the end of the next Parliament. The Lords on one of their schedules responded to various local pressures by permitting foreign wine merchants to visit the Isle of Man, Chepstow and the ports of Wales, reconfirmed the duties leviable on wines, and made sure that nothing in the act extended the jurisdiction of the lord admiral. Lord Cobham, though absent from the House on the day in question (24 March), secured a further proviso protecting the rights and dignity of the warden of the Cinque Ports.

This medley of matters was in essence held together by the desire to guard English shipping against foreign competition. English merchants, using English vessels, gained trading advantages and fisheries were variously encouraged. The rest got tacked on as opportunity arose. Though the first initiative had not come from the Council, thanks to Cecil's chairmanship it then took the act over. Messy or not, the act stood, being regularly renewed well into the seventeenth century. Proclamations tried to enforce observance of various parts of it – for the price of wine

[220] *CJ* I, 68; the three clauses in question were drafted by Cecil (SP 12/27, fos. 286r–v).

(1564), the export of grain (1565), the growing of hemp (1579).[221] It stood virtually unaltered. An attempt made in 1566 (in the Lords!) to repeal the Wednesday fast found no support, however much 'puritans' may have continued to abominate it, but in 1585 the continuance act repealed that much debated clause.[222] Two acts of 1571 tried to introduce modifications. One brought back the ban on small vessels engaging in the seafaring trade which had been enacted in 1559 (now expired) and taken away by section 6 of the 1563 act.[223] This restoration of the prohibition was time-limited and not continued in 1585 when it should have been. Also in 1571 a further act amended parts of the navigation statute to the greater benefit of the herring fisheries.[224] The triumphant herring fisheries act of 1581 saw no reason for referring to 1563 at all: the two acts stood side by side.[225]

SOCIAL REFORM

If at one time it used to be supposed that the regulation of trade and manufacture represented a deliberate and consistent government policy, it has been even more firmly held that attending to the structure of a society in the throes of transformation stemmed from official sources. The first turns out not to have been the case: most economic measures (though not all) at best demonstrate official acceptance of sectional demands. What then is the truth about the social reform? The predominant aspects of this set of issues and measures are the maintenance of the existing social structure and assistance to the poor. We shall look at them in turn.

A number of unsuccessful bills, all plainly of private promotion, tried to prevent various social groups from changing their place in the scheme of things. In 1559 it was proposed to compel craftsmen in Kent and Sussex to live in seacoast towns where they would be subject to guild regulations; living outside town limits gave them opportunities to undercut townsmen whose work was stinted in quantity and supervised in quality. The bill got all the way to a third reading in the Lords before it was voted down.[226] A bill of 1566 for enforcing the same upon all shoemakers dropped out after one reading.[227] In the same year two readings were given to a proposal that artisans should be restricted to

[221] *TRP* II, 257–8, 262–3, 435–8.
[222] *LJ* I, 656; 27 Eliz. I c. 11, sect. 3.
[223] 13 Eliz. I c. 15.
[224] 13 Eliz. I c. 11. Privately promoted by one Valentine Harriss who persuaded Burghley to support it (SP 12/77, fo. 104).
[225] 23 Eliz. I c. 7; see note 209 above.
[226] *CJ* I, 54, 56–9; *LJ/EHR*, 536; *LJ* I, 574.
[227] *CJ* I, 77.

owning one tenement and husbandmen to two.[228] And in 1572 someone tried to make a reality of the widespread feeling that merchants must be prevented from turning themselves into landed gentlemen: those assessed for the subsidy below £500 were to be confined to one house, one garden and one orchard, those worth more than that to £51 worth of land, and aldermen could acquire land to the value of £100.[229] The bill got the fate it deserved in a House full of merchants, lawyers and gentlemen anxious to keep the land market open.[230]

The best known bill pursuing the ends of social stability, of course, was the vast statute of artificers, passed in 1563.[231] It has been discussed so often that there is no need to review its contents at length. Summing up and superseding much earlier legislation, it constituted a general code of labour law which attended to three particular issues: contracts of service in agriculture and manufacture, wage assessment by local magistrates, and standardized rules for apprenticeship.[232] At present it appears to be agreed that, although government policies played a role in creating the act, it was really in the House of Commons that its magnificent profusion and confusion were created: it was there that it grew by stages as a variety of matters kept getting added to the bill. This view rests on the careful analysis undertaken by S. T. Bindoff, and if one could accept his reconstruction there would be no more to be said.[233] Unfortunately, however, essential evidence goes counter to the fundamentals of his argument, and it must be said that he got the history of the act wrong. He held that it started with a privately promoted and minimal bill which by four stages of augmentation, under the guidance of committees chaired by privy councillors but engaged upon proposals fed in by private members, turned into the act as passed. In this interpretation the clauses on apprenticeship, which Bindoff held did not get drafted until the third stage reached the Commons in 22 March 1563,[234] become an afterthought; yet the evidence that a bill for this purpose existed even before the opening of the session is conclusive. On 21 December 1562, three weeks before the Parliament, there met at York a steering committee of thirteen men, including the mayor and five aldermen, to prepare for

228 Ibid. 76, 80.

229 Ibid. 101. Cf. the similar proposals in the official programme of 1559 (*TED* I, 326).

230 *CJ* I, 101; *Proc.* 392.

231 5 Eliz. I c. 4.

232 Cf. the summaries in C. G. A. Clay, *Economic Expansion and Social Change: England 1500–1700* (Cambridge, 1984), II, 230–1, 234–5.

233 S. T. Bindoff, 'The Making of the Statute of Artificers', *Elizabethan Government and Society*, ed. S. T. Bindoff et al. (London, 1961), 56–94. See his conclusion: 'Whatever truth there is in the criticism that the statute of artificers was out of date before it was passed, that criticism attaches... to the royal councillors... Whatever it had which was new and forward-looking it owed to the House of Commons'.

234 Ibid. 72.

the forthcoming meeting at Westminster. The first item in their programme reads: 'As touching the act of apprentices, a like proviso made for York as is for London and Norwich.'[235] York's rulers therefore knew of a bill to be put into the Parliament; they knew it concerned the rules of apprenticeship; and they knew that it contained the proviso (section 33 in the act as passed) which permitted London and Norwich to continue using their established practices in the taking of apprentices despite the restrictive rules of the act.[236] It is hard to avoid the conclusion that the mayor and his committee had a copy of a bill before them which was not so different from what ultimately emerged.

York, moreover, receives support from the other end of the country. On 31 January 1563, Geoffrey Tothill, one of the members for Exeter, reported to John Hooker, town clerk there, on the state of affairs in Parliament. He remarked that, 'as for prentices', there was a bill in hand 'for servants' which had been committed to the master of the Rolls and others. This fits the evidence of the Journal: it called the original bill 'Touching servants to serve their masters' and recorded committal to the master of the Rolls (Sir William Cordell).[237] That committee did not report until 24 February, and when Tothill wrote, the bill for servants was still in committee. But Tothill thought it was about apprenticeship; that was the aspect that concerned him, for he went on to say that if the bill passed he meant 'to get a proviso for all cities in England to take apprentices, and so Exeter not named'. Thus he, like the men of York and London and Norwich, disliked the restrictions in the bill and hoped to gain exemption for his city, though diplomatically he meant to hide a particular interest behind a general clause. In the end there was no general clause, nor did York get its exemption, if ever it actually tried.[238]

Thus Bindoff's analysis, subtle but confusing, cannot be right; he made the story much more complicated than in fact it was by ignoring certain bills of 1559 and by various dubious convictions about Commons' procedure, in part because he accepted Neale's views about an obstreperous and ever-rising House.[239] As its short enacting clause also

[235] *YCR* VI, 50.

[236] In Bindoff's reconstruction (p. 72) that clause first appeared in the last revision of the bill, as one of the points added at the third reading on 6 April.

[237] HMC, *Exeter*, 51–2; *CJ* I, 62.

[238] York behaved strangely in the quest for an exemption clause. After moving for an act to that effect in 1559, it did nothing that we know of in 1563, nor did any bill emerge in 1566 and 1572 when the same resolution was taken in the city council (*YCR*, VI, 118; VII, 46). In 1576, when the Parliament was expected to reassemble, they so resolved once more (ibid. VIII, 22) and this time produced a failed bill in 1581 (*CJ* I, 127).

[239] Cf. his categoric treatment of the House cited in n. 233 above. Some of his assumptions touching procedure are at least doubtful; thus every 'reading' did not mean that the whole bill was read again, and committal at first reading to a privy councillor does not

indicates, the statute of artificers stemmed from Council initiatives and it did not start in 1563. The official programme for 1559 contained two particular items that produced bills put into the session: one for 'a good order for servants of husbandry and artificers and their wages', the other 'for taking and having apprentices and journeymen'.[240] Both appeared very late in the session thanks to the primary concern, the ecclesiastical settlement; they therefore got nowhere but it was evidently decided in official circles to reintroduce them in the next Parliament. York even then knew enough about what was in hand to have produced a bill for exemption several days before the relevant bill reached the Commons,[241] and as we have seen it also knew beforehand about the government's intentions to try again in 1563. Nor is there any difficulty in explaining this level of information, seeing that the Speaker of the 1559 Parliament was Sir Thomas Gargrave, knight for Yorkshire and one of the most influential men in the North. Evidently it was he who kept York informed and provided them with a copy of the lapsed apprenticeship bill to help them in their preparations for the next session. And those preparations show that the exemption clause for London and Norwich was in the bill for 1559.

The session of 1563 opened on 11 January; on the 16th the last session's bill for servants and wages was brought back – the very first bill to appear after the bill *pro forma*. This time the government meant to get its legislation. The bill was at once handed to a committee chaired by the master of the Rolls.[242] This committee sat for nearly six weeks and on 24 February reported a bill expanded into one 'of many articles'.[243] It had taken quite a while to produce an amalgamation of the two labour bills of 1559, for that had been the purpose of the committee: Cordell manifestly took the apprenticeship bill into the committee in order to tie the two together. That that is what happened in the first committee on the bill is conclusively proved by Tothill's testimony, by

prove the bill to have come from private sources. The detailed analysis of discrepancies and repetitions, useful in itself, does not prove the gradual accumulation of fresh topics but rather indicates the consequences of merging two bills and then meeting piecemeal objections in the course of passage.

240 *CJ* I, 60; the first could be a *nova* emerging from Sir Anthony Cooke's committee on a bill for 'men servants and women servants' (ibid. 59). For the pre-sessional planning cf. *TED* I, 325–6 (points 2 and 6).

241 *CJ* I, 54.

242 Ibid. 62.

243 Ibid. 66. All the complicated growth clause by clause which Bindoff deduced rests on no positive evidence but on ingenious inference starting from false assumptions. It actually makes the structure of the act incomprehensible. Nothing can be argued from the bill titles in the Journal: the clerks always tended to keep to the first title used throughout the history of the bill because this made tracking it easier. As Bindoff's tabulation shows (p. 70), the Journal never mentioned apprentices, even after by his own reconstruction that subject had got into the bill.

the failure of the apprenticeship bill to reappear in its own right, by the fact that only the Cordell committee produced a *nova* (so that by 24 February all the essentials of the act must have been in the bill), and by the structure of the act as passed. Its preamble, as Bindoff pointed out, says nothing about apprenticeship,[244] but his conclusion – that the issue entered the bill later, under pressure from the House – is mistaken. The preamble does not mention apprenticeship because it belonged to the bill for servants and wages. There is a second, brief, preamble in the act, in section 18 which introduces the regulations for apprenticeship. Cordell's committee simply tied the two bills together, after inserting a first clause after the preamble to the servants' bill to clear the ground by repealing all earlier legislation. Sections 2–17 are that bill (servants 2–10, wages 11–17). Then follows the original apprenticeship bill with its original preamble either in full or quite possibly a little shortened (sections 18–32). The remaining eight clauses are afterthoughts and particular provisos, the last two being separate provisos added after engrossment.

The bill certainly provoked doubts and debates with additions and amendments during passage in the Lower House. The bill coming from Cordell's committee was on first reading once more committed but only for minor amendment, for it was back within a week for those amendments to be brought in line by the correct procedure of a first reading.[245] Further debate compelled the appointment of yet another committee, with Sir James Croft in the chair, the third councillor to chair committees on this Council bill. This time it took nearly three weeks for the committee to report and a further ten days before a split second reading obtained the order to engross, but none of the changes were such as to call for a *nova billa*.[246] Not too much should be made of those relatively long intervals because it was notoriously difficult to get committees together; moreover, at the time the House was very busy over the problem of the succession which even in the councillors' minds took precedence over the artificers' bill. Nevertheless, they do indicate argument and probably further amendments. Once the bill was engrossed, on 2 April, the Commons altered nothing further in it but added their separate proviso, for the capture of absconding servants.[247] The Lords dealt expeditiously with the bill, adding one proviso to save court sessions held by high constables, and rewriting section 12 (for the punishment of J.P.s who failed to attend wage-fixing sessions), the correction making it impossible to read the original clause on the parchment

[244] Bindoff, 67–8.
[245] *CJ* I, 66. The chairman was Thomas Seckford, master of Requests.
[246] Ibid. 66–71.
[247] Ibid. 72.

bill.[248] It is not now possible to say with confidence what parts of this very long act represent additions or modifications, or even gaps created by deletion; that changes occurred during the debates and the two bill committees need not be doubted. There are plenty of clauses within each of the three parts that make up the final act which could well be interpolations produced by arguments. But the basic structure of the bill as it emerged, new, from Cordell's committee did not alter, and that structure reflects the joining of two government bills inherited from the previous session. Thus, to repeat, the statute of artificers was a Council measure, somewhat modified and equipped with reservations and exemptions in its passage through both Houses.

Its endeavour to freeze society and force everybody into employment – or, using Tudor concepts, to preserve good order and offer everybody a place in life – went, as is well known, counter to the nature of events and well beyond the powers of Tudor government to maintain. The act offered opportunities to the less than scrupulous exploiter. Thus in 1572, two men, Edmund Mathew and Richard Carmarden, sought a patent for a monopoly in the issuing of the certificates which under the act anyone wishing to change his employer and place of employment needed to possess (section 7).[249] Burghley did not respond, but the enterprising pair were right in declaring the ban on mobility unenforceable. Nor did this conservative and restrictive act cure unemployment, and its clauses touching apprenticeship proved much too inflexible to become general reality, though they helped to set proper standards and prevent some abuses.[250] The one part that proved effective was the second half of the original servants' bill: no sooner had the act passed than J.P.s all over the place and the London magistrates set about fixing wages and publishing lists of them which, if they did not please journeymen, are very valuable to economic historians.[251]

The problem of the poor and unemployed remained. The acts passed have, of course, been thoroughly discussed before, but the parliamentary history of the campaign to assist the helpless and prevent criminal vagrancy needs a brief look.[252] Especially one needs to know how far the

[248] *LJ* I, 614–17, and see OA. The addition of the Lords proviso necessitated a return to the Commons but caused no further delays.

[249] SP 12/88, fos. 20, 22–3.

[250] Margaret Gay Davies, *The Enforcement of English Apprenticeship* (Cambridge, Mass., 1956).

[251] E.g. *TRP* II, nos. 501–7, 509, etc. Cf. F. A. Youngs, *The Proclamations of the Tudor Queens* (Cambridge, 1976), 121–3; R. H. Tawney, 'The Assessment of Wages in England by the Justices of the Peace', *Vierteljahrschrift für Sozial- und Wirtschaftsgeschichte* 11 (1913), 307–37, 533–64.

[252] All later discussion of the Tudor poor law (culminating in the measures of 1597 and 1601 which lie outside this book's concerns) still rests on E. M. Leonard, *The Early*

legislation enacted resulted from government initiatives. All thinking on this grave problem stemmed from the distinction made between the able-bodied and the impotent poor – unemployed and unemployables – which was first worked out in the 1530s; though no one revived the ambitious plan for a major scheme of public works, the intended coping-stone of the programme then put forward, the idea that work of a sort might be artificially provided also survived.[253] In 1563, one side of the problem, vagabondage, was tackled in the act against gypsies, already discussed.[254] More important was the long act 'for the relief of the poor' which organized the collection of supposedly voluntary contributions from parishioners to a relief fund administered by the churchwardens under the supervision of justices of the peace and the diocesan authorities.[255] Its time-limitation clause made it expire at the end of the 1571 session. It started in the Lords but, to judge by the enacting clause, did not come from the Council; its preamble stated briefly that it was passed to avoid valiant beggars and provide for the unfit 'which are the poor in very deed'. The Commons heavily amended it.[256] In the main they sharpened its administrative clauses by attaching penalties to any remissness on the part of the supervising agencies (in the concluding portions to sections 2, 9 and 10); they also struck out an exempting proviso for the city of Chester which the Lords had accepted. In general their amendments underlined the broad hints of the act that failure to give voluntarily could in the end lead to compulsory charity. I do not think that this act derived from Council initiative, the more so as the only clause in the 1559 programme to concern itself with the poor aimed at reviving, with additions, the Edwardian act which punished vagabonds with slavery.[257] The crux of the act lies in the employment of the parish as the unit for poor relief. We are so used to thinking of the parish as a part of secular administration that we forget that that function arose from the Tudor poor law's use of it; in 1563 it was still primarily an institution of the Church. Allowing for the House of introduction and the unofficial enacting clause, I incline to think that it was a product of clerical planning entrusted to and promoted by the bishops.[258]

History of English Poor Relief (Cambridge, 1900; repr. London 1965), but see also Beier, *Masterless Men*, 146–70.

[253] Elton, *Reform and Renewal*, 122–6. [254] Above, p. 223.

[255] 5 Eliz, I c. 3; *LJ* I, 597, 601–5, 613; *CJ* I, 69–71.

[256] Three provisos in a schedule to the act, as well as a long paper of amendments filed with the OA.

[257] *TED* I, 325; the act was 1 Edward VI c. 3.

[258] Leonard, 59, tends to agree. The act really revived the charity provisions of the previous two reigns, hesitantly adding slow steps towards a compulsory poor rate.

After 1563, the story of initiatives got more complex.[259] In 1566, a bill which may have been official tried to give the earlier act better teeth by appointing special commissions to supervise the collection and use of the contributions, but it did not progress beyond a first reading.[260] On the same day, a bill against rogues and vagabonds suffered the same fate, but that came back in the next Parliament when William Strickland introduced it, thereby making a strong case for its having been unofficial from the first.[261] On introduction it dealt only with unwanted beggars and vagrants, making them felons,[262] to judge from later evidence probably on a second offence; in the debate on first reading one member declared it to be 'oversharp and bloody'. The two privy councillors who supported it did so in ways that intimate approval but not foreknowledge. Knollys suggested the erection of a Bridewell in every town, every alehouse-keeper in the country paying a shilling a year towards the costs; while Thomas Wilson, reminding the House of Christ's warning 'that poor of necessity we must have', made the point that though every country he knew had sturdy beggars he had never seen 'such looseness and lewdness' as in England.[263] Taking the advice that earlier acts should be studied (another indication that the bill had not been drafted for the Council), the House appointed a committee which added clauses for poor relief to the bill. In this form, and after further work on it, the Lords rejected it – we do not know why.

That left the problem to be tackled in 1572 when the act of 1563 expired, and so the Commons read a relevant bill on 14 May.[264] It bore some relation to the bill of 1571 but was itself a different one, for (as Cromwell, who summarized its terms, noted in the margin) it was not proceeded with 'by reason the Lords dealt with another bill which passed with us last year'.[265] That is to say, the Upper House dug out the bill it had dashed in 1571, and the product, now an official bill, suggests that they did so under pressure from the government. The Lords must have somewhat modified the bill,[266] for it had a fairly painful passage in the Commons, after shunting aside the bill started there.[267] Several committals and debates postponed acceptance, and the first reading produced some interesting comments.[268] Ralph Seckerston (member for Liverpool) called the bill partial in that it provided for big cities like

[259] Leonard (68–72) oversimplifies in supposing that from 1569 the government led the way.
[260] *CJ* I, 79; the bill is SP 12/77, fos. 197–204.
[261] *CJ* I, 84–5, 87–90, 92: *LJ* I, 690–2.
[262] So Hooker says: *Proc.* 247.
[263] Ibid. 219.
[264] *CJ* I, 95.
[265] *Proc.* 344.
[266] *LJ* I, 706, 708–10, 716–17.
[267] 13 Eliz. I c. 5; *CJ* I, 95–100.
[268] *Proc.* 366–7.

London but ignored 'Liverpool and other small boroughs'. He also demanded that the rich, including the bishops, should employ more servants and thus reduce unemployment. He was rebuked for 'ridiculous jesting' by Knollys who reminded the House that the bill before them was their own, now returned to them by the Lords; he thought it a good one and not to be held up. Nicholas St John drew attention to the habit of rogues to squat on commons, building themselves rough shelters with no land attached – one cause, he thought, of the increase in their numbers. This complaint was to produce a bill against 'the building of cottages on waste grounds and commons', rejected at second reading.[269] William Lovelace, serjeant at law, delivered a diatribe against vagabonds and called for specialist searchers to be appointed. But the man who touched the right string was Robert Slegge, burgess for Cambridge and champion there of town against gown: he was willing to have wandering minstrels punished as vagabonds but not those 'which keep a continual habitation'. For it looks as though the major bone of contention thereafter was the list of people to be included among punishable rogues. In the end the Lower House produced a few amendments in the Lords' bill, but the only one of interest removed 'players of interludes belonging to gentlemen' from the recital and added to it 'fencers, bearwards, common players in interludes, and minstrels not belonging to any baron of this realm or towards any other honourable personage of greater degree'.[270]

This long bill of 1572, inflicting severe punishment on sturdy beggars and providing very detailed rules for the collection of the first compulsory poor rate, thus stemmed from a private initiative of 1571 which at first had dealt only with the former part of its concerns, the rest having been added in the Lords and perhaps on official advice. Why it failed one year and revived in the next, both in the Upper House, cannot be confidently answered; perhaps it was the enlargement of it into a bill for poor relief as well as against vagabondage that tipped the scale. Such hints as there are do suggest that in the interval the Council, aware that something would have to be done about the time-expired act of 1563, decided to use the dashed bill to solve the problem. The act of 1572 remained the basic poor law until the economic disasters of the 1590s called for more effective measures. The code was completed in 1576 by an additional act which picked up another of the ideas of the 1530s by trying to create work

[269] *CJ* I, 97, 99. The bill is misnamed in the Journal so as to appear to be yet another bill touching vagabonds; its real purpose emerges from Onslow's notes (*Proc.* 311, and cf. 372).

[270] When the House agreed on these changes it resolved that if the Lords objected the Commons would make whatever changes the Upper House called for (*CJ* I, 99).

for the unemployed poor.[271] In this case there is no doubt about the official origin of the bill. Its first mention occurs in a set of Walsingham's notes for a Council meeting in January 1576: 'a device to be preferred to the Parliament for the relief of the poor'.[272] The chief clauses of the act provided stocks of raw materials in every county for the poor to work on and set up houses of correction, thus following up Knollys's suggestion four years earlier. Introduced into the Commons, it had a well contested passage there, including two replacement bills; the Lords proposed amendments by proviso led to a conference, but in the end the Commons accepted them.[273] To judge from Cromwell's summary of the contents of the original bill, all the palaver in the Lower House changed nothing of substance; fortunately, perhaps, a proposed proviso to make it felony to marry two wives 'wittingly and willingly' was ignored.[274] Crafty tacking was not invented in the reign of Queen Anne.

Thus after private beginnings the Council by stages turned its mind to the problem of the poor. It also showed itself concerned about another familiar social issue of the sixteenth century – sumptuary laws defining what ranks might wear what apparel. Here, however, it proved markedly less successful. A major sumptuary bill – 'the long bill of apparel, as well for temporal men as spiritual, and also for women' – was prepared on the Council's orders for the session of 1566 and caused a lot of trouble.[275] On first reading in the Commons it went into a committee chaired by a privy councillor; the new bill so produced went to another committee also chaired by a councillor; this came up with a further new bill 'of apparel for all states under the prince'. A very large Lords committee replaced this by a third new bill which was turned down on third reading in the Lower House. The theory that Cecil had used a sumptuary act to give statutory support for the Queen's stance on ecclesiastical vestments, and that a 'puritan' House of Commons tried to defeat this, is not borne out by either the probabilities or by the bill the Commons sent up to the Lords.[276] The notion that the clerk's title for the bill implies that a measure concerned with social ranks and with cloth of gold, silks,

[271] 18 Eliz. I c. 3. [272] SP 12/107, fo. 36.

[273] *CJ* I, 104, 107–13; *LJ* I, 740, 742–3, 745; *Proc.* 477–8.

[274] Ibid. 496. In the next session a bill against bigamy made some progress in the Commons (*CJ* I, 120–1, 127; *Proc.* 529).

[275] SP 12/107, fo. 146, 'an act to be made for reformation of the statute of apparel made A° 24 H. 8 [c. 13] and for great hose'. The first mention occurs in Cecil's addition to plans for 1563 (SP 12/40, fo. 149), unless this concerned the little act banning sales, discussed below. *CJ* I, 73–7, 80–1; *LJ* I, 646, 659–61.

[276] HLRO, Parchment Collection, Box 1. The strange theory was put up in Read, *Cecil*, 359. He misunderstands the Journal evidence and therefore mis-states the history of the bill. The *canard* about ecclesiastical vestments appears to have been born out of Neale's conviction that the Commons of 1566 were puritans.

embroidery and so forth could also lay down what officiating ministers should wear is as poor a reading of Tudor diction as the idea of the Queen approving a parliamentary statute on vestments is contrary to her known views on the government of the Church. The bill applied to all men and women, but all women are lay; that is why 'spiritual' is added only to men. It expected clerks to observe the same sumptuary rules as applied to the laity. Actually, the bill mentions 'the lords bishops and all others of the clergy' in a proviso which entitled them (together with an array of lay officers, lawyers and so forth of various ranks) to 'wear all such apparel and stuff in their gowns, coats, doublets, jerkins...as they have been accustomed'. The Lords cannot have rejected the bill because it left out vestments. The real problems lay rather in the fantastical, pernickety and unenforceable detail of the bill, in the desire of the socially inferior to dress themselves and their wives more elegantly, and very probably also in the protests of men whose livelihood would have been destroyed by it. The fashion for wide breeches ('great hosen') attracted special attention because it combined ostentation with a deplorable waste of cloth, but tailors and drapers would have stood up for fops. In 1563 a bill to punish both makers and wearers reached a second reading,[277] and in 1571 a single-vote majority on third reading kept in a clause in effect outlawing weavers guilty of the offence, after which the bill died without being passed even in the Lower House.[278]

The government tried again in 1576 and again in vain, but this time we know the reasons for disagreement between the two Houses, and they throw light backwards upon 1566. This bill started in the Lords, was there replaced by a new one, suffered the like fate in the Commons whence after conference the *nova* was sent up, only to be dropped upstairs after two readings.[279] The surviving report of the conference explains what went wrong.[280] The bill proposed that royal proclamations should from time to time lay down what clothing was permitted to the various ranks of society, and it appointed severe penalties for offenders – forfeiture of the offending garment and a fine of £10 for every day that it was not so handed in. Neither of these provisions is in the 1566 Commons' bill, but if they had been in the one at first moved by the Council the opposition and redrafting are fully explained. For it was these issues that troubled the Lower House in 1576. Some members opposed the bill outright because it replaced the certainty in law attached to statute by proclamations which 'should take the force of law', acceptable perhaps under so gracious a prince as Elizabeth but a dangerous

[277] *CJ* I, 68, 70.
[278] Ibid. 89–90.
[279] *LJ* I, 729–33, 749–50; *CJ* I, 106, 109, 113–15.
[280] *Proc.* 454–6.

precedent for future times. Considering James I's attitude to proclamations, those members displayed good powers of prophecy. Others objected not to the principle but to the details, especially the clause which made a proclamation proclaimed in one place binding on all the realm; this, the Lords agreed, was a poor piece of drafting which they undertook to amend. But they stuck to their guns on the allegedly excessive penalties, on the proposed manner of execution which the Commons objected would cause a lot of strife in the localities, and on the seven years' time-limit which the Commons called too long. So they buried the Commons bill when it reached them unaltered. The Council had to fall back on frequent proclamations of the existing law, which meant trying to enforce the markedly milder Henrician legislation.[281]

One bill of apparel did pass, and a very peculiar one it was. It reached the statute book in 1563 and its author was Cecil who expressed his satisfaction to Sir Thomas Smith.[282] A very short act, without any preamble at all, it deprived of any remedy at law any person who sold items of clothing to a customer without getting his money within twenty-eight days of the sale. The original bill defined the defaulting purchaser as anyone not possessed of £200 in land or fees, but the Lords raised the limit to £3000, which just about destroyed the whole purpose since now only the very rich, who least needed the prohibition, were able to buy on tick and cheat the supplier.[283] Cecil's pride in the act is not entirely comprehensible; one somehow cannot see Thomas Cromwell rejoicing over such a measure. If he supposed that self-interest would move tailors and drapers dealing with respectable gentlemen to operate a round-the-corner sumptuary law by insisting on cash on the nail, he was surely being naive. A bill appeared in 1566 in explanation (which usually meant major amendment) of the act; perhaps Cecil was trying to move the income limit back to the figure first thought of. If so, the Lords won again: they received the Commons bill but did not read it even once.[284]

Thus in the major areas of social reform and control official initiative predominated, though it could not always secure the ends fought for. In another such area, the promotion of schooling and medical care, all the initiatives came from private – usually local – interests, and both the bills passed and the failed proposals testify to some social conscience in the age. In 1563, Speaker Williams in his opening address to the Queen made

[281] Youngs, *Proclamations of the Tudor Queens*, 161–70.
[282] BL, Lansdowne MS 192, fo. 24v.
[283] 5 Eliz. I c. 6; *CJ* I, 66–7; *LJ* I, 597–8, 600. £3000 was the conventional figure of the annual income needed to maintain the status of an earl.
[284] *CJ* I, 77–9; *LJ* I, 567.

a special plea for schools and Universities,[285] and though he got nothing out of the Crown private action of a helpful sort began in that Parliament. Private acts passed for the establishment, confirmation or further endowment of schools at Guildford in Surrey (1563), Tonbridge in Kent (1572), and Coventry (1581).[286] However, more such bills failed, some for lack of time and some because the local promoters were not determined enough. St Catherine's by the Tower did not get its school in 1566 because it tied that proposal to the elevation of the church into a parish church, a notion evidently opposed by the bishop of London.[287] Southwark was twice unlucky, in 1566 and 1571, in its attempt to get a private act for the setting up of a free school.[288] On the other hand, Bletchingley in Surrey and Denbigh in North Wales abandoned their bills after one reading.[289] The attempt, in 1571, to transfer a school from one town in Lincolnshire to another was thrown out in the Lower House.[290]

Hospitals did better than schools. In 1572 two recently founded hospitals in London – Christ's and St Bartholomew's – secured a local act to protect their endowments; a Commons proviso extended this to all hospitals and bedehouses in the realm.[291] In 1571 a private act licensed the earl of Leicester to found a hospital at Warwick or Kenilworth.[292] Gloucester, Winchester, Leicester and Ledbury (Herefordshire) all used statute to give security to their hospitals, some of which had been threatened with legal actions by people who claimed rights in the endowment lands.[293] Both the London hospitals and Ledbury succeeded at a second try, having meanwhile sorted out local differences which had held things up.[294] The only such bill to fail altogether was one of 1571 against leases made out of hospital lands;[295] the proviso to the act for the London hospitals thereafter protected all such institutions against bills of this kind. Orphans, too, appeared in Parliament: Exeter's private act of 1581 for the confirmation of its liberties specially mentioned the care

[285] *Proc.* 75–6.

[286] 5 Eliz. I, OA 33; 14 Eliz. I, OA missing but see Parliament Roll, item 16; 23 Eliz. I, OA 26.

[287] *CJ* I, 66–8; *LJ* I, 603, 605 (committed to the bishop: i.e. Grindal).

[288] *CJ* I, 76, 78; *LJ* I, 651 – *CJ* I, 84, 90–1; *LJ* I, 693.

[289] *CJ* I, 90; *LJ* I, 651. Denbigh apparently followed the Welsh principle of using the earl of Pembroke as its contact man in Parliament.

[290] *CJ* I, 84, 91; *Proc.* 246, 254.

[291] 14 Eliz. I c. 14, not printed in the sessional statute. Perhaps because the proviso in effect made the act general, the governors of the two hospitals tried to evade the private bill fees demanded by the clerk of the Lords; they obtained the help of the city in appealing to Lord Keeper Bacon (CLRO, Rep. 17, fo. 342). The outcome is unknown.

[292] 13 Eliz. I c. 17, not printed in the sessional statute.

[293] 8 Eliz. I, OA 21; 18 Eliz. I, OA 28 and 32; 23 Eliz. I, OA 18.

[294] *CJ* I, 89, 96; *Proc.* 371.

[295] *CJ* I, 89; *Proc.* 252.

of orphans' affairs,[296] but a general bill to allow all towns to appoint a chamberlain to look after the property of orphans divided members between those who distrusted small-town officials and those who thought it the best bill that ever was.[297] It died in committee. One rather remarkable proposal of 1571 for the better care of the people wished to set up seven banks 'or stocks of money' in London, York, Norwich, Coventry, Chester, Bristol and Exeter. A listed group of counties was assigned to each of them. The money was to be raised from the sale of the best garment of every person who died after midsummer next, and the banks (all the details of administration being specified) were empowered to make loans repayable within a year at a maximum interest of six per cent to anyone who could prove his need. If the stock in the bank reached £100,000, £7000 was to be set aside to provide work for the unemployed. We do not know whose brain conceived this idea – very probably influenced by experience of continental *montes pietatis* – but one reading was all it achieved.[298]

[296] 5 Eliz. I, OA 34.

[297] *CJ* I, 100, 102; *Proc.* 389. On the growth of care for orphans in the sixteenth century, cf. C. Carlton, *The Court of Orphans* (Leicester, 1974).

[298] *CJ* I, 85; for the bill see SP 12/77, fos 113–30. One stated purpose was to fight against usury, a problem here omitted because it is being studied by Dr Norman L. Jones.

11

Law reform

THE LAW AND THE JURY

In one sense, of course, all that Parliament did changed the law of England, but it is legitimate to distinguish between such measures as altered the condition of the courts and the law there administered from the making of laws for the other purposes already discussed. The half-century ending around the 1540s has quite recently been revealed as one of the great periods of transformation in the common law, a time when the judges and the practitioners, by argument and decision, over-hauled the law of the land in order to bring it into a closer relation to reality than it had possessed for some time.[1] In addition, the application of printing to the records and literature of the law introduced a new degree of definition, a means for making current decisions march in step with agreed authority; put into print, the texts of statutes, of the old Year Books, of the new Abridgments and Reports, accompanied by a proliferation of authoritative textbooks, provided a general guide to the law as it stood.

At the same time, this drastic revision of the system also created a new kind of uncertainty leading to argument, as inherited interpretations came into conflict with what the transformation was trying to make of them. Altering the remedies available to litigants, redefining the rights of landowners and tenants, moving uses and copyhold – hitherto a preserve of Chancery – into the arms of the common law, developing the law of contract and obligation, and doing all this while ostensibly maintaining the continuation of immemorial custom led to much doubt especially concerning title to property and the means of establishing it. Of this doubt the great increase in litigation was both a consequence and a cause. The growth of equity in new courts similarly offered new forms of help

[1] See the introduction to J. H. Baker, ed., *The Reports of Sir John Spelman*, vol. 2 (Selden Society, 1977).

to litigants but at the same time set up new questions touching its relationship to the common law. In the history of the law, the sixteenth century seems matched only by the thirteenth and nineteenth as an age of turmoil. One might therefore expect a frequent resort to statute, the ultimate instrument for settling doubts and fixing the rules, and before the reign of Elizabeth a quantity of acts had indeed been passed which tried to do precisely that. The years 1536–40 had been exceptionally active, with statutes that defined enfeoffment to uses, permitted testamentary disposal of real property, assured lessees of rights hitherto reserved to those who held by seisin, settled the limitation in time within which claimants could challenge possessors, and so forth. However, there are signs that the flood had begun to ebb. The seven sessions here under review are in these respects more notable for piecemeal attempts than for major achievements. What was done indicates rather what some people thought insufficient in the law than what the Crown, the profession or the Parliament thought in need of comprehensive remedy or settlement.

One man, whose name remains unknown, did hope to tackle the problems more fundamentally and comprehensively, an intent which he announced in a long memorial on 'Reformations proposed in Parliament by the Queen's majesty, in favour of justice and of her well beloved subjects'.[2] Despite this superscription, the paper did not come from government circles, nor did all its details ever reach the Parliament. It was a policy document airing views on old and novel notions, put together by someone who, to all appearance, knew the law only from the outside, in the manner of an educated and experienced Elizabethan who could claim no expert authority. In addition he was a good protestant who felt strongly about idolatrous remnants still to be found in the practice of his Church. Inevitably, a man of this sort displays some characteristic signs of crankiness, typical of major schemes proposed by self-appointed reformers, but while there was some nonsense in his paper it also contained sensible ideas, and some of his proposals did find reflection in the work of the Parliament. In general he helps us identify the areas of the law where in the view of an intelligent layman the problems stood out, for which reason it is worth rehearsing his points.

1 Uncertainty in the law. 'The judges in every season presume their bosoms to be the chests of those laws'; their decisions, even when contrary to what the Year Books tell us, 'must be admitted for law'. Yet in truth the general custom always alleged as the foundation of every

[2] SP 12/107, fos. 96–8. The date of the document is uncertain because the author looks to have made new proposals as well as gathered in earlier ones; probably some time between 1572 and 1576.

judgment can arise only 'by perpetual use beyond all memory'. As a result, 'that which is known to have been law in one king's government is become no law in another's'; litigants and practitioners alike are lost 'as in a net'. Thus he put his finger on the uncertainty which marked an age of transformation. He called for a total codification of the law of England. Panels of experts were to have sectors of it assigned to them; their drafts were to be corrected by consultations with judges and serjeants; the product was then to be made the binding law of England by royal ratification.

2 Juries, misconducting themselves and rendering dubious verdicts, formed an obstacle to justice. The memorialist complained of two sides to this problem. Sheriffs, compelled by law to impanel freeholders, picked the poorer sort (yeomen) whom they or the party they favoured could manipulate by gifts and influence. The memorialist, no democrat, proposed for remedy that when men of higher ranks were involved in the case the jury should include a quota of gentlemen. On the other hand, the old method for punishing corrupt juries (attaint) had ceased to work, and the memorialist, who clearly had no faith in the court of Star Chamber which he never mentioned, called for a new supervisory machinery staffed by the gentlemen of the shire.

3 There was far too much litigation – expensive, dilatory and encouraged by the legal profession to the detriment of people in general. For a remedy he proposed to give formal reality to the extra-curial and informal arbitration by agreement which was widely practised, but which, not being binding, did not necessarily lessen resort to the law. There were to be regular shire commissions to settle minor disputes expeditiously; their decisions 'shall bind as effectually as if the sentence was given formally and judiciously in any court of record'. The insertion of a number of reservations to prevent abuse of this machinery seems not to have warned him that the remedy could easily produce as many problems as it was designed to resolve.

4 Local customs concerning the payment of tithe should be established by enquiry and recorded for the future.

5 Fraud in conveyances of lands needs urgent attention.

6 Writs of exigent (the means of summoning defendants which, if disobeyed, would lead to outlawry) should be carefully proclaimed in the defendant's parish church, to make sure that he knew of the summons.

7 Licences exempting from the penal laws (those controlling agriculture, manufacture and trade) should be revoked and the laws themselves be reviewed in Parliament, to distinguish the necessary from the superfluous.

8 The collection of fines and amercements, estreated out of the court

imposing them to the sheriffs, should be tightened up for the sake of the Queen's revenue.

9 'The Romish and profane prohibition of marriage in time of Advent and Lent', retained for the profit to be made from dispensations, should be abrogated.

10 The Church courts' excessive use of excommunication as a means to compel attendance should be replaced by 'a simple sentence of contumacy', enforced through the common law by a new writ 'de contumace capiendo', so as to reserve excommunication for its proper purpose against those who offended against the law of God. 'And the papistical form of absolution and benediction to cease'; instead, a contumacious person's surrender to the writ should simply be registered.

11 The Queen may freely alter and dispose of the court of the Duchy of Lancaster and all the revenues administered there, a power (allegedly) enjoyed by her two predecessors. It is hard to say why this minimal point got into the list, but it might perhaps be a clue to the author's identity.

12 The deans of Windsor and Westminster should be merged into a new bishop for the Queen's court 'and almoner to her majesty', with powers of spiritual discipline over the royal Household.

13 'Lastly, her majesty specially recommendeth to the consideration of the estates[3] how to convert that heathenish trial by battle into some more Christian form.'

The last five paragraphs strayed rather from the primary purpose of the memorial, and no action seems ever to have been taken on any of them. Nor were they the only notions that left no mark anywhere. The idea of a general code proved as impossible even to contemplate as it had been forty years before when Thomas Starkey had vaguely advocated and Richard Morison had tried his hand at it.[4] The very fact that the memorialist thought it feasible renders his association with the legal profession questionable. On some of the issues he included, however, he at least did not stand alone. Thus his complaint about licences *non obstante*, which interfered with the proper enforcement of restrictive (penal) legislation, echoed Lord Keeper Bacon's repeated complaint about the enforcement of existing laws; in 1566 someone – probably Bacon – introduced a bill into the Lords 'for the better execution of certain statutes and for the reformation of certain disorders in the law'.

[3] I cannot recall the use of 'estates' in any unquestionably official proposal to the Parliament.

[4] *Studies*, II, 246–40. Nicholas Bacon had a scheme for codifying the statutes but even this proved too much for the profession to attempt (BL, Harleian MS 249, fos. 117v–118v). In preparing for the Parliament of 1589 the Privy Council revived the plan and even appointed committees of lawyers to work under the direction of the judges (*APC* XVI, 416–7); nothing came of it.

It disappeared in committee.[5] Its title suggests an attempt at major reform, perhaps even something to deal with the confusions created by the renovation of the law in the previous century; it certainly recalls paragraph 1 of the memorial, but since we know nothing else about the bill all speculation is rather futile. In 1559, a bill for doing away with licences *non obstante* actually passed the Commons;[6] thereafter nothing is ever again heard of a reform which by interfering with the prerogative of dispensation would have trenched upon both the powers and the income of the Crown. The bill may nevertheless have inspired the memorialist to make his proposal. In respect of penal laws, however, policy turned towards the better control of informers in whose hands enforcement lay, a policy culminating in an official act of 1576 which also did not succeed in alleviating complaints.[7]

Juries did attract attention, but not altogether along the lines suggested by the visionary memorialist. True, a bill 'for trials by juries', calling for 'more indifferency', was introduced in the Commons in 1576 and reintroduced in 1581; on the first occasion it got to a third reading without the question being put, and on the second it was dashed at that stage.[8] In fact, in 1581 it was revived in the committee which had been considering a bill on the behaviour of undersheriffs, and it was then put to the House by Sir Walter Mildmay.[9] All this suggests that the Council may have been behind the bill since 1576. The connection with the attack on undersheriffs further links this one with that 'for impanelling juries' promoted in 1571, which was dashed on second reading.[10] This derived from a careful draft proposal, itself (to judge from its appearance) a piece of private enterprise. Its burden recalls the memorial: jury trials defeated justice because undersheriffs, 'for private lucre and favour do omit the better, richer and wiser sort and return men of weak judgment and very mean estate'.[11] The remedies proposed ran into much detail, but basically the reformer wanted J.P.s from all the counties to prepare lists of fit persons (£4 a year clear revenue from land being the criterion) from which the jury panels should be chosen. A complex machinery of record and control was appended. This does look like the working out of the second paragraph in the memorial and was evidently submitted to the government for action, though the hand that wrote it is not the same. When that action came it took over the complaint but not all the

[5] *LJ* I, 628. [6] *CJ* I, 57–8.
[7] 18 Eliz. I c. 5, preceded by a failed bill in 1566 and one vetoed in 1572.
[8] *CJ* I, 109, 111, 114, 129, 133–4; *Proc.* 484, 545.
[9] *CJ* I, 129; *Proc.* 530.
[10] *CJ* I, 84–5; *Proc.* 207, 237, 246.
[11] SP 12/77, fos. 101–2. The summary of the bill in *Proc.* (previous note) establishes the connection with this paper and the differences in terms.

machinery. It meant to commit the impanelling of juries at the assizes to the judges of the Westminster courts on the basis of lists of the freeholders sent up by the sheriffs, and it provided that the writ summoning the jury should go to J.P.s rather than to the sheriff. The memorial had complained of the monopoly for jury service of freeholders, many of them poor and simple, to the exclusion of better and wealthier men who held land on other terms; the draft proposals had not considered where the *venire facias* was to be directed. Thus the bill in Parliament differed from both on essential points of substance, however well it echoed their complaints. When Thomas Sampole in the House argued that sheriffs' ill-doings were not 'so great but the doings of the justices may be as well doubted of' – avoiding Charybdis, he warned, we might fall into Scylla – the bill was lost.

That is about as far as any influence on major reform by the private memorialist can be traced. Other bills for juries owed nothing to him. The two measures which dealt with the possibility that a panel might, by illness or challenge, lose more jurors than could be supplied from those formally summoned for service picked up from the Henrician statute which had authorized the calling in of properly qualified bystanders by what came to be known as *tales de circumstantibus* (impanelling among those present).[12] In 1563 its provisions were extended to Wales, Chster, Lancaster and Durham, all of which, being franchises, had been left out in 1543;[13] and in 1572 a brief official bill granted the right to ask for such a *tales* also to defendants.[14] It had been poorly prepared. The list of the franchises mentioned in the act of 1563 had to be added in committee, and before engrossing a proviso extended to informer actions on statutes penal the occasions when a person accused could so complete a jury and therefore feel free to challenge the first panel.[15] But the really odd thing is that except for the proviso the act would seem to have been superfluous: that of 1543 had permitted the use of *tales de circumstantibus* at the request of either complainant or defendant.

Juries turned up in the bill of 1571, rejected by the Lords after the Commons had passed it, which tried to relieve all persons on the checker roll of the Queen's Household from jury duty,[16] and in another for speeding up trials in Shropshire and Herefordshire by improving the range of people suitable for impanelling, which the Lords let die in committee.[17] One suspects that it tried to do something about the

[12] 35 Henry VIII c. 6, sect. 3.
[13] 5 Eliz. I c. 25. Durham was added by the Lords (OA).
[14] 14 Eliz. I c. 9. [15] *CJ* I, 85–6; *Proc.* 367.
[16] *CJ* I, 84, 89, 91; *LJ* I, 694, 697; *Proc.* 208, 247.
[17] *CJ* I, 89, 91–2; *LJ* I, 695–6; *Proc.* 254.

influence of faction in those fairly turbulent counties. More interesting is the repeated attempt to legislate for the jurors of Middlesex (1566, 1572, 1576). It was alleged that their labours had been greatly increased by what were called foreign actions – that is to say, actions by bill of Middlesex, that fictitious device by which the court of Queen's Bench enormously extended the range of its capacity, acquiring so much business that in the course of half a century it moved from rapid decline to becoming the most favoured of all the central courts.[18] But one result undoubtedly was that cases that should have gone to *nisi prius* in the country were heard in Middlesex, before juries of that shire. The bill proposed to compensate any juror compelled to try matters not truthfully pertaining to Middlesex with eighteen pence paid by the victorious party upon verdict being rendered.[19] In 1566 the bill sniffed out the air,[20] but thereafter its promoters were serious about it, though no more successful. In 1572 the bill called forth some legal luminaries, one of whom suggested that it were better to abolish all actions by bill of Middlesex, while another claimed that the jurors' costs were already covered by a charge on the winning party. Though committed, the bill did not reappear.[21] Revival in 1576 brought exactly the same result.[22] The only remedy provided for the overburdening of the central courts – Queen's Bench and Chancery, both of which might be called to hear cases from all over the realm – was an act of 1576 which on the face of it added to the labours of Middlesex juries.[23] It authorized the lord chief justice and the chancellor to hear pleas at *nisi prius* (that is, sent down from the centre) issued into the county of Middlesex during and briefly after the end of term, sitting in their normal places in Westminster Hall. How this was to help the congestion complained of is hard to see, except that the judges did not have to move out of Westminster Hall to some assize town; juries would certainly still have to attend.[24]

We can now depart from the memorialist, recognizing that some of his more sensible complaints either matched discontent entertained elsewhere or influenced failed attempts to provide reform. However, there were, of course, quite a few moves for law reform independent of him, and they fall into four categories, to be discussed in that order: defects

[18] Marjorie Blatcher, *The Court of King's Bench 1540–1550: A study in Self-Help* (London 1978), esp. ch. 3.

[19] *Proc.* 362, 483.

[20] *CJ* I, 77.

[21] Ibid. 95–6; *Proc.* 362, 372–3.

[22] *CJ* I, 108; *Proc.* 483.

[23] 18 Eliz. I c. 12.

[24] Holdsworth, *History of English Law*, IV, 539, seems also to have been baffled: he records the act without useful comment. Perhaps the four days allowed for *nisi prius* sessions after the end of term were thought sufficient to clear backlogs; on the other hand, they postponed some judges' departure to the assizes in the country.

in the structure of the courts, difficulties over process issued, details of the positive law, and crimes.

THE COURTS

Considering how preoccupied historians of government and law have been with the system of rivalling law courts in the sixteenth century, it causes some surprise to find how very little thought was given to any of this in Parliament. The act for speeding business in the Admiralty has already been noted.[25] The only major reform by statute in the reign instituted a court of Exchequer Chamber to adjudicate upon writs of error out of the Queen's Bench. Passed in 1584, the bill had had a trial run in 1581; it was not a Council measure but must have come from the judges.[26] Common Pleas came under attack in 1581 on a charge of permitting too many attorneys to work there; moreover, those admitted overcharged their clients and allegedly obtained their places by fraud. The bill prohibited anyone who was servant or retainer to a judge from practising there, nor was the total number to exceed double that fixed hitherto. Any attorneys beyond that number, if they continued to act in court, were to be declared guilty of maintenance, that is of illegally participating in an action in which they were not party. A new bill produced in committee added five years' work as an attorney as a qualification for practising in Common Pleas; and no one was to be admitted unless he had spent five years of employment as a clerk of the court or had been a member of an Inn of Court or Chancery, by way of guaranteeing professional skills.[27] The bill reflected contemporary convictions about the multiplicity of lawyers and their evil doings, charges which recent research has shown to derive from mistaken prejudices. On the contrary, at least until the end of Elizabeth's reign, there were not enough attorneys in the counties, with the right to practise at Westminster, to satisfy the needs of clients.[28] The bill lapsed – not surprisingly, in a House full of lawyers. More surprising was the fate of a bill of 1571 'touching the limitation of fees for counsellors and others towards the law'. It had been considered by the Council in its preparations for the session of 1563; it reached the Commons from the Lords with

[25] 8 Eliz. I c. 5; above, pp. 66–7.
[26] 27 Eliz. I c. 8; for 1581, see *CJ* I, 121.
[27] Ibid. 124, 127, 130; *Proc.* 535–6, 540.
[28] C. W. Brooks, 'Litigants and Attorneys in King's Bench and Common Pleas, 1540–1640', *Legal Records and the Historian*, ed. J. H. Baker (London, 1978), 41–59; 'The Common Lawyers in England, *c.* 1558–1642', *Lawyers in Early Modern Europe and America*, ed. W. R. Prest (London, 1981), 42–64. There were 100 attorneys in Common Pleas in 1480 and at most double that number in 1560 (ibid. 24, 46).

a special commendation from the Queen and passed there swiftly; at the assent Elizabeth vetoed it, saying that she would 'in time see [to] the reformation and take order therein'.[29] One must suppose that at a late stage the profession rallied its ranks and scared off the Council. The court of Chancery appeared in a bill of 1563 which proposed to set up a new office of two clerks for the enrolment of recognisances; it was rejected at second reading.[30] One might guess that the Lower House virtuously stopped some corrupt seeking of a needless but profitable place, but in actual fact the enrolment of recognisances was poorly served in the Chancery. Even without the help of Parliament the necessary reforms were carried out in 1574–5 by Sir William Cordell as master of the Rolls, using existing officers. It is quite possible that this reforming master (and ex-Speaker) stood behind the failed bill of 1563.[31]

Among the central courts we may include the two justices of the forests, one north and one south of the Trent, because between them their jurisdiction covered all the lands technically comprehended within the designated forests of the whole realm.[32] A bill to increase the authority of the justices of the forests, chases and parks (1576) left so little trace in the Journals that only the fortunate survival of a separate report on a conference between the Houses explains why, having been urged for expedition by the Lords, it should have died in the Commons.[33] According to the bill, the present arrangements which compelled the justices to travel around the various forest courts, there to hear pleas and deal with offences against the forest laws, put an intolerable burden of costs and labour upon those justices and much delayed the execution of justice. In future, therefore, justices should be allowed to administer their whole charge from one place by sending for the court books and dealing with the cases there registered. When the bill came down from the Lords the Commons as requested acted at speed, reading it twice in one day, morning and afternoon. But by then a number of members had collected themselves sufficiently to allege that the bill contained 'many things not meet to pass'; it was committed for amendment. However, the committee

[29] *LJ* I, 696, 698, 701; *CJ* I, 93: SP 12/40, fo. 149; *Proc.* 257. Probably in 1584, Francis Alford offered a general bill for the reform of all the courts to Burghley, but since it was never even introduced he renewed his offer in November 1585 (Ellis, III, iv, 54–7).

[30] *CJ* I, 66.

[31] Cf. W. J. Jones, *The Elizabethan Court of Chancery* (Oxford, 1967), 59, 130.

[32] By the thirteenth century the royal forests were defined and equipped with a separate legal structure for the protection, in the main, of the Crown's interests. In the course of time, much land there ceased to be afforested and in effect became normal shire ground, but it remained subject to the special jurisdiction – a long-standing grievance. For a useful summary cf. Holdsworth, *History of English Law*, I, 94–108.

[33] *LJ* I, 741–3; *CJ* I, 111–12; *Proc.* 448–51 (printed also in D'Ewes, 255–7: Neale, *EP* I, 355–6 makes little of it).

thought it wise to discuss the proposed changes in a conference with the Lords. Thirty-seven men from the Lower House, among them such familiar men of business as the comptroller (Croft), the chancellor of the Exchequer (Mildmay), Recorder Fleetwood and so forth, thus met three earls, two barons, the two chief justices and the attorney general to consider the import of what looks to have been an official bill.

The Commons' representatives attacked the bill on four counts. It was unnecessary, inasmuch as by an act of 1540 (32 Henry VIII c. 35) the justices could avoid travel and delays by appointing deputies – which in fact they were doing. To this, the earl of Sussex, chief justice of forests south of the Trent, replied that the deputies also incurred great costs; besides, their judgments did not carry the authority of those of their principals. Secondly, the Commons said, the bill was chargeable to the subject: it would now be litigants and jurors who would have to do the expensive travelling. Next, it was dangerous because the presentments recorded in the court books often rested upon dubious or malicious depositions; trials could not be conducted impartially unless such evidence was tested locally. Lastly it was dangerous because it spoke of judging cases by the laws, customs, usages and ordinances of the forests, of which foursome only the first, set down in parliamentary statute, was certain and uncontestable; the rest left the doors wide open to uncertainty and chicanery. 'To bind the subjects to things that neither they do nor may easily get knowledge of, the Common House do think it a matter very inconvenient.' Sussex regarded all these fears as exaggerated; certainly the Lords had not intended any such consequences, though he agreed that 'the bill might be penned contrary to their intentions'. He committed the Lords to a total willingness to consider whatever the Commons wished to propose.

When all this was reported back to the House next day, the Speaker suggested the appointment of a committee to undertake the reforming of the bill, but 'the whole House, a very few excepted, said they would hear no more of it'. The bill vanished and management had lost the day. On the face of it the Commons' doubts had some force. A bill preoccupied with inconveniences caused to judges and approving of the uncertainties which the use of unwritten custom might introduce deserved at least very thorough inspection. However, Sussex's reply had really drawn the sting from it: if all that bothered objectors were the remediable defects listed, they should have allowed the bill to be amended. In most areas of the common law, for instance, references to the custom of the realm were regarded with approval; why not in the forest law? The answer lies there: the forest jurisdiction had long been very unpopular since its original purpose – the preservation of the king's hunting rights – had long ceased to be at the heart of it, while people holding farming lands technically within the ancient limits of the forest lived under distinct disadvantages. Very probably only the uncertainty and inefficiency of enforcement had preserved the forest jurisdiction into the later sixteenth century; its contribution to the unpopularity of Charles I's personal rule is familiar enough. The bill meant to readjust matters for the convenience of the judges and the more effective collection of fines for offences; it was certainly tactless, and the Privy Council in the Commons would seem to have recognized that fact by leading the committee to the conference and not putting much effort behind the bill in the House.

Most of the other bills touching the behaviour of the courts dealt with problems of the localities, especially of Wales. In 1566, an attempt was made to abolish the special arrangement organized during the joining of Wales to England in the 1530s by which felonies committed in Wales could be tried in the adjoining shires in the Marches. The original reason had been the backwardness of machinery in Wales and the risk of biased trials; the bill now meant to provide in the Welsh shires that full panoply of gaol delivery, sheriffs and justices of the peace common in England. In 1566 it passed all stages but was vetoed; reintroduced in 1571 to a Parliament now better aware of whatever unsatisfactory aspect had stood in its way, it was allowed to die in a committee in the Lords which included several privy councillors.[34] But Welsh reformers succeeded in 1576 with a bill to permit the Queen to appoint more than one judge to each of the five courts which between them composed the Great Sessions of Wales and Cheshire, a measure much needed to prevent delay or failure of justice. The bill, advocated by the chief justice of Chester, anticipated further reform proposals put up by Richard Price of Brecknock in a letter to Burghley.[35] Another palatine problem arose from the fact that fines and recoveries – the traditional method for the sale of lands – could be registered in the courts there, but without the publicity enjoined upon the central courts by various acts of Parliament. This led to strife and disputes, or so we are told. Durham led the way with an empowering bill which, read once in 1559, passed as a private act in 1563.[36] Much encouraged, Chester and Wales followed suit, separately,

[34] 1566: *CJ* I, 77–80; *LJ* I, 660, 662–3. 1571: *CJ* I, 89–92; *LJ* I, 695–7; *Proc.* 252.

[35] 18 Eliz. I c. 8 (started in the Lords); P. H. Williams, *The Council in the Marches of Wales* (Cardiff, 1958), 263. Price wrote to Burghley on 31 January 1576, just before the session opened (Ellis, II, iii, 42–8) but did not get his proposals (SP 12/107, fos. 2–3, 5–33) to the lord treasurer till after the end of it; someone working through them noted that part of the programme had in fact been dealt with 'by an act in this late Parliament'.

[36] *CJ* I, 53; 5 Eliz. I OA 28 (later printed as c. 27). The first reading in the Commons (*CJ* I, 63) speaks of the bill as providing also for 'two knights from thence into the Parliament', but no such clause remained in the act. We cannot tell when or why it dropped out, thus postponing Durham's representation in Parliament until 1834.

in 1576, but their two bills were stayed in the Lords, after a conference.[37] In the same session, another initiative from the palatinates (Durham, Lancashire and Cheshire) not surprisingly won through when lords complained of the loss of feudal rights because inquisitions *post mortem* touching inheritance failed to get certified from there into the court of Wards. Seeing that the lord chiefly to benefit was the Crown, and that of the court attracting the business Burghley was master, the passage of the bill becomes understandable.[38]

One ambition which invariably failed to get through looked to the transfer of sessions or assizes in various counties from the place hitherto used to another: assizes and sessions brought wealth to the town they sat in. Pembroke tried in 1559 to get the county's quarter sessions held there;[39] Worcester, Aylesbury and Stafford all failed in 1571 and 1572 to become assize towns.[40] Stafford was a bit unlucky. Its bill really tried only to renew an act of 1559 which had made it an assize and sessions town and which had expired by dint of not being included in the continuation act of 1571. This was pointed out in debate, as was also the backing the bill had received from the earl of Essex, Lords Stafford and Paget, and the whole community of the shire. So, despite doubts raised over the exclusive appointment of any place for the assizes which might cause havoc if that place proved for any reason unusable, the Lower House passed the bill.[41] It was vetoed. To judge from the parchment, the 1559 bill had passed after much amendment and deletion; no doubt the local difficulties thus hinted at (it looks as though all the shire did not back it after all) caught up with it in 1572. The veto also disposed in 1576 of a bill to allow Middlesex sessions to be held 'at Justices Hall in the Old Bailey'.[42] The Cornwall tinners twice tried in vain to get the same privileges of hearing pleas and making ordinances in their stannary courts as their counterparts held in Devon;[43] but Lostwithiel in Cornwall got a private act which authorized its doubtful practice of taking legally enforceable bonds for debt in its town court, in reliance on the statute of Acton Burnell (1283).[44] Matters of this kind

[37] *CJ* I, 108–11; *LJ* I, 741–2; SP 12/107, fo. 190.

[38] 18 Eliz. I c. 13; cf. J. Hurstfield, *The Queen's Wards* (London, 1958), 101–2.

[39] *CJ* I, 55, 58: the bill was read a third time but was not put to the question.

[40] Worcester: *CJ* I, 85. Aylesbury: *CJ* I, 99, 101–2; *LJ* I, 721–2. Stafford: ibid. 711, 714–15, 723; *CJ* I, 100, 102–3.

[41] 1 Eliz. I, OA 37; *Proc.* 409–10. The bill did allow for plague closing Stafford to the assizes (ibid. 406) but made no specific appointment of a substitute; this conflicted with the need to have a known place to which to send cases on *nisi prius*.

[42] *CJ* I, 108, 110–12; *LJ* I, 744, 746; *Proc.* 484.

[43] 1571, 1581: *CJ* I, 89, 129–31; *Proc.* 252, 539.

[44] 13 Eliz. I, OA 24. The town claimed that it lay too far for convenience from the places authorized to take the bonds called statutes merchant – London, York and Bristol.

depended on the favour a locality could mobilize and on its securing general agreement in the county affected.

PROCESS

Proposals to improve the means by which the courts exercised their authority and offered opportunities of redress to litigants were fairly numerous, but only two of them made it to the statute book. Both were official bills, very short (the second had no preamble at all), and directed against chicanery in the law.

The first act concerned the writ of *latitat*, the instrument by means of which the Queen's Bench circumvented the normal difficulties met in getting defendants to come to the court, most commonly in actions by bill of Middlesex.[45] The writ enabled the court to reach an accused person if he 'hid himself' or 'lurked' in a shire other than that in which his alleged trespass had been committed or debt incurred. Ordinarily, summons (writ of *capias*, followed by three writs of exigent, followed by outlawry, days for each return being given term by term) issued to the sheriff of that county who too frequently returned 'non est inventus' – he cannot be found – on the grounds, true or not, that the man lived in some other shire. *Latitat*, awarded to the sheriff of the county of residence, got round this and seems to have worked. For the Bench its importance derived from the manner in which it extended its competence in matters raised from outside Middlesex through actions which pretended a litigable event within that county; without the *latitat* all writs would have had to be directed to the sheriff of Middlesex who in all honesty would have had to return *non est inventus* in all such cases. The *latitat* made possible the defendant's arrest, real or pretended, in an action raised by bill of Middlesex, even though he was not to be found in Middlesex; once he was taken into the custody of the court's marshall, the matter really at issue could be legitimately brought against him in the Queen's Bench.

In the eyes of the law, the basic flaw in this use of the writ lay in the fiction: it was being sued out for one issue as a preparation for the trial of quite another. However, to attack that abuse would have been equal to demolishing the fiction which had helped to restore the Queen's Bench as a court of major importance. The act therefore spoke in somewhat ambiguous terms. To any person improperly vexed it gave costs and damages to be rated by the court, but it defined vexing as the failure of the party pursuant within three days of the arrest to prosecute his suit

[45] 8 Eliz. I c. 2. See Marjorie Blatcher, 'Touching the Writ of *Latitat*: an Act "of no great moment",' *Elizabethan Government and Society*, ed. S. T. Bindoff et al. (London, 1961), 188–212.

against the defendant or in some other way to continue the action. Since in the bill of Middlesex procedure the original action was never pursued, the intention plainly was to render the *latitat* invalid in that procedure, but the act did not expressly say so and thus left open the possibility that any action brought on within the stated time would satisfy the statute. Litigants continued to prefer the speed and cheapness of the bill of Middlesex and *latitat* to the oldfashioned process by original writ (of debt or detinue, of entry or novel disseisin) with the long-drawn-out mesne process to follow; between them, the court and the lawyers working for interested parties soon drove the usual coach-and-four through the act.

A failed bill of 1576 also looks like an attack on the bill of Middlesex procedure, though we do not know enough about it to be sure. Started in the Lords and out of time in the Commons, it gave compensation to anyone 'wrongfully vexed by slanderous and untrue suits' – suits, as the diary tells us, 'upon English bill'.[46] Bills English opened a suit in an equity court (Chancery, Star Chamber, Requests, the equity side of the Exchequer), but it seems very unlikely that these are meant here, for what was complained of was the unjust or false accusation in the bill, that falseness appearing in plaintiff's failure to make good his bill; surely no one wished to impose 'double costs and damages' on anyone who simply lost a suit at equity. On the other hand, the bill of Middlesex, alleging an offence that was never tried, meets the case: an accusation so levelled and never taken further could be called not only untrue but also slanderous. If the bill had passed it would have stopped the Middlesex device of the Queen's Bench more effectively than the act for the reform of the *latitat* had done.

The chief victim of the bill of Middlesex was the court of Common Pleas which should have been the place for the trial of most of the actions so transferred. It particularly lost actions for debt which since the latter part of the fifteenth century had become the mainstay of its business.[47] People were discouraged from going to Common Pleas by the endless delays of its mesne process, which defendants had no difficulty in evading for years if they did not mind the harmless effects of a technical outlawry,[48] and by the court's inability to enforce its judgments upon

[46] *LJ* I, 746, 748; *CJ* I, 114–15; *Proc.* 491.

[47] 'Debt' had acquired a very wide meaning. The action was used to recover movables and lands, and was regularly prescribed as the means by which informers were to bring breaches of penal statutes into the courts. Cf. also D. J. Guth, 'The Age of Debt, the Reformation and English Law', *Tudor Rule and Revolution*, ed. D. J. Guth and J. W. McKenna (Cambridge, 1982), 69–86.

[48] Outlawry was the final stage in common law mesne process; the outlaw could not sue or be sued at law, but he could clear himself any time he wished by a technical surrender to the court and a small fine.

recalcitrant debtors. The champions of Common Pleas moved for three different improvements in its process, without any success at all. In 1572 a bill failed which could have improved the summoning machinery by insisting on public proclamation of the writs of exigent in parish churches, so that the defendant should not be able to claim ignorance of the process.[49] The bill did not return from committee 'for that [it was] thought more inconvenience would grow thereby than before'. One can only ask, what inconvenience? In the same session it was proposed to give Common Pleas the power possessed by other courts of extracting a bail bond from the defendant on his first appearance in court 'to satisfy the plaintiff of his judgment or yield his body to prison', peers only being excepted. The bill came back in 1576 but on both occasions never got beyond a first reading.[50] Plaintiffs thus lost the chance of a guarantee of execution against a defendant if they had won their case. The third endeavour passed the Commons in 1581 but was dropped in the Lords. This bill really tried to tackle the procedural inadequacies of an action in Common Pleas. Mesne process was to be shortened by imposing immediate return of writs upon the sheriff, and after trial no writ of error, seeking to invalidate verdict and judgment, was to issue until the plaintiff had his money. No doubt this would not have abolished all the advantages that plaintiff enjoyed in the Queen's Bench, but in any case it did not please the Upper House.[51]

The other successful bill, 'for the reformation of jeofails', seems to have been a little more effective.[52] It passed in 1576, after the bill had failed for lack of time in 1571.[53] Between those two occasions, a bill of 1572, though differently entitled, was probably the same measure ('against delays of judgment at the common law'); it too ran out of time but in the Lords.[54] Passage at the third attempt is thus not surprising. Jeofails were motions for arrest of judgment on grounds of technical errors alleged to have been committed during the formal pleading or at the joining of issue – the stages which preceded the gaining of a decision, by the jury on a question of fact or by the court on a question of law. In the ancient traditions of the law, small mistakes of no significance

[49] *CJ* I, 94; *Proc.* 342. The bill corresponds to the point made in para. 6 of the memorial. A part of a draft survives: SP 12/147, fos. 68–74.

[50] *CJ* I, 94, 107; *Proc.* 342. The paper bill of 1576 survives in HLRO, Papers Supplementary 1576/1593.

[51] *CJ* I, 120–1; *LJ* II, 27; *Proc.* 529. The parchment bill sent up by the Commons is also in HLRO (see previous note).

[52] 18 Eliz. I c. 14.

[53] *CJ* 87, 89–91.

[54] Ibid. 97, 102–3; *LJ* I, 726–7 (day of the prorogation). Cromwell described it in terms which well accord with the act as passed (*Proc.* 379): errors to stay a judgment after trial or admission had to be in the verdict or the judgment, not in an earlier stage.

could very easily delay or even defeat the course of justice, as the possibilities listed in the act indicate: 'Any default in form or lack or form, touching false Latin, or variance from the Register [of Writs], or other defaults in any writ original or judicial, count, declaration, plaint, bill, suit or demand', and so forth. In future such defects were not to be successfully advanced to stay judgment after verdict or to reverse it if already given, except that jeofails remained available in actions for felonies or upon statutes penal. Thus the traditional means of defeating a good case was abolished when no more was at stake for the defendant than possession of a piece of property or payment of a debt; if he stood at the risk of his neck or of forfeitures, the merciful law continued to offer him a last resort of escape arising out of highly technical defects in the course of the trial.

There remain seven bills under the head of process, the first four of which had only one reading in the Lower House. Their titles – which is all we know about them – at least indicate the sort of problems in the law which somebody thought it worth his while to draw a bill for. 'To reverse judgment in *praecipe quod reddat* for lack of summons' (adding to the uncertainties of actions for the recovery of landed possessions); to amend an act of Edward II 'for duress by imprisonment for assurance of lands' (proof of duress rendered void any agreement made); 'that upon demurrers in the law the causes shall be specially entered at the time' (demurrer terminated the trial of facts and committed the parties to abide by the court's decision on the law); 'to avoid delays in real actions' (how?).[55] The other three bills were followed beyond the first reading but also failed in the end. One wished to improve the law's handling of slander by words or writings, commonly tried in the Church courts or Star Chamber; it ordered trial in the county where the offence was committed and allowed traverse of the verdict.[56] Another for once left the common law alone and tried to help defendants in equity courts who had to swear to their answer to plaintiffs' bill: bills too should be sworn to in future.[57] And the third, which did pass the Commons, prohibited the use in land disputes of witnesses' depositions taken in the courts of corporate towns if the lands in question did not lie within that town's confines.[58] One can hardly call this a major age of parliamentary reform in the cumbersome procedures of the common law.

[55] *CJ* I, 55, 64, 70, 79, all in 1559–66.

[56] 1576: ibid. 104–5; *Proc.* 476, 478.

[57] 1576: *LJ* I, 744–6. Star Chamber commonly exacted such an oath, but Chancery, for whom presumably the bill was intended, never came to do so.

[58] 1581: *CJ* I, 124, 129–30; *LJ* II, 41; *Proc.* 534.

THE LAND LAW

All the bills and acts for substantive changes in the law concerned real property, its transfer from one person to another, and the fraudulent practices which could arise in the course of such transactions.[59] Grievances turned upon the possibilities of deceiving purchasers by tricks dependent on secret conveyancing which left the buyer ignorant of encumbrances (especially concealed future rights) resting upon land he acquired. The main concern of parliamentary activity lay with the two leading forms of conveyancing one of which was in process of superseding the other.

The reform, in the 1530s, of the law relating to enfeoffment to uses had promoted 'bargain and sale', the simplest means by which after the statute a use could be created, into the commonest method of transferring ownership. The makers of the statute, recognizing this, had added the statute of enrolment which compelled the registration of such transactions in one of the courts at Westminster.[60] In 1563, in one of the few successful moves for an improvement in the law of real property, a private act extended this duty to enrol to the palatine courts of Lancaster, Chester and Durham.[61] However, if there was one thing that both landowners and attorneys liked it was secret conveyancing, though purchasers and the more thoughtful lawyers working for the Crown remained ever conscious of the potential for fraud. The former soon invented devices to escape the duty to register indentures of bargains and sales; the latter contemplated extensive schemes of general oversight like the ambitious proposal for a body of county registrars headed by a general recorder whose deputy would look after London and Middlesex. Their function was to inspect, correct and enrol all title deeds for every property in the realm.[62] That sort of thing was well beyond the means of Elizabethan government, but the general principle of putting an end to secret conveyancing by providing better machinery of enrolment found support also in bills in Parliament. Thus a bill of 1572 proposed that every assurance (a declaration of all encumbrances resting on lands bargained

[59] Cf. the general demand in para. 5 of the memorial.

[60] 27 Henry VIII cc. 4, 16. Cf. A. W. B. Simpson, *An Introduction to the History of the Land Law* (Oxford, 1961), 177.

[61] 5 Eliz. I c. 26 (not at first printed).

[62] SP 12/77, fos. 236–43: 'Mr Lupton's device for avoiding forgeries and cozenages' (date uncertain). Perhaps the Lupton in question, of whom nothing else is known, was the Thomas of that name who round about 1580 wrote various pamphlets, including one describing an imaginary commonwealth (E. Rose, 'Too Good to be True: Thomas Lupton's Golden Rule', *Tudor Rule and Revolution*, ed. Guth and McKenna, 183–200). Very little is known about him too! His commonwealth did, however, own a network of registers for deeds (ibid. 198).

and sold) should be made before two justices of the peace whose clerk would endorse the deed and register an abstract of it, the information being sent to a central register in London within six months of the transaction. This would have created a comprehensive land register at least for one popular kind of conveyance where intending purchasers could institute the necessary search. Fees were kept low; a search, for instance, would cost only 4*d*.[63]

The bill never got beyond a first reading, but when it was brought back in 1576 it led to a debate, and the arguments advanced against it, with answers to them, were sent to the Council – attached to the paper bill, which means that Speaker Bell sent it up.[64] There had been the usual misunderstandings, only too likely when members relied on ear and memory for the terms of a bill. Edward Flowerdew had protested at the enormous scope of a bill which, he thought, covered not only bargains and sales but also all fines and recoveries; but in fact it dealt only with secret bargains and sales, a point that might perhaps be made clearer in the draft. Much the same answer applied to John Popham who accused the bill of rendering all *bona fide* conveyancing void unless registered: not so, only secret practices were involved. It had been objected that the bill would put intolerable labours upon the greater landowners if they had to register every grant they made, but the bill specifically provided for the grantees or lessees to see to the recording. Objections touching the difficulties created for corporations were irrelevant, seeing the bill 'extends only between party and party', and objections about the mass of paper created – Westminster Hall would be full up in four years' time – mistook the effect of summarizing detail in the registration books. As for searches being too troublesome in all that welter of records, 'if a skilful man have the office and divide his records according to the counties, and keep skilful calendars, the search will be most easy and certain'. Good advice for anyone organizing a record office. It had been put that the bill would lead to fraudulent evasion by conveyances without deed, by word of mouth before witnesses (*parol*); this should be attended to by adding a clause to render illegal all leases *parol* for more than ten years. 'Or if the House like to have conveyances and leases *parol* to continue', a written record of the terms agreed might be kept.

The House was not contented by any of these arguments, and the bill died. However, another attempt was made in 1581 which more specifically attacked the chief risk of secret conveyancing by bargain and sale while

[63] *CJ* I, 95; *Proc.* 361.

[64] *CJ* I, 105–6; SP 12/86, fos. 169–82. The Journal entry notes that thirteen named persons spoke in the debate; several names there listed recur in the report to the Council.

avoiding the much disliked principle of registration. That main problem was shifting and springing uses – conditions placed on entailed lands which would come into effect only after a lapse of time and in previously hidden circumstances, thus activating claims from unexpected heirs or forgotton remaindermen that would defeat the titles of purchasers.[65] It was therefore proposed that all limitations (conditions) imposed on lands 'by uses or wills' which prevented the owner from alienating or from giving assurances to the buyer should be void: shifting and springing uses were to be abolished.[66] Surprisingly enough, the bill passed the Commons in this form, but the Lords, though inclined to approve its purpose, wanted its details more fully set out and in conference asked the Lower House, as in such matters better qualified, to amend it. After debate, the Commons instructed two serjeants-at-law among their members to advise their helpless lordships in a private capacity, 'not by appointment of the House', but nothing further came of it all.[67] Secret conveyancing triumphed over the hope for a general land registry, and for the moment it also triumphed over a ban on imposing future conditions on land which created 'perpetuities' (never dying but hidden rights).[68] The second victory was soon overset: in 1584 a much amended version of the 1581 bill passed into law.[69] However, it too was soon enough outflanked by the conveyancers.

Before the statute of uses far and away the most popular conveyance was the device known as fine and recovery. This involved a collusive action between vendor and buyer in the court of Common Pleas, and it could be further improved by a voucher of warranty by which the vendor guaranteed the purchaser's title against any claim that might thereafter arise.[70] Originally the device had the advantages of publicity and certainty. It needed an original writ upon which the action (known as levying a fine or suffering a recovery) was raised, and that writ remained on file in the court. It concluded with a tripartite indenture called a final concord (or fine for short), the foot (bottom part) of which also remained on record in the court. Needless to say, it was nevertheless not immune to fraud, more particularly for employment in the breaking of an entail which defeated the interests of heirs and remaindermen. Against this an act had passed in 1540 which in 1572 was replaced by a slightly more

[65] Simpson, *Land Law*, 184–6.
[66] SP 12/147, fos. 155–6.
[67] *CJ* I, 118, 120–4; *LJ* II, 27.
[68] A general bill 'against secret conveyances and deceitful sales of land', the terms of which are unknown, was introduced a little later in the session but vanished in committee (*CJ* I, 131, 133).
[69] 27 Eliz. I c. 4.
[70] Simpson, *Land Law*, 115–17. If vouched to warranty the original seller became the defendant in the action; if he lost he had to compensate the buyer, whom he had warranted, with lands to the same value.

elaborate version.[71] A bill to help remaindermen against fraudulent vouchers of warranty failed three times.[72] But with the rise of bargain and sale, which eased the life of the ingenious conveyancer, these problems began to dwindle.

Nevertheless, there remained difficulties besetting the fine, especially as so many titles rested upon pretty ancient transactions of that kind. Every one of our seven sessions, therefore, witnessed the introduction of a bill for fines and recoveries, until at last an act passed in 1581.[73] Both the fortunes and the contents of the bills varied, though about most of them we know very little. In 1563 and 1566 the disappearance of the original writs troubled the lawyers; a draft bill to that effect indicates that they could be stolen ('embezzled') by searchers tearing them off the file, but the remedy offered – to prevent deficiencies in the record from affecting the rights at law of the owners – also occurs as the special concern of the bills of 1572 and 1576.[74] Much of the difficulty arising from error in the record, much emphasized in that bill, was removed by the 1576 act for jeofails, but a remnant of the point was incorporated into the second section of the 1581 act. The main thrust, however, of that act comes as a surprise: it establishes a system of registration for all transactions by fine and recovery.[75] This indicates that the old publicity and certainty of the device had indeed been lost with the disappearance of relevant records in Common Pleas (and some local courts), but the success of a bill concerned to reduce secrecy in land transactions also underlines the decline of the fine as a conveyancing method. Secret conveyancing had become the special concern of grants to uses made by bargain and sale, with their superior capacity to break entails and free landowners to dispose of property at their pleasure, by sales or by testamentary demise.

Another chance of cheating also came before the Parliament: it was alleged that people made bogus gifts and conveyances of lands and other property so as to defraud their creditors and, by hiding their possession at death of lands held in chief from the Crown, also the Queen. A bill

[71] 32 Henry VIII c. 31; 14 Eliz. I c. 8. Tenants in tail collusively suffered recoveries which terminated the title they held and opened the door to obtaining the fee simple. See Simpson, *Land Law*, 118–29.

[72] 1571: *CJ* I, 88, 90; *LJ* I, 688, 690. 1572: *CJ* I, 97, 101; *Proc.* 380, 397. 1576: *CJ* I, 109, 111; *Proc.* 486–8.

[73] 1559: *CJ* I, 55. 1563: ibid. 65–6, 68, 70; *LJ* I, 106. 1566: *CJ* I, 74, 78, 81; *LJ* I, 629, 631–3. 1561: *CJ* I, 87–8; *LJ* I, 686. 1572: ibid. 711, 713. 1576: *CJ* I, 104–7, 111 (below, p. 307); *LJ* I, 734–6, 740. 1581: 23 Eliz. I c. 3.

[74] The draft bill is SP 15/11, fos. 181–7; it looks likely to be the bill introduced in 1563 and tried again in the next session.

[75] The innovation provoked a long and reasoned protest on behalf of the existing system, which was ignored (SP 12/147, fos. 31–2).

of 1563, which imposed the penalties of praemunire on anyone who gave away the eighth part of what he owned within eight days of his death, specifically aimed to protect such feudal rights; the Commons rejected it by 89 votes to 63 on third reading.[76] The more general purpose was served by an act of 1571 against collusive gifts intended to defraud creditors; though enforceable by informer action, it offered much future amusement as the courts might strive to define collusion in such cases.[77] Bills for the act started virtually simultaneously in both Houses, but when the Commons ran into difficulties over theirs they gratefully accepted the official one coming from the Lords.[78] It did not take long for dissatisfaction to be voiced; in the very next Parliament the Commons passed a bill amending and extending the act which the Lords contented themselves with reading once.[79] It proposed to include gifts made by private agreement and without any record, the consequences of which could come home to roost with people who later acquired the property in all good faith. Its promoter was Francis Alford who had suffered from a fraud committed by Ludovic Greville and William Porter; the private act of 1571 which had tried to unravel the skein had failed to remedy his grievance. When the bill of 1572 failed upstairs, he obtained a kind of arbitration before a Commons committee.[80] His bill occasioned hot debate, some saying that it called every conveyance in doubt and others that it dealt with an infamous kind of fraud which before this had deceived even the lord keeper and the lord chief justice. Alford related his troubles; Fleetwood gave an irrelevant and inaccurate history lesson. Norton was for the bill because Alford deserved assistance: 'better many little bills than one long bill, lest by doing so many good things at once one good thing may not go forwards'. Coming from one of the Council's chief draftsmen this is an interesting observation. Norton, it seems, preferred the specific and private bill over general reform. This attitude retreated from the position taken up by Thomas Cromwell forty years before and forecast the eighteenth century's dislike of general bills. On this occasion, a new bill produced in committee still did not satisfy those who feared that people might slip out of undertakings by alleging that these had been fraudulent in the first place, though others continued to back the bill. The debates, too long to be fully rehearsed here, throw an

[76] *CJ* I, 67, 69, 70, 72. It was almost certainly an official bill, drawn by Dyer J. by order of the Council (SP 12/107, fo. 147).

[77] 13 Eliz. I c. 5. As the debates (below) showed, the crucial question was whether the gift had been made for an acceptable consideration, a term which included paternal affection (cf. Simpson, *Land Law*, 167–90).

[78] *LJ* I, 673, 675–6, 688; *CJ* I, 84, 87, 89, 90.

[79] Ibid. 95–6, 99, 101–2; *LJ* I, 722; *Proc.* 343, 358, 362, 386–7.

[80] Above, p. 129, n. 124.

impressive light on the legal sophistication which such issues called forth in the Commons, but the trouble of cheated creditors and unfortunate purchasers remained unresolved.[81]

One problem linked precariously to the possibility of fraud was that of bankruptcy, and our period witnessed the passage of the act of 1571 which is reckoned to be something of a landmark in the history of that branch of the law.[82] It had a prehistory in earlier sessions; in fact, its gestation was far from easy. The programme of 1559 wished to make bankruptcy felony, though if all his creditors put up a joint petition for mercy the bankrupt might be pardoned for the first offence. Thieves, who get hanged, steal a sheep or cut a purse; bankrupts smuggle away hundreds and thousands of pounds and 'undo many an honest man'.[83] Bankrupts were not much more popular in the city where the court of aldermen in December 1562 appointed five of its members to 'draw some good bill against such citizens of this city as hereafter of a corrupt mind and lack of good conscience shall... become bankrupt without any good, just or reasonable cause, having great quantities of store of other men's goods and substance in their hands'.[84] Most probably this was the bill introduced into the 1563 session where it was replaced by a *nova* which set up commissions out of Chancery for the trial of bankrupts; the committee which produced this was chaired by John Marsh, one of the team responsible for the city's bill. It passed all stages but was vetoed, perhaps because the Council, with harsher measures in mind, thought it insufficient.[85] The city, however, did not give up and during the 1566 session asked the original draftsmen to revise their bill and reintroduce it. This time the Council beat them to it, with a bill in the Lords which after much labour was rejected in the Commons by sixteen votes in a House of 136.[86]

Next time round, at last, the Council, having come to terms with the city, settled matters. The bill – official, to judge by the enacting clause – was no doubt somewhat amended, but it still proposed to solve the problem by the use of a special commission out of Chancery which was made responsible for selling up the bankrupt's goods and settling his debts. The bill again started in the Lords, but this time care was taken

[81] A special act of 1576 (18 Eliz. I c. 4) disallowed conveyances made by the rebels of 1569; thus the Crown got the full forfeiture.

[82] For the whole story see W. J. Jones, *The Foundations of English Bankruptcy: Statutes and Commissions in the Early Modern Period* (Transactions of the American Philosophical Society vol. 69, part 3; 1979).

[83] *TED* I, 328.

[84] CLRO, Rep. 15, fo. 158v.

[85] *CJ* I, 68–70; *LJ* I, 615–16, 618.

[86] CLRO, Rep. 16, fo. 118 (3 Oct. 1566: the bill was read a first time on 1 Oct.); *LJ* I, 627–8, 630–1, 634; *CJ* I, 74–5, 79–80.

to avoid trouble in the other House: the bill committee was authorized to take advice from members of the Commons or any other person 'who may best inform touching any doubts or other matter that may rise upon the said bill'. Even so it all took nearly seven weeks from first to last, in a session that lasted only just about nine weeks.[87] In the end, genuine rather than fraudulent bankruptcy became the real issue, and ideas about felony had gone by the board; people who had themselves arrested or outlawed to escape action by creditors and afterwards came to reclaim the property confiscated were punished by a fine of double the value of the goods involved. From that time the management of bankruptcy lay in the hands of those special commissions. Immediately, however, the law had one weakness. While it offered relief to native creditors it seemed to leave out the claims of foreigners. At least, though the act said nothing expressly hostile to aliens it could be read as forgetting about them. In the years after its passage, merchants from the Low Countries vigorously argued this complaint,[88] and in 1581 they got a bill 'to make bankrupts' goods liable to strangers' debts as well as the debts of our own country' into the Lords. The Commons, unsympathetic as usual to the foreigner, dashed it on third reading.[89]

Lastly, a few bills touching matters of real property, none of which got very far, may just be mentioned. In 1576, fines levied at common law on lands in ancient demesne were to be declared valid, saving all the other privileges which tenants holding by that title enjoyed.[90] In 1581 it was proposed to extend to copyholders the limitations in time for suits brought in various forms of tenancy (1540), while another bill hoped to limit action by formedon in descender (the action by which an heir to entailed lands could claim against strangers who had somehow entered upon his rights) to sixty years where hitherto it had been unlimited.[91] In the same year, a bill to enable tenants in tail to make certain longish leases despite their having only a life estate in the land, also failed in the Lords.[92] One success: a private bill which passed at second attempt, after running out of time at the first, changed the custom of Exeter which had favoured partiple inheritance (gavelkind) to the common law of primogeniture.[93] Generally speaking, these seven sessions had done nothing much to the law of real property; the consequences of the

[87] 13 Eliz. I c. 7; *LJ* I, 670, 672, 685, 687, 695; *CJ* I, 90–2.

[88] HMC, *3rd Report*, *App.*, 48a.

[89] *LJ* II, 28, 33, 49; *CJ* I, 133–4; *Proc.* 545.

[90] *CJ* I, 104–5; *Proc.* 477. Ancient demesne comprised the Crown lands vouched for in Domesday Book; tenancy there provided various privileges.

[91] Copyholds: *CJ* I, 124–5, 128–9; *LJ* II, 38; *Proc.* 534. Formedon: *CJ* I, 124, 127, 129–30; *LJ* II, 40; *Proc.* 534.

[92] *CJ* I, 129–31; *LJ* II, 43; *Proc.* 540.

[93] 1572: *CJ* I, 102–3; *LJ* I, 723. 1581: 23 Eliz. I c. 17 (not at first printed).

Henrician legislation took a much longer time to provoke serious revision.

CRIME

The medieval law on crime left a good deal to be desired. Precise only on felonies, defined by their carrying the penalty of death by hanging and forfeiture of all moveables to the Crown, it was very uncertain about misdemeanours some of which could be tried as trespass while most of them occupied no place in the common law but might be punishable locally by custom. Like so much else on the social scene, the concept and treatment of crime underwent much scrutiny and some action in the sixteenth century. However, the lead was here taken by the court of Star Chamber, applying its equitable principles; in the law of the land, criminal offences still remained insufficiently accommodated. Notoriously, the reign of Henry VIII sought to solve the problem by massive additions to the category of felonious crimes, but the propaganda statute of Edward VI's first Parliament repealed just about all of them. At common law, juries tried crimes, but as long as action lay with Star Chamber, where juries were liable to appear only as defendants, they had too little opportunity to learn their business: at a time when they finally became independent judges of facts supplied by evidence and increasingly felt the need to modify rigour by the sort of compassionate concessions which it should have been the task of the law to define, juries remained in a state of transitional uncertainty.[94]

The programme of 1559 made no mention of felonies; its only oblique reference to a possibly criminal offence concerned perjury in trials at law on which an act passed in 1563, imposing a varied range of fines, with imprisonment and pillory waiting for those unwilling or unable to pay.[95] The act professed to be an amendment to a statute of 1540 which, it was claimed, had been too mild to stop the suborning or giving of false evidence. In this claim it set the note for all the bills creating felonies which passed in our seven sessions. There were only three of them; all passed in 1563 and all revived Henrician felonies which it was thought had been illadvisedly repealed in the previous two reigns. They were the acts for servants who embezzled their masters' goods, against witchcraft, and touching sodomy.[96] Each of them restored to the list a crime first identified in the reign of Henry VIII, and none of them originated with the Council. As has already been shown, they began as a single,

[94] Cf. T. A. Green, *Verdict according to Conscience: Perspectives on the English Criminal Trial Jury, 1200–1800* (Chicago, 1985), esp. ch. 4.

[95] 5 Eliz. I c. 9.

[96] 5 Eliz. I cc. 10, 16, 17,

comprehensive bill, privately promoted, 'to revive diverse acts repealed anno primo Edwardi and anno primo Marie' which in the Lords was replaced by separate measures drawn out of the general bill,[97] and they exhausted the Council's and the Parliament's willingness to return to the drastic policy of the Queen's father's reign. Other proposals of a like kind failed to find support. In 1563 the act for boiling poisoners alive (1531) was offered for revival; one reading terminated interest.[98] A new witchcraft bill did as badly in 1571.[99] Sexual offences raised no serious concern: the Lords read a bill for adultery and incest once in 1576, while the Commons in 1581 gave just a little more attention to bigamy.[100]

Bills for crimes below the rank of felony matched this paucity and lack of success. One wished to punish extortion by the officers of the Crown – demanding money for things done or favours shown in the execution of an official duty.[101] Another, starting in the Lords, set a sliding scale of monetary and humiliating punishments for people spreading slanders, the scale reflecting the ranks of the persons slandered; this caused some annoyance in the Commons and died there in committee.[102] Efforts to improve the preservation of the peace came before the sessions of 1576 and 1581: the former tried to make the pursuit of traitors and murderers more effective along the Scottish border by compelling lessors to take from all their tenants recognisances to answer charges,[103] while the second tried to extend pursuit by the hue and cry beyond the hundred in which the crime had been committed.[104] A bill of mercy failed in 1566 for an interesting reason. It proposed to save from all forfeiture a person who accidentally killed another by shooting arrows at a target set at a long distance (240 yards or more). The Lords gave it two readings but at the second decided that a bill concerning the Crown's prerogative of mercy and its rights to forfeited goods trod upon sensitive toes; they would not proceed further with it until the Queen's pleasure was known.[105] Apparently she was pleased to let the bill drop.

Even as the reign of Henry VIII had done much work in identifying crimes in need of punishment, so it also led the way in the attack on aspects of the law which stood in the way of effective repression, especially the privileges derived from the special claims of the Church.

[97] Above, pp. 110–11.

[98] *CJ* I, 69.

[99] Ibid. 90.

[100] *LJ* I, 740; *CJ* I, 120–1, 127.

[101] Ibid. 124; *Proc.* 534.

[102] *LJ* II, 23–7; *CJ* I, 120–1; *Proc.* 530.

[103] *CJ* I, 107, 111, 113; *LJ* I, 746; *Proc.* 490.

[104] *CJ* I, 131, 134; *Proc.* 542–3, 545.

[105] *LJ* I, 630–1. The law recognized the possibility that a verdict of homicide by a coroner's jury could involve non-culpable accident, but until the nineteenth century it still imposed forfeiture and the need of a pardon (paid for) upon the accidental killer (Green, *Verdict according to Conscience*, 123–5).

So far as guilty criminals were concerned, those claims had produced the ancient escape hatches called benefit of clergy and sanctuary.[106] Nothing was done about sanctuary in our period, the law for which remained unsure, but a problem arose over the recovery from people who had fled there, more particularly into the sanctuary of Westminster Abbey, with intent to evade their creditors. In 1563 a reforming bill reached the Lords too late for action,[107] and when it was reintroduced in 1566 the dean of Westminster, as successor to the abbot, stood ready to defend the rights of his liberty even for the good of defaulting debtors. One might add that among the criminal confraternity gathered at Westminster defaulting debtors were probably relatively harmless and attractive. When the bill was ready for engrossing, the claims of the Westminster enclave, a burden for centuries to law-enforcers, were mentioned in the debate, and the House decided to hear the dean defend them. Given time to prepare his arguments, he appeared with Edmund Plowden in tow and spoke forcefully of grants going back to King Lucius. Plowden, rather more realistically, grounded the sanctuary on a grant of Edward the Confessor in 1066, 'with great reasons in law and chronicle'. The common law received the support of the law of Rome: 'Mr Forde, a civilian, also alleged diverse stories and laws for the same'. This sufficed to raise doubts about the bill which was committed to the master of the Rolls 'to peruse the grants and to certify the force of the law now for sanctuaries'. Cordell's report gave the bill sufficient support to get it engrossed but no more; at third reading it failed by 60 votes to 77.[108]

Benefit of clergy, unquestionably a much more serious obstacle to law enforcement, attracted more attention, especially in two official bills which passed. These abolished the benefit for cutpurses working in gangs on the one hand, and for persons convicted of rape and burglary on the other; both started in the Lords and underwent much discussion and amendment in both Houses.[109] The second act also attended to the standard grievance which benefit regularly aroused – the fact that a criminal who successfully pleaded it in effect had his first crime free. Ever since 1489 care had been taken that the privilege could be claimed only once; branding in the thumb made sure that the fact would be known on a second occasion. However, that first and successful plea meant that the beneficiary was handed over to the ordinary of the diocese to be

[106] Thomas Cromwell had been particularly exercised over both: Elton, *Reform and Renewal*, 135–8.

[107] *CJ* I, 67, 72; *LJ* I, 617. [108] *CJ* I, 73–4, 76, 79.

[109] 8 Eliz. I c. 4 (prepared by the lord chief justice: SP 12/107, fo. 146); 18 Eliz. I c. 7 (a substantial paper of Commons' amendments to this short act is filed with the OA; and see above, pp. 63–6).

punished by the spiritual law. Once before the ordinary (in the bishop's court), the man could usually clear himself by compurgation, that is by bringing his own oath and that of willing helpers in proof of his innocence. The consequent prevalence of perjury was often complained of, and Thomas Norton tried for an act to end the practice in 1563, 1566 and 1571.[110] The remedy he proposed took care not to attack the Church courts directly, though in opening the issue in 1571 he minced no words; it was hoped to control clerks convict by demanding that in addition to being set free by compurgation they should be compelled to obtain a pardon out of the Chancery, the sueing out of which might offer a better chance to keep an eye on what happened to them.

This, however, was still not a very effective remedy, and the act of 1576 concerning benefit of clergy (which may well have derived from Norton's previous efforts) instead dealt drastically with perjured clerks and feeble Church authorities. The pleas of clergy would still be accepted if the crime remained clergiable and the plea has provably not been used before. But instead of being handed over to the spiritual arm the offender could, at the court's discretion, be imprisoned for one year. A Commons proviso also saved the right to try him for any other crime of which he might stand accused even if, having been tried on one, he had escaped by the benefit. In effect this concluded the legislation on benefit of clergy by means of which the sixteenth century tamed a potentially capricious right while retaining it in order to soften the harshness of the law on felony. Though most really serious crimes had by this time been declared not clergiable, the benefit remained available; it could be pleaded only once in a criminal career; and its lifesaving capacity was modified by the threat to life which imprisonment implied in Tudor England. Above all, the act of 1576 effectively severed benefit of clergy from the Church and acknowledged this inheritance from a very different past as the term of art in the secular law which it had become.

110 Norton is not mentioned in 1563 (*CJ* I, 63) but appears as the promoter on the other two occasions: ibid. 75, 84, 89–90; *LJ* I, 686, 688, 691; *Proc.* 224, 252.

12

Private legislation

A great deal has already been said about private bills and acts – their character, the distinction between personal and local, and the parliamentary time they occupied. Private acts matter in this analysis because they offered to individuals a definitive settlement of particular problems and thus extended the usefulness of Parliament beyond the concerns of the great agglomerates of Queen, Church and commonwealth. Though they cost money they often saved much higher costs of litigation. As a subdivision of parliamentary legislation, with its own rules and sometimes its own procedures, they appear to be a unique bequest of late-medieval representative institutions; other assemblies of estates and Parliaments enacted measures for similar purposes but did not distinguish them in their general law-making activity as the English Parliament did. It is therefore necessary to provide a brief conspectus of the kind of thing that was done by private act in these seven sessions. Most of the bills promoted for and by individuals caused no difficulties at all, but those for the settling of estate and local concerns could be troublesome because they involved more than one person or interest. It is within these last two categories that one finds a relatively high number of failed bills.

RESTITUTION IN BLOOD

In the first place, private acts served to restore people to normal legal rights lost through the attainder, by act or at law, of ancestors whose blood, as the phrase went, had become corrupted through condemnation for treason and very occasionally for felony. In theory at least a person through whose veins such corrupted blood flowed stood outside the law: though it could be used against him he could not himself use it or acquire property. Twenty-four acts of restitution passed between 1559 and 1581. The bulk of the work was done in the sessions of 1559 and 1563, as the aftermath of rebellions in the reign of Mary had to be cleaned up. The duke of Northumberland's conspiracy at the beginning of that reign yielded two such acts, for Sir Henry Gates, son of that Sir John who had been executed with the duke, and for Lord John Grey, uncle to Lady Jane and involved sideways in his family's disaster.[1] The duke's own family, which after all included the future earl of Leicester, had been restored in Mary's last Parliament.[2] The people who cleansed themselves of the disabilities caused by Wyatt's rebellion and the conspiracy of Sir Henry Dudley (a different family of the same name) included descendants of fathers executed as well as people themselves sentenced but never put to death. Amongst the former we find the four sons and five daughters of Edward Lewkenor who died in the Tower under sentence of death,[3] the daughter of that William Thomas who wrote *The Pilgrim*,[4] the son and daughter of Archbishop Cranmer,[5] the offspring of the brothers Isley of whom one had only sons and the other only daughters,[6] Thomas and James Digges whose father Leonard (the mathematician) had been pardoned under Mary for his rebellion,[7] and the three children of Sir Thomas Wyatt himself who came in rather belatedly.[8] A multiple restitution was effected in a single act for six esquires and five gentleman, all from Kent, whose fathers had made the mistake of marching with Wyatt.[9] Five petitioners, however, had themselves been condemned and had managed to survive; they included two members of the Parliaments which passed their bills.[10] It would appear that corrupt blood did not stop a man from sitting in the Commons, though such an election clearly made it desirable that he should remove the taint at the first opportunity.

Four acts of restitution removed the effects of condemnations incurred

[1] Eliz. I, OA 22, 24. Grey was the youngest son of Thomas, marquess of Dorset, who had died in 1530, and therefore brother to Henry, duke of Suffolk, father of Lady Jane Grey, who was executed in 1554. Unlike his brother, Lord John did not appear in the only act of attainder of Mary's reign (1 Mary st. 2 c. 16). But he was active in the conspiracy and had been pardoned after sentence, a pardon he evidently thought insufficient without an act of Parliament (D. M. Loades, *Two Tudor Conspiracies* [Cambridge, 1965], 27–8, 104).

[2] 4 & 5 Philip & Mary c. 15.

[3] 1 Eliz. I, OA 32; Loades, *Conspiracies*, 233.

[4] 5 Eliz. I, OA 44. Cf. E. R. Adair, 'William Thomas, a forgotten clerk of the Privy Council,' *Tudor Studies presented...to A. F. Pollard* (1924), 133–60.

[5] 5 Eliz. I, OA 46.

[6] 5 Eliz. I, OA 43 (the five daughters of Thomas Isley), 47 (the two sons of Sir Henry Isley); Loades, *Conspiracies*, 113, 127.

[7] 5. Eliz. I, OA 45; Loades, *Conspiracies*, 120.

[8] 13 Eliz. I, OA 29.

[9] 5 Eliz. I, OA 51.

[10] Sir James Croft (1 Eliz. I, OA 23) and Sir Peter Carew (5 Eliz. I, OA 40) both had been in exile under Mary. For the other three acts see 1 Eliz. I, OA 27 (Robert Rudstone), 5 Eliz. I, OA 41 (William West, of the family of Lord De la Warr) and 48 (Robert Turner). All these had been pardoned by Mary: Loades, *Conspiracies*, 119, 234.

during Elizabeth's own reign; they form a mixed bag. Anthony Mayne, who had robbed his father, had escaped the consequences of his conviction by pleading his clergy, after which the victim procured a pardon for him; the act was needed to complete his restoration to a normal gentleman's life.[11] Two Londoners, John and Dudley St Leger, had been attainted and outlawed for the death of one Roland Vaughan or Owen; though they were clearly an unsatisfactory pair of brothers, their loyal father Sir John, a member of every Parliament from 1559 to 1584, joined them in a petition for pardon and restitution which passed in 1581 without anything being explained about the death of Roland.[12] Treason accounted for the troubles of Philip, earl of Arundel, eldest son of that duke of Norfolk whom the axe got in 1572; he cleared himself in law in 1581, just four years before vanishing into the Tower, a suspect traitor himself, for the rest of his days.[13] That case of treason is well known, but nothing seems discoverable about the treasons committed by Sir Ralph Chamberlain and John Harlston of which they were convicted at law in 1560 and cleared by statute in the next Parliament.[14] The Queen signed the bill, as she signed all the rest in this category.

More surprising are five acts freeing some of the Queen's subjects of the consequences of attainders passed in her father's bloody reign; one wonders why they waited so long. Thus the descendants of two victims of the Boleyn purge of 1536 – Henry Brereton and Sir Henry Norris – obtained final restitution acts in 1571 and 1576 respectively, after apparently managing to live for decades in an at least partially blood-corrupted state.[15] Although they might have had difficulty in persuading Edward VI or Mary to help them, they could have sat at the door of the Privy Chamber from November 1558 onwards. Norris sat in the first Parliament of Edward but spent much of the next quarter-century on various duties abroad. In 1571 he got elected once more (as knight of the shire for Oxfordshire, no less) and in the following year was elevated to the peerage. He regularly attended the Upper House in 1572, but perhaps something was said to him there, so that in the next session he finally took the necessary steps to correct his status. Loyal servant and ambassador on behalf of Queen Elizabeth, his wife one of her closer friends, a man of means, knight in Parliament for a shire, Lord Norris of Rycote and summoned in that title to the Lords: one must ask just what effect the misfortune of being corrupted in blood really had. True, the attainder of the ancestor forfeited the family lands to the Crown, but neither Norris

[11] Above, p. 92.
[12] 23 Eliz. I, OA 17; see HPT, under Sir John St Leger.
[13] 23 Eliz. I, OA 20.
[14] 5 Eliz. I, OA 42.
[15] 13 Eliz. I, OA 30; 18 Eliz. I, OA 24 (cf. above, p. 91.).

nor Brereton seems to have starved during the long years when technically they remained unable to resort to the law. At any rate, it is clear that a man could wait as long as he wished until some particular need or circumstance arose which made it advisable to remove the supposed disabilities.

Much the same mystery hangs about the family of Lord Hussey, executed for his share in the Lincolnshire rising of 1536. They decided at last to go to Parliament in 1563.[16] The act cleared a motley collection, including the traitor's widow, still alive, his two sons, four grandchildren (offspring of his deceased daughter Dorothy Docwra), and four daughters – all married or widowed. All the daughters had married well, and it does not seem to have worried the countess of Rutland, Lady Throgmorton, Lady Browne or Mrs Dymmocke one little bit (nor their husbands either) that all this time their blood was corrupted. In the case of George Fiennes, lately restored to the family title of Lord Dacre of the South which his grandfather's execution for murder had forfeited in 1542, we are told why the act was promoted in 1559: he needed it in order to recover some of the lands that went with the title.[17] But he had become Lord Dacre before the corruption was removed from his blood. In this first year of Elizabeth, the younger children of that earl of Surrey whom Henry VIII had put to death for treason in January 1547 terminated their unfortunate condition;[18] the older brother, in due course the fourth duke of Norfolk, had been restored by Mary in 1553.[19]

One such bill failed to pass, and since its fate is one of the best documented episodes in the history of private legislation in this reign it deserves attention. In 1576, the then Lord Stourton petitioned the Queen for an act to remove the taint created when his father was convicted of murder in the reign of Mary and executed.[20] Elizabeth 'graciously inclined' to his suit, and the Lords let the bill through in two days. In the Commons, however, it met heavy weather on second reading, to the astonishment of its sponsor and probably the embarrassment of the clerk, for it had evidently been agreed to despatch it quickly by giving it the first

[16] 5 Eliz. I, OA 39.

[17] 1 Eliz. I, OA 38. A bill of the next session, described only as 'touching the Lord Dacre of the South', may have tried and failed to deal with the estates (*LJ* I, 611–12).

[18] 1 Eliz. I, OA 39.

[19] 1 Mary st. 2 c. 26.

[20] The case (briefly discussed by Neale, *EP* I, 356–7) is fully described in a memorial 'of a cause happening in the Parliament by which the Commons in the Nether House thought their liberties touched', copied for the use of early Stuart antiquaries (BL, Cotton MS Titus F. i, fos. 214r–217v; printed in *Proc.* 457–61). Hakewill printed it as an appendix to his *Manner how Statutes are Passed*, pp. 80–97; he disguised Stourton throughout as 'a noble lord' and reduced some verbiage, but otherwise gave a faithful copy. Neither Neale nor the editor of *Proc.* seems to have been aware of this printing. For the parliamentary history of the bill see *LJ* I, 742–3, 749; *CJ* I, 111, 113–15.

two readings in one day. Some members objected to Stourton personally: in their view, he 'had given cause for men to think that he would not hereafter be worthy of so much favour'. Others argued that the saving clauses of the bill did not sufficiently protect those who had bought lands from his father and his ancestors further back. The first objection was quashed with a reminder that the Queen had thought it right to favour him,

> and therefore no cause that this House should mislike her gracious favour to be extended to any of her subjects in such cases but rather to hope that he, being a young nobleman, would prove a good servant to her majesty and the realm as divers of his ancestors had done.

Including, one supposes, his father the murderer. The second objection, however, carried enough weight to get the bill committed, for the drafting of an additional proviso. Reading the bill with care, hearkening to doubts raised, and also recalling similar problems from their own experience, the committee added a proviso to bar Stourton from ever taking advantage of any errors found in any conveyances executed by any of his ancestors: 'he should be in that respect as though his blood was not restored, in which state he can bring no writ of error'. It is not at all improbable that it was precisely the desire to exploit writs of error that had moved Stourton now, some twenty years after the event, to seek oblivion for his father's crime. But even if this was so and the committee had grounds for apprehension, everybody at the time evidently knew that what the Commons were doing was to repay the Lords for dashing, a few days earlier, a general Commons bill touching errors in fines and recoveries which would have stopped the likes of Stourton going back on ancestral dealings.[21]

Such a blatant act of revenge naturally led to trouble. The Lords enquired angrily why the Commons insisted on ill-treating a nobleman who was only seeking what others had always got. This message did not spring from their lordships unprompted. When Stourton, whom the Commons committee had incautiously allowed to present a case before them, saw that he had lost he moved his peers into action. The Commons took a high line. Thinking 'the manner of dealing very strange', they resolved to stick to their proviso. Stourton riposted by obtaining another message from the Lords, this time asking for a conference to resolve the disagreement in the bill. Instead of humbly deferring matters until they were better instructed, the Commons promptly rushed through both bill

[21] Passed in the Lower House on 21 Feb (*CJ* I, 107) but rejected by the Upper House on 3 March (*LJ* I, 740). Even a conference between the Houses on 7 March (*CJ* I, 111) did not get the bill revived.

and proviso on 13 March, an action which earned them a peremptory request for a delegation to explain their doings to the Upper House. The delegates were left for some time cooling their heels in the lobby outside the Parliament Chamber before the Lords (of whom 'there were many and the persons of the principal noblemen') emerged to take their places solemnly, and very slowly, at a long table. Acting as spokesman, Burghley reproved the Commons for passing the bill and proviso without waiting for the explanation to be offered at the conference, by which precipitancy the Lords 'took themselves greatly touched in honour and thought that the Common House did not use that reverence toward them which they ought to do'. More practically, he could see no reason for the proviso, 'for the bill being signed by her majesty, he said, none might presume to alter or add anything to it without the assent of her majesty'. Such tampering was more than the Lords would venture to risk. He offered for precedent various provisos signed by Henry VIII. Besides, the judges thought the general saving clause (standard in such bills) to be fully sufficient, and he wished to know why the Commons should dissent from that authoritative opinion.

When the Lords wished to get huffy the Commons could always out-huff them. The committee dourly replied that their charge was only to hear what their lordships had to say; before they could make answer they would have to consult the House again. Their report there caused an uproar: it 'moved them all greatly and gave occasion to many arguments and speeches, all generally misliking this kind of dealing with them and thinking their liberties much touched'. Their determined sentiments were conveyed to the Lords on the resumption of the meeting, through the mouth of Sir Walter Mildmay – one privy councillor confronting another. Although he poured a little balm by assuring the Lords that 'the Nether House did not want consideration of the superiority of their estates' and would 'yield unto their lordships all dutiful reverence', he emphasized the Commons' duty to pass on the liberties of the House 'to their posterity in the same freedom they received them'.[22] The Lords, truth to tell, collapsed. After a hurried consultation Burghley replied. He accepted the assurances of the Commons' deferential respect and hinted very plainly that the Upper House felt they had been misled about attitudes in the Lower by Stourton's slanted reports. He did try once more to discover why the proviso was thought so essential but again ran into the stonewall protecting the supposed secrecy of the Commons' proceedings. And that, in effect, was the end of it. The Lower House, receiving their committee's further report, showed themselves delighted 'that so great a storm was so well

[22] Cf. below, pp. 335–6.

calmed and the liberties of the House preserved', but they did not withdraw the proviso. The Lords refused to accept it, and Stourton's bill lapsed, never to be revived. Burghley's admission that Stourton had duped his peers into a needless quarrel evidently lost the petitioner the whole of his case. Oddly enough, this little tempest did not raise a word from the Queen whose sign manual had been drawn into dispute and whose favour to Stourton had started the business; even odder is the fact that the defeated 'young nobleman' never tried again – unless, perhaps, he did and Elizabeth refused to sign him any more bills.

NATURALIZATION

Children born abroad to English fathers, as well as any foreign wives they had married there, could employ an act of Parliament to give them full native rights (naturalization) or the slightly lesser rights of a denizen.[23] The acts in question could be drawn for the benefit of a single person or for a whole collection of them; if the latter, all the names with their ancestry had to be recited. Among the individual acts were three for the sons of Marian exiles – Gersome Wroth, sixth son of Sir Thomas and Lady Mary, born at Strassburg; John Stafford, son of Sir William and Lady Dorothy, born at Geneva; and Peregrine Bertie, son of Robert and Lady Katherine, late duchess of Suffolk, born at Wesel.[24] Jane Sibilla, wife of Lord Grey de Wilton, was born at Augsburg in 1552, when her father, Sir Richard Morison, was ambassador to the Emperor Charles V.[25] Bulk naturalization became commonplace from 1563. In that year six Londoners engaged in trade at Antwerp and Bremen clubbed together to get thirteen children made 'free denizens'; all but one of the six had married foreign wives (daughters of citizens of Antwerp, Berghen-op-Zoom and Bremen), and two of them had had children before going abroad for whom, of course, there was no need to do anything.[26]

The continuance of settled trading with the Low Countries quickly expanded the numbers in need of this assistance, and 1576 turned out to be a champion year for naturalization. So many applicants stood at the door that two bills were needed. One dealt with the children of 'her majesty's faithful subjects in Antwerp married with strangers'. The twelve fathers included two officers of the Merchant Adventurers

[23] Denizens could not inherit land in England though they could buy it, but it was only in the reign of William III that they were declared unable to hold office under the Crown or sit in Parliament. Denization, unlike naturalization, could be obtained by letters patent, but under Elizabeth acts of Parliament seem to have been preferred.

[24] 1 Eliz. I, OA 26; 8 Eliz. I, OA 29; 13 Eliz. I, OA 28.

[25] 18 Eliz. I, OA 26.

[26] 5 Eliz. I, OA 49.

Company, eight freemen of London, and one man each now living at Ipswich and Antwerp; their wives came mostly from Antwerp with a small sprinkling from Bruges, Flushing and Berghen thrown in; between them they had produced thirty-nine children.[27] The other bill, actually introduced a week earlier, included among the fathers one belated Marian exile and eleven Londoners still at the crucial time resident in Antwerp; among their wives there were five Englishwomen who had accompanied their husbands abroad, and seven Netherlanders. They were nothing like so prolific as the other bunch but still put up twenty-one children born abroad.[28] One might have supposed that this would have exhausted demand, but 1581 witnessed yet another such bill whose twenty-six beneficiaries had been born in Danzig and Hamburg to eight English fathers with two English and six foreign wives.[29] A point to note about this last act is the absence of the sign manual which had hitherto appeared on every naturalization act. This was no accident, for the 1581 act was the first of its kind to be introduced as a paper bill and engrossed during passage;[30] Elizabeth had never seen it. Evidently such acts had now moved even formally out of the region of special favour and were recognized as the routine measures they clearly had become.

These naturalization bills passed both Houses without difficulty. Apart from the genealogical information they contain, their chief interest lies in the fact that they were of necessity private and could be nothing else. The rule that everyone who took benefit from private act must pay £2 to each clerk, £5 to the Speaker of the Commons, and £10 to the Speaker of the Lords thus assumed a formidable potential. Even though some at least of the people naturalized very likely were still under age, the rule called them and not their fathers (a few of whom had died) the beneficiaries. That means that in 1576 the clerks should have collected £120 each, the Speaker (fortunate Mr Robert Bell) £300, and Lord Keeper Bacon a most agreeable £600. Each child cost his or her father £19 in these major fees alone, not counting the money laid out in getting the bill to move on. Naturalization bills were thus the parliamentary bureaucracy's cherished darlings. It causes no surprise at all that a general bill to simplify the process, introduced in 1566 'to enfranchise Englishmen's children born beyond the sea', died after one reading.[31]

[27] 18 Eliz. I, OA 35. The bill lists wives' fathers as well.
[28] 18 Eliz. I, OA 37.
[29] 23 Eliz. I, OA 21.
[30] *CJ* I, 128.
[31] Ibid. 74.

ESTATE ACTS

Private legislation was the most convenient instrument for resolving problems of landownership, provided the parties were agreed; statute could provide the least contestable title available at law and thus terminate or prevent litigation when uncertainty, rival claims or indeed deceit had muddied the waters. By the same token, getting an act to settle ownership of land was bound to be less straightforward than repeal of attainders or naturalization, since by definition the interests of more than one person or one family were likely to be in dispute. Bills for estate acts did most to compel the adoption of court-like procedures of investigation, with parties in the House and represented by counsel; for this reason also they stood high among those private matters that took up an inordinate amount of parliamentary time in either House. Among the most tiresome bills of this kind were the contentious efforts of 1559, spilling over into 1563, to sort out the disputes over ownership in both freehold and leasehold which resulted from the religious changes between 1547 and 1558. Grants and leases made by protestant bishops had been superseded by their catholic successors' grants under Mary, and with the return of protestantism much uncertainty clamoured to be sorted out especially with respect to the two sees of London and Winchester. The efforts of rival claimants, together with especially Bishop Bonner's tenacious defence of his supposed rights, largely accounted for the delays in the ecclesiastical settlement and the length of the first Parliament of the reign. However, these matters have been thoroughly analysed before this and therefore call for no further discussion here.[32]

Of course, not all estate acts were troublesome. The most straightforward simply ratified agreements already made, the act of Parliament forming a simple but effective means of registration. Such acts could terminate very lengthy disputes, as did the ratification of a Chancery decree made in November 1571 by an act passed ten years later. The decree had resolved disputes between the copyhold tenants on certain Worcestershire manors and their lord, who happened to be the dean and chapter of Worcester cathedral, but seemingly relations had not thereby become perfect. The tenants therefore promoted a bill of ratification, putting the whole Chancery file, from bill to decree, by way of evidence into the Parliament.[33] The same session also passed an act to ratify an award made in a land dispute by Sir Walter Mildmay and Sir James Dyer CJCB, commissioners out of Star Chamber.[34] That is to say, two of the great equity courts of the land had offered a solution to a legal dispute,

[32] Jones, *Faith by Statute*, passim.

[33] 23 Eliz. I, OA 22. [34] Ibid. OA 33.

but the parties preferred to obtain the ultimate security of the highest court of record in the realm. Two rather fascinating acts of 1576 ratified complex arrangements made for the rescue of hopelessly indebted landowners, William Isley esq., and Lord Howard of Bindon. In both cases powerful committees mostly of privy councillors were given authority to take over the debtor's lands and sell what they could so as to satisfy his creditors.[35] On one occasion, Parliament did not settle an argument but authorized an arbitration by a body of privy councillors as agreed to by the parties. The dispute, a very complicated one, had arisen out of a settlement made by Sir Richard Wenman of Carswell in Oxfordshire which after his death had led to every conceivable conflict of interests between the widow (who had remarried) and her third son; one can only hope that the councillors, appointed because the short duration of the Parliament prevented a conclusion during the session, brought peace to the family scene. The proceedings on the bill included lengthy meetings of a Commons committee with parties and counsel.[36]

Members of the nobility found statute a useful means for confirming family arrangements, especially jointures settled on wives at marriage, though the terms of the acts sometimes hint at quarrels now tided over. No problems seem to lie behind such a settlement of a jointure for Anne, wife of Ambrose Dudley, earl of Warwick, or the reassignment of the first Lady Cobham's jointure after her death to her successor.[37] But things do not seem to have been altogether peaceful in the household of Edward, Lord Stafford. When he married he had no lands upon which to erect a jointure for his wife (Lady Mary), because his widowed mother (Lady Ursula) still held on to hers and all the rest of his lands were entailed. The act therefore assigned Lady Ursula's jointure to Lady Mary when the dowager should die, thus avoiding attempts – always highly contentious – to break the entail.[38] Even so, one feels that the settlement cannot have created best relations between the husband's mother and her daughter-in-law.

The marital arrangements of the fourth duke of Norfolk and his second wife, Lady Margaret, daughter of Lord Audley, were complicated, among other things, by the Church. Norfolk had married Margaret and settled a jointure upon her by enfeoffing trustees to her use, with

[35] 18 Eliz. I, OA 25, 34. Isley (presumably the Marian conspirator who had been pardoned: Loades, *Conspiracies*, 119) was said to be some £10,000 in the red and all his property had got into a tangle of mortgage bonds, to a point where he could find no purchaser and thus could raise no cash. The Howard problem involved other members of the family; the commissioners were empowered to sell selected lands and assign the proceeds to the contestants in stated proportions.

[36] 18 Eliz. I, OA 30; *CJ* I, 110–13.

[37] 8 Eliz. I, OA 26, 27.

[38] Ibid., OA 28.

remainder to himself. Then two different sets of doubts had arisen. The settlement was poorly drawn: it had failed to follow through on all the technicalities demanded by the law. It was defective 'for lack of livery and [*sic*] seisin, attornment and such other ceremonies which the law requireth to the perfection of the said conveyance and jointure', not to mention earlier conveyances made by the duke's ancestors. That great nobleman does not seem to have had very good legal advice. But that was not all: the marriage itself had been called in doubt 'by reason of certain decrees and canons of the pope's law'. Margaret was a cousin of Norfolk's first wife, and the canon law brought this relationship within the prohibited degrees by extending the biblical ban on marriage with a dead wife's sister. As the preamble explained, Norfolk's marriage did not contravene the law of *Leviticus*, and with Rome once more expelled the duke and duchess hoped to clear up their wedded state. The act therefore confirmed both the marriage and the jointure, removing all hindrances as only a parliamentary statute could. Introduced into the Lords in 1559, the bill passed with only one small contretemps. The Commons added a proviso enabling Norfolk to make leases out of his wife's jointure lands, leases which would be good in law against the duchess, and it was this proviso, not the uncanonical marriage, that six of Mary's bishops plus the last abbot of Westminster refused to approve.[39] Very odd.

The largest number of estate acts did not ratify an agreement but imposed a solution where uncertainty had previously prevailed. A Surrey gentleman, Thomas Brown (quite a regular and active member of the Lower House), together with his uncle George, held lands in Kent where the inheritance custom of gavelkind prevailed. In 1559 they obtained an act which converted this into 'the course of the common law', that is primogeniture. Then, it seems, George died, because in 1566 Thomas for safety's sake repeated the operation on his own behalf alone. The Parliament's power to override this local custom was first proven in 1539.[40] On the other hand, when Lord Latimer died he left a group of coparceners with rights of inheritance. This caused predictable difficulties between the next Lord Latimer and his brother-in-law, Sir Robert Wingfield, which they tried to settle by statute in 1572. The bill passed all stages but was vetoed.[41] A second attempt in 1581 proved successful, but since we do not know the terms of the first bill we cannot tell whose interests had been sufficiently neglected on the earlier occasion to persuade the Queen to withhold her assent.[42] Estate acts were a favourite means for breaking tiresome entails, though any attempt so to use them

[39] 1 Eliz. I, OA 31; *LJ* I, 567.

[40] 1 Eliz. I, OA 28; 8 Eliz. I, OA 30; and see above, p. 35.

[41] *CJ* I, 97–9, 100, 102; *LJ* I, 717–18, 720–2.

[42] 23 Eliz. I, OA 28.

was likely to bring reversioners and remaindermen into action. I have found only one such act in these seven sessions: in 1563 Henry Neville, Lord Abergavenny, secured the right to make twenty-one-year leases out of his entailed lands. There was so far no heir to the entail, and various remaindermen (so the act said) objected to all leases made out of lands held in tail; nevertheless the bill passed at speed.[43] Entails caused the difficulties which Lord Berkeley resolved by a private act of 1571. He was the remainderman in a grant in tail by which his ancestor had made over all his lands to Henry VII, and which had, of course, ended with Edward VI's death in 1553. While the lands were in the hands of the Crown (or so Berkeley claimed) the title deeds had somehow vanished, which left him, now again possessed, uncertain of his rights. Therefore the act set them out. Some of the lands in question had been subject to litigation some years earlier, with Queen's Bench finding for the Berkeley interest against Henry VIII's treatment of entailed property as though it were held in fee simple.[44] In 1572 an act was needed to resolve difficulties that had arisen out of unexpected deaths and minorities.[45]

One man used an act to seek security against his difficult Queen. This was the earl of Sussex who in 1576 confirmed his acquisition of the house and manor of New Hall in Essex, for a time one of Henry VIII's favourite country seats. The manor had belonged to the earl of Ormond who died in 1515; in his will he had set it aside for sale to cover some debts. It had been bought by Sir Thomas Boleyn, Anne's father, who in 1517 (probably under pressure) sold it on to the King. In order to acquire it, Sussex therefore needed to sue to the Queen who proved most reluctant. Burghley and Mildmay urged the suit upon her till 'she thought it best that you should have it, but therewith she mixed speeches, also after her accustomed manner, what a notable house it was and with what charges her father had built it'. The intermediaries explained that Henry had abandoned it in his later years and that in consequence it no longer was a house suitable for a prince. 'Then she wore a new doubt, whereof I never heard, whether she should not have a rent for the park.' Burghley countered by reciting the sacrifices of income imposed upon Sussex by the deal. 'In the end she changed her talk and, being by me pressed, would give no resolved answer of yea or nay.' However, two months later, in May 1574, she did sign the grant, further enlarged in December of that year. Sussex thought it best to tie her down by statute as soon as the Parliament met again.[46]

[43] 5 Eliz. I, OA 37.
[44] 13 Eliz. I, OA 33. For the case of Willion *v.* Berkeley cf. above, pp. 37–8.
[45] 14 Eliz. I, OA 16.
[46] 18 Eliz. I, OA 33; Burghley to Sussex, 29 March 1574 (Ellis, III, iv, 15–16).

Some of these settlements by act dealt with far more contentious and difficult matters. In 1571, an Essex gentleman, John Tyrell, brought a bill in which he accused the late William Porter of Gloucestershire of abducting his daughter Mary (aged about thirteen) and forcibly marrying her; in the process Porter allegedly forged grants of various of Tyrell's manors to himself and his accomplices. Suits before Privy Council and Star Chamber failed because Porter could not be found. Now that he was dead, Parliament was asked to declare void all alleged conveyances by Tyrell to the criminals, and it did so.[47] In 1576 Sir John Rivers needed an act to protect legitimate purchases of lands which the vendor's heirs were contesting by means of a doubtful indenture between their late father and the bishop of Ely.[48] In 1572, a dispute between the earl of Kent and Lord Compton over a single manor led to endless proceedings and arguments in the Lower House, with the parties, their counsel and witnesses at one point being heard at the bar; in the end, the matter never concluded because the Queen sent Compton to Dover to attend upon an envoy from France, so that he could not appear when summoned. The business took up a lot of time in a short session supposedly devoted to the fate of the Queen of Scots – and that although, as the solicitor general argued at one point, the earl, with suits in the Queen's Bench and in Chancery, could have justice at either law or equity without troubling the Parliament.[49]

The earl's bill was not the only one of 1572 to lead to quasi-judicial proceedings in the Lower House. The parties to an action over a fraudulent sale of lands were heard at the bar, after the defendant had been threatened that the hearing would proceed in his absence if he failed to appear. After the hearing the bill lapsed – rightly so, I should say, because the plaintiff had in fact various remedies available after Chancery had found for him and the defendant's forcible entry had produced an indictment which had not yet been tried.[50] These sorts of proceedings rarely came to a conclusion, though they enlarged the Commons' claims to act as investigators and judges. In 1563 a bill for the assurance of certain lands acquired by Richard Bertie and his wife, previously duchess of Suffolk, produced a Speaker's summons to the other party to come and protect his interest, but no one came and the bill lapsed.[51] On the other hand, in 1571 Henry Sacheverell, at the bar, confessed his fraud in a land deal on William Skeffington; the House passed the bill but ignored Fleetwood's wordy demand that the trickster should be punished.[52]

[47] 13 Eliz. I, OA 34.
[48] 18 Eliz. I, OA 31.
[49] *CJ* I, 96, 98–102; *Proc.* 313, 369, 388, 396–7, 399–401.
[50] *CJ* I, 96–7, 101; *Proc*, 371–2, 395.
[51] *CJ* I, 63.
[52] 13 Eliz. I, OA 31; *CJ* I, 84–7; *Proc.* 219–20, 241.

LOCAL

Local bills and acts – that is to say, those affecting not this or that individual but a town, one to three counties, or a special interest in a locality (a craft guild, a school, a hospital) – formed the largest sector of the technically private legislation. We have already found that they were distinguished from strictly personal acts by being given the 'public' assent, *la reine le veult*.[53] A great many of these proposals, passed or failed, have been used in the course of this study, and no good purpose is served here by analysing them in full. An approximate count shows that in these seven sessions Parliament passed forty local acts and saw another seventy-six local bills fail. The count must be approximate for two reasons. Some manifestly and provably private bills resulted in local acts that were printed in the sessional statute and were therefore technically public, and the local status of failed bills has nearly always to be guessed from their contents, a method which is reasonable but not always demonstrably accurate. Still, altogether close on 120 bills of the 885 handled in these Parliaments (just over 13 per cent.) were local, many of them causing problems in passage. As Norton pointed out, those bills put up by special interests could form the most palpable obstacle to getting any programme of public bills through.[54] It is therefore necessary to illustrate the most salient points about them by a few examples.

The first question to be asked concerns those private bills turned into public acts. We have seen that 'special favour' achieved this for the 1581 act for the draining of Plumstead marshes,[55] but no such explanation was offered in the other cases. Seven acts are here involved – two in 1571 and five in 1576.[56] For the latter group we have it positively stated that they started as private bills;[57] for the first two such an origin may be safely assumed because they started in an afternoon sitting which had expressly been set aside for private bills.[58] All seven of these acts passed with no contretemps whatsoever, and six of them served very similar purposes. The exception here was 18 Eliz. I c. 21 which secured freedom to trade in wool in the borough of New Woodstock (Oxon.) in order to bring business and employment to an economically moribund town. The remainder authorized the levying of a local rate to finance the paving of streets at Ipswich, Chichester and outside Aldgate in London, as well as the building and maintenance of bridges at Chepstow, Rochester and Oxford. Their easy fortunes in Parliament prove that the respective

[53] Above, pp. 128–9.
[54] Below, pp. 326–7.
[55] Above, p. 46.
[56] 13 Eliz. I cc. 23, 24; 18 Eliz. I cc. 17–21.
[57] SP 12/107, fo. 144.
[58] *CJ* I, 89.

towns had taken care to secure a united front at home. The printing of the acts saved the promoters the expense of a good many certified copies, though one must suppose they they paid in some way for the privilege. Perhaps such measures were treated as younger cousins of subsidy acts, also printed for the convenience of collectors. The only comparable act which remained private provided for the paving of Kentish Street in Southwark; it differed from the others by not raising a rate but instead imposing on the owners of the street fronts a duty to carry out the necessary repairs, with a penalty specified for negligence. This gives some support to the speculation which ascribes the printing to the fact that a tax was in question.[59]

Two very different examples may be cited to show the range of local bills that fell by the wayside. Many of them were cloth bills and other measures to secure economic advantages at the expense of some other identifiable interest, but the bill for punishing 'certain lewd persons' fleeing from Great Yarmouth by putting them in irons rightly deserved no more than a single reading.[60] What seems like a sensible bill (of 1572) for diverting the Severn to augment the water supply of Worcester, after agreement with the landowners through whose properties the diversion would have to pass, ran into rather typically meanminded objections in the Commons. It was engrossed, as was a belated proviso, but the debate on third reading did for it. Robert Newdigate, a wealthy landowner in distant Buckinghamshire, objected to 'any man's inheritance' being taken away 'especially for so small a commodity as increase of water', while with respect to compensation he did not like it 'that commissioners should set price on other men's lands'. Sir Nicholas Arnold thought that the Severn was already over-exploited; Worcester could get its water at a tenth of the cost by bringing it in by carriage or horses. He suspected that the town planned to build mills. Sir James Croft would never agree to anyone else valuing his lands; he had, he said, 'some property not worth twenty years' purchase which he would not sell for sixty years'. Thomas Atkins (of Gloucester and thus concerned) ponderously regarded it 'a great matter to alter the course of a stream' and shared Arnold's suspicions concerning the town's real intentions. Only Robert Snagge supported the bill. He pointed out that most of the land in question belonged to the elderly earl of Worcester who approved of the scheme, and that the bill contained all necessary safeguards against sharp practices. It did no good: on third reading the House divided and the bill went down by six votes. The town had done its best, but not even

59 8 Eliz. I, OA 32. This bill ran out of time in the previous session, probably because it was sufficiently contentious to be committed (*CJ* I, 67–8, 70, 72; *LJ* I, 617).

60 1571: *CJ* I, 90; *Proc.* 252.

two cheeses, worth 4*s*, between them, bestowed on the Speaker could turn the tide.[61]

Four harmless looking local bills passed both Houses but failed at the assent. Evidently they were promoted over local opposition that did not bother to fight them in the Parliament but instead raised support by appealing to the Queen. As a result, the endeavour to equip Bury St Edmunds with an adequate gaol failed, as did the attempt to reform the payment of tithe at Reading on the model of London's practice.[62] The town of Cringleford near Norwich, on the other hand, at a second attempt got its act to finance rebuilding after a fire and to settle lands there as copyholds held of the manor (of which the corporation of Norwich was the lord).[63] Whosoever it was that backed the incorporation of Hexhamshire into the police and court organization of Northumberland won through at a third attempt.[64] However, most local bills either passed without much ado or failed, often after long arguments, never to be revived. It took money, after all, to promote a private bill, and one effort could exhaust coffers or willingness.

[61] *CJ* I, 95, 97–8, 100; *Proc.* 362, 389–90; HPT I, 280. Snagge spoke of 'the lord of Worcester' which just possibly could have been the bishop, but I think the earl more likely.

[62] Both in 1576. Bury: *CJ* I, 106, 108; *LJ* I, 737–40, 745. Reading: *CJ* I, 107–9; *LJ* I, 740, 744–5; *Proc.* 483.

[63] *CJ* I, 107, 111–12; *LJ* I, 745–6: *Proc.* 483, 489; 23 Eliz. I, OA 19.

[64] In 1559 the bill ran out of time (*CJ* I, 54, 57, 60; *LJ* I, 537–9); in 1566 it was vetoed (*CJ* I, 76, 79, 81; *LJ* I, 635, 640–1, 643); in 1572 it passed as 14 Eliz. I c. 13 (not printed in the sessional statute).

PART IV

Politics

13

Duties and rights

MANAGEMENT

In the course of this study, problems of parliamentary management have cropped up frequently enough. Nevertheless, a particular look at what was involved in managing will be appropriate, the more so because one can still meet the conviction that there was something improper, or at least dubious, about tactics which can be called interference with the freedom of either House to act at will or according to conscience. Throughout this investigation it has been emphasized that Parliament met to do certain things – to provide money, to pass bills, to discuss matters of concern. If it was to fulfil those purposes it needed organization and guidance; to have failed to provide these would have been a plain dereliction of duty on the part of those who governed under the Queen and recognized the Parliament for what it was – a part of the Queen's administrative machine. Much of the method used is familiar. Interested parties, including the Council, prepared bills; lord chancellors and Speakers, assisted by their clerks, controlled the programme; 'men of business' cooperating with the councillors in Lords and Commons provided motions, advice, explanations and instructions. Peers, knights and burgesses who came to the Parliament with a view – to quote Thomas Cromwell in 1529 – to get themselves better regarded looked to that embryo Treasury bench for leadership. Parliament time was a time of hard work for the Privy Council, nor did the hard work always pay off; however, in the main the Council remained in control.

The Council's supervision of parliamentary business has been demonstrated again and again in the course of this discussion, but attention should be drawn to less familiar and somewhat surprising involvements. Speakers, we all know, were Queen's men chosen by the Council, but how often did councillors go so far as Burghley did when he prepared a full draft of the address the Speaker was to deliver to the Queen at the end of the session?[1] The Council made it its business to know who came to Parliament – no problem in the Lords, of course, but a policy which regularly involved purchasing copies of the Crown Office list of members of the Commons.[2] When leading councillors moved upstairs they took care to remain informed about what went on in the Lower House, using the clerk and their own clients among burgesses to do so.[3] At times their guidance could appear fussy. In welcoming Sir Thomas Gargrave as Speaker in the 1559 Parliament, Lord Keeper Bacon especially laid stress on Sir Thomas's 'long experience...in Parliament matters', but a little later instructed this old hand on so obvious an aspect of management as the order of business: 'that in sorting of your things...matters of the greatest moment and most material to the state be chiefly and first set forth'.[4] We know very little about management in the Lords where the task was, of course, easier: a much smaller House whose members were likely to know one another well, closer to the Queen, conscious of its superiority, and well served not only by its clerks but even more so by the eminent lawyers who stood by to assist in scrutinizing, redrafting and ferrying bills cannot have called for much effort by the Council, even if the notion of the Lords as obedient rubber stamps for government has by now gone to the rubbish dump from which it should never have emerged. The history of bills has shown sufficient difficulties of passage to assure us that the silence of our sources does not prove the absence of any need for managerial activities in the Upper House. Nevertheless, the real task unquestionably lay in the Commons.

The best introduction to an understanding of what managing the Commons really meant is found in 'A Discourse importing the assembly of a Parliament', extant only in a later copy and there quite wrongly ascribed to Mr Francis Tate of the Middle Temple.[5] Tate, one of the circle of Elizabethan antiquaries, born in 1560 and never in Parliament until 1601, may have copied this Discourse, but he certainly did not write it. There is little difficulty about the date of the document. It refers to Richard Onslow, Speaker in 1566, as dead: he died in April 1571. It describes the current master of the Rolls as one who had been Speaker under Mary: this can only have been Sir William Cordell MR, Speaker in Mary's last Parliament, who died in 1581. Since the Discourse deals with the meeting of a forthcoming and new Parliament, it must have been

[1] BL, Lansdowne MS 104, fos. 150–5: in Burghley's hand but drafted in the first person singular. It has not been possible to identify the session to which this speech belongs.
[2] BL, Additional MS 5756, fo. 40, in a list of warrants for payment signed by Lord Treasurer Winchester.
[3] Above, pp. 12–15.
[4] *Proc.* 41, 43.
[5] BL, Harleian MS 253, fos. 32r–36v (in a volume of Ralph Starkey's collection which reached the Harleian Library by way of Sir Simonds D'Ewes).

written in the spring of 1572, after the election but before the assembly of the one new Parliament called in that span of time. Its whole tone makes its purpose plain: it offers advice to someone closely concerned with the running of the House but altogether new to the job. This description perfectly fits Sir Christopher Hatton who had sat inconspicuously in 1571 but next year became one of the government's leading men in the House.[6] This identification is strengthened by the discovery that Hatton was in the way of seeking expert instruction when catapulted into a position of leadership in the Parliament. In 1587, when against all the probabilities he became lord chancellor and thus had to lead the Parliament of that year, he commissioned a long paper of guidance from the clerk of the Parliaments about his duties in the Lords, especially at the opening and close of the session.[7]

The author of the Discourse cannot be identified quite so certainly, though the probabilities point one way, to Thomas Norton, 'the Parliament man', whom a cynic described in 1566 in the phrase 'do, judge, speak, read, write, in and out of season'.[8] Norton's close relationship with Hatton is well attested in their correspondence; whereas Norton's letters to his other patron, Burghley, tend to be formal and deferential, those he wrote to Hatton breathe an air of relaxed friendship.[9] Unlike other correspondents, Norton always addressed Hatton as 'your honour', a form of address also used in the Discourse which, moreover, clearly reflects some of Norton's experiences of the previous session as over the treason bill and the uncertain guidance of Speaker Wray. The document being a copy, there is no way of positively proving Norton's authorship, but neither can any other candidate be found who would fill the role as well as he does. For simplicity's sake, therefore, Norton shall here be treated as Hatton's adviser.[10]

[6] E.g. *Proc.* 333–4: Hatton conveys the Queen's instructions concerning the bill against Mary Queen of Scots. Hatton became captain of the Guard, his first office of importance, soon after the end of the session.

[7] Folger Shakespeare Library, MS V.b.303, fos. 145–6: 'Mr Mason his advice to me of my manner of proceeding in Parliament – Sir Christopher Hatton, Lo. Chancellor' (a later copy). A charming paper of technical detail which passes over everything except the formal rules with the words 'As for other things, the daily experience will thoroughly inform your lordship.'

[8] In the well known 'lewd pasquil' on forty-three members of the House, which is discussed further in the next chapter (Cambridge University Library, MS Ff.5.14, fo. 82v): 'age, iusta, loquere, scribe, tempestive et intempestive'; the author also calls him 'Norton the scold' (ibid. fo. 84).

[9] E.g. N. H. Nicholas, *Memoirs of the Life and Times of Sir Christopher Hatton, K.G.* (London, 1847), 161–2, 234–5.

[10] I have discussed the document with Michael Graves, engaged on a biography of Norton. We are agreed about the date and the recipient, but Professor Graves doubts whether the remarks about London bills could have come from this leading London citizen in Parliament. I think they could, easily.

Norton started off with the crucial question – how 'to have a Parliament least offensive'. That was the issue, that was the aim of management: not a subservient or even obedient Parliament, a thing not possible nor for Norton in the least desirable, but one that could be guided and did not raise needless trouble. Throughout, Norton was in the main concerned to avoid waste of time, since the Queen's desire for short sessions was well known and a very large number of bills were sure to come before the House. He offered the opinion that prorogued Parliaments usually prove more convenient than new ones,

> for every dissolution driveth the next assembly to a new choice of new men who...are commonly most adventurous and can be gladdest of long Parliaments to learn and see fashions, where the old continuers have among other things learned more advisedness.

Evidently he thought that both the wonders of London and the enjoyment of mornings spent in the House could wear off with experience. Besides, new Parliaments meant a heavy charge for the Queen in new fees and a lot of bother with the swearing-in 'and other matters of ceremony that prolong time'. This part of his advice was taken for the Parliament of 1572, prorogued more than twenty times with only two more sessions intervening, until it was finally dissolved while standing prorogued. It contrasted markedly in this with its one-session predecessor, somewhat disturbed by reforming passions.

Next Norton turned to the election of the Speaker and debated whether it were better to choose a councillor or another. Obviously the Speaker must prove agreeable to the Queen who had to appear willing to accept the Commons' nominal choice and also had to be ever ready to receive him throughout the session: 'it may be thought that a councillor were meetest'. But since the House would surely continue to accept whomsoever the privy councillors presented for election the problem of acceptability is in any case solved, so long as the councillors work the trick with skill, 'not arrogating to themselves the right of nomination but leaving the House to their full liberty, who in their greatest liberty will be most frankly obsequious'. In any case, there were many reasons for not choosing a member of the Council. 'The Speaker loses his voice' and councillors' contributions to debates and votes are essential 'to her majesty's service'. 'In some heads' the suggestion of electing a councillor will seem contrary to the liberty of the House since such a man is specially sworn to the royal service:

> and thereupon some man may move question, and of such question may raise a pike in the beginning of the session, which cannot be but perilous, ominosum, and to all discreet men very grievous, and would be carefully foreseen.

Sound management consists in avoiding such needless confrontations. As we have several times seen, the opening days of the 1571 session had been especially mismanaged, with much time wasted; clearly this memory lay behind this advice. Furthermore, a non-councillor in the chair would add a useful agent of government in the House, 'and one councillor's voice the more saved'; and councillors were essential in committees where the Speaker could not sit. Fourthly, the Speaker must be a skilled lawyer 'or else there will be many matters that he shall hardly well deliver'; the Privy Council did not have many such experts. A councillor also, however hard he tried, could not be as freely available to members and suitors, for which reason he would never 'find and disclose the humours of the House' as well as another could.

Right: no councillor for Speaker – as indeed had been the almost invariable practice since the organization of the restricted Privy Council in 1536, from which incidentally a good many legal experts had been excluded that had used to serve on the earlier large Council.[11] Norton went on to consider possible candidates. He could think of only two, John Popham and George Bromley, of whom the latter was attorney of the duchy of Lancaster whereas the former held no office. Though there was nothing between them in respect of 'zeal of religion, in settled mind to hold the religion set forth by law without alterations, in the skill of the laws of England, in honesty and discretion,' he preferred Bromley. He thought him 'far superior' in other forms of learning and the more accomplished speaker; since he already held a good office, 'her majesty may better burden him with such a service'. Above all, he was now 'a small practitioner' who would suffer less loss of clients than Popham, 'nor so hurtful to poor clients for losing their counsellor'. Norton put these revealing reasons forward because he knew 'there will be a difficulty to persuade him to like the place' – a place which had so harassed Onslow that he fled even with the loss of his life, 'and commonly the fittest men do least seek for office, though they were gainful'. Norton's preference is a little surprising. Popham had already left his mark in debates, but Bromley never attracted any diarist's attention. However, he was an old hand who had sat regularly since Mary's last Parliament and had often enough served on committees. We do not know whether he was approached and refused, but in fact neither man got the Speakership which went to Robert Bell whom a legend derived from Peter Wentworth regards as having highly displeased the Council only

[11] The exceptions are Sir John Baker (Speaker in 1545 and 1547) and Sir William Cordell (Speaker in 1558), both mentioned by Norton as proving that councillors could hold the office. Before 1536, members of the large and unreformed King's Council regularly became Speakers, as Sir Thomas More did in 1523 and Sir Thomas Audley in 1529.

a year before. In 1581, when Bell had doubly disqualified himself by accepting a judgeship and dying, Popham did succeed, with a good deal of delaying confusion because he had meantime become solicitor general and had to be brought back from the Lords.

The main body of the Discourse offered advice on how to handle matters in the Commons 'if her majesty's meaning be to have the session short'. In the first place, the number of private bills advanced for individuals needed to be controlled. But Norton advised strongly against any hint that a selection of what was to pass and what to be put back sprang from any command of the Queen's – 'for so would by and by be raised some question of the liberty of the House and of restraining their free consultation'. Things might well be said that would offend the Queen, and at the least there would be 'long speeches to the troublesome prolonging of the session'. Instead he thought it best that someone should speak in praise of a short session as a piece of royal graciousness, with the stress laid on the expenses of a long meeting, on the late season with its threat to health (1572 was the only session in the period to sit through May and June, with the plague season coming very near), on the calls of home upon members' time, and anything else of that sort that Hatton might think of. It was particularly desirable that in drawing any conclusion about reducing the number of bills not a word should be said about rejecting any private bills out of hand – 'although indeed it amounts to a rejecting of those that be of small importance' – since private bills 'ever be eagerly followed and make factions'. A remark based on experience the truth of which we have had occasion to note. Private bills did take up time. In this Parliament, halfway through the session, afternoons were to be set aside for them, and it was ordered that if they concerned any particular locality they should not be put to the question for passage or rejection unless the relevant knights and burgesses were in the House.[12] The zeal of promoters was not always reflected in the behaviour of supposedly concerned members, but no doubt the dashing of a bill in the absence of its particular friends would have caused special annoyance.

Norton further recommended that the many bills put in by guilds and companies, especially from London, should be reduced in number by asking the London members to refer the issues back to the mayor and aldermen; a solution which had been occasionally adopted after the bill had already taken up much time might have proved more effective at an earlier stage. Since some bills are known to have been prepared in London which then did not appear in the Parliament, it is possible that this recommendation was sometimes followed. Sudden motions, Norton

[12] *CJ* I, 101.

went on, concerning this or that topic 'makes disputations'; anyone anxious so to raise issues should be instructed to consult with others before bringing in a written motion. Members showing a desire to speak to the issue should take their part in this writing up and the House could thus be saved their orations. This strikes one as over optimistic, but Norton added a point gained from experience: 'The more committees that you make in any case the longer it will be ere the matter come in again, specially if you will appoint lawyers in term time'. Lawyers, of course, usually formed an important part of every bill committee, and that last remark should therefore warn us against suspecting trouble and disagreement just because a committee, with its lawyers finding it hard to make time to attend, was slow in concluding its business.

With equal realism, Norton recommended that if long arguments seemed likely on a bill they should be delayed until towards the end of the sitting. This, he admitted, really would test the Speaker who would have to avoid any suspicion 'of overruling or straitening the liberty of the House'. He would have to arrange a 'discreet interposing of committees' and especially prevent any too rapid reappearance of bills which at earlier readings had shown themselves 'to be so large walking fields'. Delays could further be avoided by careful drafting of important bills (especially the subsidy bill) before the session opened; failure to do so would give their chance to those who hoped to prolong the session by keeping the Queen's chief business unfinished. Lastly, he advised against too many conferences with the Lords. Conferring, he thought, served well but it could be overdone; because of it, leading members were too often absent, talking with the Lords, and the 'true liberty of the House' was threatened by 'terrifying of men's opinions'. Not that 'the Lords terrify men', but the Commons' delegates will feel out the views of their betters, 'and knowing that in the Common House nothing is secret they gather other advisements' (that is, adjust their opinions to those they find up there). 'Howsover it may be, over-many conferences work many courses to prolong the session'. It was Norton's motion in 1581 which led to the resolution that at conferences the Commons' representatives must not go beyond their exact brief.[13]

All this was sound enough advice for the management of the business of bills in the Lower House. Norton called for the purposeful and sensible handling of a volatile and selfcentred body of men, but no part of his Discourse even hints at the possibility that the House might fall under the sway of an organized and disruptive opposition. So far as Norton was concerned, such a thing could not exist. Individuals might flare up, and according to the Discourse a manager's chief task consisted

[13] Above, p. 117.

in keeping a loyal House in a good temper. All the emphasis is on tact. When the Queen issues some command it is a good idea for the order, if possible, not to be communicated by a councillor: 'not that I think her majesty's subjects mislike her commandments but because I suppose her people do love her more than they fear her' – for which reason she ought to be made to look like a gracious patron rather than like a disgruntled governess. Everything must be done 'to avoid long questions of liberty'. 'Hard messages make speeches, questions, petitions and great delays.' People naturally incline to love the Queen and obey her, but tactlessness can cancel out such feelings. Councillors need to mix; they should call to themselves 'some mean men of the House and use their advises' and they should bind private members to the management by helping them in singing their praises to the Queen. It remains true, of course, that the best part of the Commons' business is done in the bars. But some councillors were much better at handling members than others; too many of them caused needless trouble by appearing arrogant and standoffish; care must be taken in choosing who was to manage what. 'The perfectest way to have a Parliament short and not offensive...is to cherish the tenderness and good affection between her majesty and the House.' It was the task of the councillors and their helpers, the 'men of business', to preserve this amity and thus manage bills through the House.[14]

What Norton so clearly understood did indeed lie at the heart of things. The Elizabethan House of Commons did not include a group of opposition members anxious to raise issues displeasing to the Queen, or simply to delay proceedings. What it did include were men of strong views on major issues, men with specific interests, public or private, to serve, as well as men always ready to respond to affronted cries of liberty. If such men happened to hamper the purposes of Queen and Council it was important to treat them with respect, even when comprehensible exasperation suggested a kick in the teeth. That type of man was often strikingly selfimportant – very touchy, very voluble, and ever on the alert for an infringement of liberties. Just about anything could upset his kind. In May 1572 the House was asked to send forty of its members to join twenty-one peers in hearing Nicholas Bacon explain the position with respect to the Queen of Scots. This was not only the main business of the session but also the business the more ardent spirits in the House were desperately anxious to see launched. No one on the Council can have expected that invitation to lead to trouble, 'but the Lower House, not thinking good to be directed in their number did choose forty-four for

[14] M. A. R. Graves, 'The Management of the Elizabethan House of Commons: the Council's men-of-business,' *Parliamentary History* 2 (1983), 11–38.

the same purpose'.[15] This sort of childishness remained, and remains, characteristic of the knights and burgesses of the House of Commons, and the degree to which such tiresome behaviour was avoided constituted the test of successful management.

Elizabeth's managers faced the additional problem that the Queen herself often hindered easy relations rather than assisted them. Time and time again she showed her contempt for these little men who dared interfere in the counsels of princes, and it did not help that much of that contempt was very thoroughly justified. If time and again her gracious speeches poured oil at the end of a session, it is too often manifest that she herself had been responsible in the first place for stirring up the troubled waters. In 1566 she had not even tried to be gracious. The draft of her closing speech fully expressed an undisguised exasperation and a haughty superiority. Could the members really suppose that their liberties should prove a bondage of their prince? They had pontificated on things they knew nothing about; some of them, 'yielding their judgements to their friends' wits', had gone about echoing everything they heard.[16] In the event, perhaps, she abandoned this degree of severity, for the speech as reported swerved from the draft, but modification did little to moderate a furious discourse which ended by warning the House to 'beware how ever you move your prince's patience as you have now done mine'. Her pointed conclusion threw the goats into the discard when she dismissed to their homes only 'the most part of them' as still in their prince's grace.[17] She could have done with Norton's reminder that the House's affection responded best to kindness, though she would not have liked to be told that people did not fear her. The tale of Queen Elizabeth's skilful handling of the Commons is a bit of a legend, though she did in time learn to speak more circumspectly. But in 1566 she provided a full explanation why she dissolved the Parliament rather than prorogued it, as well as a vigorous justification for the sort of advice that Norton directed at her through Hatton. Whether her reaction was justified is something that we shall try to discover in the next chapter.

At any rate, as both Elizabeth and Norton made plain, the watchword of discontent and injured pride was liberty – the trigger with which a skilled operator could always release the hurt feelings of selfimportant and opinionated men. Did it have any meaning, and did the fears that it was under attack, which became vocal on several occasions, have any justification?

[15] *Proc.* 345. *CJ* I, 94 disguised the minor rumpus by pretending that forty-four had been asked for from the first.

[16] *Proc.* 174–5.

[17] Ibid. 172–3.

PRIVILEGE

In the historiography of Parliament, the word privilege has played a role of some importance; the rights of those who came to the King's Parliament have attracted some attention. Yet they are not easily identified, especially not for the House of Lords which put forward few claims, none grandiloquent, and assumed certain rights that in the absence of dispute needed no defining. For the Commons, on the other hand, historians came to measure independence and self-government by the privileges and liberties of which members spoke and which by stages enabled some to speak of the Lower House by itself as a high court of the realm.[18] In that House the story of privilege has a starting point and a means of definition because every Speaker, after his election and in his address to his monarch, made a petition for the established privileges of the House. In 1559, Sir Thomas Gargrave, petitioning for the 'ancient liberties', listed four of them: The Speaker's right of access to the Queen and the Upper House in order to convey the opinions of the Commons, his freedom to correct any mistakes he might make in carrying out that duty, 'liberty of speech for the well debating of matters propounded', and freedom from arrests and suits at law for members and their servants. In reply, Bacon confirmed the Queen's grant of these 'as largely, as amply and as liberally' as ever her predecessors had given them, but added 'admonitions and cautions'. Access would be allowed so long as it was not importunate, concerned only necessary matters, and took place at convenient times, qualifications which sounded needlessly haughty. The mind drifts off into a scene of Elizabeth caught at some most inconvenient moment by an importunate Speaker with nothing much to talk about. As for the correction of error, Gargrave should have it so long as he was careful not to err too frequently. Speech was to be free 'so as they be neither unmindful nor uncareful of their duties, reverence and obedience to their sovereign'; and as for freedom from arrest at the suit of parties, care was to be taken that 'no evil disposed person seek of purpose that privilege for the only defrauding of his creditors and for the maintenance of injuries and wrongs'.[19]

Both the petition and the responses are not without interest. Two of Gargrave's points touched only himself; they had been the standard substance of the Speaker's petition since the fourteenth century. If one

[18] For summaries along these lines see Holdsworth, *History of English Law*, IV, 177–84; Wallace Notestein, 'The Winning of the Initiative by the House of Commons,' *Proceedings of the British Academy* 11 (1926), 125–76; J. E. Neale, 'The Commons' Privilege of Free Speech in Parliament,' *Tudor Studies...Presented to A. F. Pollard* (London, 1924), esp. p. 258.

[19] *CJ* I, 53; *Proc.* 42–3.

were to trust the Roll of Parliament, they formed the only components of that petition as late as 1523 and 1539.[20] However, it is thought that we cannot believe those formulaic entries because we know that in 1523 Sir Thomas More, apparently innovating, also asked for a limited right of free speech in the House.[21] That occasion, often commented upon, is odder than seems to have been realized. For More did not repeat the hallowed phrases of his predecessors. He asked expressly for two things, one for himself and one for the House.[22] The first – equal to Gargrave's request for the right to correct error – appears on the Roll, with a rider that the petitioner asked for it to be so recorded; did More omit to ask for access because he forgot or because as a man sworn of the Council he had that right anyway? The second request, for a carefully circumscribed freedom of speech (inadvertent offence given in debate should be pardoned), was, according to Hall's *Chronicle*, also granted and also accompanied by a plea for enrolment, but it never, then or later, made it into any official record.[23] This looks like a rather striking refusal to acknowledge More's innovation and reduces the significance of his plea; perhaps the clerk of the Parliaments (Sir Brian Tuke, civil servant and courtier) received orders from his departmental head, Lord Chancellor Wolsey. Between that date and the first Parliament of Elizabeth's reign we are poorly informed about the Speaker's petition. Only three are recorded, all in short notes in either the Lords or the Commons Journal, and only the fact that they are not all identical encourages a hesitant belief that the entries may really summarize what was said. If that is so, Richard Rich in 1536 was the last man before 1559 to mention the excuse for misleading reporting, but he had nothing to say about speech or arrest. In 1542 and 1554, on the other hand, speech is mentioned and on the last occasion arrest too. It is really too dubious and exiguous a body of evidence on which to rest general theories, except that every Speaker seems to have asked for the one thing omitted by More – access to the monarch – while freedom from arrest was never remembered until 1554.

However, we should be warned by the fact that we know of Gargrave's four requests only because Bacon, in his reply, summarized them. All we can say, therefore, is that by 1559 those four points had acquired something like conventional currency, with Bacon's responses indicating that the Crown had no intention as yet to grant them without very careful reservations. Gargrave's successors did not all follow his example. In

20 *LJ* I, pp. lxxvi, clii.

21 *Tudor Constitution*, 270–1.

22 *Two Early Tudor Lives*, ed. R. S. Sylvester and D. P. Harding (New Haven, 1962), 202–5.

23 Edward Hall, *Chronicle*, ed. H. Ellis (London, 1809), 653. For the three petitions recorded between More and Gargrave (1536, 1542, 1554) see *LJ* I, 86, 167; *CJ* I, 37.

1563, Thomas Williams, according to the Journal, made 'the accustomed petitions'; thanks to an unofficial account, we know those to have been the same four, all being granted.[24] It therefore comes as a surprise to find that Richard Onslow, in 1566, confined himself to the old pair of requests on the Speaker's personal behalf; not a word on speech or arrest.[25] Very probably we have here the Queen's solicitor general carefully avoiding points she regarded as touchy. Christopher Wray, in 1571, obtaining what the Journal calls a grant of 'the ordinary petitions', mentioned all four points, with arrest leading.[26] But in 1572 Robert Bell rested content with three, saying nothing of arrest, though the Journal again speaks of 'the ordinary petitions'.[27] Bell was still Speaker in 1576, and in the confusion of the election of Popham in 1581 the Journal entirely omits his address for privilege. That he did make one appears from Cromwell's diary which mentions 'the three ordinary petitions' but in fact they were all four, the diarist amalgamating the two old requests for the Speaker's own person.[28] It looks as though Gargrave's four points had become reasonably standardized as the subject matter of the Speaker petition, but that some Speakers did not mention them all and no one knew of a particular order or phrasing that had become obligatory. As yet there was no common form.

In any case, those four 'privileges' are not of a kind, nor were they so regarded. The two concerning the Speaker's access to the monarch and his right to be forgiven for error in reporting, the only truly pre-Tudor ones, had lost all real meaning. The Queen might warn that he should not abuse his right to come into her presence and hope that he would not often misrepresent the Commons, but those medieval relics meant nothing in an age in which Queen and Council relied in part on the Speaker to keep them informed about what was going on. The only trouble was that he got summoned to the presence more often than suspicious men in the House really liked. On the other hand, the two 'privileges' concerning all the House do not exhaust the general concept of liberties, as the word was so often used in debates and protests. A revealing remark occurs in the anonymous diarist's comment on Bell's petition: 'The first for liberty of speech only, and so omitted to speak for the liberty of the House in other matters'.[29] Bell had in this respect followed precedent fairly enough; what were those other 'liberties' in that member's mind? His comment, like many an outcry in the House itself, recalls the vagueness of times long gone by, as when in 1401 Speaker Arnold Savage, having prayed for the two traditional privileges

[24] *CJ* I, 62; *Proc.* 77–8.
[25] *CJ* I, 73; *Proc.* 127.
[26] *CJ* I, 82; *Proc.* 199.
[27] Ibid. 318, 341; *CJ* I, 92.
[28] *Proc.* 526.
[29] Ibid. 318.

for himself, added a request that the Commons might have 'their liberty in Parliament as they have had before this time'.[30] In 1572, as in the reign of Henry IV, there would appear to have been an area of 'traditional' liberties less well defined and presumably less well agreed than those included in the Speaker's petition.

The first point to make about all this is that the traditional treatment, which uses the terms privilege and liberties as synonymous, will not do. Privilege could at most cover the Speaker's four points, but in actual practice it had a much narrower meaning still. Whenever it occurs in Elizabethan evidence it means freedom from arrest and nothing else. This freedom (as is well enough known) rested on the principle that those who came to Westminster at the monarch's bidding and for her service should not be prevented from doing their duty by the intervention of private affairs, especially by litigation in lower courts which might be asked by aggrieved parties, especially by creditors, to secure the presence of the accused burgess of the Parliament by means of an arrest. When the Commons Journal records such a case it has the member ask for his privilege and the House grant it to him. In this respect, members of both Houses were very much in the same position as ambassadors sent abroad who obtained letters of privilege to prevent them being sued at law in their absence, or as officers of the Queen's courts who commonly enjoyed a right to be litigable only in the courts in which they served since attendance in another court would interfere with the discharge of their duties. As the Queen's and the lord keeper's comments pointed out several times, the privilege could be abused by members and their servants, the best known case being that of Edward Smalley, servant to Arthur Hall, burgess for Grantham, who in 1576 demonstrated the technique.[31] Charged with a debt really owed by his master, he procured his arrest for it and then applied to be set free by the privilege, such liberation being sufficient to bar further action by the creditor. In Smalley's case, the trick did not work properly because the House, having indeed got him out of the Compter, then by its own authority sent him to the Tower, but people less unpopular than Hall could and did defeat their creditors by these means. We have seen that Bacon in 1559 warned against the practice; he repeated the caution in 1563 and 1571, on the second occasion with special reference to men 'who

[30] *Select Documents of English Constitutional History 1307–1485*, ed. S. B. Chrimes and A. L. Brown (London, 1961), 201.

[31] *Tudor Constitution*, 278–80. The discussion in the House turned on the means for releasing Smalley, not on his right to be released; advised that a writ should be sought out of Chancery, the House sent its serjeant (warrant of the mace), as it had done in Ferrers' case (1542) which the advisers had ignored (*Proc.* 480–2, 484, 488–9, 496). Ferrers' case had been remembered in 1572 (ibid. 381, 411).

under their shadows untruly protect any other'.[32] Nevertheless, there was no question that members of both Houses enjoyed that right for themselves and their servants, and that they claimed it. The matter has been sufficiently discussed not to require any lengthy exposition here, especially as the privilege raised no political issues and did not affect the relations between the Crown on the one side, the Lords and Commons on the other.[33] For the privilege applied between party and party; a successful claim defeated and damaged only the subject.

In the seven sessions under review, no member of the Lower House was arrested by command of the Crown. Peter Wentworth's visit to the Tower came by order of the House itself, and Strickland's case (in 1571 he was briefly ordered into attendance upon the Council) constituted not an arrest but a sequestration from the House. The move may have been unwise but it did not offend the privilege which no one raised in connection with it.[34] When problems arose they were of a technical and legal sort, as when the House refused to extend the privilege to the member who had his horses confiscated at Gravesend for the use of a French embassy, but granted it to another who had been fined £10 for failing to obey a jury summons.[35] The Lords firmly asserted the privilege even against the protest of their own president. In 1572, Henry Lord Cromwell failed to obey an injunction out of Chancery and was arrested by the sheriff of Norfolk. Nicholas Bacon put up a strong case for treating contempt of Chancery as equal to contempt of the Queen's prerogative; he also argued that preventing Chancery from acting in the case offended against natural justice and that granting the privilege in this case would hinder anyone involved in a Chancery suit with a nobleman from obtaining the remedy due to him.[36] However, the Lords, taking the opinions of judges and serjeants, asserted the claims of the high court of Parliament over those of the high court of Chancery. One problem that was to cause difficulties was the time during which the privilege was available in law. In 1572, it was agreed that it existed during adjournments – and by implication not if the House stood prorogued – as well as during a member's journey to and from the Parliament, 'though the Parliament be ended'; in the latter case, no warrant of the mace being possible in the absence of a Parliament, the clerk of the Crown in

[32] Ibid. 78, 199. [33] For a summary see *Tudor Const.*, 262.

[34] *Proc.* 225. Against another form of arrest, at the suit of a private party for something said in Parliament and after its dissolution, members were protected by statute (4 Henry VIII c. 8), not by privilege; as regular practice was to prove in the 1620s, the law did not bar arrest by King and Council.

[35] *Proc.* 402, 414 (1572).

[36] Ibid. 265–6. In a case of 1585 the Commons failed to save a member from a subpoena out of Chancery, issued while the House was sitting (Cook's case: *Tudor Const.*, 280).

Chancery would issue the necessary writ. The comment recorded speaks of 'the privilege of the House', which automatically meant freedom from arrest and no more.[37]

That leaves the liberties of which only free speech, to be discussed in a moment, appeared in the Speaker's petition. Were there any others? Certainly the House of Commons thought so. The few attempts to specify those supposed rights make it plain what really was at issue: various procedural practices which were held to guarantee the independence of either House, but more particularly of the Commons, in conducting its business. In 1576, in the dispute between the Houses over Lord Stourton's bill,[38] Sir Walter Mildmay, leading the Commons committee in conference, expressed regret that the Lords had taken umbrage at what the Lower House had done. 'They would,' he said, 'yield unto their lordships all dutiful reverence so far as the same were not prejudicial to the liberties of the House, which it behoved them to leave to their posterity in the same freedom they received them.'[39] The Lords had complained that the Commons had behaved badly in altering a bill agreed in the Upper House and moreover graced with the sign manual; they had not only questioned its validity but had after protest returned it with two damaging provisos. In addition they had refused several requests for a conference before finally sending up the members now in conference with the peers.[40] After the first message from the Lords, asking why the bill was being tampered with when it provided only for what other noblemen had before this obtained without difficulty, the House had resolved that such interference was 'perilous and prejudicial' to its liberties, and by this term they clearly meant their rights to assess the contents of a bill and decide whether they harmed anyone else, to dash a bill let alone to alter it, and to regard the Queen's signature 'but as a commendation thereof'. As for conferences, they took it to be the order of the Parliament that those could be asked for only by the House in whose hands the bill in question happened to be. It was emphasized that the Lords could not 'by ordinary means take notice of our doings'.[41]

Those, then, were the liberties of the House, agreed by them in debate and later explained by Mildmay to the Lords' representatives: to treat each bill as a proposal to be studied and at need amended, whether or not the Queen had signed and the Lords had passed it, and in such cases to reserve to themselves the right to call for a conference. Mildmay further excused himself from explaining the Commons' reasons for

[37] *Proc.* 334. [38] Above, pp. 306–9.
[39] *Proc.* 459–60; for the debate see ibid. 492.
[40] *CJ* I, 114–5. [41] *Proc.* 492.

adding the disputed proviso because to do so 'were to yield an account of their doings and of things passed in their House which they could not in any wise agree to, being so prejudicial to their liberties'. The conduct of their business must use the proper processes (which they claimed they had done) but in particular must not be interfered with from outside.

By giving in, the Lords had in effect recognized the liberties claimed, though their surrender owed most to their realization that Stourton had deceived them. How sound was the Common's case? They could show that they had before this added provisos to a sign manual bill (as for instance to that of 1563 for the Queen's Household). Though one such proviso, safeguarding the rights of wards' families, had come very close to a tack, no one had then protested against their treating the Queen's signature as a licence to proceed, not as an order to pass without alteration.[42] On the other hand, despite this precedent, it was categorically stated in about 1585 that 'a bill signed by the Queen and sent to the Lower House may not be altered in any part there without her Majesty's licence',[43] a point of view which echoes Burghley's remarks in Stourton's case and may indeed be based on them. If that was so, the Commons' challenge of the Lords would seem to have led to a novel limitation over the Commons' 'liberties' rather than the vindication which the House thought it had obtained. Sign manual bills were certainly treated with special respect by the managers of business – both Seymour and Onslow marked their every appearance in the Journal with a 'Q' as reminder that they were not as other bills – and they were virtually never tampered with; where the 'liberty' stood after 1581 will not be known until later sessions are investigated. On the point touching conferences the Commons were entirely in the right; presumably only Stourton's importunity had led the Lords into taking so false a step. As for the secrecy of the Commons' proceedings, that was assuredly a rule (perhaps a liberty) of the House but one that lacked reality. On this occasion it had to be invoked not because members of the Lower House were ever men of high principle but because the disputed proviso had plainly come up for no more respectable a cause than the Commons' desire to pay the Lords back for rejecting one of their bills. Since the judges thought everybody's interests quite sufficiently protected in Stourton's bill as it stood, the proviso probably did lack justification. The episode reveals much about the ease with which the Commons could be made to rise in defence of their liberties, but more about how limited the liberties of the House were supposed to be. They notified its independence as part of the legislature and would be defined to suit any case where that

[42] 5 Eliz. I c. 32, sect. 14–15, added on separate schedules; cf. *LJ* I, 613.
[43] *Lambarde's Notes*, 68.

independence was deemed to have suffered. They had never been specifically petitioned for, were not confirmed by royal grant, and in their nature were protean enough to fit any circumstances. And in this period at least they had no political significance.

Of course, the Lords too could play that game if they felt like it, and we have several times had occasion to draw attention to tensions between the Houses which usually arose from impatience in the Upper and dignified pomposity in the Lower. In 1581, the Lords similarly managed to stand on their dignity – the dignity of what they might have called their liberties if they had been in the habit of pounding that drum – when they refused to reconsider a bill until the Commons' amendments bore the formula of transfer without which the Upper House had 'no warrant to deal therewith any further'. In the same session they recorded their protest at the Commons returning a Lords' bill together 'with a new one of their devising', a proceeding they thought 'both derogatory to the superiority of the place and contrary to the ancient course of both Houses'; they did not wish to see it hereafter 'abused as a precedent'.[44] What matters is a general attitude: each House highly valued its dignity which it regarded as protected by procedural rights to be called liberties, but behind these spats there lay no political conflicts nor any new growth of independence. At issue was the proper conduct of business which had always been governed by practical conventions, as the Commons showed when they collected precedents from Henry VIII onwards to prove that they were fully entitled to add important provisos to bills sent down to them.[45]

The impression which some historians have gained from these assertions that the Commons were engaged upon an aggressive expansion of their role grew out of the peculiar circumstances of the case. Privileges and liberties were supposed to be proved by precedents, but where could such precedents be found? Even by the end of our period, the Commons' record, such as it was, stretched back barely thirty years: before that they had only the medieval Roll in which the only point relevant to their claims was the Speaker's petition. Events in Parliament from Edward III's reign onwards were sometimes cited, with notable inaccuracy and general irrelevance. The uncertainty about Ferrers' case, remembered by some committees and forgotten by others, can be understood: it was not on record at all, being vouched for only in a short passage in Hall's *Chronicle* and possible memories of surviving participants in the event. Indeed, it was Smalley's case of 1576 that moved Ralph Holinshed to investigate and to produce the detailed account on which ever since our knowledge

[44] *CJ* I, 132; *LJ* II, 46.

[45] *Proc.* 492.

of the case has rested.[46] When William Hakewill wrote his careful book on Commons procedure in 1611, he had much more to go on, but even so he could rely on nothing before the reign of Edward VI. It was as true of the liberties of the House as of its procedure that 'every rule of order ever made was a response to a particular, perhaps momentary, need'.[47] We must not treat these issues of privilege as though the Elizabethan Commons had their Erskine May to hand. What actually happened differed altogether from the tidiness of precedents and established claims which our textbooks tend to reflect. As Norton knew, the House was easily upset (touchiness on matters of honour constitutes one of the more enduring characteristics of any status-based society); and on such occasions quite a few members could be trusted to complain about an infringement of liberties, whether or not they had anything definable in mind. A general conviction certainly existed that the House had some such rights. And yet hardly any of those famous rights could be confirmed, even approximately, from precedent, the sole justification which both doubters and defenders recognized. Paul Wentworth did well to frame his protest of 1566, alleging breaches of 'liberty', in three questions to which there simply were no agreed answers.[48]

Of course, uncertainty has its advantage; as in procedure so in 'liberties' innovations could easily come in on a vague notion that they were anciently established. Such 'precedents' sprang from the particular problems of the moment, but if entered in the Journal would in due course acquire a quality of legitimizing authority. Take the Commons' right to control and adjudge their own membership which in the course of the century grew into a claim to decide contested elections. Yet the only firm grounds for any of that growth was the act of 1515 (6 Henry VIII c. 16) which forbade departure from the Parliament without the Speaker's licence; everything else got somehow added by conveniences and necessities creating 'precedents'. In 1571 it was left to a Commons committee, with the help of the attorney and solicitor general, to approve returns from boroughs which had sent no members to the previous Parliament; in 1563, a similar action had required the lord steward's agreement.[49] A question arose in 1576 over the knight for Sussex, John Jeffrey, elected in 1572 but in the meantime promoted to Queen's serjeant and as such attendant as assistant in the Lords. Which House was he to attend? On 17 February it was resolved that since he had no

[46] *Tudor Const.*, 261, n. 96.
[47] Lambert, 'Procedure', *EHR* 95 (1980), 753.
[48] *Proc.* 154. Cf. Neale, *EP* I, 152–3, and ibid. 188 where the unanswered questions have turned into a new definition of free speech.
[49] *CJ* I, 83; BL, Cotton MS Titus F.i, fos. 196–7. For 1563 see *CJ* I, 63.

voice in the Upper House 'nor is any member of the same' he should continue to stay in the Commons, and the entry declared the resolution of this first-time event to be 'according unto the old precedents of the House'.[50] In fact, Jeffrey's case became an unprecedented precedent. Just before they had settled it, the Commons had actually found a precedent to deal with the case of Lord John Russell, recently by the death of his elder brother heir to the earl of Bedford and therefore given a courtesy title. Could he remain as an elected member? Since he had received no summons to the Upper House the question should never even have been raised; however, on those grounds he was allowed to stay – according to the precedent set by his own father twenty-seven years before.[51] But no precedents existed or were even alleged when the House decided to allow two of its members, one 'in execution' (pursued or even arrested, probably for a debt), the other indicted for felony but not yet tried, to remain elected burgesses.[52] On the first occasion it was agreed 'that neither for absence for sickness, by reason of ambassage, or other accidental cause, any alteration of the burgesse[s] should be made'. To call an indictment an accident is a fine piece of effrontery but this enlargement of a particular event into a general rule enabled the Commons in the next session to allow a member to sit who at the time was outlawed, a decision they justified on the grounds that he had got into that unhappy condition only by standing surety for a defaulting debtor and was not the debtor himself.[53]

The claims to the 'right' soon spread in circles. In 1581, yet another member indicted for felony was kept in the House by resolution, and on this occasion the lord chancellor, by refusing a writ for a bye-election till the House should decide, had acknowledged the Commons' 'liberty'.[54] He had probably done so because two days earlier his right to issue such writs even when the Parliament was not sitting had been called in question. For in this session the House faced a more general problem produced by the length of this Parliament. The nine years that it had been in existence had naturally worn away some of the original membership, by death or by employment elsewhere in the Queen's service. Everyone seems to have agreed that it was right to allow bye-elections for dead members, but the replaced members yet living

[50] Ibid. I, 106; *Proc.* 479.

[51] *CJ* I, 15, 104; *Proc.* 477. Russell received a writ of summons for the session of 1581 when he was introduced into the Upper House on the first day of the session; he sat regularly from the third day (SP 12/147, fo. 23; *LJ* II, under dates).

[52] *CJ* I, 104; *Proc.* 477–8. The second case was not entered into the Journal and thus constituted no precedent.

[53] *CJ* I, 122, 124; *Proc.* 553.

[54] *CJ* I, 118; *Proc.* 526. These sources mention no name but D'Ewes, 283, says that the matter was raised by Robert Broughton, member for Stafford, on behalf of 'his companion or fellow-burgess'. The other member for Stafford was Thomas Purslow.

caused a long and seemingly acrimonious debate. Some maintained that the Chancery had had no business to issue writs for constituencies whose representatives remained alive; others did not wish to insult the lord chancellor by questioning his actions. In the end, however, all bye-elections, for whatever reason they had occurred, were confirmed; any other decision would have led to much confusion, nor did it seem likely that replaced members would allow themselves to be dragged back.[55] Two months later, on the last day of the session, the House had to consider much the same question once more. Faced with the report of a committee on absentees and uncertainties among the existing membership, they resolved to fine regular absentees but to confirm the original members so far as they were yet living.[56] Since the Parliament was then prorogued and not dissolved, the decision had a technical significance, but there were no practical consequences because that Parliament never assembled again. In this way, without real precedents but creating some along the way as specific queries arose and called for action, the House moved towards the claim of jurisdiction over disputed elections which in due course was to cause plenty of trouble.[57]

A similar assumption of 'liberties' without precedent, and certainly without any search for precedents either, enabled the Lower House at times to act like a court towards non-members. It explicitly arrogated this term to itself in 1572 when it called Andrew Fisher to the bar to explain why he had told the Lords that the Commons had passed a bill to which Fisher had agreed when in fact he had not done so.[58] In 1576, two outsiders were hauled up at the bar of this 'court': one Charles Johnson of the Inner Temple for attending a sitting of the House, and one Williams who had struck Robert Bainbridge, burgess for Derby, with a dagger during a political argument. Both were committed to the

[55] *CJ* I, 117; *Proc.* 524–5. The diarist must have left before the end of the debate because he thought that the matter had been left undecided. A 17th century collector of precedents drew up a list of bye-election writs sent out during the prorogations of this Parliament (SP 12/147, fos. 19–20). He found nine, all according to him to replace a member who had died. However, he missed some, included one in error, and ascribed the replacement of Lord John Russell falsely to death.

[56] *CJ* I, 135; *Proc.* 546. It is quite plain what the real problem was. By 1581 quite a few members who had been glad to be elected in 1572 had grown heartily sick of what was beginning to look like a commitment without an end. If they had not succeeded in getting themselves replaced by what the House was to resolve were illegitimate interlopers they just stayed away.

[57] A leading case is that of Norfolk in 1586 (*Tudor Const.*, 264); and cf. the Buckinghamshire election case of 1604, most recently reviewed by Linda L. Peck, 'Goodwin v. Fortescue: the local context of parliamentary controversy,' *Parliamentary History* 3 (1984), 33–46.

[58] *CJ* I, 101; *Proc.* 392. The Journal says that he was told to appear again 'in the court' on the following day; the diary has him committed to the serjeant. Nothing further is recorded.

serjeant, but nothing further happened to either.[59] For Johnson a species of precedent existed, promptly trotted out by Fleetwood, probably in the committee appointed to consider the right course of action, of which committee both he and the diarist were members. In 1397 and 1461, so Fleetwood claimed, the acts of the session had to be repealed because non-members had been present at the making of them, though no such steps were taken in 1576; nor does even Fleetwood seem to have been able to produce any precedents for proceedings by the House against intruders. Here was another new 'liberty', further extended in 1581 when two porters of Serjeants Inn, who had tried to stop Thomas Norton from entering the House, were arrested by warrant of the mace; described as prisoners at the bar, they apologized and were let go.[60] All these dubious innovations – dubious by the Commons' own standards because unprecedented – arose from occasions and not from principle, and all served the purpose of getting on with business. Nevertheless, the House certainly built itself an identity out of such bricks, without displaying any visible political ambitions. Self-love, self-importance, a proper appreciation of what was due to a member of the legislative trinity – such feelings produced developments which, naturally, could be exploited very differently if ever the need arose.

FREEDOM OF SPEECH

The liberty of free speech is another matter. For one thing, it was asked for in the Speaker's petition and therefore explicit; for another, it was evidently an accepted right in Parliament by 1559, if not sooner. Indeed, the principle that in either House members could express their views without fear of the consequences, so long as they minded their manners, cannot have been very new. As was to be said again and again on later occasions, what point was there in arguing over issues of importance in Parliament unless people felt able to give their advice honestly? Free speech, though not of an unrestricted kind, had prevailed long before Elizabeth came to the throne, and the chances are that More's sole innovation lay in expressly defining it. In 1529, when John Petite, citizen for London, opposed the bill which retrospectively turned a forced loan into a parliamentary grant, Henry VIII responded only by asking jocularly, as other bills came forward, whether 'Petite were of his side'; in 1547 Stephen Gardiner reminisced about the Parliament House 'where was free speech without danger'.[61] In the debates on the

[59] *CJ* I, 105–6, 109; *Proc.* 478, 485.

[60] *CJ* I, 121; *Proc.* 531.

[61] *Narratives of the Days of the Reformation*, ed. J. G. Nichols (Camden Society, 1859), 25; *The letters of Stephen Gardiner*, ed. J. A. Muller (Cambridge, 1933), 392.

ecclesiastical settlement of 1559, Lord Montague, determinedly opposing government policy, sought 'the privilege of the House' in speaking his mind, with a sideswipe at others who kept their mouths shut for fear that their words would get reported outside the House, 'to their displeasure'.[62] In the debate on the succession in 1566, one contributor took the right of free speech to the highest authority: 'The providence of God, I say, hath ordained by law that in this House everyone hath free speech and consent.'[63] Evidently unable to find any human ordinance to serve his purpose, he also forgot to cite the relevant text from Scripture. At any rate, freedom of speech was generally accepted as one of the 'liberties' enjoyed by both Houses, and one never finds it denied.

What one does find is a discussion of its meaning which turns on two points. In the first place, could a man be attacked for abusing the right by speaking without proper respect and outside the bounds of decency? And secondly, did it mean freedom to speak frankly to all matters put before the Parliament, or would it entitle any member to raise any issue he wished? As to the first point, as we have seen, Bacon as early as 1559, before Elizabeth had had any experience of Parliament, warned the Commons to observe their duty, reverence and obedience towards the Queen, a warning which reflects unfortunate experiences during the previous two reigns.[64] The warning became one of the standard *topoi* in Bacon's replies to the Speaker:[65] 'so that it be reverently used' in 1563, to avoid meddling in matters of state in 1571, a reminder of warnings ignored in 1572. It is ironic that Onslow's caution in not asking for the privilege prevented Bacon from uttering his commonplaces in 1566, the session during which free speaking in the House came nearest to ruining relations with the Queen altogether. What people feared was the point made more than once in that session, namely that their words would be revealed to Elizabeth and bring serious consequences for themselves. In the debate on the treason bill of 1571, Henry Goodere hoped that nothing said would cause 'dislike between her majesty and this House, which were hateful'. In reply Thomas Norton demanded that since speech was free so long as it did 'not exceed the bonds of loyalty' it should also 'be free of unjust slanders and undeserved reproaches'. But of course the trouble was that anyone who found out that his words had offended the Queen regarded himself as unjustly slandered; the limits of decorum remained sufficiently uncertain to make this condition thoroughly unhelpful.

On the question of initiatives in the House the case was clearer; it was

[62] *Proc.* 8.
[63] Ibid. 130.
[64] Ibid. 43.
[65] Ibid. 78, 199, 341.

to be worked out by stages into a firm doctrine held by Elizabeth that members of Parliament could speak freely to anything raised in the proper fashion. In her view this meant that matters of state had to be introduced on behalf of the Queen and with her permission, whereas anybody could introduce matters of the common weal. The doctrine was stated plainly by Bacon in 1571 and most starkly expounded by Lord Chancellor Puckering in 1593.[66] Though Neale supposed that 'historically' Elizabeth was right, it should be said that no monarch before her ever to our knowledge laid down such a distinction. No doubt she was forced into inventing it because, unlike her immediate predecessors who used Parliament to make and debate policy on great affairs, she always wanted to keep Parliament out of the act. The precedents, such as they were, spoke against her. Thus in 1533, when private members in the Lower House moved for an address to ask Henry VIII to restore Catherine of Aragon to her rightful place, they were certainly not speaking in a debate initiated on behalf of the Crown but suffered no rebuke or other ill consequences.[67] In effect, Elizabeth was out of historical step from the first. By 1584 a member of the House recorded the surprise widely felt when after decades of handling the affairs of the Church the Commons were suddenly told not to meddle with them.[68] Elizabeth's rigorous distinction on initiative constituted an innovation which caused resentment.

The correct meaning of free speech in Parliament was carefully debated in 1572, during an attack on the duke of Norfolk, and was tested to destruction by Paul and Peter Wentworth. The 1572 discussion followed in the wake of a major debate in which a number of members urged an approach to the Queen to have the duke executed; after trial by his peers he stood condemned for treason, but the Queen remained reluctant to have the sentence carried out, the more so because his fate was involved with that of Mary Queen of Scots, the assault on whom was the major business of the session.[69] In the course of the debate, Arthur Hall made himself into a marked man by speaking against the majority opinion in the House. An expert in ill-timed tactlessness, he unquestionably said some very rash and provocative things. The duke's offence, he claimed, touched the Queen but not the House; it was therefore for her to decide what to do. Indeed, very possibly Norfolk had done no harm to either Queen or realm, and members 'will hasten the

[66] Neale, *EP* II, 249–50.
[67] Hall, *Chronicle*, 788. For another such unscripted intervention see *Letters and Papers...of the Reign of Henry VIII*, ed. J. S. Brewer et al., VI, no. 324.
[68] Northants Record Office, MS F(M), P.2, fo.1.
[69] The story is told in Neale, *EP* I, 252–5, slanted to fit his preconceptions.

execution of such whose feet hereafter you would be glad to have again to kiss'. Some people would not now be where they were if the severe justice applied to Norfolk had been meted out to others.[70] Next day, the gauntlet so thrown down was predictably taken up, and Nicholas St Leger, a solid protestant, rose to ask whether a man who had declared the duke's proven treason possibly not harmful to the realm was 'a fit member to be one of this House'. Hall had shown himself 'to be of that faction' and deserved imprisonment. As for free speech, 'it ought to be contained in bonds'.[71]

Other business distracted the House, but on 17 May Thomas Honywood (the man whose horses the House soon after refused to release by the privilege) reopened the matter. He repeated St Leger's points and asked that Hall should be made to answer for his speech. Sir Francis Knollys firmly put him down. While not wishing to offend anyone so zealous in defence of the Queen's safety, he held that speech in Parliament should be free; for one thing, he would 'rather know men by their speech than not know them by their silence'. It would be wrong to give some members the chance to pretend that they would have spoken but had not dared: 'Therefore give them scope, let them speak their fill'. This defence of freedom of speech did not go down too well. George Ireland, another ardent anti-papist, declared that Hall had spoken treason; he trusted 'that the liberty of this House will not permit a man to speak treason'. He called for advice from the lawyers. Support came from Thomas Sampole, known as a convinced protestant, who defined freedom of speech as not meaning that 'a man might say what he listed'. Hall's remarks, he added, 'called in question the proceedings of the Lords and overthrow the resolution of this House', and he produced (irrelevant) historical precedents to show that the offender should therefore be called upon to explain himself.[72] George Grenville, who had sat on the committee to whom the abominations of the Queen of Scots were revealed, confirmed how dangerous to the realm the treasons in question were and then strayed off into a bloodthirsty fancy concerning the decapitation of the duke and Mary Stuart, but Thomas Norton, who originally had been the cause of Hall's speech, brought the debate back to the point. He liked, he said, *sine acerbitate dissensionem* – disagreement without bitterness. Men can inadvertently say things they do not mean, for which reason 'it were good the gentleman were called to answer, and to hear how he can explicate his own meaning'.

[70] *Proc.* 273, 354 (15 May 1572).
[71] Ibid. 355.
[72] Among other things he alleged that in Henry VIII's reign Bishop John Fisher had been forced to retract when he implied that the Commons were heretics. This is true, but it was the King, not the Commons, who had made Fisher take back his accusation.

As so often, Norton was followed by Fleetwood who, as so often, produced a bit of only thinly relevant history but went on to advocate toleration for misliked remarks in the House when such great matters as the arraignment of a queen were before them. Of course, if Hall (as was alleged) had repeated similar remarks outside the House 'the case is changed'; and he cited the example of a man who felt that a judge had given a wrong judgment against him. He should not complain at large but seek his remedy by writ of error. One man in such a situation had in fact brought the matter to Star Chamber and found the court willing to listen, but when he said the same things 'upon his alebench' the judge sued him for slander by an action on the case. 'Words tolerable in this House are not sufferable at Blunt's table'. Fleetwood had admitted that he did not hear Hall's speech; Francis Alford, who spoke next, laboured under the same handicap. He thought the words as reported – and the reports varied – ill considered, but the place of their delivery needed consideration. Alford described himself as 'jealous of the liberties of the House'. If the words were spoken in the Commons, Hall should be called to answer. This brought on Robert Snagge, a radical who usually thought the House the proper place for raising all the causes he cared about; his contribution revealed that in his opinion there was 'no liberty to be granted to licentiousness'. He had heard Hall's remarks and felt that if they were tolerated 'let sedition be sown'. A remarkably balanced opinion came from John Marsh, the London mercer and alderman. The motion had asked whether there was treason in the words, and that should be investigated. It further asked whether treasonable words might be spoken, and he would answer that 'the House has no such liberty'. On the other hand, he thought the House of Lords had 'unjustly condemned the duke', a remark for which he was not taken up. Then Edward Fenner, a conservative and reasonably eminent lawyer, declared for liberty, 'infinite in estimation'; it would be best to maintain it by holding Hall to be mad. No, said Sir Nicholas Arnold, who had started his career as a client to Thomas Cromwell and had suffered for the protestant cause under Mary; calling Hall to answer would not infringe the liberty of the House. It was then decided that Hall should be summoned and on the day set he made a humble and successful submission, Knollys having explained to the House that Hall's father had also been 'somewhat inclined to madness'.[73]

Thus there had been a clear division of opinion on the proper extent of free speech in the Commons and how far its practice constituted a liberty of the House. The absolute position had been defended by the

[73] *Proc.* 359–61, 365–6.

official side (Knollys, Fleetwood, Norton) with the support of good conformist conservatives. Against them, the more radical men had upheld the view that that liberty must be limited: neither offensive remarks nor treason could claim its protection. It may well be that the government speakers allowed Hall's connection with Burghley, whose ward he had been, to influence them, and the radicals may have enjoyed themselves echoing the reservations regarding free speech which the Queen caused to be uttered at the opening of every Parliament. None of this alters the basic fact. Freedom of Speech was generally regarded as one of the valued liberties of the House, and its meaning adapted itself to whatever any interpreter thought to the advantage of his cause.

Since ordinarily talk of limits aimed to contain the manoeuvres of more radical men like the Wentworth brothers, it is no wonder that they battled for the widest possible interpretation, though that debate of 1572 should instruct us that they did so not for principle but for advantage – or perhaps, in the best tradition of House of Commons radicals, by presenting their advantage as a fundamental principle. Paul and especially Peter Wentworth have had quite sufficient attention before this to render a lengthy investigation here superfluous. The old standard view of the Elizabethan Commons as an ancestor of the House bored by Cobden and Bright elevated the Wentworths to the position of heralds and heroes; at least there does seem to be this much truth in the fantasy that they rarely found the House very sympathetic. They belong to a tribe much favoured by whiggish historians – the people 'ahead of their time'.[74] Their campaign they concentrated on the maintenance of freedom of speech in the largest possible sense because they recognized in the Queen's ability to restrict them by narrow definitions, and by the 'rumours and messages' with which she influenced the House, the major obstacle to their own ambitions in Parliament. Unless they could initiate the discussion of any topic they chose and could rely on debate to remain uninfluenced by threats of royal displeasure, they could not hope to promote the causes they cherished – the elevation of the Commons above the Lords, and the promotion of puritan reform against the bishops. In fighting for both these lost causes the Wentworth brothers arrived at a definition of free speech which later ages, unwilling to recognize the role which influence and profit have always played in the running of the House, came to think the only proper definition and the truth.

Paul Wentworth's three questions of 11 November 1566 were skilfully framed.[75] The first asked whether a command from the Queen to cease debating the succession was 'a breach of the liberty of the free speech

[74] See esp. J. E. Neale, 'Peter Wentworth,' *EHR* 39 (1924), 36–54, 175–205; this is absorbed into *EP* 1, passim (see Index).

[75] *Proc.* 154.

of the House', the second whether the councillors transmitting that command had the authority 'to bind the House to silence', and third what offence a man would commit who declared an opposite opinion if the answer to the first two questions was yes. There could be only one way of dealing with such leading questions: they remained unanswered. Peter seems to have been the more activist of the two. He also might carry the liberties of the House forever in his mouth, as when, citing Scripture, he proclaimed them to be threatened by Sir Humphrey Gilbert's sycophancy towards the Queen and by the practice of misrepresenting to her what had been said; he did so 'for the credit of the House and for the maintenance of free speech'.[76] But in his famous oration of 1576 – 'sweet indeed is the name of liberty and the thing itself a value beyond all inestimable treasure' – in which he attacked Elizabeth's whole policy and person, he put the Wentworth definition to the test.[77] Well launched into the speech he was stopped; a powerful committee was appointed to interrogate him about his meaning and reasons; he went to the Tower whence he could be delivered, by the Queen's licence, only two days before the end of the session; on his return he was made to listen to an edifying discourse by Mildmay who reminded him that the well-attested and necessary freedom of speech did not mean that 'a man in this House may speak what and of whom he list', as well as to a stern rebuke by the Speaker and annoying praise for Elizabeth's compassion.[78] Hall, who had spoken something like treason, had been allowed to make his peace; Wentworth, whose ringing tones did not conceal offensive contempt for House and Queen alike, spent most of the session in the Tower. Both of them had proved that so far as the age went there were indeed limits to the liberty of speech and that these liberties depended on circumstances. There was some justice in the fact that Hall, who had spoken like a fool, got off lightly, whereas Wentworth, seeking martyrdom, underwent a little suffering.

Of course, the government was entitled to influence debate in either House, and if normal methods of warning or persuasion failed to manage the conduct of business it went without saying that the monarch, one of

[76] Ibid. 237.

[77] Ibid. 425–34 – the whole speech, including the part (nearly half of it) he was stopped from delivering. The account of his interrogation by the committee (ibid. 435–9) was written by himself and must be treated with a caution not applied to it, e.g., in Neale, *EP* I, 326–9. If Wentworth had so dominated the committee and won all the debating points, a body displayed as so cowed and deferential would have had some difficulty in imprisoning him.

[78] *CJ* I, 114; BL, Cotton MS Titus F.i, fos. 220r–221v. The whole business is transmitted to us in ways that make judgment extremely difficult. Everything that Wentworth allegedly said – and we know the bulk of the story from his pen – reeks of a selfsatisfied conceit.

whose institutions of government the Parliament was, felt bound at need to intervene. As Norton pointed out, such intervention should always have been tactful and not hectoring: an aspect of good and successful management. Did Elizabeth abuse her right to intervene? We can give no absolute answer to this question. Much of her action came in the rumours and messages complained of: the first escape the record while the second may not have been regularly noted there. The fact that her interventions caused at least some resentment, together with the often combative tone of her set speeches, supports the conclusion that she could have done better. The Queen's sour temper at times hampered management. This, after all, was not the only region of policy in which she could drive her councillors to despair. Direct intervention in proceedings on actual bills remained rare; I can find only six such cases, three in each House, all of which have been mentioned in earlier chapters.[79] The tally is modest. Not even Peter Wentworth would have denied her right to veto bills passed in both Houses. As for messages, so far as we can discover them they were at least impartial. In 1559, Lord Montague complained that matters of the faith had been banned – 'utterly forbidden' – from debate.[80] In 1566, a message from on high stopped further debate on the succession, but this was quickly recognized as a bad move and graciously withdrawn.[81] In the same session, an outburst of James Dalton's got him into trouble, but Elizabeth extricated herself from the possibility of a real clash by accepting his explanation that he had been misreported. However, she also sent a message asking the House to find out if he really had not said what she had been told.[82] In 1572, two privy councillors conveyed her message about two versions of a bill for religion, a message which stopped further proceedings.[83] Speaker Popham's address at the start of the 1581 session, with its call for no more wasting of time and its injunctions touching discreet speaking and sticking to the point, sounds very much like his mistress's voice speaking through him.[84]

No doubt there were more messages, not now found in the record or not readily identifiable for what they were, but the final impression suggests that, except perhaps in 1566, a session which taught her much about the handling of Parliament, Elizabeth did not overdo her intervening. The ordinary business of Parliament, which occupied far and

[79] In the Lords: sheriffs' accounts (1563), respite of homage (1571), against the Prayer Book (1571); in the Commons: dispensations (1572), for the earl of Kent (1572), discipline in the Church (1576).

[80] *Proc.* 9.

[81] Ibid. 160–2; see below, p. 372.

[82] *Proc.* 158–9, 163.

[83] Above, pp. 215–16.

[84] *CJ* I, 118.

away most of its time, raised disputes and difficulties on quite a few occasions, but proved manageable. What really caused trouble were, naturally enough, 'greater' issues of policy and politics, those conflicts which at present are the thing best remembered about the history of those Parliaments.

14

Great affairs

THE MYTH OF AN OPPOSITION

Though the main bulk of the Parliament's business consisted in the passing of bills, it must not be forgotten that it also found itself involved in high politics – in matters of national interest which did not necessarily arise out of its legislative function. Those great affairs, which were all bound to be the occasion of discussion and even conflict, whether between members of both Houses or between the Houses and the Queen, form the main content of Sir John Neale's analysis of the history of the Elizabethan Parliaments. He devoted almost all his two volumes to them and told the resulting story vividly and with full assurance that he had got it right. General accounts have followed the lines he constructed. If that were all, it would be pointless to go over the story once more, but it has to be said that Neale was greatly mistaken. Occasionally his remarks are not borne out by his evidence, but the fundamental trouble lies elsewhere. The sources rarely leave no doubts about purposes and motives, and our understanding of what happened consequently depends to a high degree on our assessment of those less than factual aspects. Though at times Neale recognized other influences he operated mainly on one basic assumption. He had persuaded himself that the first two Parliaments of the reign witnessed the consolidation of a genuine and coherent opposition to the Queen's policy – loyal but endlessly troublesome – and that what moved that body was what he called 'puritanism'. Having emerged and coalesced in the 1560s, this opposition was then discovered at work in subsequent Parliaments. Neale rested his interpretation first of all on his identification of a radical group which in 1559 forced a protestant settlement of the Church upon the Queen, but that this group and its victory were figments of the imagination has been fully shown by Norman Jones.[1] Secondly Neale declared that a list

[1] This is the general conclusion of his *Faith by Statute*.

of members of the Commons, described, with some scurrility, in a 'lewd pasquil' of 1566, constituted a roster of that puritan opposition. This was the 'choir' which before and after 1566 enabled him to see the machinations of an organized opposition behind the evidence. Time and time again, without any further grounds given for its existence or its doings, he brought it forward to build up his picture of an independent leadership to an opposition battling in the House against the Queen and over all sorts of issues. He saw it as preparing the scene for the kind of role which, he believed, the House played in the early seventeenth century.

The myth of this 'choir' has been briefly shown up before,[2] but in view of the importance it holds in Neale's account – as the key for interpreting all events – it needs to be considered rather more carefully. The document from which the myth was constructed is exceptional in Tudor constitutional history. Described in the only complete copy extant as 'a lewd pasquil set forth by certain of the Parliament men 8 Eliz'., it is in fact the equal of a skit in a satiric magazine.[3] It lists forty-three members of the 1566 House of Commons with brief comments. The first part attached to thirty-five of them often witty tags in Latin, many of them from Scripture; the second, partly in English doggerel verse, gives all of them a one-word ascription. For example, of William Fleetwood, talkative lawyer and later recorder of London, we learn in Latin that 'the law was given by Moses' (*lex data est per Moysem*), while later he is called simply 'the pleader', to rhyme with 'The Hanse feeder [supporter]' attached to John Marsh, the London Merchant Adventurer. The author did not always manage even rough rhymes, but sometimes the search for something like it clearly played a greater part than psychological accuracy. In the Latin section he ran out of time or inspiration – or Latin. Even so, there are some neat phrases. John Foster, once a member of a religious order from which he escaped after an affair with a nun, is called 'the friar'. This makes Robert Newdigate ('I shall sound like a trumpet') into 'the crier'; James Dalton, 'the denier' perhaps for the rhyme's sake, grew into the tag when he was charged with making a speech he maintained had been misreported. Was Thomas Norton 'the scold' because Francis Alford had been called 'the bold', or *vice versa*? Or did the words say something true about both? The shoes fitted. On the other hand, while Richard Grafton unquestionably was 'the printer' it is hard to see why Thomas Fleetwood (a second Fleetwood) was called

[2] *Studies* III, 175–6; Graves and Silcock, *Revolution, Reaction and the Triumph of Conservatism*, 355–8.

[3] Cambridge University Library, MS Ff.5.14, fos. 81v-84r: from a commonplace book temp. Eliz. I, probably put together not later than *c.* 1580.

'the minter' except to make the rhyme – unless an illusion is lost on us.

Anyway, that is the kind of chat this paper consists of. Can we agree with Neale that the whole group, called 'our choir' at the end, constituted a coherent body of puritan activists? The biographies collected in the relevant volumes published by the History of Parliament Trust (and inspired by Neale) enable us to check up on them, and the results firmly deny Neale's supposition. Of the forty-three only twenty-two can safely be called firm protestants, and few of them – perhaps two or three – were really ardent enough in religion to merit the puritan accolade. Five had strong links with the old religion; one of these, Henry Goodere, became notorious as a devoted admirer of the Queen of Scots. Eleven held government office or were clients of privy councillors; three more, in 1566 at the start of their careers, later became judges. Thirteen were practising lawyers, and one – Francis Alford, the conservative – had studied the law of Rome. Perhaps the most interesting sort of members included are those whom from their work in the House at other times we know to have acted as men of business for the Privy Council: seven or eight of them, with two more who came to play that part in later Parliaments. There are two future Speakers – Robert Bell and Christopher Yelverton. And, of course, there is Thomas Norton whom we already know to have been the leading man of business in the Parliaments of the 1560s and 1570s, with the session of 1581 crowning his career.

Thus there is no visible coherence, no clear-cut identity or common purpose, about this collection of individuals. Certainly the larger part of them supported the reformed Church, but so naturally did the largest part of the House; few enemies to the established Church either sought or were likely to gain election to Parliament. As historians have gradually become aware, a passion for protestantism and a dislike for Rome did not make a man a puritan or even eager for further reformation, unless the bishops gave a lead. Norton's faith merits another brief glance. He felt exceptionally, even pathologically, hostile to the pope and inclined to see Jesuits under every bed. Part-author of the play *Gorboduc* (about which more in a moment), he also wrote violent pamphlets against the Antichrist at Rome.[4] There is no doubt about his zeal in the cause of true religion. But does that make him a puritan, wound up ready to oppose on principle? Some evidence exists for his beliefs which has not so far been considered. In 1574, as the lord mayor's remembrancer, he composed a paper of guidance for the incoming mayor, James Hawes.[5] Hawes was told that he must do 'what in you lies to suppress the boldness

[4] Graves, 'Norton,' *Hist. Journal* 23 (1980), 30.
[5] BL, Additional MS 33271, fos. 28r–31r.

and growing of dangerous sects and especially the heresy of papistry' – an interesting phrase because it is very rare in the reign of Elizabeth to find Roman catholics described as heretics. However, Norton also knew of non-catholic sects he regarded as dangerous. But he could distinguish. Only traitors, he went on, were papists, 'for you well may know that no Christian – so call I a gospeller – will be enemy to this state'. Outright radicals also need to be watched, but at least they are Christians – though no true radical would have used that rather contemptuous word, gospellers, of his own kind. Elsewhere Norton made it sufficiently plain that he thought the controversies launched by genuine puritans deplorable. This comes out in a long, earnest, pompous composition put together for the attention of the Privy Council, probably early in the seventies.[6] While Norton there favoured reforms in the clergy, at the Universities, and at the Inns of Court, in order to prevent popish infiltration, he insisted that he disliked innovations and changes in the law; there was no need for drastic measures. 'As Bucer used to say of Germany, *o maledictam questionem sacramentariam*, so I say of England, *o maledictam questionem vestiariam.*' Anyone willing to curse the vestiarian controversy of the 1560s was not a puritan of any sort. And neither were nearly all the rest of the good protestants in the lampoon.

So the puritan choir is a myth and should be removed from the annals of history. However, somebody thought it a handsome trick to run down this list of forty-three worthy members of the Commons. Can we find some other common identity for what were in effect forty-four people – forty-three taken off and one taker-off? That forty-fourth appears in the last line of the Latin section: 'Pasquillus – et omnis populus dicat amen.' In conclusion, the satirist asked all the people to say Amen to his skit. Now in the history of the conflict in 1566 over the succession the figure forty-four does have significance. On 19 October in that year the Commons appointed a committee of all the privy councillors and forty-four members to consider an approach to the Lords over renewing the campaign for a settlement of the uncertain state of the throne; that committee later drew the petition presented to the Queen.[7] The gathering in the pasquil looks very much like a committee, the usual mixture of experts and amateurs, with those anxious to tackle the question in a majority but accompanied by others less determined and with enough lawyers to help if any drafting was to be done. The suggestion that that was the character of the 'choir' gains further support from a small and

[6] SP 12/177, fos. 155–80: 'a book of Mr Norton's devices'.

[7] *CJ* I, 75. Neale (*EP* I, 140) says that twenty-one of the forty-four were members of his 'choir' but I cannot see what evidence he thinks he has for the names of the committee; I think he was dreaming at this point.

hitherto mysterious detail. The second part of the lampoon ends with a little quatrain, 'As for the rest, they be at devotion, and when they be pressed they cry "a good motion".' This has been interpreted as meaning no more than that everybody else in the House was in effect asleep, just waiting to applaud what the 'choir' might propose, but that would ill describe a much disturbed House, nor do the likes of William Bowyer ('the antiquary') or Sir John Chichester ('the fool') qualify as manifest leaders of debate. On the other hand, the committee appointed on the 19th was ordered to meet on the next day, a Sunday, so that while they were deliberating the rest of the House were indeed 'at devotion'. Obviously, the theory that the 'lewd pasquil' gives us an important committee list cannot be proved conclusively, but it makes some sense: there is a bit of supporting evidence, and it would account for so higgledy-piggledy a collection being brought together. Even Pasquillus might well hesitate before lampooning her majesty's councillors, but he let himself go on his non-conciliar colleagues. He had a whole afternoon to put his doggerel together. If I am right, we now know all the members of the committee of 19 October except one, and I cannot begin to guess who the poetaster might have been.[8]

At any rate, we are rid of the illusion which supported Neale's determination to ascribe argument and conflict to the emergence of a puritan opposition. As we shall see, without that distorting glass the available evidence suggests a very different interpretation. The issues that led to serious clashes were very few. Those that arose out of the Queen's refusal to allow Parliament further to reform the Church and the clergy were discussed in an earlier chapter, and it appeared there that theories about the leadership of a puritan pressure group in the Commons cannot be sustained. Certainly the Lower House, or rather some members of it, at times made a noise about religion, but in the main they echoed the desire of Church leaders for reforming legislation. Elizabeth, anxious to avoid provocative measures that might disturb the peace and herself unimpressed by many of the precise principles current among her people, on several occasions resisted demands made in both Houses and supported by her Council. Only in the rather pointless skirmish at the start of the 1581 session, when a bare (and temporary) majority supported Paul Wentworth's proposal for a public fast, by way of seeking divine assistance in those troubled days, did Elizabeth face a disunited House of Commons with the realm on her side.[9] She regarded this resolution as an invasion of her rule over the Church and for once was able to administer a sharp rebuke which was meekly accepted; she might also

[8] Unfortunately, George Gascoigne, the poet, who sat in 1559, did not get elected to this Parliament.

[9] *Proc.* 526–7; SP 12/147, fos. 33–4.

have asked what puritan opinion was doing calling for a fast when they abominated Cecil's weekly fish days. It remains to be seen how the difficulties arose over the other two issues which in those Parliaments troubled relations with the Queen: the succession to the Crown, and the fate of Mary Queen of Scots.

SUCCESSION

The accession of an unmarried Queen, with an unhappy mix of claimants around the place, from the first worried the political nation. History told of too many examples of what a disputed succession could lead to, but it also offered warnings about the sort of consort, foreign or domestic, that a queen regnant might find herself marrying. Since the best title for the inheritance lay with Mary Queen of Scots, champion of Rome, the continuation of the protestant religion in the Church of England was vested in Elizabeth's life and the hope that she would furnish an adequate heir of her body, but that required that she should marry in the teeth of bad omens, not to mention her own desire. Thus through the first thirty years of her reign much of public life, of international relations, and of faction disputes in her Council was dominated by the Queen's possible marriage and the uncertainty of the succession, and naturally enough the anxieties aroused spilt over into the Parliament – assisted (as we shall see) by councillors' ploys. In Neale's interpretation, the succession question provided the opportunity for a loyal but obstreperous opposition to form and make itself effective. As he saw it, it was in the 1560s that the kind of confrontation between government and opposition originated that in the end was to bring down the Stuart monarchy. However, that is not what happened – though what did happen perhaps fits better revised views of the events of Charles I's reign.[10]

All our seven sessions produced some reference to the succession and to the Queen's hoped-for marriage. The Parliament could lay a claim to a right to consider at least the former. As Robert Monson, an experienced member of the Commons and one of the Council's men of law there, pointed out in 1571, it would have been treason to assert that Parliament had 'no authority to determine of the Crown', for that would have meant attacking Elizabeth whose right to the throne rested on the third Henrician succession act and the 1559 confirmation thereof.[11] What Monson did not mention was the very recent history of this power, a

[10] The general background and setting for the supposed clashes in Parliament are most effectively displayed in Wallace T. MacCaffrey, *The Shaping of the Elizabethan Regime* (Princeton, 1968), esp. chs. 7–9; for the supposed role of Parliament see Neale, *EP* I, 101–13, 129–64.

[11] *Proc.* 216; 35 Henry VIII c. 1; 1 Eliz. I c. 3.

history which went back no further than to the act of 1534 that replaced the issue of Catherine of Aragon by that of Anne Boleyn.[12] Before that, parliamentary statements concerning the Crown had been simple recognitions of accomplished fact, with no legislative element in them, as in the so-called act of 1485 confirming Henry VII's occupation of the throne: though its formulation should have made it chapter one of 1 Henry VII it did not even get into the printed statute of the session.[13] And Monson also passed over the crucial question of Elizabeth's attitude to acts touching the Crown: could either House initiate discussion or even legislation on this topic without waiting for instruction from the Queen?

It was on the fifth day of the first Parliament of the reign, 4 February 1559, that the Lower House debated the proposal for a request to be put to the Queen that she should marry, and since Elizabeth replied to it six days later we know that the request was made.[14] The Commons here followed the example of their predecessors in Mary's reign who in October 1553 had petitioned their Queen to marry within the realm; for their pains, they had been savagely rebuffed.[15] On that occasion the House had been manoeuvred into petitioning by those members of the Privy Council who objected to the proposed marriage with Philip of Burgundy, and it is obvious that the request of 1559, put up before the House had had time to gather itself together, also sprang from a Council initiative. Everybody in politics expected this young woman of twenty-five to marry and wondered only whom she would choose.[16]

Fortunately, in a way, the parliamentary petition presented to the Queen avoided mentioning any particular husband, a sensible caution (after the experience of Mary's reign) which enabled Elizabeth to return a soothing answer. She went out of her way to appreciate the Commons' good sense in speaking of 'no limitation of place or person'. At the same time she uttered a warning in one of the frankest and least devious speeches she ever made. She declared that she had deliberately chosen the state of permanent celibacy. Had she wanted to marry she could have done so before this time, but since she came to 'years of understanding', and much influenced by what she had seen in her sister's reign, she meant to remain 'in this kind of life in which yet I live'. If ever she did change her mind she would be sufficiently careful of the interests of the nation to render superfluous all fears on the part of the Commons: 'therefore put that clear out of your heads'. Then – and this turned out to be

[12] 25 Henry VIII c. 22.
[13] *Tudor Const.*, 4.
[14] *CJ* I, 54; *Proc.* 44–5.
[15] D. M. Loades, *The Reign of Mary Tudor* (London, 1979), 120.
[16] Jones *Faith by Statute*, 58–60.

unwise – she promised to see about finding a successor 'in convenient time'; a promise once made not so soon forgotten. She added a very un-Tudor-like preference for the adoptive over the hereditary principle: she would promise to rule well, 'yet may my issue grow out of kind and become perhaps ungracious', for which reason it might be better to allow God to find 'a fit governor'.[17] A lot of trouble would have been prevented if the listeners – councillors and the rest – and the foreign envoys attendant had taken her peroration to heart: 'that in the end this shall be for me sufficient that a marble stone shall declare that a Queen, having reigned such a time, lived and died a virgin'. Forty-five years later, that prophecy came true. Meanwhile, however, both the apprehensions of the protestant nation and her own exploitation of her unmarried hand in diplomatic games both serious and frivolous closed ears to that message, and her failure promptly to attend to the provision of an assured succession made it impossible for responsible advisers to let the issue rest.

Before the next Parliament met, several events conspired to produce a crisis. In 1562 Elizabeth nearly died of the smallpox, and at the same time the claims of Mary Queen of Scots raised the spectre of a catholic succession. It should be emphasized that there existed no authoritative rule in law concerning the succession. By and large, a principle of legitimacy, derived from the principles of primogeniture that governed the inheritance of land, was vaguely supposed to apply, but – as the judges declared in the Parliament of 1460 when Richard duke of York claimed the Crown – a question touching the king's estate and regality 'is above the law and past their learning'.[18] For close on a hundred years – in 1399, 1460, 1483 and 1485 – usurpation by force of arms had taken the place of legitimacy. The consequent resort to statute from 1534 onwards, while it demonstrated the existence of a tribunal which could and would decide what the judges of 1460 had refused to touch, complicated doctrine by consistently overriding such notions of legitimacy as existed. The Henrician succession acts deprived heirs hitherto totally legitimate, and the King's will, whose efficacy rested on statute, destabilized things further by preferring the heirs of his younger sister to those of his elder. The coalescence of threats to the realm with a variety of claims produced the agitation over the succession which filled the 1560s with pamphlets and debate. Elizabeth found it impossible to name an heir. Her personal preference was, if anything, for that fellow-Queen of Scotland whom her protestant subjects abominated, but above all she had in her person sufficiently experienced the menace of conspiracies and plots that would gather around heirs-apparent. She wished to have no

[17] *Proc.* 44–5. [18] Chrimes and Brown, 215.

such centres of disaffection in the realm – or outside it. Yet she could very easily have been dead when the Parliament of 1563 met, and those who remembered that disputed successions led to civil wars had history and sense on their side.[19]

So in the two sessions of the second Parliament, in 1563 and 1566, the demand that she should marry and that, so long as no heir of her body existed, she should name her successor, grew vociferous and took up endless time. That fact is not in dispute; what needs to be established is the source of those loud and time-consuming protests. The issue came up at once, in the sermon preached at the opening of Parliament on 12 January 1563 by Alexander Nowell, dean of St Paul's. After pious prayer and an outline of a legislative programme that would help create a godly commonwealth, Nowell adverted to the absence of a safe succession. Addressing the Queen directly, he did his preacher's duty by reminding her of the fact of mortality so recently brought to mind by her illness. 'When I heard,' he went on, 'of the calling of this Parliament I was thereby encouraged, hoping and not doubting that there shall be such order taken and good laws established' – one of them, he hinted, to settle the succession to the Crown.[20] Exiled under Mary and one of the truly long-lived men of the century, Nowell was unquestionably a radical in religion of whom Elizabeth came to disapprove, though his failure to obtain a bishopric would seem ascribable to his own reluctance to seek that promotion. More to the point, however, he belonged to the clientage of the Dudley family at a time when Lord Robert had reason to think that a call to the Queen to marry might promote himself into a royal consort.[21] Nowell's homiletic discourse on the uncertain succession is most unlikely to have been totally spontaneous and without ulterior purpose; rather it suggests that someone used him to foreshadow the revival of the petition presented in the previous session. If that was so, the future earl of Leicester and his supporters offer themselves as the most likely Council faction to work up steam for the general hope that Elizabeth might act. Dudley had been engaged since January 1562 in preparing the ground for a campaign to get the succession settled. In that month he brought the tragedy *Gorboduc* from the Inns to Court, so that the Queen might hear its message to responsible rulers who wished to

[19] Cf. Mortimer Levine, *The Early Elizabethan Succession Question, 1558–1568* (Stanford, 1966); Marie Axton, *The Queen's Two Bodies: Drama and the Elizabethan Succession* (London, 1977).

[20] BL, Cotton MS Titus F.i., fos. 61r–64v (printed in *Nowell's Catechism*, ed. G. E. Corrie [Parker Soc. 1853], 223–9). Neale (*EP* I, 95) regards the sermon as an 'incitement' to the agitators in the Commons.

[21] Collinson, *Puritan Movement*, 46, 63; cf. William Haugaard, *Elizabeth and the English Reformation*, index s.n. Nowell lived from *c.* 1507 to 1602.

avoid disaster after their own demise.[22] One of the authors of that tragedy was Thomas Norton whose parliamentary career had begun in Mary's last Parliament and resumed in 1563; the other was Thomas Sackville who sat for the last time in 1563–6, being created Lord Buckhurst in 1567. The outlines of a temporary Dudley faction in the Commons are certainly discernible.

It is therefore no wonder that the issue of the succession quickly came up again in the Parliament when it met in January 1563. Councillors not of Dudley's faction were only vaguely prepared for it but even so not surprised. On the 14th, Cecil, writing to Sir Thomas Smith in France, expected a short session, 'for the matters of moment like to pass are not many'. He named the revival of felonies first enacted under Henry VIII[23] and the subsidy, but not artificers. However, he knew enough of other people's intentions to add. 'I think somewhat will be attempted to ascertain the realm of a successor to this Crown, but I fear the unwillingness of her majesty to have such a person known will stay the matter.'[24] The attempt came promptly on the 16th when 'a burgess' (perhaps Norton?) moved in a long speech for action on the succession. The motion was debated 'by divers wise personages' on the 18th, and on the following day a committee chaired by the comptroller (Sir Edward Rogers) was appointed to cooperate with the Speaker in drawing up articles for a petition to the Queen.[25] We have record of only one speech in the debate, an address by Sir Ralph Sadler, an established bureaucrat trained by Thomas Cromwell and a privy councillor at least since 1540.[26] Speaking from long experience, he delivered a diatribe against the Scots, that is to say against the candidature of Mary Stuart: no right-thinking Englishman should contemplate having a person from north of the Tweed on the throne. He related a conversation he had had in the 1540s with Sir Adam Otterburn, Scottish envoy to Henry VIII, who had assured him that despite the treaty of Greenwich (1543) the Scots would never suffer an English monarch. 'Now,' cried Sadler,

> if these proud, beggarly Scots did so much disdain to yield to the superiority of England that they chose rather to be perjured and to abide the extremity of the wars and force of England than they would consent an Englishman to be their king by such lawful means of marriage, why should we for any respect yield to

[22] Levine, 39–44; Axton, 39–41.
[23] Above, pp 110–11.
[24] BL, Lansdowne MS 102, fo. 18.
[25] *CJ* I, 62–3.
[26] *Proc.* 87–9. Sadler had been of the Privy Council since 1540, and, after intermitting attendance during Mary's reign, resumed his seat on Elizabeth's accession. The statement sometimes made that he was off the Council between 1559 and 1567 is in error. The Council register is missing between 23 January and 10 August 1563; both before and after these dates, Sadler, engaged on Scottish affairs, was rarely if ever at court.

their Scottish superiority or consent to establish a Scot in succession to the crown of this realm?

Apart from abominating Scotsmen, Sadler rested his case on the law which did not permit a foreigner to own land in England and by that same token much more prohibited him ruling the land. He is unlikely to have been egged on by Dudley, but his opinion chimed well with the favourite's who hoped that when the Queen had named an English heir she would be free and eager to marry him. It also, of course, suited well the likes of Norton who wanted to make sure that there should be no catholic queen. In fact, the agitation of 1563 aimed quite as much at keeping out Mary as at preventing uncertainty in case the Queen died; the 'party' calling for action came together from a mixture of motives and under the guidance of a councillor (Dudley) who was not even a member.

On 26 January the committee reported to the House and Norton read out the petition they had drafted. The privy councillors in the House were instructed to ask the Queen for an audience at which the whole House, through the mouth of the Speaker, would present that petition. Rogers, about to carry some bills to the Lords, was told to seek the cooperation of the Upper House, which he did; he was able to report that the Lords liked the Commons' proceedings well.[27] So on the 28th, Speaker Williams presented the Commons' document at court, with the House in attendance.[28] He thanked the Queen for assembling her Parliament not only to remedy defects in the common weal but also for securing the safety of the realm, as (he said) the lord keeper had instructed them at the beginning. Bacon had indeed mentioned such need but he had given no hint of the interpretation which Williams now put on his words, namely that in this respect the Commons could see nothing more urgent than the settling of the future of the Crown. Therefore: would she please marry whomsoever she pleased and declare her successor, for in the last act to declare the descent of the Crown (1543) she had formed the end of the chain appointed by Henry VIII. Elizabeth spoke gently.[29] So great a matter, she said, needed careful thought; she could not reply at once. She knew she was mortal and had a duty to think about what might happen if she died. She would therefore let them have their answer after due deliberations. However, she took the opportunity to aim a blow against those whom she regarded as particular trouble-makers. Hoping to 'discharge some restless heads in whose brains the needless hammers beat with vain judgment that I should mislike this

[27] *CJ* I, 53–4.
[28] Ibid. 64; *Proc.* 90–3.
[29] Ibid. 94–5.

their petition', she made it clear that 'of the matter and sum thereof' she approved very well – a plain and diplomatic untruth.

The initiative now passed to the Lords who four days later, on 1 February, presented their parallel petition through their Speaker, the lord keeper. It looks very much as though the promoters of the cause thought themselves more likely to succeed if they hammered Elizabeth twice in quick sequence. Bacon spoke at greater length and with more orderly skill than Williams but to the same purpose; and according to the Spanish ambassador Elizabeth took no trouble to conceal her anger at finding her nobility support the 'restless heads' in the Commons.[30] She plainly knew that the agitation really came from within her Court and Council and hoped to put an end to it. But the organized campaign continued. Her sharp words did not prevent the elderly Lord Rich from next day backing up the petition with a private – and rather fatherly – letter of his own.[31] Another peer, whom ill health had prevented from attending the audience, wrote in even more patronizing terms to press the need for action. His licence to absent himself he had obtained through the good services of Robert Dudley: one wonders who had suggested that he might do some good by writing.[32] The Lords were not united – the Spanish ambassador reported after this meeting that some disliked Dudley's motives and manoeuvres[33] – but just about all agreed about the need to move the Queen to abandon her inactive and contemplative posture.

If Elizabeth thought that she could hide behind the pretence that she was giving the matter deep thought, she was mistaken. As Cecil reported to Smith on 7 February, 'the heads of both Houses are fully occupied with the provision of surety of the realm, if God to our plague should call the Queen's majesty without leaving of children'.[34] He preferred to profess a neutral attitude: 'The matter is so deep that I cannot reach into it; God send it a good issue.' That is to say, he was aware of the forces at work but knew Elizabeth well enough to prefer for the time being to sit on the fence. He was pulled off it when five days later the Commons urged the privy councillors among them to remind the Queen of the need to answer their petition, but got a predictable rebuff. Rogers and Cecil, coming from the Court, reported her as saying that the senior men in

[30] Ibid. 58–62. For the date see Neale, *EP* I, 109.

[31] Ibid. 110–11. Rich, solicitor general at the trial of Sir Thomas More, but lord chancellor under Edward VI, had with age lost his earlier suppleness of conscience and acquired self-importance.

[32] John Strype, *Annals of the Reformation* (ed. Oxford, 1824), II, ii, 652–8.

[33] Levine, 56.

[34] BL, Lansdowne MS 102, fo. 20v. By 'heads' he did not here mean the leading members but the brains of all the members of both Houses.

the House knew well enough that she had not forgotten; as for the 'young heads', they might 'take example of the ancients'.[35] And that was all that the Commons got out of her in this session. In the Lords another attempt was made to resolve the deadlock when on 24 March a bill was introduced to provide against a vacancy of the throne. If the Queen would not settle the succession, perhaps she could be persuaded to agree to an act which set up a regency government in case of her demise and left it to the Parliament to choose her successor. The one extant part of that bill was drafted and heavily corrected by Cecil, now off his fence,[36] and the move was followed up with yet another address from Bacon (with all the Lords present) who urged that if she could not bring herself to choose a successor she should comfort herself and the realm by marrying.[37] He had to admit that the bill had found no favour in the Lords, perhaps because it did not in fact settle the central point at issue, or because the suggestion that the Parliament might appoint the occupant of the throne was entirely unprecedented, assigned a totally new role to it, and in its likely production of strife was distinctly dangerous. But Elizabeth stood them all off. At the close, Speaker Williams alluded to the most obvious part of the session's business only by hoping that the Queen would take the Commons' 'doings in good part'. Elizabeth, at her most gnomic, declared that as a prince she was not vowed to the unmarried state which as a private woman she would prefer, and that the problem of the succession was too serious to be quickly decided. At least, that is what she seems to have been saying; she encapsulated her meaning in verbiage.[38]

The agitation had solved nothing because the Queen had not wished to solve anything. Cecil had felt sure of this outcome by 18 February, and as the session drew to a close he declared it to have been unsatisfactory.[39] As we have seen, in the end he and Bacon tried to save something by their regency bill which avoided the immediate issue of the succession and could not, therefore, satisfy the Dudley faction. Neither secretary nor lord keeper had been responsible for bringing the issue to the boil at the beginning of the Parliament but they had been in there fighting at the end. Initiatives had come from Dudley and his client Nowell, from Norton who, as we know, always looked to cooperate with the Council and proved agreeable to Dudley because one had delivered and the other absorbed the message contained in *Gorboduc*, from Sadler and from Rich. These are the only names mentioned in the affair, and

[35] *CJ* I, 65. [36] SP 12/28, fos. 68–9.
[37] *Proc.* 63–5. I accept the dating of these events in Neale, *EP* I, 112.
[38] *Proc.* 109–10, 114–15.
[39] BL, Lansdowne MS 102, fos. 22, 29v.

four of them were councillors. Everything else must be conjecture, especially the dreams spun by Neale about an independent Lower House. The ascertainable facts point to action from within the Council which used the impatience current in both Houses to put pressure on the Queen. If there was any planning afoot, the evidence points only to the immediate revival of the issue in the Commons and to the careful wheeling of the Lords into the firing line after the Commons had mounted the first assault. All in all, though the Queen knew that the Commons contained hot-headed men who needed cooling off, no one at the time can have supposed that the demands had been spontaneous or put forward by an opposition fighting against the Council.

That the Queen also knew who had heated up those hotheads emerges from her actions after the Parliament had been prorogued. As late as November 1564 Bacon fell into Elizabeth's ill graces 'upon suspicion that he had dealt in the matter of succession'; though he denied the charge, he had not been innocent in 1563.[40] Another man, much closer to the Queen, felt her displeasure much earlier. Late in March 1563 she began to hint to visiting Scottish envoys that she knew of a good candidate for the hand of the Queen of Scots, and though for nearly a year she did not reveal the name she had in mind everybody knew from the first that she meant Robert Dudley. This bizarre move has called forth varied reactions, from thinking it 'a diplomatic comedy' to calling it a result of 'the mental torment' into which the session of 1563 had thrown her.[41] To me it seems a good deal more likely that we have here one of Elizabeth's cruel jokes. If her Robin would try to force her hand in Parliament and thus obtain his seat on the throne, he would be taught a lesson by being offered to the Queen of Scots and a throne he did not want. This revenge had agreeably varied uses. It proved helpful in Elizabeth's endeavours to stop Mary from marrying at all, and it kept Dudley quiet because he could hardly make a scene when it was suggested that he should marry a queen, even though it was the wrong one. Elizabeth did not keep the game going until Mary outflanked her in July 1565 by marrying Lord Darnley; she indicated that she had tired of it and that all was again well between her and Dudley when at Michaelmas 1564 she made him earl of Leicester. But meanwhile she had played with his self-respect for some eighteen months because she knew well enough that it was Dudley who had 'made' the Parliament of 1563 against her.

When Elizabeth prorogued this Parliament she left behind two

[40] BL, Harleian MS 36, fo. 348v (in Cecil's private diary of political events).
[41] MacCaffrey, *Shaping*, 162–6; Neale, *EP* I, 111.

promises: she meant to marry if she could find the right man, and she would settle the succession when the issue became manageable. At the time those loose commitments looked like a handy way out of trouble, but they stayed in the memory and could be raised against her. Moreover, the prorogation left her with the prospect of again encountering the same people, now trained in disbelieving her promises and in parliamentary ways possibly effective in frustrating her escaping tricks. Before need for money compelled her to recall the Parliament in the autumn of 1566, the issues of marriage and succession continued to rumble at the centre of politics; indeed, both grew more troublesome in ways that made a future confrontation in Parliament more likely and more difficult.

In those years, the negotiations for Elizabeth's hand to which Cecil had pinned his hopes and his policy became ever less convincing; it seemed ever more likely that she really intended to stay unmarried. As for the succession, that developed into a straightforward contest between the descendants of her two aunts, and the problems of opting for either grew no fewer. The senior, Stuart, line improved its position when Mary married in Darnley a man entitled to inherit land in England and then produced a son who would be available to keep the succession safe for another generation. Mary, always given to overplaying her hand, grew so confident that she made peaceful relations with her English cousin depend on being 'by Parliament established heir apparent, or adopted daughter of the Queen's majesty'.[42] The junior, Grey, line, represented by the imprisoned Catherine countess of Hertford, could still claim under Henry VIII's will. The first claimant remained a catholic, a fact which made the second the choice of apprehensive protestants. Both the options so posed were distasteful to the Queen who also continued to fear the creation of a reversionary interest as a centre for disaffection. Yet the failure to solve the problem caused widespread fears for the stability of throne and realm, apprehensions certainly shared by the Privy Council which also was split between the two potential heiresses. It was certain that the recalled Parliament would revive the agitation, and as soon as its forthcoming assembly became known pressure mounted in pamphlets and flysheets. Some popular opinion blamed Cecil for the Queen's failure to act, but that overrated his influence.[43]

The interval between the two sessions had been well analysed before this, and the 1566 session itself has received thorough attention. However, previous accounts have depended on the theory of an organized puritan pressure group in the Lower House, a nonexistent entity.[44] It

[42] BL, Harleian MS 36, fo. 348. [43] Ibid. fo. 352.

[44] Esp. Neale, *EP* I, 129–64. The account in Levine, ch. 10, is better but understandably accepts too much of Neale's interpretation. Some of the extant documents are undated

is therefore necessary to go through the main events once more, so as to identify the sources of the violent agitation which brought relations between the Queen and the two Houses very close to a real breakdown. Several scholars have pointed out that the session started hesitantly, with the first fortnight devoted to sorting out the position of members brought in through bye-elections and to a number of bills, and this hesitancy has been ascribed to fears at court of giving independents in the Commons a chance to make trouble. True, for a while the great matter which everybody expected to come up again remained dormant. This, of course, suited the Queen, but it was not she who directed the business of Parliament. The real cause seems to have been a division in the Privy Council where Leicester apparently favoured the Queen of Scots while Norfolk supported Catherine Grey.[45] These divisions also delayed the introduction of the subsidy, from the Queen's point of view the main business of the session. Divided as it was, the Council simply could not get the Queen to take the kind of action that would prevent trouble in Parliament. Finally the duke of Norfolk took the cow by the horns and reminded Elizabeth of her unfulfilled promises; he begged her to allow the Parliament to resume discussion but drew only a furious rebuff.[46] The Council therefore decided to introduce the subsidy bill even at the risk of starting independent action in the Lower House which had been sure to remain quiet so long as a continuing session was guaranteed by the absence of the money bill. The House was likely to get alarmed if it seemed possible that, with supply granted, the session might end and the great cause still remain unsettled.

On 17 October, the senior privy councillor – Sir Edward Rogers, comptroller of the Household – took up the lord keeper's introduction of Elizabeth's financial needs; his motion was supported in a brilliant speech by Cecil.[47] We have already shown that Neale's treatment of the subsidy as an instrument used by an opposition determined upon the settlement of the succession is mistaken; the money bill went its own way and, because it imposed an unusually heavy tax, encountered its own difficulties, though a few people tried to tie the two things together.[48] Immediately, reaction to the demand was hostile, which explains the motion made next day which Neale read as a prearranged manoeuvre to use supply against the Queen. In effect, the opposite was nearer the truth. On the 18th, John Molyneux moved 'for the reviving of the suit for succession and to proceed with the subsidy'; that is to say, he wished

and placing them must involve conjecture; my conjecture now and again differs from Neale's.

[45] Levine, 172–3.

[46] Ibid. 174.

[47] *CJ* I, 74.

[48] Above, pp. 162–5.

to see no further deadlock over supply which might prevent the House from renewing the petition concerning marriage and succession.[49]

Who was Molyneux? He never sat in any Parliament but this one; he played no other known part in it or anywhere else in politics; and he had not been involved in the succession debates of 1563. Nor was he a radical protestant but rather inclined to conservatism. The pasquil, for obvious reasons, called him 'the mover' and attached to him a biblical tag – 'who shall rule over the people of Israel' – which also reflects his taking of the initiative over the succession but assigns to him no identifiable opinion. Insofar as he had any connection with an aristocratic patron it lay with the earl of Rutland, and the link was somewhat tenuous. However, the current earl (Edward Manners) had only in 1563 succeeded to the title and had not yet taken up any position in politics, nor was he of the Council, but he had been a ward of Cecil's. Cecil had taken the decision to bring in the subsidy and urgently wanted it to prosper. Cecil had earlier recorded his resentment at being blamed for the Queen's prevarications over the succession. Cecil, moreover, as was his habit, had sorted out his ideas on the subject in a paper of reflections which dissected the issues quite prophetically.[50] The most, he argued, that could be desired was 'both marriage and stability of succession'. 'The uttermost that can be denied' was the refusal of both. To ask for marriage 'is most natural, most easy, most plausible' to the Queen. On the other hand, 'the certainty of succession is most plausible to all the people'. Yet the second 'is hardest to be obtained' because the rival candidates are difficult to discuss in view of the factiousness involved and the uncertainties hanging about the pretenders' rights. Also, the Queen's consent is most unlikely in view of her suspicions against any named heir. He concluded that it would be best to concentrate on the marriage and to proceed to the second topic only if every approach on the first were to fail. In the true Cecilian manner, the note spells out the obvious but also indicates a line of policy adopted from the first and in essence adhered to by him through the session.

Thus much the most probable conjecture makes Molyneux act on behalf of a councillor – indeed, the councillor most concerned to see policy accomplished. The aim then would have been to get the current marriage negotiations brought to fruition and to hold the dangerous issue of the succession in reserve. That these were the tactics adopted is indicated by the immediate intervention of Sir Ralph Sadler, one of Cecil's allies

[49] *CJ* I, 74.

[50] SP 12/40, fo. 195, in Cecil's hand. The paper looks much more like Cecil's accustomed analyses for his own use than like the notes for a speech which Neale seems to have taken it for.

on the Council, who forcefully backed the secretary's policy.[51] Molyneux's double-headed motion gave him the chance to concentrate on the subsidy, for which he offered reasoned support at some length. Turning to the succession, he hoped that it would not be linked with the money bill; he advised against even appearing to be offering a deal – 'if her majesty will grant us the one we will the more willingly grant her the other'. Thus he spelt out the distinction rather than the merging, which (it has here been argued) was what Molyneux had been after, who also meant to separate the two. Sadler agreed that like everybody else he too hungered and thirsted for a settled succession, but he could not see 'how we can deal with it unless it came from the Queen's majesty'. It should be left to the Queen and the nobility, being 'a matter far out of our reach and compass'. Like every good diplomat he hinted that if everyone knew the scene as well as he did they would follow his advice; and seeing how involved he was in the intricacies of Anglo-Scottish relations, he probably spoke the truth. He had heard the Queen promise to marry: that should be enough for the present.

So the whole business was revived by a conciliar manoeuvre which accepted that if the money bill was to go forward marriage and the succession would have to be allowed back on the agenda, which recognized the advantages to Council policy if parliamentary pressure could be brought to bear on Elizabeth, and which hoped to minimize potential damage by concentrating at once on marriage and avoiding a petition for the succession which, as these councillors knew very well, would merely infuriate the Queen. But though Cecil could set the stage, he could not immediately control the play. Against advice, the House decided it wished 'to recontinue their suit and to know her highness' answer'.[52] This decision reflects less a united House led by a single and organized group who knew what they wanted than a collection of interests who for the moment all worked in the same direction. One could support a petition to the Queen to settle the succession because one wished to promote the Grey interest or the Stuart interest, or – and this seems to have been the commonest motive – because anything seemed better if the Queen should die than no known successor at all. No one was more convinced of that fact than the Privy Council, saddled with the responsibility, and they really made the moves. Elizabeth's inflexibility, however, ensured that less pliable or less well informed members of the House would take advantage of such moves to press their own refusal to abandon the chase after the unobtainable.

In the first instance, the privy councillors tried once more to prevent

[51] *Proc.* 141–4; *CJ* I, 74 confirms that this is the speech made on 18 Oct. and adds an important detail.

[52] *CJ* I, 74.

a serious clash between the Commons and their Queen. On the 19th, Cecil spoke again; in an attempt to allow tempers to cool while maintaining pressure on Elizabeth, he made some concessions to the prevailing mood.[53] He once more advocated securing the Queen's marriage but agreed that the security of the succession mattered greatly and should be petitioned for. However, seeing that at present there was no hope of achieving it, he suggested a short prorogation in the course of which the marriage, well under way, would be achieved; after that, when the Parliament reconvened, they might take another look at the succession in new circumstances. Sir Francis Knollys, Sir Ambrose Cave and Sir Edward Rogers all spoke in support: the Privy Council now stood united in their tactical use of Parliament to break down the Queen's obstinacy. A long debate ensued and the House stood firm; a majority wished to go on with the petition and to send a committee (all the privy councillors and forty-four members) to consider cooperation with the Lords, a step accepted two days later (Monday, 21 October).[54] It looked as though it might be awkward to coordinate things with the other House; if the Spanish ambassador judged correctly (and in this case he probably did), the Lords under Leicester's guidance contained a party for the Queen of Scots, while the Commons, predominantly good protestants, mostly favoured the countess of Hertford.[55] Here lay the weakness of the moderate councillors' plotting: as his private memorandum had made plain, Cecil had little love for either interest. The Queen had hoped that the Lords would not come in at all with the Lower House, and she proved right to the extent that they tried to get a settlement from her before necessity compelled them to accept the Commons' invitation. A deputation waited upon Elizabeth on the 21st, to ask for a decision or an end to the Parliament before any money was voted: the tactics of pressure. But manifest pressure never worked with Elizabeth who confined herself to angry words. Several peers, especially the earls of Pembroke and Leicester, went through a period of severe disfavour.[56]

So, at last, on the 23rd, the Commons committee conferred with the peers and presented their draft petition. The occasion was reported back to the Lower House by a privy councillor (Rogers) but, as he explained, the reading to the Lords had been left to three of the forty-four non-Council members: Robert Bell, Robert Monson and Richard Kingsmill.[57] The last named, a member of the most powerful protestant clan in Hampshire, can be called a genuine independent; Bell owed his seat at King's Lynn at least in part to the duke of Norfolk, and Monson,

[53] *Proc.* 164–5. [54] *CJ* I, 75. [55] Levine, 173.
[56] Ibid. 176; Neale, *EP* I, 141–3; BL, Harleian MS 36, fo. 352v.
[57] *CJ* I, 75.

who sat for the city of Lincoln, had patronage connections with the earls of Rutland and Bedford, both supporters of the protestant cause and the latter a councillor and good friend to Cecil.[58] Bell and Monson were to make careers in the law under government sponsorship and most of the time acted as policy agents in Parliament on the Council's behalf. Thus it would be very rash to treat any of the three as playing at this time the game of opposition and independent initiative, though they had a deep concern for the cause of religion and the safety of the realm. But it should by now be plain that such attitudes did not distinguish them from the conciliar leadership of the House. Very probably they had taken a lead in the drafting of the petition and for that reason were chosen to explain the document to the Upper House; in the pasquil's review of that drafting committee they follow as a group straight after Molyneux the mover, being called orator, prover and collector, terms which indicate that they had done the serious work of putting the petition together. No doubt the activists were at this point running a little ahead of the councillors (who after all sat in that committee too but would be careful not to let their guiding hand appear in public), but those three were men who normally served Council politics. Their prominence may suggest the existence of Council factions impatient with Cecil's Fabian tactics.

In the course of the next week the two Houses worked out a joint strategy and petition, in the slow-moving manner of large committees, but just as they were ready to ask for an audience, Elizabeth, clearly kept informed of every move and speech made, beat them to the draw.[59] On 5 November she summoned thirty members from each House to hear her views. There was no petition ready, and on this occasion all the talking was done by the Queen, in a blistering speech.[60] She poured out her anger at protests which seemed to suggest that she did not have the good of the realm at heart, protested that once she had promised to marry her good faith should not be called in question by constant reminders and grew sarcastic at the insolence of the foot eager to direct the head in so weighty a cause as the succession. She exaggerated a valid point when she questioned the good sense of a demand over the details of which the demanders themselves were widely divided: 'They would have twelve or thirteen limited in succession, and the more the better.' At the present,

[58] Read, *Cecil*, 243.

[59] Levine, 179–80. It seems clear that it was in late October that Cecil's suggestion of a prorogation was fruitlessly brought to the Queen's attention.

[60] *Proc.* 146–9. All the accounts speak of 30 peers and 30 commoners, but the committee named in the Lords ran only to 28 names (*LJ* 1, 641). The Commons delegation selected by the Speaker (*CJ* 1, 76) included all eight privy councillors and only six of the first drafting committee; Molyneux, Bell, Monson and Kingsmill were not on it (*Proc.* 145–6).

she repeated, the succession could not be discussed without serious danger to herself, and she wished to hear no petition for it. But even in her fury she employed guile. She must have known the role played in the agitation by her councillors and great men of the realm, but she wanted no quarrel with them and found scapegoats. Though she directed her anger indiscriminately at both Houses, she singled out 'Mr Bell with his accomplices' in the Commons, and two unnamed bishops – 'domini doctores' – in the Upper. Bell's group, she pretended, ruined the chances of an agreement by running away with a cause which proper gravity could have brought to a happy conclusion: a manifest flag of truce for the councillors quaking at her fury. As for the bishops, how could they talk about the settlement of the succession when in 1553, after Edward's death, they had preached sermons in which she and her sister were declared to be bastards? Which bishops she had in mind we do not know, and her attack gave the activists in the Upper House a chance to retreat more or less unscathed; but it is of interest to hear that protestant fears about the Queen of Scots were backed in the Lords by leaders of the spiritualty.[61]

Next day, Rogers and Cecil reported a bowdlerized version of the speech to the House: the Queen would marry but the time was not ripe to consider the succession.[62] Perhaps it had been a mistake to leave Bell and his 'accomplices' out of the thirty members brought to court; hearing the Queen's own words might have abashed them, as clearly the experience ended the Lords' willingness to pursue the matter further. As it was, the attempt to put an end to the agitation misfired: the House received the report in mutinous silence. And two days later the whole business revived with a vengeance. This second phase of the dispute saw the Commons go it alone, but even this more explosive situation reveals the successful revival of Cecilian management.

On 8 November one William Lambarde made 'a learned oration' for the resumption of the suit concerning the succession 'and thereupon reasoned strongly for both parts'.[63] The text of the speech, lost for a long time in unsorted papers, turned up at the Public Record Office in the

[61] The only person to hold a bishopric both in 1553 and 1566 was John Scory, bishop of Chichester on the first occasion and of Hereford on the second. The Queen's words, however, say no more than that two clerics, now bishops, had thirteen years earlier preached against her rights.

[62] *CJ* I, 76; *Proc.* 150–3.

[63] *CJ* I, 76. Despite Neale and the HPT, this was not William Lambarde the famous antiquary. The very strong case against this identification put up by Retha M. Warnicke, *William Lambarde: Elizabethan Antiquary 1536–1601* (London, 1973), 17–22, receives further support from the speech rediscovered since that book was written. The speaker referred to a political dispute in which he had become involved in 1554 when the antiquary was only eighteen years old.

early 1970s.[64] It was indeed a powerful discourse which at length argued away the various reasons the Queen had offered in explanation of her inability to deal with the succession at that time. The House, he proclaimed, also had a duty to look to the safety of the nation. His crucial point came towards the end: 'I have prepared a bill...' That bill was to offer a supply (the subsidy and two fifteenths already in hand) 'to obtain her majesty's loving, willing and favourable consent unto this weighty cause'. Thus the threat, present from the first, that the succession might be traded for a money grant appeared to have become real, but in a very curious way. Subsidy bills were very long indeed and required highly expert attention; it is difficult to see what Lambarde's bill may have looked like. Was it a full-scale instrument the preamble of which recorded the terms of exchange? Was it for an act settling the succession in whose preamble the promise of a grant was mentioned? The simple fact is that a bill doing what Lambarde claimed his did was totally impossible, a fact which indicates that he did not so much have a bill as made a move to get things going again.

The real subsidy bill of the session had been read a first time on 28 October, and although it was evidently held up by the business of the succession the nine working days that had elapsed since then do not constitute a major delay.[65] Nevertheless, something seemed advisable if the timetable of the session was not to get into real confusion. According to the Spanish ambassador, the man who broke the dam was Cecil who, de Quadra had learned, had got the House to restart on the money bill.[66] That makes it very likely indeed that he was behind Lambarde's move. We know very little about this William Lambarde, but what we know is suggestive. He sat for Aldborough in Yorkshire, a duchy of Lancaster borough where at this time Sir Ambrose Cave, Cecil's conciliar ally, exercised the patronage, and he later had contacts with Cecil.[67] The secretary's fine Italic hand (considering Cecil's handwriting, perhaps an unfortunate metaphor) appears out of the murk. If this was what happened, Cecil was playing a potentially dangerous game, though certainly not one outside his proven capacity to take chances. No one knew better than he how implacably opposed his sovereign was to any further talk of the succession, or how she would react to blackmail. On the other hand, no one also knew better how urgently the money was needed, in addition to which he certainly shared the general desire to

[64] SP 46/166, fos. 3r–11v, printed in *Proc.* 129–44. The editor inclined to ascribe the speech to John Molyneux and treated it as the opening shot in the whole campaign (ibid. 120); for some reason he missed the identification of Lambarde as the orator which appears at the head of the manuscript, itself a later copy.

[65] *CJ* I, 75.

[66] *Cal. SP Span. 1558–1567*, 588.

[67] Warnicke, *Lambarde*, loc. cit.

provide for a settled succession. Thus, deprived of a peaceful solution by Elizabeth's fierce reaction on the 5th, though possibly also encouraged by her aside on the chances of an agreement if everything was left to wise heads in the House, he took the risk.

In actual fact, the manoeuvre incorporated in Lambarde's move was subtle enough to stem from Cecil's mind. There could be no question of reading, let alone passing, a bill for the succession, and one may wonder if anyone ever saw this spectral bill, but the apparent introduction of one put the hotter heads in the House into a joyful mood. Lambarde was soon on his feet again to thank members for their reaction to it.[68] But that is the last we hear of the bill. In his speech of thanks, Lambarde also revealed that he had in addition the draft of a petition ready prepared, and he asked the Speaker to have the clerk read it to the House, so that after a quick word with the Lords it might be presented to the Queen that very afternoon. This was to rush things beyond the feasible, but the House had now been put into a mood of believing that a petition – the move that had already proved pointless – would be a sensible thing to attempt once more, and Cecil stood prepared to get one written. First, however, he had to sit out a major storm. The news of the proposal goaded Elizabeth into another Tudor-style fury, and on the day after Lambarde's speech Knollys reported the Queen's 'express commandment' to cease all discussion and rest content with her promise to marry. Cecil and Rogers supported him, to wait for quieter waters.[69] But it was this command which provoked Paul Wentworth's three questions and with them further troublesome delays; the earlier champions of the cause also revived as 'Mr Bell and Mr Monson made troubles over motions in the Parliament about the succession'.[70] On the 12th, Speaker Onslow, coming late into the House from a clearly hair-raising interview with the Queen, repeated her interdict on further debate – her answer to Wentworth. At this point Cecil came into the open. Whatever petition it was that Lambarde had prepared dropped out of sight; instead one was drafted by the secretary and brought to the House on 16 November.[71] A quite new tone had entered the discussion. The petition was full of humble devotion and profound apology for any unfavourable impression created; it accepted the Queen's instruction to drop all talk of the succession; and it looked forward to a happy and fruitful marriage. A diplomatic concession to the more radical members appeared in a brief

[68] *Proc.* 140. [69] *CJ* I, 75.

[70] BL, Harl. MS 36, fo. 353. Cecil dated the event to 14 Nov., and while not all his dates are entirely correct this dating at least indicates that we are not hearing about the first phase of the dispute.

[71] *Proc.* 155–7. The three drafting stages reveal Cecil's responsibility for the document: SP 12/41, fos. 38–48.

reference to freedom of speech, Cecil himself adding the words accustomed lawful liberties'. In effect Cecil called off the revival of the issue which he had himself instigated and returned to the position he had occupied at the beginning of the session. Peace was now the first consideration, but if his tactics had worked he might have obtained the marriage in return for peace.

It seems unlikely that this petition was ever presented, but it received sufficient acceptance in the House for the Queen also to withdraw from her dangerously exposed position. On the 24th she went over a draft of Cecil's for a message to the House and next day delivered it to the Speaker. In it she cancelled her earlier demands and in turn made her peace with the Commons. The move worked perfectly. The House received her message 'most joyfully' and at last turned to the second reading of the subsidy bill.[72] Except for a ludicrous and abortive attempt to tie the Queen to her vague promises in the preamble of the subsidy bill,[73] the great agitation was over. However, looking back Cecil was not happy. As he noted in his diary, the duplicitous role he had played had first got him into trouble in a House unwilling to accept his emollient lead and then got him attacked by Sir Anthony Brown, justice of the Common Pleas and one of Mary Stuart's supporters.[74] Nor had his activities behind the scenes escaped the attentions of his difficult sovereign who was told that it was he who had lurked behind the Commons' obstinacy. Though he denied this in Council and she accepted his word, at least the events since 8 November supported the tale-bearers.[75] While in the end he abandoned the campaign as hopeless, he had certainly from the first taken his share in reviving the issue of the succession, as had other men in high places who used various members of the House. Interestingly enough, Norton seems to have played no part; either he had learned the lesson of 1563, or whoever had moved him before preferred to lie low in 1566. The final outcome left Cecil still dissatisfied, and his notes on this point strongly support the suspicion that he had tried to organize the whole session for the purpose of making the Queen give way. Instead, as he put it at the head of the 'memorial to the Queen at the end of the Parliament', 'The succession not answered, the marriage not followed.'[76] In the end Elizabeth had de-

[72] *CJ* I, 78; *Proc.* 160–2. The 'addition' to the message, which ordered the Speaker to stop at once any further speech on behalf of this or that particular successor, is very peculiar. The apparent signatures of eight privy councillors and four judges are all in Cecil's hand. Did he copy a real letter or invent a missive not used? It did contradict the restoration of free speech.

[73] Above, p. 164.

[74] BL, Harleian MS 36, fo. 353.

[75] Read, *Cecil*, 369.

[76] SP 12/41, fo. 76.

feated his purposes by breaking off the matrimonial negotiations which Cecil had confidently expected to be completed before the end of the year.

The full inwardness of the noisy disputes of 1563 and 1566 will never be entirely clear; absence of evidence makes sure of that. But all the indications are against the thesis of an independent initiative promoted from within the House of Commons. It was the Privy Council that originally advised the Queen to marry and name a successor; when it got nowhere with her at the Council Board it used the Parliament to augment the pressure on her. However, Elizabeth was quite prepared to stand out alone, against both Houses of Parliament as well as her Council, in a matter so particular to her royal person. In addition, using the Parliament on these issues turned out to be an unusually dangerous enterprise. Some members especially of the Lower House proved capable of reckless and politically unproductive action: egged on in the first instance by conciliar manoeuvres, they could not thereafter be restrained and came close to wrecking all relations with the Queen. At the end, Cecil managed to forestall that disaster, to provide for both sides a road back to normality, and to save the subsidy (at the cost of abandoning the exceptional demands first made).[77] But over the political issue it was the Queen who won. She did not at once forgive: her speech at the close, as we have seen, barely hid her fury.[78] Nor did she ever forget. The experience of 1566 perhaps taught her to be more careful about the management of the Commons, but above all it taught her to avoid long sessions thereafter, to the detriment of the promoters of many a useful bill. As for the man who unleashed it all, he too seems to have had enough. 'Regnaturus...super populum Israel' or not, John Molyneux never again sat in Parliament.[79]

MARY QUEEN OF SCOTS

In 1566 Elizabeth had forced both her Council and her Parliament to accept her determination to leave the succession uncertain, and she owed this Pyrrhic victory in great part to their belief that she really meant to marry. However, the problems did not go away, especially since she had no intention to take a husband from the admittedly deplorable specimens paraded before her. In 1568 tensions increased as the legitimate heir and the one candidate whom protestant opinion most decidedly did not want

[77] Above, p. 164. [78] Above, p. 329.

[79] Another petition to marry was presented by the Lower House in 1576, in an atmosphere of decent calm. It had been moved for by one John Croke, another Cecilian by the looks of it, and the Queen received it with gracious but empty words. A curious aftermath. (*CJ* I, 113–14; *Proc.* 462–4, 490).

to succeed fled her country and took refuge in England. The Queen of Scots was a nuisance in Scotland; as a guest or prisoner of Elizabeth she became an inescapable menace, a focal point for conspiracies against the Queen of England. The Queen's government overcame the crisis of 1569–71 – the northern rebellion, the papal bull of deposition, the Ridolfi plot and the treasonable dealings of the duke of Norfolk – without resort to Parliament, though that of 1571 assisted in sweeping up some of the aftermath with acts against traitors and importers of the bull.[80] Although one would have expected the still unsettled succession to come up again in those circumstances, it put in only an oblique appearance in the addition to the treason bill which Thomas Norton promoted. That general silence, so striking after all the noise of 1566, helps as much as the analysis of that earlier session's inwardness to illumine the truth about the political role of Parliament. In 1571 the Council did not want to add to the crisis by once more tackling the Queen's determination to leave her successor unnamed; therefore, the Commons never raised the point specifically. Norton's intervention, which sufficiently angered Elizabeth, may reflect the presence on the Council of a more determined section; someone (Burghley?) thought it would do no harm to test the temperature of that sea of troubles. Though Norton got some support in the Commons the ill-advised experiment was quickly dropped, and even the chance of at least eliminating the most disliked competitor from the race went by the board.

However, in the autumn and winter of 1571 the truth about the Ridolfi plot came into the open; by 16 January 1572, the duke of Norfolk stood condemned to a traitor's death, and Mary's involvement in treasonable plotting had been proved to a point where even Elizabeth could no longer avoid taking action. One result was the calling of the emergency Parliament which met on 8 May. In his opening address Bacon left no doubt that this was an extraordinary meeting. No money would be asked for and the purpose of the session he declared in the first place to be the making of laws for the Queen's safety, the risks to which had been revealed by the recently discovered conspiracies.[81] It is clear that in calling the Parliament Elizabeth had given way to pressure from her Council who had vainly tried to persuade her to allow the death sentence on Norfolk to be carried out and to do something about the standing threat posed by Mary Stuart.[82] These were to be the two great issues of

[80] Above, pp. 181–4.

[81] *Proc.* 317, 336.

[82] Neale, *EP* I, 241–2. Cf. Shrewsbury's letter to Burghley – absentee councillor to Council leader – expressing satisfaction at the calling of a Parliament (*Cal. SP Scotland*, IV, 311). The Queen agreed in part because alleged pressure from Parliament enabled her to put pressure on Mary (ibid. 325–6). The same trick was worked on James I in

the session, a session which is unusually well documented in memorials, draft bills and records of debate. The story does not need to be told again. Sir John Neale's account relates what happened, and Michael Graves's brief analysis conclusively proves that what did happen was orchestrated by the Privy Council.[83] Having obtained the creation of their instrument of pressure, the councillors, well assisted by their usual men of business, used it to the hilt. There was plenty of unorganized support in the Lower House for the demand that Norfolk be executed and in both Houses for steps against Mary, though even the Council was divided over the question whether she should die by the law. That division became manifest with the introduction of two bills against her – one for an act of attainder which would have procured her death, and another merely declaring her permanently incapable of inheriting the Crown of England. As usual, when her Council could not wholly agree Elizabeth knew how to exploit the difference, and as usual the Council's use of the Parliament against her ended in a compromise. Elizabeth sacrificed the duke of Norfolk and by allowing his execution to go forward on 2 June, halfway through the session, assuaged the clamour. Offered a choice of bills against Mary, with a majority in Council and Commons favouring the more drastic one, she accepted the lesser and then vetoed it, using the regular formula – *la reine s'avisera* – to pretend that in so terrible a matter she needed further advice before she could make up her mind to consent.[84]

The session of 1572 really provides a beautifully clear commentary on the function of parliamentary meetings in the handling of public affairs. The Parliament need never have got involved in the first place; neither law nor politics demanded its participation in the crisis created by Elizabeth's virgin state and the Queen of Scots' ambitions. The duke of Norfolk was dealt with by the ordinary processes of the law; Parliament could contribute nothing to his conviction, execution or pardon. Nor

1581 (ibid. 597). It, too, was not new: in the early stages of his quarrel with Rome, Henry VIII liked to pretend that opinion in Parliament forced him into adopting policies he did not like. It also had a long life, being e.g. still used by Castlereagh at the Congress of Vienna in 1815.

[83] Neale, *EP* I, 247–90; Graves, 'Management,' *Parliamentary History* 2 (1983), esp. 24–9.

[84] The bill she vetoed (*Proc.* 302–10) was a fairly extraordinary piece of drafting. Cast in the form of a petition from both Houses, it had a preamble well over half its total length in which the recent troubles were rehearsed in detail. This was evidently meant to provide the justification for proceeding without trial against a foreigner, possibly still a monarch (if the Scottish deposition were not to hold). This preamble would have acted as a major propaganda device, at home and (if translated) abroad, if the bill had passed. Thus the bill copied an invention of Thomas Cromwell's who had in effect prefaced the attainder without trial of the Nun of Kent and her accomplices (25 Henry VIII c. 12) with a propaganda pamphlet.

could Parliament usefully engage itself in the fate of Mary Stuart; condemnation by attainder, even without Elizabeth's refusal to contemplate it, was only doubtfully available in law against someone who was not a subject. When fifteen years later the tragedy finally had to be concluded by the axe, no one bothered to give Parliament an active part to play in it. It was to act solely as an instrument of propaganda, as Burghley said when he explained the reason for its assembly. Parliament was not called to do anything positive, but the Council, he remarked, thought it best to have one so as 'to make the burden better born and the world abroad better satisfaction'.[85]

Thus Parliament assembled in 1572 solely because one party in the real political conflict between the Queen and her advisers wished to use it as an arena in which to proclaim its purposes and as a weapon to force the other to give way. When it met, this party from first to last supervised all that was done or said, achieving complete success for its original intention, only to see that success wiped out at one blow by the other party: the simple device of exercising her right to withhold her consent enabled Elizabeth to do as she pleased, no matter what had been debated and resolved in eight crowded weeks. Without the monarch, the Lords and Commons had no power; without the Council, they even lacked the means for organizing themselves for any political purpose or for initiating a policy.

This degree of powerlessness, this dependence on sources of power outside itself, had always been the truth about the Parliament as a participant in national politics, and so it was to remain at the very least until the early nineteenth century. Parliament could be useful in marshalling opinion in support of a policy or discovering the degree of opposition to it; it could be employed in bringing an apparent consensus to bear on the agencies of power. But by itself it had neither power nor policies; it had no function apart from the granting of supply and the making of laws both general and private. Inasmuch as the courts refused to acknowledge the existence of new law not made in Parliament, and inasmuch as that body was technically in a position to provide or withhold the financial means of government, its function matters and mattered greatly. Interposed against arbitrary taxation and arbitrary legislation – though it by no means always succeeded in exercising these protective powers – it may fairly be said to have been an instrument for guarding certain liberties of the subject, though the liberties it was

[85] Cited Neale, *EP* II, 104. Neale went on to speak of 'the overwhelming pressure of Parliament'. As his own narrative shows, the Queen was not in the least influenced by events in Parliament when at last, and very reluctantly, she agreed to let Mary go to the block.

forever parading around the place were its own, to be most commonly used against the subject. But if it did stop a powerful executive from becoming an absolutist monarchy, it did so not by forming a counterpoise to the Crown but by assisting the Crown in lawful government.

In politics, Parliament was only a secondary instrument to be used or ignored by agencies whose real power base and arena of activity lay elsewhere – at Court or in Council. And even as in taxation and legislation the House of Commons took a greater share of the action than the House of Lords, so in matters of politics it was even weaker and more irrelevant than the peers upstairs. Many members of the Lords did have other power bases and institutionalized arenas of operations in which to give effect to policy: after all, the Upper House contained the leading councillors, the leaders of the localities, and the leaders of the Church. The ancillary role of the whole Parliament in assisting the Crown's policy, as for instance in the legislation which established the framework of the separate Church of England, was matched by the ancillary role which the Commons could play in assisting the politics of an aristocratic society. Both Crown and nobility at times found it useful to gain voice and noise from the Lower House where policy could become public and likely reactions could be sounded out. Parliament continued to exercise that function which had induced Edward I to summon it: it made the government of the realm more smoothly effective. And it also continued a function which the baronage of Edward II's reign had found so useful: it enabled an exasperated governing order to turn the king's instrument against him. But all talk of the rise of Parliament as an institution, or, worse, the rise of the House of Commons, into political prominence is balderdash.

In the reign of Henry VIII, politics in Parliament achieved their aim because the monarch, proprietor of Parliaments, took the lead. In the reign of Elizabeth, political debates in Parliament and especially in the Commons never achieved anything because the monarch was entirely free to ignore them and usually did so. In both reigns, politics in Parliament reflected the purposes of non-parliamentary agencies, resorting thither either because laws enforceable in the courts were needed or because failure had attended action in the normal places of political debate and strife. The old-established search, beloved by historians, for some growth or development in the political power and authority of Parliament and especially of the Commons is chimerical because in fact that power never changed in its fundamental characteristics: institutionally it remained near zero in 1640, 1649 and 1688, though on each occasion the House offered a convenient battlefield for the contestants and on the first the Lords provided a roof over the heads of a suddenly homeless Privy Council. The seventeenth century was to replace civil war and revolution by an apparently constitutional means to sanctify transfers of power which occurred elsewhere, usually the court, and occurred for reasons in which that constitutional means played no part; and the seventeenth century needed two civil wars and two revolutions to achieve that much. Ultimately the existence of Parliament, and especially of the Commons, made it possible to bring the raw contest for power out of the closet and make it look like orderly government – not an inconsiderable achievement but a very different one from that which traditional historiography ascribed to Parliament in the familiar story of the 'rise' of constitutional rule and a limited monarchy. And of that achievement no genuine trace can yet be found in the reign of Elizabeth. In that age of a strong monarchy wisely using the inherited institutions of government, the Lords and Commons, with the agreement and toleration of the Crown, formed a convenient and really rather ingeniously devised instrument for raising supply by consent and for making laws binding upon the agencies of enforcement. Its lawmaking power further offered a useful service to private and local interests, while its aura as the Queen's high court attracted respect from all sectors of political society. The availability of Parliament brought forth an embodiment of sovereignty and introduced flexibility as well as considerable sophistication into the ways of government. In addition, as a gathering of men of standing and influence it could be useful to its manipulators – usually the monarch but sometimes others. The rest was pretence, even if that pretence could at times deceive the pretenders.

Index of Bills

Index of Acts

General Index